Crafting Selves

Dorinne K. Kondo

Crafting Selves

Power, Gender, and
Discourses of Identity
in a Japanese
Workplace

The University of Chicago Press/Chicago and London

Dorinne Kondo holds the MacArthur Chair in Women's Studies and Anthropology at Pomona College, Claremont, California. She has taught at Harvard University and has held fellowships at the Institute for Advanced Study, Princeton, and at the Center for Cultural Studies, Rice University, where she is a Rockefeller Fellow during the academic year 1989-90.

The University of Chicago Press, Chicago 60637
The University of Chicago Press, Ltd., London
© 1990 by The University of Chicago
All rights reserved. Published 1990
Printed in the United States of America

99 98 97 96 95 94 93 92 91 90   5 4 3 2 1

Library of Congress Cataloging-in-Publication Data

Kondo, Dorinne K.
    Crafting selves : power, gender, and discourses of identity in a
Japanese workplace / Dorinne K. Kondo.
        p.   cm.
    Includes bibliographical references.
    ISBN 0-226-45043-0 (alk. paper)
    1. Women—Employment—Japan.   2. Women—Japan—Social conditions.
3. Women—Japan—Economic conditions.   4. Group identity—Japan.
5. Self-perception—Japan.   I. Title.
HD6197.K658   1990
305.42′0952—dc20   89-38547
                                                                    CIP

♾ The paper used in this publication meets the minimum requirements of the American National Standard for Information Sciences—Permanence of Paper for Printed Library Materials, ANSI Z39.48-1984.

To my families, in America and in Japan

Okagesama de

Contents

Contents

Acknowledgments

That texts, like selves, are constructed in relationship seems abundantly clear when I look back over the many people who had a role in shaping this book. My first and greatest debt is to the many people in Japan who allowed me to become part of their lives: the "Satōs," the "Hatanakas," the "Sakamotos," and my co-workers and neighbors who put up with the quasi-*gaijin* in their midst and offered me their generosity and hospitality. Their kindness, friendship, and care have indelibly touched my life. The Economics Division of the Arakawa Ward Office and Mr. Katō of the Subcontractors' Association were gracious and helpful in introducing me to owners of small companies in the ward. Since I first stepped off the plane in September of 1978, some of my most treasured *sensei,* without whom this project could never have been completed, have died, and with profound feelings of sadness I note their passing: Wagatsuma Hiroshi, who introduced me to people in Arakawa; Hirayama Kuni-sensei, who in her kindness acted as my guarantor, introducing me to the "Hatanakas" and the "Sakamotos"; Sada Eiko-sensei, my landlady before I moved to Arakawa and a friend whose generosity, humor, artistry, and wisdom were inspirational; my relatives, Suzuki Mikihito and Suzuki Noriko, who so generously looked after me during my years in Tokyo. I know they would be happy to see that Dōrin-san finally finished the book they all worried so much about. I wish they could know how much I miss them.

My research from 1978 to 1981 was generously funded by a grant and a renewal from IIE Fulbright, and by supplemental funds from the Department of Anthropology at Harvard University. The Social Science Research Council provided support for the initial write-up phase. A leave from Harvard University and a grant from the Rockefeller Foundation enabled me to spend a year at the Institute for Advanced Study in 1987–88, without which this manuscript could never have been completed. To all, a warm thanks.

During my years of training, I benefitted greatly from the example of S.J. Tambiah, who taught me what anthropology could be, and whose the-

oretical approach was critically important in shaping my thinking; Ezra
Vogel, whose knowledge of Japan was an indispensable guide to an unfamiliar terrain; and Evon Z. Vogt, whose ethnographic and comparative
questions helped me to refine my argument. John C. Pelzel retired while I
was in Japan, but his insights into Japanese culture and his concern and
interest in my work come to mind whenever I think of the term *sensei*.
Harumi Befu has provided support and encouragement since my undergraduate days. I have always benefitted greatly from his insider's knowledge of Japan, and his unflagging concern over the years could not be
more appreciated. Chie Nakane acted as my academic sponsor while I
was in Tokyo. Her perspicacious advice helped me to focus my study and
to manage many a fieldwork problem. While in Japan, I "held hands" with
Matthews Hamabata as we both negotiated our wonderful, yet often exhausting, fieldwork situations. His friendship and scholarly acumen
sustained me through the trying times of fieldwork, writing, the job
search, and the first years of teaching, and they continue to sustain me.
Monique Djokiè, close friend and colleague since our first year in graduate school, has helped to keep my life in balance, generously offering her
judicious counsel and brilliantly incisive critical comments. Life without
the presence of these friends would be difficult to imagine.

But it was my year at the Institute for Advanced Study in 1987–88 that
allowed me to finish the book and to reshape its theoretical framework.
Like fieldwork, the Institute promises to live in memory as a magical time
that changed my life. To Clifford Geertz and Joan Scott go special thanks.
If there is a foundational point of departure for many anthropologists,
myself included, it is the tradition shaped by Geertzian interpretivism,
and though I make few specific references to it in the text, the influence
of that tradition should be obvious in what follows. Too often, authors
neglect to acknowledge the critically important practical factors that enable writing to take place, and here, too, my thanks go to Cliff and to
Karen Blu for giving me a cool, quiet place to live and work during the
sweltering Princeton summer—a gift without which I could never have
finished my manuscript before leaving the Institute. Joan Scott opened
new worlds of scholarship to me, in feminist and poststructuralist theory
and in the literature on artisanal work. I learned immeasurably from her
expertise, and her generously given comments were invaluable in shaping this work.

To everyone who participated in the gender seminar at the Institute I
extend my warm appreciation. Their creative input is especially visible in
the chapter on artisanal identity, which I presented at the seminar. A few

people should be singled out. The perspectives of Judith Butler and Donna Haraway were inspirational in innumerable ways, and my understanding of poststructuralism owes much to them. Donna's ability to bring together scientific discourse, feminist theory, race, imperialism, colonialism, poststructuralism, and science fiction in such a compelling way transformed my ideas of what "social science" could be. Judith Butler's writings on identity gave me another perspective and another language in which to cast anthropological critiques of "the self." The influence of her important work on "the subject" suffuses this book. Emily Sher's critical insights and her novelist's sense of style helped me craft my ideas and my writing, and her sympathetic encouragement kept my spirits from flagging at crucial moments. It is to Julie Taylor and Elliott Shore I owe the greatest debts, both scholarly and existential. I could count on both friends for thorough readings at a moment's notice—Julie may still have a pile of my work near her phone, for ready consultation. In addition, both provided essential practical help, crucial but usually so little acknowledged, like rides to the supermarket during a year when I was without transportation. Julie always provided sensitive insights into a problem and creative ideas that spurred my own thinking. Her encouragement has informed this book at every turn and brought me through the often trying process of completing what has seemed to be an endless piece of work. Elliott Shore generously read the entire draft, both as it trickled out of the word processor and as new installments appeared via Federal Express. His ideas, editorial expertise, and scholarly judgment helped me shape the manuscript and make crucial changes; his enthusiasm persuaded me I was on the right track even when I was convinced otherwise. The friendship and intellectual companionship provided by these people have enriched my life.

Since I began rewriting the manuscript, many other people have generously given much-needed support, from reading and offering comments on the entire work or parts thereof, to other, more intangible forms of encouragement. To all these people, my deeply felt thanks: Chester M. Pierce, who has been there, and whose politically informed scholarship, sense of humor, and consistent, warm support transformed my experience of Harvard and sustained me over the years; Lisa Rofel, whose close, creative readings of the entire manuscript greatly shaped the revisions, particularly the chapter on part-time workers; Jane Collier; Karen Smyers; Maya Dumermuth; Linette Poyer; Vincent Crapanzano; Elizabeth Eames; Susan Hogue; Jane Bachnik; Takie Lebra; Nancy Rosenberger; Robert J. Smith; William Kelly; and an anonymous reader for the

University of Chicago Press. My sponsoring editor offered his enthusiasm for the project and his indispensable editorial and scholarly guidance. Throughout the writing process, Fraelean Curtis helped to keep my priorities in view. Without her wise counsel, my life would be different indeed.

Since 1982, funds from the Reischauer Institute, the University of Chicago Press, the Northeast Asia Council of the Association for Asian Studies, and the Graduate School at Harvard University have enabled me to benefit from the assistance of various people. They helped me keep research and teaching together: John G. Russell, Deborah Finn, Leslie Tamaribuchi, Elizabeth Roberts, Steven Kusumi, Mark Pleas, and Daniel Pentlarge. Linda Blair must be thanked for her patience and assistance as I made innumerable last-minute emergency requests requiring her immediate attention, as she sent out package after package via Federal Express.

Portions of chapter 1 appeared as "Dissolution and Reconstitution of the Self: Implications for Anthropological Epistemology" (1986), *Cultural Anthropology* 1 (1): 74–88. Chapter 3 appeared in altered form as "Creating an Ideal Self: Theories of Selfhood and Pedagogy at a Japanese Ethics Retreat" (1987), *Ethos* 15 (3): 241–72. These sections are reproduced by permission of the American Anthropological Association. A paragraph of chapter 1 appeared in a review article on Takie Lebra's *Japanese Women: Constraint and Fulfillment* (University of Hawaii Press, 1984), entitled "Gender, Self and Work in Japan" (1985), *Culture, Medicine and Psychiatry* 9: 319–28.

A last note of thanks to the people who contributed most centrally to this project: my parents, Roy and Midori, and my brother Jeff, whose love and support gave me the confidence that enabled me finally to reach the end of what has been a long, sometimes trying journey. My understandings of the meanings of family would be much impoverished without their concern and without the concern of all the people in Japan who allowed me to become, even if temporarily, a member of their *uchi*. To these people for whom I care so much, my families in America and in Japan, I dedicate this book.

Note on Romanization

In rendering Japanese terms, I have followed the Hepburn style of romanization. Macrons indicate long vowels. However, macrons are omitted in commonly used words: e.g., Tokyo rather than Tōkyō.

Part

1

Settings

1   *The Eye/I*

A walk down the streets of the Tokyo neighborhood where I lived would impart to the casual observer the impression of bustling, noisy, yet somehow comfortable chaos. The main thoroughfare is usually clotted with traffic, congested to a degree surprising even for Tokyo, for cars, trucks, buses, and bicycles must defer to the electric trolley, the last of its kind in the city, as it slowly wends its way through the crowded intersection. A subway line connects the neighborhood to the cosmopolitan downtown areas of the Ginza, the Diet Building, and the financial district, luring new residents to the area. The infusion of newcomers has spawned the usual cluster of business establishments: several banks, two *pachinko*[1] parlors, and a variety of fast food restaurants, from stand-up counters where you can have a quick bowl of noodles to MacDonald's and Kentucky Fried Chicken. Lining the streets are innumerable *kissaten,* or coffee houses, where the price of a cup of coffee entitles you to sit as long as you please, perhaps chatting and laughing with friends, or—if you are in a more contemplative mood—reading a novel or a comic book, stopping occasionally to stare out the window as the passing crowds emerge from underground.

The main street is a covered arcade shading a long row of small specialty stores. Merchants pool their resources to buy decorations for each of the lampposts, from which they suspend a plastic branch representing the flower of the season. The bright, artificial colors add a festive touch to the urban scene: shocking pink cherry blossoms in the spring; the silvery green willow fronds of summer; autumn's scarlet and golden maple leaves; and in midwinter the auspicious New Year symbols of pine, bamboo, and plum blossoms. Sheltered in the shadows of the plastic boughs are a bewildering variety of shops, among them the capacious tea store, a resplendent example of commercial prosperity. Always crowded with customers, it was for me a place of endless fascination, where you could pass many pleasant moments desultorily inspecting the rows of shelves stocked with special teas and the arrays of ceramic pots and cups, some of delicate porcelain painted in brilliant hues, others rough, asymmetrical, and somber.

A little closer to the subway stop, beckoning customers as they walk home, are the sparkling windows of the Satō confectionery, offering to passersby the soft, plump rice cakes and elegant French pastries we made in the factory across the alleyway in back. I worked there as a part-time laborer for a year, along with thirty-odd other employees. Together we made and packaged the delicacies gracing the gleaming display cases. Around the corner, on the second floor of a modern three-story building was the beauty salon where I also worked for a month or two part-time, acting as occasional receptionist, helper, floor sweeper, and laundress for Yokoyama-sensei and the younger women who worked in her salon. Even on this part of the main thoroughfare people are usually hurrying here and there, though they will sometimes stop to chat or to murmur greetings as they pass. The atmosphere vibrates with bustling commercial activity.

A turn down any of the side streets reveals settings of a somewhat different sort. The houses lining the narrow, asphalt-covered roads are crammed so close together that they touch, and the fronts of the houses themselves abut directly onto the street. A few potted plants and flowers placed outside the front doors give the otherwise muted grays and browns a splash of occasional color. Early in the mornings on sunny days, housewives put out their *futon*² to air, hanging them out the windows, folding them over poles, or—an especially ingenious method my landlady used—draping them over the family car. The local elementary school is not far from the main street, and when children play in the schoolyard, their exuberant shouts and laughter offer a welcome contrast to the sternly institutional concrete facade. At the corner candy shop, the neighborhood senior citizens often gather to trade tales.

When I am reminded of everyday life in the neighborhood, it is often a *sound* that jogs the memory. Turning the corner on the way to my apartment, I would always hear the clanking of the metal presses in the distance, as they stamp out parts for heavy machinery or cut out food containers, belt buckles, even Snoopy medallions from sheets of plastic. Most of these *puresuyasan,* as they are called, are one- or two-person operations, where the machines beat out their insistent rhythms in a room adjoining the main house. Our days were punctuated by the relentless pulsing of the presses. If you were to venture beyond the bounds of the neighborhood and take a walk to the station, other sounds would provide accompaniment. The whine of machines at the neighborhood shoe factory deafens passersby, and a penetrating aroma—glue for the soles, I was told—emanates from the open windows and doors, assailing the nostrils. And mornings I associate with the cool, metallic ring of a bicycle bell as it slices through the air, a signal that the *sake* shop's delivery man is making his rounds. He would stop in at the houses of his regular customers to take orders, exchange a few pleasantries, and deliver bottles of *sake,* beer, and soy sauce. No ordinary apprentice, this— rumor had it that he and his wife were well-to-do landlords of an apartment building in a part of Tokyo about five stops away on the Yamanote electric train line.

The sounds of urban life signaled busy activity, and in my immediate neighborhood, almost every house seems to be filled with people working. Around the corner live the *tatamiyasan* and his helper, who patiently weave their plaited mats, allowing the fresh, grassy fragrance of rushes to waft through the open windows and transport the passing pedestrian momentarily to a more rustic setting. Just a few doors down the street, a woman stands all day, tending a machine that does nothing but sharpen pencils. She feeds in the pencils, the machine buzzes as it hones the lead into a point, and she in turn carefully stacks the pencils as they emerge from the sharpener. Fujimoto-san, who owns the dry-cleaning shop directly across from my apartment, listens to the radio blaring as she irons piles of shirts. She has the reputation of being unusually dedicated to her work, for even when she was exhausted and ill to the point of collapse, she insisted on sweeping the floor of her shop before she would allow herself to be taken to the hospital. "My God, what can you do?" her husband says, shaking his head. "That's just the way she is." He himself is a former executive with a famous multinational trading company, who quit the corporate grind in order to become the boss of his own machine shop.

Appearing quiet from without, even the most conventional-looking residences house workshops of one kind or another. On the corner, in a house indistinguishable from others on the street, sits a craftsman. After going to the elementary school for the 6:30 A.M. broadcast of radio exercises on the school loudspeaker, he comes home to his small workshop at the front of the house, where he makes hand-carved umbrella handles from cherry and camellia wood, sculpting them into intricate shapes: renderings of classic patterns, or of animals and flowers. Just a few doors away from him lived Mr. Tanoue, a sixtyish craftsman who worked all day making trays and wooden accessories for restaurants specializing in *soba,* Japanese noodles. The fresh, pungent fragrance of Japanese cypress—*hinoki,* the most durable and precious of Japanese woods—greets the visitor to his workshop. Mr. Tanoue would sit among the clean, white shavings as he put the finishing touches on his trays. From here, he piled them onto the back of his son-in-law's pickup in order to deliver them to the middlemen, the people who painted the trays with black and red lacquer. *Akebono,* dawn, I found especially beautiful, the crimson deepened and burnished by its undercoating of black. In the old days, Mr. Tanoue says, he used to stack the trays and containers on the back of his bicycle, twenty or more at a time, and pedal to Shitaya, some miles away. The truck, he laughs, makes life easier for an aging body. After many coatings of lacquer, his handiwork eventually finds its way to the finest *soba* restaurants in the country.

Within five minutes of my apartment were a host of family-owned factories. In the soap factory down the street, an unfortunate incident a year or two earlier had created explosive tensions that still underlay the seeming cordiality of neighborhood relationships. A fire had started under a vat of melted tallow and lye, threatening to spread to other houses. The wrath of the neighborhood descended on the Sekiguchis as they were condemned for their "carelessness." Badly burned and still bandaged, the husband and wife walked from door to door, apologizing to all the people for whom they had "caused so much trouble." On another corner was a garment factory that made uniforms, mostly—as my landlady and I discovered when we headed over for their annual sale. Every day, women would deliver bundles of the piecework they had sewn at home, balanced precariously on the handlebars of their bicycles. In a slightly larger factory, several middle-aged women ran machines that stamped out plastic accessories, while men carried in new materials and took out the finished products, gingerly stepping over the snappish Yorkshire terrier who guarded his territory near the door. The boxmakers, who—among other things—made the boxes for the confectionery where I spent my days working, were tucked away from the street at the end of a cul-de-sac. Sheets and sheets of cardboard leaned against the factory walls, and I could often discern the high-pitched drone of the lathes as I walked past. The owner was a ruddy-faced, kindly-looking man, one of the officials in the local "block association" (*chōnaikai*) along with the grandmother of the Hatanaka family, my neighbors and landlords.

All around me was a community alive with people at work.

The "Setting" Trope

A jumble of unfamiliar buildings when I first moved in, the Tokyo neighborhood where I lived began to take on increasing familiarity and significance as impersonal facades gave way to homes populated by friends and acquaintances. It is this sense of increasing familiarity I think anthropologists invoke when we begin our ethnographies by describing the "setting," where we lay out the map of "our" country, "our" community, and retrace the journey that brought us to those communities. We try, I think, to recapitulate our experiences of primary disorientation and of trying to find our feet in a place where our own common sense assumptions about the world take us exactly nowhere. I would suspect that many of our first journal entries highlight sensory impressions, superficial descriptions, and feelings of the strangeness and mystery of a place. But "the setting" eventually becomes populated with people you grow to know, sometimes to love, sometimes to dislike, almost always to respect. The gray house down the street was not just any gray house; it was Tanoue-san's home, where I might be invited to have a cup of tea and have a chat, if I happened by at the right time. The cardboard-cutting factory I used to pass on the way to my tea ceremony lessons turned out to be the home of dauntingly energetic Sekine-san, who regaled me with tales of her family's history and insisted on serving me a bowl of her handmade noodles, garnished with the scallions the vegetable seller personally delivered. And the Satō factory, initially to me just the place that supplied the delicious sweets I would buy as gifts for my relatives or bring home for dessert, turned out to be my world of co-workers and friends during the year I spent there as a part-time worker.

Consequently, the setting trope—a narrative convention both shaping and shaped by experiences of fieldwork—is one of a journey, more or less linear, where order and meaning gradually emerge from initially inchoate events and experiences. Sometimes, as other anthropologists and I have argued, order and meaning can be imposed when you have left the field, in a sometimes violent attempt to recover meaning in the flux and chaos of everyday life (Crapanzano 1977; Kondo 1986). The narrative convention of the "setting" thus compels, even as I strain to avoid it, precisely because it evokes the experience of fieldwork by locating the author and the reader in a world that is initially strange, allowing the author to render that world comprehensible to the reader just as it became familiar to her in the process of doing research. Through the act of writing, complexity is inevitably simplified and assimilated to the familiar, often unconsciously reproduced conventions by which we have learned to make sense of that complexity. In this case, the "setting" trope recalls not only the conventions of ethnographic writing but also those of realist fiction—as I discovered, to my surprise and discomfort, upon rereading Balzac's *Eugénie Grandet*.

Mine is a (totalizing) story of emerging order, then, and of epiphanal moments of understanding sparked by particular events. Consequently, the theoretical/rhetorical strategy I deploy is to begin *evocatively* in the form of vignettes—settings and events that lead us into a world. Evocation establishes a mood and calls up images (cf. Tyler 1986, 130–1). My strategy of evocative writing is also designed to call attention to itself—not only through self-consciously reflexive passages such as this, but through an intentionally overwritten quality of the descriptions I offer. The evocative language I use should suggest or call forth a world, but I deploy it in order to problematize it, indeed to problematize the notion of "description" as the transparent inscription of reality on the blank page.

So I begin with the unfolding of *this* story, of *this* book: how the shape of experience, the questions I asked and the responses I received, even the writing of the ethnographic text, occupy a space within a particular history of a specific ethnographer and her informants as we sought to understand each other within shifting fields of power and meaning. To begin evocatively highlights the complexity and richness of experience. And to examine that complexity and richness in its specificity leads toward a strategy that expands notions of what can count as theory, where experience and evocation can *become theory,* where the binary between "empirical" and "theoretical" is displaced and loses its force. So I tell the story of how I came to center my project on notions of identity and self-hood, through an "experiential" first-person narrative I deploy in order to make several "theoretical" points: first, that any account, mine included, is partial and located, screened through the narrator's eye/I; second, to emphasize the processual and emergent nature of ethnographic inquiry and the embeddedness of what we call theory in that process; and third, to argue that the liveliness and complexity of everyday life cannot be encompassed by theoretical models which rely on organizational structures, "typical" individuals, referential meanings, or invocations of collective nouns like "the Japanese." Rather, my strategy will be to emphasize, through shifting, multiple voices and the invocation of the "I," the shifting, complex individual identities of the people with whom I lived and worked, and the processes by which I became acquainted with them.

How the Problem Emerged

When I first made my acquaintance with this Tokyo neighborhood, the air was still warm and humid, awaiting the cleansing winds and rains of the September typhoons. I had come to study the relationship of kinship and economics in family-owned enterprises. Thinking about "kinship" and "economics" in abstract, organizational, structural-functionalist terms, but drawn by the emphasis on cultural meanings in the writings of interpretivists like Clifford Geertz, I began with questions concerning the ways people thought about and enacted the meanings of "company" and "family" in their everyday lives. By the following autumn—the time of *zanshō,* the lingering summer heat—I was a resident and worker in the community I have described, and the focus of my study had shifted to accommodate my year's experiences and observations. For although it was true that company and family, economics and kinship, were vibrantly meaningful arenas of everyday life for the people I knew, the idiom in which they were cast was always, ineluctably, centered on persons and personal relationships. In the factory, in the family, in the neighborhood, in language, in the use of space, in attitudes toward nature and toward material objects, the most insistent refrain, repeated over and over again and transposed into countless different keys of experience, was the fundamental connectedness of human beings to each other. It was a conception that exploded my Western ideas about the relationship between self and social world, and it was an inescapable motif in the everyday lives of people I knew. Abstract organizational charts of company hierarchies; kinship diagrams; neat divisions of social life into domains of kinship, economics, politics, and religion; and the use of abstract individuals like "the Japanese woman" or "the Japanese man," seemed less and less compelling, less and less able to capture the complexity of what I saw around me. By the time I left Japan, during Taikan, the coldest days of the winter season, it had been twenty-six months since I first arrived, and the problematic of kinship and economics had come to pivot around precisely what I perceived to be even more basic cultural assumptions: how *selfhood* is constructed in the arenas of company and family. My work of that historical moment concentrated on delineating "the Japanese concept of self" and on trying to experiment with narrative voice, to begin to evoke some of the vividness of life as I had seen it in the factory.

Now, some years later—the luxury of reflection and memory shaping and reshaping my re-encounter with the people who shared their lives with me—the presupposition that informed my problematic at that moment is clear. I assumed my goal as anthropologist to be a description of a "concept of self" characteristic of all members of any particular culture. Collective identities like "the Japanese" or "Japanese concepts of self" no longer seem to me to be fixed essences, but rather strategic assertions, which inevitably suppress differences, tensions, and contradictions within. Given these moves toward practice, nonessentialism, and radical cultural and historical specificity, I develop in the present inquiry the themes of personhood, work, and family by asking a slightly different question: How did the people I knew craft themselves and their lives within shifting fields of power and meaning, and how did they do so in particular situations and within a particular historical and cultural context? In framing a reply to this query, I detail the dynamically engaging, everyday contests over the meanings of company and family, the two most salient sites of symbolic struggle in the Satō factory, and the ways identities are asserted in those struggles. In turn, these terrains of contest cannot be understood without reference to the larger movements of what we would call history, politics, and the economy.

In attempting to enlarge the boundaries of what counts as theoretical, I attempt to build on feminist scholarship that expands our definitions of what counts as political. Power can create identities on the individual level, as it provides disciplines, punishments, and culturally available pathways for fulfillment; nowhere were these forces more evident to me than in my relationships with the Japanese people I knew. At stake in my narrative of emerging order are the constantly contested and shifting boundaries of my identity and the identities of my Japanese relatives, friends, and acquaintances. We participated in each others' lives and sought to make sense of one another. In that attempt to understand, power inevitably came into play as we tried to force each other into appropriately comprehensible categories. This nexus of power and meaning was also creative, the crucible within which we forged our relationship. In turn, our negotiated understandings of one another enabled me to shape the particular problematic that now animates my research. The sites of these struggles for understanding were located in what we might call salient features of "identity" both in America and in Japan: race, gender, and age.

On Being a Conceptual Anomaly

As a Japanese American,[3] I created a conceptual dilemma for the Japanese I encountered. For them, I was a living oxymoron, someone who was both Japanese and not Japanese. Their puzzlement was all the greater since most Japanese people I knew seemed to adhere to an eminently biological definition of Japaneseness. Race, language, and culture are intertwined, so much so that any challenge to this firmly entrenched conceptual schema—a white person who speaks flawlessly idiomatic and unaccented Japanese, or a person of Japanese ancestry who cannot— meets with what generously could be described as unpleasant reactions. White people are treated as repulsive and unnatural—*hen na gaijin,* strange foreigners—the better their Japanese becomes, while Japanese Americans and others of Japanese ancestry born overseas are faced with exasperation and disbelief. How can someone who is racially Japanese lack "cultural competence"?[4] During my first few months in Tokyo, many tried to resolve this paradox by asking which of my parents was "really" American.

Indeed, it is a minor miracle that those first months did not lead to an acute case of agoraphobia, for I knew that once I set foot outside the door, someone somewhere (a taxi driver? a salesperson? a bank clerk?) would greet one of my linguistic mistakes with an astonished "Eh?" I became all too familiar with the series of expressions that would flicker over those faces: bewilderment, incredulity, embarrassment, even anger, at having to deal with this odd person who looked Japanese and therefore human, but who must be retarded, deranged, or—equally undesirable in Japanese eyes—Chinese or Korean. Defensively, I would mull over the mistake-of-the-day. I mean, how was I to know that in order to "fillet a fish" you had to cut it "in three pieces"? Or that opening a bank account required so much specialized terminology? Courses in literary Japanese at Harvard hadn't done much to prepare me for the realities of everyday life in Tokyo. Gritting my teeth in determination as I groaned inwardly, I would force myself out of the house each morning.

For me, and apparently for the people around me, this was a stressful time, when expectations were flouted, when we had to strain to make sense of one another. There seemed to be few advantages in my retaining an American persona, for the distress caused by these reactions was diffi-cult to bear. In the face of dissonance and distress, I found that the desire for comprehensible order in the form of "fitting in," even if it meant sup-pression of and violence against a self I had known in another context, was preferable to meaninglessness. Anthropological imperatives to im-merse oneself in another culture intensified this desire, so that acquiring the accoutrements of Japanese selfhood meant simultaneously construct-ing a more thoroughly professional anthropological persona. This required language learning in the broadest sense: mastery of culturally appropriate modes of moving, acting, and speaking. For my informants, it was clear that coping with this anomalous creature was difficult, for here was someone who looked like a real human being, but who simply failed to perform according to expectation. They, too, had every reason to make me over in their image, to guide me, gently but insistently, into properly Japanese behavior, so that the discrepancy between my appearance and my cultural competence would not be so painfully evident. I posed a challenge to their senses of identity. How could someone who *looked* Japanese not *be* Japanese? In my cultural ineptitude, I represented for the people who met me the chaos of meaninglessness. Their response in the face of this dissonance was to *make* me as Japanese as possible. Thus, my first nine months of fieldwork were characterized by an attempt to re-duce the distance between expectation and inadequate reality, as my informants and I conspired to rewrite my identity as Japanese.

My guarantor, an older woman who, among her many activities, was a teacher of flower arranging, introduced me to many families who owned businesses in the ward of Tokyo where I had chosen to do my research. One of her former students and fellow flower arranging teachers, Mrs. Sakamoto, agreed to take me in as a guest over the summer, since the apartment where I was scheduled to move—owned by one of my class-mates in tea ceremony—was still under construction. My proclivities for "acting Japanese" were by this time firmly established. During my stay with the Sakamotos, I did my best to conform to what I thought their ex-pectations of a guest/daughter might be. This in turn seemed to please them and reinforced my tendency to behave in terms of what I perceived to be my Japanese persona.

My initial encounter with the head of the household epitomizes this mirroring and reinforcement of behavior. Mr. Sakamoto had been on a business trip on the day I moved in, and he returned the following eve-ning, just as his wife, daughter, and I sat down to the evening meal. As soon as he stepped in the door, I immediately switched from an informal posture, seated on the *zabuton* (seat cushion) to a formal greeting posture, *seiza*-style (kneeling on the floor) and bowed low, hands on the floor. Mr. Sakamoto responded in kind (being older, male, and head of the household, he did not have to bow as deeply as I did), and we exchanged the requisite polite formulae, I requesting his benevolence, and he welcoming me to their family. Later, he told me how happy and impressed he had been with this act of proper etiquette on my part. "Today's young people in Japan," he said, "no longer show such respect. Your grandfather must have been a fine man to raise such a fine granddaughter." Of course, his statements can hardly be accepted at face value. They may well indicate his relief that I seemed to know something of proper Japanese behavior, and hence would not be a complete nuisance to them; it was also his way of making me feel at home. What is important to note is the way this statement was used to elicit proper Japanese behavior in future encounters. And his strategy worked. I was left with a warm, positive feeling toward the Sakamoto family, armed with an incentive to behave in a Japanese way, for clearly these were the expectations and the desires of the people who had taken me in and who were so generously sharing their lives with me.

Other members of the household voiced similar sentiments. Takemi-san, the Sakamotos' married daughter who lived in a distant prefecture, had been visiting her parents when I first moved in. A few minutes after our initial encounter, she observed, "You seem like a typical Japanese woman" (*Nihon no josei, to iu kanji*). Later in the summer, Mrs. Sakamoto confided to me that she could never allow a "pure American" (*junsui na Amerikajin*) to live with them, for only someone of Japanese descent was genetically capable of adjusting to life on *tatami* mats, using unsewered toilets, sleeping on the floor—in short, of living Japanese style. Again, the message was unambiguous: my "family" could feel comfortable with me insofar as I was—and acted—Japanese.

At first, then, as a Japanese American I made sense to those around me as a none-too-felicitous combination of racial categories. As fieldwork progressed, however, and my linguistic and cultural skills improved, my informants seemed best able to understand me by placing me in meaningful cultural roles: daughter, guest, young woman, student, prodigal Japanese who had finally seen the light and come home. Most people preferred to treat me as a Japanese—sometimes an incomplete or unconventional Japanese, but a Japanese nonetheless. Indeed, even when I tried to represent myself as an American, others did not always take heed. For instance, on my first day on the job at the confectionery factory, Mr.

Satō introduced me to the division chief as an "American student," here to learn about the business and about the "real situation" (*jittai*) of workers in small enterprise. Soon it became clear that the chief remembered "student," but not "American." A week or so later, we gathered for one of our noon meetings to read from a pamphlet published by an ethics school. The owner came, and he commented on the theme of the day, *ketsui* (determination). At one point during his speech, he singled me out, praising my resolve. "If Kondō-san had been an ordinary young woman, she might never have known Japan." I stared at my shoes, my cheeks flaming. When the exercise finished, I hurried back to my work station. Akiyama-san, the division head, approached me with a puzzled expression on his face. *"Doko desu ka?"* he asked. (Where is it?—in other words, where are you from?) And after my reply, he announced loudly to all: "She says it's America!"

My physical characteristics led my friends and co-workers to emphasize my identity as Japanese, sometimes even against my own intentions and desires. Over time, my increasingly "Japanese" behavior served temporarily to resolve their crises of meaning and to confirm their assumptions about their own identities. That I, too, came to participate enthusiastically in this recasting of the self is a testimonial to their success in acting upon me.

Conflict and Fragmentation of Self

Using these ready-made molds may have reduced the dissonance in my informants' minds, but it served only to increase the dissonance in my own. What occurred in the field was a kind of fragmenting of identity into what I then labeled Japanese and American pieces, so that the different elements, instead of fitting together to form at least the illusion of a seamless and coherent whole—it is the contention of this book that selves which are coherent, seamless, bounded, and whole are indeed illusions—strained against one another. The war was not really—or only—between Japanese and American elements, however. Perhaps it had even more to do with the position of researcher versus one of daughter and guest. In one position, my goal had to be the pursuit of knowledge, where decisive action, independence, and mastery were held in high esteem. In another, independence and mastery of one's own fate were out of the question; rather, being a daughter meant duties, responsibilities, and *inter*dependence.

The more I adjusted to my Japanese daughter's role, the keener the conflicts became. Most of those conflicts had to do with expectations sur-rounding gender, and, more specifically, my position as a young woman. Certainly, in exchange for the care the Sakamotos showed me, I was hap-py to help out in whatever way I could. I tried to do some housecleaning and laundry, and I took over the shopping and cooking for Mr. Sakamoto when Mrs. Sakamoto was at one of the children's association meetings, her flower arranging classes, or meetings of ward committees on juve-nile delinquency. The cooking did not offend me in and of itself; in fact, I was glad for the opportunity to learn how to make simple Japanese cui-sine, and Mr. Sakamoto put up with my sometimes appalling culinary mistakes and limited menus with great aplomb. I remember one particu-larly awful night when I couldn't find the makings for soup broth, and Mr. Sakamoto was fed "*miso* soup" that was little more than *miso* dissolved in hot water. He managed to down the tasteless broth with good grace—and the trace of a smile on his lips. (Of course, it is also true that although he was himself capable of simple cooking, he would not set foot in the kitchen if there were a woman in the house.) Months after I moved out, whenever he saw me he would say with a sparkle in his eye and a hint of nostalgic wistfulness in his voice, "I miss Dōrin-san's salad and sautéed beef," one of the "Western" menus I used to serve up with numbing reg-ularity. No, the cooking was not the problem.

The problem was, in fact, the etiquette surrounding the serving of food that produced the most profound conflicts for me as an American wom-an. The head of the household is usually served first and receives the finest delicacies; men—even the sweetest, nicest ones—ask for a second helping of rice by merely holding out their rice bowls to the woman nearest the rice cooker, and maybe, just maybe, uttering a grunt of thanks in return for her pains. I could never get used to this practice, try as I might. Still, I tried to carry out my duties uncomplainingly, in what I hope was reasonably good humor. But I was none too happy about these things "inside." Other restrictions began to chafe, especially restrictions on my movement. I had to be in at a certain hour, despite my "adult" age. Yet I understood the family's responsibility for me as their guest and quasi-daughter, so I tried to abide by their regulations, hiding my irrita-tion as best I could.

This fundamental ambivalence was heightened by isolation and de-pendency. Though my status was in some respects high in an education-conscious Japan, I was still young, female, and a student. I was in a so-cially recognized relationship of dependency vis-à-vis the people I knew. I was not to be feared and obeyed, but protected and helped. In terms of my research, this was an extremely advantageous position to be in, for people did not feel the need to reflect my views back to me, as they might with a more powerful person. I did not try to define situations; rather, I could allow other people to define those situations in their culturally appropriate ways, remaining open to their concerns and their ways of acting in the world. But, in another sense, this dependency and isolation increased my susceptibility to identifying with my Japanese role. By this time I saw little of American friends in Tokyo, for it was difficult to be with people who had so little inkling of how ordinary Japanese people lived. My informants and I consequently had every reason to conspire to recreate my identity as Japanese. Precisely because of my dependency and my made-to-order role, I was allowed—or rather, *forced*—to abandon the position of observer. Errors, linguistic or cultural, were dealt with impatiently or with a startled look that seemed to say, "Oh yes, you are American after all." On the other hand, appropriately Japanese behaviors were rewarded with warm, positive reactions or with comments such as "You're more Japanese than the Japanese." Even more frequently, correct behavior was simply accepted as a matter of course. *Naturally* I would understand, *naturally* I would behave correctly, for they presumed me to be, *au fond,* Japanese.

Identity can imply unity or fusion, but for me what occurred was a fragmentation of the self. This fragmentation was encouraged by my own participation in Japanese life and by the actions of my friends and acquaintances. At its most extreme point, I became "the Other" in my own mind, where the identity I had known in another context simply collapsed. The success of our conspiracy to recreate me as Japanese reached its climax one August afternoon.

It was typical summer weather for Tokyo, "like a steam bath" as the saying goes, so hot the leaves were drooping limply from the trees surrounding the Sakamotos' house. Mrs. Sakamoto and her married daughter, Takemi, were at the doctor's with Takemi's son, so Mr. Sakamoto and I were busy tending young Kaori-chan, Takemi-san's young daughter. Mr. Sakamoto quickly tired of his grandfatherly role, leaving me to entertain Kaori-chan. Promptly at four P.M., the hour when most Japanese housewives do their shopping for the evening meal, I lifted the baby into her stroller and pushed her along ahead of me as I inspected the fish, selected the freshest looking vegetables, and mentally planned the meal for the evening. As I glanced into the shiny metal surface of the butcher's display case, I noticed someone who looked terribly familiar: a typical young housewife, clad in slip-on sandals and the loose, cotton shift called "home wear" (*hōmu wea*), a woman walking with a characteristically Japanese bend to the knees and a sliding of the feet. Suddenly I clutched the handle of the stroller to steady myself as a wave of dizziness washed over me, for I realized I had caught a glimpse of nothing less than my own reflection. Fear that perhaps I would never emerge from this world into which I was immersed, inserted itself into my mind and stubbornly refused to leave, until I resolved to move into a new apartment, to distance myself from my Japanese home and my Japanese existence.

For ultimately, this collapse of identity was a distancing moment. It led me to emphasize the *differences* between cultures and among various aspects of identity: researcher, student, daughter, wife, Japanese, American, Japanese American. In order to reconstitute myself as an American researcher, I felt I had to extricate myself from the conspiracy to rewrite my identity as Japanese. Accordingly, despite the Sakamotos' invitations to stay with them for the coming year, I politely stated my intentions to fulfill the original terms of the agreement: to stay just until construction on my new apartment was complete. In order to resist the Sakamotos' attempts to recreate me as Japanese, I removed myself physically from their exclusively Japanese environment.

Thus, both the fragmentation of self and the collapse of identity were results of a complex collaboration between ethnographer and informants. It should be evident that at this particular point, my informants were hardly inert objects available for the free play of the ethnographer's desire. They themselves were, in the act of being, actively interpreting and trying to make meaning of the ethnographer. In so doing, the people I knew asserted their power to act upon the anthropologist. This was their means for preserving their own identities. Understanding, in this context, is multiple, open-ended, positioned—although that positioning can shift dramatically, as I have argued—and pervaded by relations of power. These power-imbued attempts to capture, recast, and rewrite each other were for us productive of understandings and were, existentially, alternately wrenching and fulfilling.

"Epiphany" and a Shift in the Problem

This moment of collapse was followed by a distancing process. I returned to the United States for a month, and upon returning to Japan, I moved into the apartment promised me, next door to Hatanaka-san, my landlady and friend from the tea ceremony class. This arrangement turned out to be ideal, for I could enjoy the best of both worlds: the warmth of belonging to a family and the (semi)privacy of my own space. I immersed myself in research, finding contacts through Hatanaka-san. In fact, I ended up working in businesses owned by two of her grade school classmates: a hairdressing salon owned by Yokoyama-sensei, and the Satō confectionery factory, the focus of this book.

I have written "collapse of identity" and "distancing process." But the distancing was only relative, for the same pressures were there, both internal and external, the pressures to be unobtrusively Japanese. In most cases my informants still guided me into these roles and at times refused to let me escape them. In moving to a different neighborhood and away from the Sakamotos, I had simply exchanged the role of daughter for other culturally meaningful positions—those of guest, neighbor, worker, young woman—that demanded participation and involvement.

Indeed, the shift in the focus of my study lay precisely in this participation. As time wore on, it seemed to me that the relationship of kinship and economics in these family-owned firms—the problem I had initially set out to study—was always filtered through an emphasis on personal relationships. An awareness of this person-centered universe impressed itself upon me in myriad ways. Certainly anyone who lives in this Shitamachi (downtown) district cannot help but be aware of the constant presence of others. In my neighborhood, the houses were so densely packed that the walls almost touched. Though I lived in my own apartment, I shared a wall with Akemi-chan, Mrs. Hatanaka's daughter, and we would try to be solicitous of each other's daily routines: I was especially careful to refrain from typing when she was practicing the piano. Whenever I opened my back window to air my *futon* or to hang up my clothes to dry, I inevitably ended up conversing with the gracious, elderly woman next door, who was always out tending her garden. "Cold, isn't it?" "Beautiful morning." "They say it's going to rain again." "Today feels like another scorcher." As the seasons passed, we exchanged the conventional yet somehow comfortable and comforting greetings about the weather, before branching off into other topics of mutual interest. Less pleasant were my next-door neighbors' fights. They quarreled every morning, and without ever really getting to know the nine year old son, I formed a distinctly unfavorable opinion of the young man. He complained constantly about his paltry allowance, yelling at his mother one morning, "How could this be enough?" (*Tarinē ja nē ka yo!*). The mother was able to give as good as she got, upbraiding him with great relish. Quarrels sometimes became neighborhood affairs. One summer evening, when everyone left their windows open to admit the cool night air, the screams from a family fight two houses away drifted in with the breeze. Alarming in its intensity, with the drunken father threatening to hit someone with baseball bats and beer bottles, the fight kept all of us up and prompted neighborhood concern and intervention. The next morning, everyone within a five-house radius was bleary-eyed from lack of sleep.

Minute details of everyday life also attracted people's attention. I was able to smell the cooking from the two houses nearest me, and I am certain that others could take note of my daily menu. No visitor could passed unnoticed. I could easily have kept, had I chosen to do so, a highly accurate accounting of the comings and goings from the Hatanakas and at least two other houses near mine. And the Hatanakas never failed to comment on the appearance of each of my visitors. When a former (male) student of mine from Harvard came to visit of an afternoon, Akemi-chan observed, "He sure was here a long time, wasn't he?" (*Zuibun ita n desu, ne*). When my phone rang, the Hatanakas took note. If I happened to be out, a head would emerge from their door just as I arrived home, to inform me that I had received a call. People were able to observe what time everyone else arose in the morning, by the presence or absence of the morning paper in the mail slot in the front door. What is more, they never hesitated to comment, "Oh, you were up early this morning," or "You must have been tired; you took it easy today, didn't you?" In an area where early rising is equated with moral virtue, the latter statement was calculated to provoke shame and embarrassment, and I always tried to arise much earlier on the following day. Hatanaka-san and her family noticed how often I did my wash and when I aired my *futon;* if it were a properly sunny day, there would invariably be a tap on my door, telling me that I could, if I wished, air my *futon* on their laundry pole or, even better, lay it flat on top of their tiny Suzuki automobile so that the *futon* would be especially fluffy.

It may seem that I am describing a society where everyone meddles in everyone else's business, where privacy is breached at every turn. This is, indeed, one of the stereotypes of this Shitamachi, or downtown area, that I often heard from people who lived in the Uptown, or Yamanote, section of Tokyo. Yet I should not neglect to convey the sensitivity and care that so often animated social life in my neighborhood. The Hatanakas, for instance, were especially solicitous. After a hard day at work, I could almost always count on a tap on the door, and the cheery Mrs. Hatanaka would be there, bearing some wonderful concoction—more often than not, a delicious, hot meal. And on special occasions, I knew I could expect my favorite dish, beautifully prepared: *buri no teriyaki,* rich, buttery yellow-tail in a gleaming *teriyaki* sauce. If I were sick, they looked in on me. When I began to go to an acupuncturist for my back and neck ailments, the Hatanakas plied me with all sorts of remedies, from Tiger Balm to medicinal plasters to a piece of bamboo I was supposed to place under my feet as I stood at my sink doing dishes. "It will relax you," they reassured me. The Hatanakas' concern sometimes manifested itself in amusing ways. One summer night, a huge cockroach appeared in my kitchen (the Japanese species has a nasty way of flying at its attackers), and my piercing screech of *"Gokiburi!"* (Cockroach!) brought Mrs. Hatanaka over the next morning with a *gokiburi hoi hoi* (come here, cockroaches!)—a roach motel complete with smiling cockroaches waving a hearty welcome from their cardboard windows.

All this was more than mere passive awareness arising from sheer, unavoidable physical proximity. Rather, life in Shitamachi was animated by active involvement and interest in the lives of others. I initially feared that, in the case of the Hatanakas, curiosity about my "foreign" ways and their responsibility for my welfare perhaps exhausted the explanations for their concern for every detail of my life. Certainly these were important factors. But some of my fears on this score were laid to rest when, after I left, I received a letter from Akemi-chan, my landlady's teenage daughter, whose bedroom had been on the other side of the wall from my own. She described in hilarious detail the living habits of the young man who had inherited my apartment: "He gets up at six, takes a bath in the morning,[5] and then sings off key while he dries his hair with an unbelievably noisy blow dryer. How is a person to sleep?"

As an American accustomed to privacy, I sometimes found even the kindnesses were difficult to accept. Even in my own apartment, I was not able to totally relax, for my menu, sleeping and bathing habits, and housekeeping all seemed open for public inspection. But perhaps nothing symbolized this frustration more eloquently than the way my Shitamachi neighbors and friends had of paying calls. In this area, doors are never locked if someone is at home; delivery persons, friends, and visitors will simply open the door, enter as far as the *genkan,*[6] and announce their presence with a *"Gomen kudasai"* (Excuse me). On more than one occasion, such unexpected visits awakened me from a much-needed nap on my day off from the factory. In the winter months, this was particularly painful, for like many Japanese, I would snuggle under the *kotatsu*[7] as I napped. Not only was it an excruciatingly rude awakening to have to emerge into the freezing room (Japanese houses by and large do not have central heating), but I was embarrassed by having been caught fast asleep in the afternoon, when I should have been working or otherwise making myself useful.

One incident epitomized these encounters with Japanese notions of privacy and caring concern. I had fallen ill with the flu, exhausted by my hectic schedule. I had made plans to call on an artisan and his family, but because of my sickness I canceled our appointment. During the middle of the day, I was fast asleep on my *futon*. My apartment was in total chaos. For two days I had been unable to summon the energy to wash the dishes or even to hang up my clothes, which were strewn about the *tatami* room in utter disarray. As I lay there, blissfully lost to the world, the door was suddenly flung open and two voices chorused, "*Gomen kudasai!*" I leaped out of my *futon,* on the verge of heart failure from the shock. There were the artisan and his wife, all smiles, bearing armfuls of mandarin oranges, sweets, and loaves of bread. They announced their intentions to take care of me and urged me to go straight back to bed. I was mortified, for not only had I been caught in bed, sickness notwithstanding, I had been caught with a disorderly apartment and disheveled hair and clothes. I was even more mortified when Mrs. Hayashi began to wash my dishes. I scurried out to the kitchen, assuring her that her efforts weren't necessary, and thanked them profusely for the food and for taking the trouble to call on me. After a short time they left, leaving me with lists of suggestions on how to care for my flu. I was ready to cry from embarrassment, frustration, and exhaustion. I felt shamed at having been discovered in this *uchi* or informal, inside state, and constrained by the bonds of their caring and concern. I felt guilty, too, for I knew their concern to be genuine, yet I could not rid myself of the feeling of having been invaded by these expressions of kindness.

The demands and obligations of Japanese social life came to assume increasing importance in my life. The time I was living in my own apartment, I was an active member of many different social networks: relatives, acquaintances from work, classmates from tea ceremony lessons, and fellow participants in community activities. The hospitality and graciousness that were my initial due as guest were tempered with growing demands on my time. As I grew to be more of a participant in these relationships, rather than a mere observer, it came my turn to reciprocate. I was bombarded with requests to teach English, a story familiar to any Americans who have been in Japan. People asked me to take part in many social gatherings, commensurate with my positioning within social networks: a relative's funeral, another relative's memorial service, the coming of age of my neighbor's daughter, the elementary school graduation ceremony of Fusae-chan, Mrs. Hatanaka's younger daughter. Though at the beginning stages of my field research I welcomed all such invitations, the requests and solicitous care shown for me occasionally elicited feelings of invasion. I felt bound by chains of obligation to my sponsors, my relatives, my friends, and my co-workers, and though I appreciated their concern for me and realized my responsibility to return the kindnesses they had shown me, I simply did not have enough hours in the day to accommodate all of them.

The situation came to a climax one day when I received a phone call from a local teacher who had arranged a number of interviews for me. He began with *"Jitsu wa . . ."* (actually . . .) a phrase that almost always precedes the asking of a favor. My antennae went up, sensing danger. Well, said he, there was a student of his who would love to learn English conversation, and well, he would like to bring her over to meet me the following evening. Since he had been of so much help to me, I knew I could not refuse and still be considered a decent human being, so I agreed. But I was in a foul mood the entire evening. I complained bitterly to my landlady, who sympathetically agreed that the *sensei* should have been more mindful of the fact that I was so pressed, but she confirmed that I had no choice but to comply. She explained that the *sensei* had been happy to give of his time to help me, and by the same token he considered it natural to make requests of others, who should be equally giving of themselves, their "inner" feelings notwithstanding. *"Nihonjin wa ne,"* she mused, *"jibun o taisetsu ni shinai no, ne."* (The Japanese don't treat themselves as important, do they? That is, they spend time doing things for the sake of maintaining good relationships, regardless of their "inner" feelings.) I gazed at her in amazement, for her statement struck me with incredible force. Not only did it perfectly capture my own feelings of being bound by social obligation, living my life for others, it also indicated to me a profoundly different way of thinking about the relationship between selves and the social world. Persons seemed to be constituted in and through social relations and obligations to others. Selves and society did not seem to be separate entities; rather, the boundaries were blurred. This realization, coming as it did through intense participation in social life, led me to shift my research problem from kinship and economics to what seemed to be an even more fundamental assumption: how personhood was defined in a Japanese context, and how, more specifically, people at the Satō factory crafted themselves in the practices of everyday life.

Participation in the field was thus a necessary step in the process of understanding, and in fact it was instrumental in shifting the focus of my research. But in the cases I describe, it also produced a threat to the self: one of fusion or dissolution in my collapse of identity, and one of invasion in the second epiphanal moment. My ambiguous insider/outsider position in the field may have made the issue of identity and threat to coherent selfhood especially acute, but other studies by white female ethnographers and by Japanese American men suggest that my experience was not a unique one (cf. Bachnik 1978; Bernstein 1983; Hamabata 1983 and forthcoming; Okimoto 1971). The ways my informants preferred to treat me, my increasing sense of ease in "belonging" to Japanese society, the recognition of cultural skills I had retained as a Japanese American—all led to the weighting of what my Japanese informants and I labeled my "Japanese" self. I collaborated in this attempted recreation with various degrees of enthusiasm and resistance.

In fact, my decision about when to leave Japan was linked to this re-writing of identity. The final months of fieldwork are generally the best and most productive: the months of laying groundwork pay off in the increasing intimacy and comfort in your relationships and in the depth of the insights you are able to reach. This fact made me ever more reluctant to say that my research was "finished." I kept extending my stay at the factory; it became something of a joke, as the older women would tease me about my parents, whose "neck must be sooooo long," the expression one uses to describe someone who is waiting impatiently. "You must have found a boyfriend," they would tell me, or, laughing, they might suggest, "Why not find a nice Japanese boy and settle down here?" I laughed with them, but I continued to stay on as research became more and more productive, until one event convinced me that the time to depart was near. At a tea ceremony class, I performed a basic "thin tea" ceremony flawlessly, without need for prompting or correction of my movements. My teacher said in tones of approval, "You know, when you first started, I was so worried. The way you moved, the way you walked, was so clumsy! But now, you're just like an *ojōsan,* a nice young lady." Part of me was inordinately pleased that my awkward, exaggerated Western movements had *finally* been replaced by the disciplined grace that makes the tea ceremony so seemingly natural and beautiful to watch. But another voice cried out in considerable alarm, "Let me escape before I'm completely transformed!" And not too many weeks later, leave I did.

My experiences of identification, fragmentation, and self-transformation eloquently demonstrated for me the simultaneously creative and distressing effects of the interplay of meaning and power as my friends, co-workers, and I rewrote our identities. Yet I would argue that enthusiastic participation in my friends' lives was essential before I could step back to discern the meaningful order in everyday life and thereby understand its significance. Engagement and openness could throw into relief wrenching contradictions, but it was also productive of meaning, of identity, of change. Through participation, one had to open oneself to others and remain willing to change one's perceptions through this intimate contact. Only then could difference be truly realized. And only then could the issue of identity and of crafting selves emerge as my central theoretical problem.

Consequently, experience, and the *specificity* of my experience—a particular human being who encounters particular others at a particular historical moment and has particular stakes in that interaction—is not opposed to theory; it *enacts* and *embodies* theory. That is to say, the so-called personal details of the encounters, and of the concrete processes through which research problems emerged, are constitutive of theory; one cannot be separated from the other. Deconstructing the binary between personal/private/experiential/interior on the one hand, and political/institutional/theoretical/exterior-to-the-self, on the other, is a key motif in the critique of individualism and the self/society, subject/world distinction.

My "personal" account of the emergence of the problematic of selfhood is thus the product of a complex negotiation, taking place within specific, but shifting, contexts, where power and meaning, "personal" and "political," are inseparable. Identity is not a fixed "thing," it is negotiated, open, shifting, ambiguous, the result of culturally available meanings and the open-ended, power-laden enactments of those meanings in everyday situations. The crafting of this text; the crafting of my identity; and the crafting of the identities of my Japanese friends, relatives, co-workers and acquaintances as represented in this book, are the complicated outcomes of power-fraught negotiations between "Self" and "Other"—the Western cultural baggage of the terms themselves being highly problematic. In the anthropological hermeneutic circle, participation eventually gives way to "observation" and reconstruction, as we anthropologists create our ethnographic texts. Writing freezes the complex dance of domination and counter-domination, of approaching and drawing back, which I have attempted to evoke in these pages. The process of making sense of each other involves active efforts to force others into preconceived categories. Just as my informants, in writing me and my identity, tried to excise traces of Americanness, I also in the act of writing inevitably fix ambiguity, and attempt to stitch together pieces of my "self," in order to construct an account of the lives of my co-workers and friends and the ways I came to "understand" those lives. And in the act of writing, culturally shaped abstractions like "theory," "power," "experience," and "identity" also emerge.

Consequently, the first-person voice is a rhetorical/theoretical strategy (again, the split between these terms is an artifact of our linguistic and cultural conventions). At stake in the choice of this strategy is the distinction between personal and political. Mine is an attempt to challenge and displace that distinction through a tactic that meshes so-called experiential and theoretical concerns. The narrative "I" is meant to problematize the very terms "first person," "personal," "private," and in its least complimentary form, "narcissistic," that might conventionally be used to characterize my writing strategy. That my book came to pivot around notions of identity is, I have argued, the result of a complex, open-ended series of interactions between a specific ethnographer, with a particular face, age, gender, "personality," and disciplinary training, and a particular agenda in mind, and specific Japanese people with their own particular faces, ages, genders, "personalities," and agendas. And these are not "merely personal," "deeply private" aspects of identity, something secret and unknowable that can never be shared, but multiple, crosscutting forces. Race, gender, age, academic training, and so on, are some of them, but others, equally important, include the historical and political agendas underlying anthropological research, the place of "East Asian Studies" in the United States and at particular institutions,[8] and the strategic, highly fraught geopolitical relationships between America and Japan, especially in the light of World War II and the recent "trade wars." These constitute the matrices of power within which, for both better and worse, my inquiry and all research done by Americans in Japan, or conversely, by Japanese in the United States, is conducted.[9]

In short, by deploying and problematizing the first-person voice, I argue that the bounded, interiorized self is a narrative convention. The "I" invoked is not clearly divisible from "the world," and no inviolable interior space, no fixed essence which we can unequivocally label "private," can be distilled out from the domains of what we call politics, economics,

language, culture, and history. Thus far I have deployed the "I" in order
to describe the processes by which the problematic of identity emerged.
But my major aim is to focus attention on the people I encountered in
Japan, and for them, as for us, language and narrative conventions provide the most striking insights into the simultaneously creative and
disciplinary production of "selves."

Japanese Selves and Their Challenge
to the "Whole Subject"

A brief consideration of work done on "the Japanese self," in the light of
my particular experiences in the factory and the neighborhood, can
point us toward the profound challenges such scholarship offers to seemingly incorrigible Western assumptions about the primacy of "the
individual" and the boundedness and fixity of personal identity. My
neighbors, friends, co-workers, and acquaintances never allowed me to
forget that contextually constructed, relationally defined selves are particularly resonant in Japan. I was never allowed to be an autonomous,
freely operating "individual." As a resident of my neighborhood, a friend,
a co-worker, a teacher, a relative, an acquaintance, a quasi-daughter, I
was always defined by my obligations and links to others. I was "always
already" caught in webs of relationships, in which loving concern was not
separable from power, where relationships define one and enable one to
define others. The epiphanal moment when I realized the lack of importance of any personal self apart from social obligations was perhaps the
most eloquent in my experience, though it simply crystallized the
themes already so much a part of life in my neighborhood. But such
selves are enacted every day, every time Japanese people speak Japanese.

A motif in the plethora of recent work on Japanese selfhood throws
into relief what Jane Bachnik has so aptly called a "sliding scale" of self
and other. This sliding scale is encoded in multiple registers of experience, most strikingly apparent in the use of language, including body
language (e.g., Doi 1986; Lebra 1976; Plath 1980; R. J. Smith 1983b; Bachnik 1982; Kondo 1982; Wetzel 1984). Moreover, Japanese linguistic
ideology highlights the permeability of selves, a "distance cline" between self and other, where selves are determined by context and
boundaries are constantly shifting. What I describe here can only begin
to sketch the outlines of the ways Japanese people I knew enacted their
identities in language use, in order to delineate the *general parameters*
within which any speaker of Japanese must operate. I concentrate on

those elements which in English are especially significant repositories of personhood, agency, and personal identity: so-called personal pronouns and so-called proper names. And I try to show that these linguistic conventions were indeed part of everyday life for the people I knew in the Satō factory, in the neighborhood, and among my relatives and teachers.

In Japanese, so-called personal pronouns offer striking evidence to support the idea of relationally defined selves. Speakers of Japanese have a plethora of different options to exercise in choosing terms of self-reference. A cursory review of available choices might include:

	Male	Female
Formal	Watakushi	
	Watashi	Watakushi (less formal
	Wasshi (for older men, usually)	than for men)
	Boku	Watashi
Informal	Ore	Atashi

Source: Modified from Harada 1975 and Bachnik 1982.

Choice of one pronoun over another is situationally negotiated and varies according to gender, class, region, and so on. *Boku,* for instance, has a middle-class, "good boy," and sometimes childlike resonance;[10] some of my upper-middle-class friends averred that they—or their husbands or sons—would never use *ore,* although longterm acquaintance revealed that their denials had to be greeted with a certain skepticism. *Ore* has a tough, informal, macho aura that *boku* utterly lacks, and among close friends or to their wives or girlfriends, these men would use *ore* quite liberally—their reports on their own behavior notwithstanding. The class resonance of these terms for self-reference is also pronounced. Indeed, my relatives even asked what term the artisans tended to use for themselves, and when I replied with *ore,* they shook their heads knowingly and said, yes, that is something that "laborers" would say. Of course, my male relatives would themselves use *ore* in informal situations. On the other hand, in the Satō factory the male artisans would rarely be caught using the "affected" or "less masculine" term *boku;* rather, they would use the "vulgar, masculine" term *ore* when they were talking amongst themselves. But when they were talking to a superior—the division chief or Mr. Satō, for instance—their language went up a level in politeness, and they either omitted terms of self-reference or used the term *boku.*

More startling to the speaker of English are the bewildering variety of terms which can serve as so-called personal pronouns. These include kin terms, proper names (both first and last), occupational titles, and other terms that could not be substituted for pronouns in most Indo-European languages (T. Suzuki 1978, 93). Usually people have no need to invoke any term for self-reference, for it can be implied through context. If such terms are used, situational factors circumscribe the available appropriate choices. For example, Mr. Hatanaka, when speaking to his children, used the term *Otōsan,* or father, to refer to himself. Occasionally, he would use the word *papa* instead, most memorably in one of his favorite puns, which used to make us roll our eyes: "*Papa iya,*" Papa (I) hate(s) it, he would say, wrinkling his nose and shaking his head, on the rare occasions when we brought out papayas for dessert. Mrs. Hatanaka usually called herself *okāsan,* mother, when she was speaking to her children. On one especially noteworthy day, her daughter Akemi-chan had forgotten her English conversation lesson with me. Mrs. Hatanaka was furious. In angry tones, she ordered Akemi-chan to apologize to me. Akemi-chan protested, "But I had to do all this work for our school club! I just lost track of time." This was too much for the usually gracious and gentle Mrs. Hatanaka, who completely lost her temper. She slapped her daughter on the face, and invoked her authority as mother: "*Okāsan ga itta deshō. Ayamarinasai!*" (Mother's told you, hasn't she? Apologize!) This, the tearful and chastened Akemi-chan immediately did. I, embarrassed, hurriedly accepted the apology.

Younger people can also refer to themselves using kin terms (older brother or sister, for instance), but they may also use a shortened version of their first names plus the appropriate diminutive suffix. My young relative, Ruriko, often referred to herself as Ruri + the diminutive *chan,* terms used most often as terms of address, usually to a child or to someone to whom you can express intimacy and affection. "Ruri-chan wants some, too," she might say as her older sister was having a snack, or "Ruri-chan has a meeting of her school club tomorrow," or "Ruri-chan read that book the other day." This was not a personal idiosyncrasy—though perhaps she did this a trifle more often than did her siblings—but a reasonably common everyday occurrence among younger people. Older people tended to define themselves in terms of their roles in the family or through occupational titles. For example, *shachō,* company president, was deployed in interesting ways. Mr. Satō, the *shachō* of the confectionery factory, might come in and say, "*Shachō* will come to the noon meetings tomorrow," referring to the meetings where we read from our ethics pamphlets and chanted the slogan of the day. Of course, *shachō* would be used to emphasize his role as the head of the organization, whereas a more inclusive, egalitarian feeling could be imparted by using *uchi,* our group, our company: "we" instead of "I." In other situations, Mr. Satō would sound rather silly referring to himself as *shachō*— around his friends, for example, most of whom are also the *shachō* of their small companies.

Suffice it to say that the plethora of available "I's" throws into relief the multiple ways people present themselves and their identities in particular situations. You are not an "I" untouched by context, rather you are defined by the context. One could argue that identity and context are inseparable, calling into question the very distinction between the two. In more technical, linguistic terms, a case could be made that identity in Japan is not linked to the use of pronouns as anaphora, where the "I" stands for a proper noun that has been registered in discourse. Rather, as Bachnik (1982) and Wetzel (1984) have argued, so-called pronouns in Japanese are indexical and deictic, shifting with social positioning and the relations between "self" and "other." The "I" is shaped by formality, kinship, occupation, other people's desires and usages, and myriad other "contextual" factors; it does not stand for a proper noun that has already been registered in discourse and remains a constant irrespective of the particularities of a given situation. As such, it provides striking contrast to pronouns in English. As Smith notes, "the use of personal referents is one of the most difficult features of the language to teach Americans, for whom the apparently irreducible 'I' presents a major stumbling block to the easy adoption of the constantly shifting, relational 'I' of the Japanese, which is not detached from the other" (R. J. Smith 1983b, 79).

Smith also demonstrates that in Japanese, even the quintessential symbol of Western logocentrism and of presence—the proper name— reveals its referentially empty, shifting, and contextual nature, for the pronunciation of proper names can also differ according to contextual factors and can be more influenced by the desires of the speaker than by those of the person to whom the proper name is supposedly attached. Smith cites the example of noted kinship scholar Ariga Kizaemon, whose last name could be pronounced Aruga or Ariga. He had written to a close associate of Ariga in order to find out the correct pronunciation of the name (ibid., 80–81). The reply he received was as follows:

> I am fortunate to be able to send you this latest answer from the professor himself. Of course we know that he is called Aruga in his local community of Suwa, Nagano Prefecture, and by his

older intimate friends from his earliest days in Tokyo. But at a later time, both in Japanese society and internationally, he became more commonly known as Ariga. . . . What is the situation today? A few persons around him call him Aruga. Some people, like myself, sometimes called him Ariga, at other times Aruga; most people call him Ariga. When he publishes in English, the professor himself uses the form Ariga, so this is probably the one your colleague should use in his bibliography.

The upshot is that there is no unequivocally correct pronunciation, and that pronunciation of the proper name may vary according to contextual factors, including the speaker's desires and the generally common usage in the group of which the speaker is a part.

First names may also be pronounced in more than one way. Many people have first names that can be read either in their Japanese or *kun* reading, or in a Japanese reading based on Chinese, the so-called *on* reading. "Masao," written in a certain way, can also be called "Seiyū," in its Sinicized reading. This Sinicized version is a term of honor or respect. When I stayed one summer with a family whose head had this name, my grandmother advised my parents to address their letters to Mr. Seiyū H., not to Masao, and in fact, he did seem to be flattered by the designation. My relatives in Tokyo, however, provided me with the most interesting example. My great-aunt's first name was written with characters that are ordinarily read "Kazuko," though she adopted a highly unusual reading of "Noriko" for the same characters. When my grandmother read the characters for my parents, who would send cards, packages, or letters to my Tokyo relatives and caretakers, she naturally assumed the reading was "Kazuko," and "Kazuko" was the name my parents dutifully printed on the outside. My great-uncle and his son not so subtly took me aside a few times to tell me that the reading was really "Noriko." Yet, to this day, my great-aunt signs her name "Kazuko" when she writes in romanized letters to my parents. She is deferring to their writing of her identity as "Kazuko," though "Noriko" she may be to those who know her better. They, as much as she, define her identity, her "proper name," in the context of that relationship.

Terms of self-reference and proper names in Japanese are clearly not the seemingly fixed essences they seem to be in English, but perhaps even more revealing are the layers of intimacy and distance, engagement and detachment, that permeate other facets of the Japanese language. A striking feature of Japanese is that the indexical meanings, the way something is said, and what that in turn says about the relationship between speakers, are often far more important than the actual content of an utterance. Indeed, Japanese "linguistic ideology" (Silverstein 1979) directs attention to levels of hierarchy, intimacy, distance, and contextuality. A mark of mature adulthood is the ability to handle different kinds of language suitable to particular situations.

To illustrate the complexity of the social calculus involved in any utterance, and the layers of distance and intimacy encoded in language, consider the four simplest possible ways of saying "to hold" or "to carry." The base form, *motsu,* is relatively informal, a form you could use with friends. The "medium polite" form, *mochimasu,* indicates more distance. It could, for example, indicate that you and the addressee are acquaintances, but not good friends. When speaking to status superiors—teachers, bosses—you would probably select *omochi ni narimasu* to refer to the superior's actions. But to offer to carry your boss's bags, for instance, you should use *omochi shimasu,* the humble form. Women, especially those with upper-middle- to upper-class pretentions, would probably select the more polite forms in order to display their refinement, and they might even use the informal forms of honorific verbs (e.g., *omochi ni naru*) to add an air of "distinction" (Bourdieu 1984) to their speech. Awareness of complex social positioning is an *inescapable* element of any utterance in Japanese, for it is *utterly impossible* to form a sentence without *also* commenting on the relationship between oneself and one's interlocutor.

In short, proper use of Japanese teaches one that a human being is always and inevitably involved in a multiplicity of social relationships. Boundaries between self and other are fluid and constantly changing, depending on context and on the social positioning people adopt in particular situations. These multiple, infinitely graded layers of selfhood are often described in Japanese in terms of two *end points* of a continuum: the *tatemae,* social surface, that which is done to smooth social relations, and *honne,* "real" feeling; *omote,* the front, formal side, vs. *ura,* the back, or intimate side; *soto,* outside, and *uchi,* inside (Doi 1973, 1986; Bachnik 1978; Kondo 1982; Hamabata 1983). Let me emphasize that the boundaries of *soto/uchi omote/ura,* are contextually constructed, shifting, and therefore referentially empty; they are *not* dualistic, essentialist categories. Using these terms invokes a complex series of gradations along a scale of detachment and engagement,[11] distance and intimacy, formality and informality. (For earlier articulations, see Doi 1973; Bachnik 1978; Kondo 1982.) The tension between the two poles is never completely resolved, however, though I will argue that the tension is often creative. Both ends of the continuum are necessary, irreducible facts of human life. These multiple, relationally defined selves offer culturally specific possibilities for human fulfillment in the intertwinings of deep feeling and the inextricable connectedness of selves. And they also, I will later argue, offer other, culturally specific possibilities for domination and for the coercive, disciplinary production of selves.

In contrast, the irreducible "I" of the English language is relatively detached from its social context; indeed, that one can even distinguish between the "I" and "the context" is revealing in itself. The linguistic ideology of American English masks what may be a discontinuous and changing self, exploiting what Crapanzano calls the "anaphoric potential" of the "I." That is, the "I" who is registered once in discourse is the referent for all subsequent invocations of the "I." The "I" who wakes up in the morning is presumably the same "I" who goes to work, who talks to a boss, who takes care of the children, who goes to bed at night. The English language encourages an assumption that "the self" is a whole, bounded subject who marches through untouched and unchanged from one situation to the next.[12] If openness and multiplicity are admitted as possibilities, if self and world are not separable, the "I" is revealed in its referential emptiness (cf. Crapanzano 1982). "The self," "the whole subject," the irreducible "I," the bounded essence separable from "society" is at least partially, then, the sediment of our own history, language, and linguistic ideology, elaborated in myriad ways in everyday and academic discourses. Furthermore, the invocation of this seemingly unchanging, anaphoric "I" may veil a self that is contextually constructed and referentially hollow (Butler 1988a; Crapanzano 1982).

Lest the reader think that these comparisons are too general and unconvincing at the level of language, let me turn to culturally shaped narrative conventions. Takie Lebra, in her book on Japanese women (1984), cites in her conclusions a series of autobiographies collected over the years from both (white) American women in Hawaii and the Japanese women she interviewed for her book. The comparisons she offers are highly instructive. For although many feminist scholars (usually associated with object relations theory, who generally take as their subjects white, middle-class American women—e.g., Gilligan 1982; Chodorow 1978) argue that American women in comparison with American men define themselves relationally, the differences between American and Japanese narrative styles are striking. Individualism and independence are played fortissimo in the American accounts, which focus on "the recollector herself as the central 'figure' . . . relegating everything else to the 'ground'" (Lebra 1984, 294). Indeed, this tendency was so pronounced, Lebra writes, that it "frustrated my intention to capture American social structure out of the individuals' biographies" (ibid.). In the Japanese autobiographies, it is clear that "the Japanese individual, in the course of life, becomes an increasingly integral part . . . of social structure." (ibid., 299) The Japanese stories of self-construction emphasize a woman's life as a single thread in a richly textured fabric of relationships. Japanese women portray themselves as accommodating to duties and to the needs of others, rather than as independent decision makers. And it is this accommodation to others that makes them fully mature human beings, that creates their "personality," as David Plath (1980) phrased it. Underlying these two highly contrastive approaches to narrative are, I would argue, fundamentally different cultural ideals about what it is to be human, a woman, and an adult—two ways of conceiving and enacting selves. Thus, although Western feminists have undertaken the important work of deconstructing "the whole subject" by pointing to differences within "Western culture," the relationally defined self of American women still remains solidly within a linguistic and historical legacy of individualism. Relationally defined selves in Japan—selves inextricable from context—thus mount a radical challenge to our own assumptions about fixed, essentialist identities and provide possibilities for a consideration of cultural difference and a radical critique of "the whole subject" in contemporary Western culture.

Displacing the Binary:
Anthropological Studies of the Self

This brief sketch of how the people I knew used language to create contextually specific, nonessentialist identities, combined with my personal, experiential account of shifts in a theoretical problematic, enacts the theoretical stakes of my project: the challenges, in various forms, anthropological studies can present to the congeries of phenomena called, in at least some of its incarnations, the Western individual, the whole subject, the master subject, and the possessive individual. Common to these conventional views of identity are assumptions that rest on a "substance metaphysics" (see Butler 1987b; Outlaw 1987). Identities are, in this view, fixed, bounded entities containing some essence or substance that is expressed in distinctive attributes. This conventional trope opposes "the self" as bounded essence, filled with "real feelings" and identity, to a "world" or to a "society" which is spatially and ontologically distinct from the self (Butler 1988a). Indeed, the academic division of labor re-capitulates this distinction in its separation of the disciplines, distinguishing "psychology" from "sociology." A burgeoning literature in anthropology undermines the substance metaphysics fundamental to conventional views of identity—present both in our "folk" understand-ings and in our "theoretical" metadiscourses—through highlighting the socially constructed features of the "concept of self" in a particular culture. Inevitably this move calls into question hegemonic American as-sumptions about identity and selfhood as a bounded essence containing inner, true feelings. The anthropological literature on selfhood is thus crucial in mounting a radical challenge to "the whole subject" by expos-ing its cultural specificity.

But the anthropological literature on "the self" is a literature alive with tension. On the one hand, its emphasis on social construction is a move to de-essentialize "the self," disengaging it from some necessary connec-tion to a universal essence or biological substrate. Such a move calls into question the boundary between "self" and "world" as a fundamental point of departure for analysis. Yet even in an anthropological literature which claims to transcend it, the trope of fixed identity and the self/soci-ety distinction persist.[13] That distinction is enshrined in the anthropological literature in the form of a split between what Marcus and Fischer (1986) call "conveying other cultural experience" through stud-ies of selfhood and emotion, on the one hand, and studies of world historical political economy, on the other. The self/society binary is transposed into yet another key in the anthropological distinction be-tween a "person"—that is, human beings as bearers of *social* roles, on the one hand, and "self"—a kind of inner, reflective psychological es-sence, on the other, recapitulating the binary between social and psychological, world and subject (cf. M. Rosaldo 1984). Yet if we take se-riously the implications of studies since Marcel Mauss and his key essay on *la notion de personne, celle de "moi,"* we are led to a series of ques-tions. Are the terms "self" and "person" the creations of our own linguistic and cultural conventions? If "inner" processes are culturally conceived, their very existence mediated by cultural discourses, to what extent can we talk of "inner, reflective essence" or "outer, objective world" except as culturally meaningful, culturally specific constructs? And how is the inner/outer distinction itself established as the terms within which we inevitably speak and act?

The inner/outer, subject/world dichotomies have been foundational in anthropological studies since Mauss himself, even as he links these notions to culture and history. The classic Mauss essay takes as a point of departure *"la notion de personne"* as *"tout simplement et provisoirement,"* an Aristotelian category, an example of one of the fundamental categories of the human mind. Traversing space and time, Mauss draws our attention to different ways of defining "persons" and "selves" in different cultures at different historical periods, but posits the evolutionary superiority of Western notions of person. "Far from existing as the primordial innate idea, clearly engraved since Adam in the innermost depths of our being, it continues here slowly, and almost right up to our own time, to be built upon, to be made clearer and more specific, becoming identified with self-knowledge and the psychological consciousness" (Mauss 1985, 20). Western notions of self as psychological consciousness and a reflexive self-awareness, based on a division between the inner space of selfhood and outer world, are clearly held up as the highest, most "differentiated" development of "the self" possible. Though Mauss's insights have been taken up and elaborated in richly varied ways, most anthropological analyses leave in place the rhetoric of "the self" or "the person" as "psychological consciousness" and "self-knowledge," continuing to impart the impression of referential solidity and the essential unity of this "self."

I have used the term "referential solidity," for it is clear that this rhetoric/theory of "the self" hangs on a spatialized ideology of meaning as reference. For example, Saussure posits the sign as a relationship between signifier and signified, between sound image as "the impression it makes on our senses" (Saussure 1966, 66) on the one hand, and the concept inside the head or "the psychological imprint of the sound" (ibid.), on the other. Meaning is thus a plenitude, a fullness occupied by certain contents, located inside our "selves." Here we find yet another permutation of a Cartesian dichotomy between reason and sense perception. And not surprisingly, Saussure's model of "the self" is precisely a rational, speaking subject, who in using language reproduces the self/world boundary. "Self" is constituted culturally, but in its presence, supported by notions of referential meaning, "the self" takes on the character of an irreducible essence, the Transcendental Signified, a substance which can be distilled out from the specificities of the situations in which people enact themselves.

Furthermore, the emphasis on referentiality and on a substance metaphysics implies the existence of a unified subject. Saussure's sign unites *a* sound image with *a* concept called up "inside" the speaking subject, in a one-to-one correspondence. The unity and coherence of the subject is reinforced in this one-to-one relationship between signifier and signified. The potential multivocality of signifiers, and even more obviously, the role of context in constituting meaning, is left untheorized or rather it is relegated to the residual category of *parole,* spoken language, the inferior partner of *langue,* the enduring linguistic system. Here, the Derridean critique of Saussure is especially apposite and possesses important implications for a theory of the "self" or "the subject" (Derrida 1976). Derrida argues that the privileging of the signified in the Saussurean sign is tied to the logocentric desire to fix and master meaning, a meaning which should be self-evident to the rational, conscious, self-identical subject. But the sign, for Derrida, always already bears the "trace" of difference; both signifier and signified are defined through difference and absence. Indeed, "the signified is originarily and essentially . . . trace, and *it is always already in the position of the signifier.*" (Derrida 1976, 73; emphasis in the original). Stated in other terms, meaning can never be fixed, for there is no transcendental signified that commands authority and exists without signifiers or beyond signification. Rather, signification involves a play of signifiers, linked in chains of substitution within systems of difference (cf. Derrida 1978, 292). And if that is the case, what happens to the self-identical subject? The subject, too, becomes a site for the play of difference, a site for the play of shifting and potentially conflicting meanings.[14] The "identity" of the subject is multiple, produced within discourse, and potentially contradictory, and though there can be "a temporary retrospective fixing" (Weedon 1987, 25) of meaning and identity, no ready form of coherence can be posited in advance. The unitary subject is no longer unified.

In the anthropological literature, the conventional assumptions of the presence and unity of "the self" and the use of the self/society binary as a foundational point of departure are reinscribed through *rhetorical strategies* which emphasize referential meaning, decontextualized examples, and totalizing narrative closure. That one can even talk of "a concept of self" divorced from specific historical, cultural, and political contexts privileges the notion of some abstract essence of selfhood we can describe by enumerating its distinctive features. The invocation of "culture and self," "a concept of self," or a "notion of person" links up with static, essentialized global traits where selves can be discussed as a category quite separable from power relations. Typically, these traits are smoothly assembled into a portrait of the "self" in a particular culture. This "self" is almost never contradictory or multiple, and traits of the "self" are held to be equally characteristic of all members of a society. Such an essence of inner selfhood preserves the boundaries between the inner space of true selfhood and the outer space of the world and leaves firmly in place the self/society, substance/attribute view of identity. Moreover, this view is extended to all members of a culture, thereby creating a homogenized, undifferentiated collective "self." Unified substance characterizes "the individual" as it also constitutes the unitary essence of a culture.

Contemporary anthropologists interested in issues of "self," emotion, and "personhood," myself included, are in the process of grappling with the difficulties and paradoxes of demonstrating the cultural specificity of selfhood, thereby de-essentializing the category, while still working within a canon and within narrative conventions that almost inevitably reinscribe a self/society distinction. The persistence of these conventional tropes of identity can be seen in a number of recent works by younger scholars on the "self," and my critical comments here should be taken as remarks made by a sympathetic participant engaged in a common collective enterprise. By examining the ways the whole, unified subject and the self/society trope insidiously persist, even in an anthropological literature that claims to transcend them, perhaps we can find ways to problematize and eventually subvert those tropes.

Take for example, the editor's comments in a volume on "culture theory," which brings together a number of scholars interested in "the self" via a Social Science Research Council conference. Richard Shweder summarizes the interpretive possibilities represented in the work of contemporary anthropologists and psychologists in a three-by-three table, lining up three theoretical stances—universalism, developmentalism, and relativism—on one side, and three approaches to rationality—the rational, the irrational, and the nonrational—on the other (Shweder 1984, 59). Shweder closes his essay with the statement, "Each interpretive approach represented in the matrix has a legitimate, although limited, role to play in the study of mind. What we must resist is the temptation to imprison all mental events in the same cell" (p. 60). What Shweder does not do, however, is to problematize his matrix or his definition of the mental, thus preserving what are highly conventional terms of discourse. A genealogical critique of the terms of the matrix itself is thereby foreclosed, and we seem condemned to remain forever within the configurations of cells he sets out for us. I would argue that what we must resist is not confinement to a particular *cell* of the matrix, but confinement to the definition of terms of the matrix itself. And the way to do that is precisely to problematize the categories and terms with which we think, to subject them to critical interrogation, and to initiate a genealogical critique.

White and Kirkpatrick, in another important anthology, *Person, Self and Experience,* bring together a number of works from ethnographers who research in the Pacific. Again, a conceptual tension is present in their introductory remarks. On the one hand, ways of defining "selves" are variable and culturally and historically specific. On the other, the fundamental distinction between subject and world, personal and social, remains foundational. Say White and Kirkpatrick:

> We do not wish to define the bounds of the personal and the social by fiat, but to explore them. Similarly we do not claim particular experience or attributes of persons to be by definition central to personhood or attributes of persons to be by definition central to personhood and subjectivity. We hope to learn on what foundations personhood may be erected in different cultures (1985, 9).

Note that the categories "personal" and "social" are relativized here, but the categories themselves are preserved. And though the authors claim no essential definition of "personhood," clearly "subjectivity"—itself deeply embedded in a Western discourse of objectivity/subjectivity, reason/sense perception, world/subject—is essential to their definitions of personhood. Finally, the invocation of "foundations" of personhood fails to critically interrogate the category of personhood itself, leaving it as a fundamental human essence that may differ in the details of its definition but remains a cornerstone of discourse in every culture. The categories "personal" and "social" are widened, but in the end, the terms themselves remain firmly in place.

Anthropological imperatives to generalize at the cultural level often mean that we construct collective identity through a similar kind of logocentrism or metaphysics of presence, positing the existence of an undifferentiated collective subject. Most of us engage in this strategy at some level or another, but I will use Kirkpatrick's article, "Some Marquesan Understandings of Action and Identity," from the anthology previously mentioned, as illustrative of common anthropological rhetorical moves. Kirkpatrick wants to understand Marquesan ethnopsychology, specifically those emotions that apparently have to do with our notions of "shame," a major preoccupation in much of the literature on selfhood and emotion. In so doing, he focuses on indigenous terms for "attitudes and processes of interaction that Marquesans find characteristic of 'persons' in general" (p. 88). He concentrates on the shared lexical features of the words, using as illustrations a number of decontextualized examples and statements from undifferentiated "informants," whose locations in a larger matrix are never specified. The problem with this approach—constructing a collective subject on the basis of composite and anonymous accounts—is striking when Kirkpatrick describes notions of "extended personal agency" in the form of desire, citing a statement from a man who describes his own phallus as an autonomous agent. One wonders whether a Marquesan woman would have quite the same perspective on the matter, or whether all Marquesan men of all ages and statuses would articulate similar views. The free use of the term Marquesan to describe what are various statements to a particular addressee from various positioned subjects living in particular historical circumstances, works to mask differences, multiplicities, and openness in the term "Marquesan" itself. In view of the inevitable differences within any collective identity and in light of a legacy of French colonialism and insertion in a global capitalist system for which "the Marquesans" produce copra and coffee, the unity and boundedness of "Marquesan culture," and rhetorical strategies that reinscribe that unity and boundedness, cannot remain unproblematized.

Others have sought ways to opening out the closure of "the self" through an alternative to approaches based on Saussurean semiotics. I have already pointed to the subject/object, reason/sense perception dichotomies operative in the concept/sound image structure of the Saussurean sign. E. Valentine Daniel sees an advance on this binarism in the openness offered by a Peircean frame, which adds a third term to the subject-object dichotomy. Peirce posits the notion of a triadic structure, composed of a sign (representamen), an object, and an interpretant (a sign called up in the mind of the addressee). What Daniel finds useful in the Peircean sign is its openness and the inclusion of an addressee in its very structure. Thus, the possibilities for dialogue and conversation are built-in, as signs "invite . . . further interpretants and further signs to partake in the open and ever-expanding semeiotic process" (Daniel 1984, 23). He makes a convincing case for the relative openness of a Peircean framework, and the ways dialogic possibilities present in Peircean signs can take us beyond a simple Cartesian or Saussurean dualism.

However, I would argue that Daniel remains squarely within a subject/object frame, which takes a self/world distinction as presuppositional. The interpretant, the third term, implies the existence of an addressee, or, at another level of abstraction, the existence of habit and culture, which mediate subject and object, self and world (Daniel 1984, 27). But mediating terms and triads are as persistent in our thought as are dualities, and two terms are by no means transcended by simply adding a third. Subjectivity/objectivity, self/society, are binaries that remain persistent in Daniel's analysis. Furthermore, he clearly desires a "systematic," indeed scientific, "proof" of the openness of the Peircean sign, manifested in his quest for "irreducible structure of the sign," or "the atomic structure of the sign" (ibid., 22). Such a quest resonates with the "search in the physical sciences for an ultimate particle of matter and that in metaphysics for essence or substance" (Shore 1982, 135). Eloquent in this regard is Daniel's schematization of the three components of the sign in a structure he compares to "chemical isomers or polymers" (Daniel 1984, 20). The wish for openness coexists with a quest for systematicity and "essence," so that Daniel is in the paradoxical position of questing for an essential kernel of openness in the atomic structure of the sign.

Perhaps one of the most compelling recent experiments in the literature on selfhood is Catherine Lutz's important work. Informed by practice theory, Lutz argues for the "emergent, contested" natures of identities and of emotions, characterizing emotions as culturally and historically constructed ideological practices. She persuasively argues, "Once de-essentialized, emotion can be viewed as a cultural and interpersonal process of naming, justifying, and persuading by people in relationship to each other. Emotional meaning is then a social rather than an individual achievement—an emergent product of social life" (Lutz 1988, 4). She goes on to critique reifications of our own conceptual categories, particularly the subject/object, emotion/reason binaries, and sensitively treats the problems of translating emotion categories across cultures. She rightfully calls into question pragmatic theories of language, based on a concern with referential meaning, and the tendency to posit a one-to-one correspondence between "word" and "thing" (ibid., 9). In the field or psychological anthropology, hers is perhaps the work most receptive to currents in social theory which emphasize practice, openness, cultural and historical specificity, and power.

The telling tension in this work lies in its rhetorical strategies. Though explicitly theoretical passages elaborate this de-essentializing move toward situational specificity and practice, the rhetorical strategies tend to follow familiar narrative conventions, reinscribing an emphasis on referential (if multivocal) meanings. Lutz discusses her perspective: "First, the lexicon of the self and interaction provides evidence about the concepts underlying ethnopsychological understanding" (Lutz 1988, 84). Especially revealing is Lutz's rhetorical focus on particular emotion words and their referents. Key words are described, as are some concrete situations and illustrations of how those words are used. But this word-oriented approach tends to draw us toward lexical definitions and notions of emotion as a static concept, and it preserves the emphasis on referential meaning Lutz has rightfully called into question. A similar relative emphasis on fixity can be see in Lutz's notion of a "scenario." Emotion words, in her view, call up conventional scenarios or plans for action, and are subjects of negotiated meanings (Lutz 1988, 10). It is important to stress the significant move Lutz makes in arguing that a word engenders practice by calling up a particular scenario. But the word + scenario writing strategy still evokes a *fixed* scenario, thereby de-emphasizing the nonessentialist, emergent dimensions of practice and the workings of power Lutz explicitly argues for in other parts of the text. The "self" implied in this account is again a unified subject who enacts these scenarios and expresses these emotional orientations in a relatively unproblematic way. The tension between practice and openness, on the one hand, and fixity, on the other, emerges in the writing strategies, which alternate between the practice-oriented technique—anecdotes, experiential accounts—and the primary writing technique, which highlights static descriptions of a word and a scenario, using particular cases as *illustrations,* instead of beginning with particulars and examining complex negotiations over meaning in their specificity. Though a scenario is a *plan* for action, it need not be seen as a fixed plan. Perhaps a writing strategy that viewed such a scenario as an assertion, enacted in specific contexts and animated by contradiction, highlighting its twists of meaning in a particular situation, might enact the theoretical argument more effectively. The text embodies a transitional moment in the writing of ethnography, where our writing strategies coexist in tension with our "theoretical" apparatus. In Lutz's book, the implicit emphasis on referentiality, fixity, and a self/world binary subverts its explicit theoretical message, which argues for contextual meanings, openness, change, and cultural and historical specificity.

These points noted, it is difficult to imagine that any ethnography written at this historical moment could escape the tensions I have so far described, and my account is one more attempt to struggle with these issues. In order for an account to be recognized as "ethnography", certain narrative conventions are inevitably preserved. Moreover, as I argued at the beginning of this introduction, the narrative conventions we have at our disposal shape our writing in a plethora of unconscious ways—as *Eugénie Grandet* brought home to me. And there are other challenges to face: for example, the difficulties of conveying the multidimensionality of experience in a linear, discursive medium, and the problems of just how we *do* go about imparting a sense of pattern in our experiences and in the materials we bring back from the field. In no way do I think it possible to "transcend" the narrative conventions of ethnography—any utopian space of "resistance" or "transcendence" is something I wish explicitly to problematize. My own account of the Japanese language as a medium for the disciplinary production of selves is itself problematic in its rhetorical strategy and in its generality, and until I or others can find more innovative ways of writing, these tensions will undoubtedly remain.

As writers of ethnography, anthropologists also confront the challenge of the ways our own accounts are constructed in and through language, history, and discourse. One could never completely jettison the semantic load of the word "self," where agency, boundedness, and fixity are indelibly inscribed in the sedimented linguistic history of the term. Any attempt to argue for openness, multiplicity, and the play of power as intrinsic to the crafting of selves easily leads to fears that agency and indeed, normalcy, will be abandoned, as selves are tossed around on the currents of history and politics and we are left with selves laid "out on the table with self-induced multiple personality disorder" (Haraway 1988, 578). We cannot simply transcend the semantic history embedded in the term "the self," even as we try to de-essentialize and open up "the self" to "the world."

However, that should not lead us to the conclusion that no further innovation is possible. Two points must be made, corresponding to two areas in which I hope *Crafting Selves* will take us one step farther toward other ways of problematizing and thematizing our material. Currents in poststructuralism, postmodernism, feminist theory, and practice theory lead us to question the ways the anthropological literature reinscribes fixity, unity, boundedness, and in particular insulates the "self" from the play of power relations. The many accounts which rely on a characterization of "*the* concept of self," "*la* notion de personne," with no reference to variation and multiplicity within "a" self, to the practices creating selves in concrete situations, or to the larger historical and institutional processes shaping those selves, share a peculiarly detached and decontextualized quality. "The self" takes on the character of an irreducible essence, which can be distilled from the specificities of the situations in

The Eye/I

which people enact themselves. The unity, fixity, and boundedness of this "self" can be challenged through explicit arguments of a conventionally "theoretical" sort, but it strikes me that the real challenge is *to enact our theoretical messages,* thereby displacing a theoretical/empirical opposition. Toward that end, my aims are first, to make issues of power central to our discussions of the "self," and second, to experiment with rhetorical strategies that might be more compatible with "theoretical" emphases on multiplicity, contextuality, complexity, power, irony, and resistance. We might do this, building on earlier studies—and in the process providing a critical appraisal of those studies—by asking how selves *in the plural* are constructed variously in various situations, how these constructions can be complicated and enlivened by multiplicity and ambiguity, and how they shape, and are shaped by, relations of power.

Power and Writing Strategies

The inextricability of power and identity links up with critiques by feminist, "Third World," and poststructuralist scholars to reveal *not only* the historical and cultural specificity of "the whole subject," or "a concept of self," but the kinds of exclusions and hierarchies upon which such a subject is constructed. (For just a few examples, see Moraga and Anzaldúa 1981; Spivak 1988; Takaki 1979; Butler 1987b; Haraway 1988; Scott 1988; Foucault 1979; DeLauretis 1986.) Such critiques would argue that "a concept of self" is inevitably implicated in relations of power and indeed, that the construction of identities cannot be discussed in the abstract, separately from power relations. Minimally, the disciplinary production of "selves" is enforced through language—and transgressions of those disciplines, if too great, risk punishment and invoke the specter of incomprehensibility and chaos.

Through experimentation with multiple, shifting voices, I undertake a project to decenter and de-essentialize selves, focusing on the ways people construct themselves and their lives—in all their complexity, contradiction, and irony—within discursive fields of power and meaning, in specific situations, at specific historical moments. Surely, investigations of "crafting selves" in the domain of work cannot ignore the fields of power, hierarchy, and discipline within which people struggle over the meanings of "company," of "family," of what it means to work in a small factory in Tokyo in the late seventies and early eighties, of what we might call "class," of artisanship, and of the conventions surrounding the

43

construction of gender. Enlarging the meanings of "personal" and "political," and displacing the opposition between them, take the form of showing the multiple definitions of selves in specific situations and the inseparability of those definitions from terms we would label economic, political, cultural, and historical. I attempt to avoid positing in advance the unproblematic existence of a unified, rational, coherent, bounded subject,[15] looking instead to see "selves" as potential sites for the play of multiple discourses and shifting, multiple subject-positions. For example, the women I knew were not members of some unproblematic category, "woman," but were constituted through a variety of specific subject-positions—wife, mother, part-time worker, resident of the Shitamachi, or downtown, district of Tokyo, and worker in a small enterprise, to name only a few.[16] And these subject-positions are shaped in history and in specific interactions on the shop floor.

Displacing the categories of "personal" and "political" through the introduction of myriad complicating multiplicities and ambiguities is a process that must occur on many different levels. One step would link these "concepts of self" to certain groups in society—usually elite or dominant groups—making them characteristic of one segment of a culture, but not generalizable to the whole. "Concepts of self" are intrinsically linked to power, then, as these elite or dominant groups derive their preeminence from exclusion and hierarchy. For my co-workers and neighbors, I argue that the qualities of self most characteristic of the dominant middle-class, "uptown," white-collar culture in Tokyo define my friends as less polished, less completely human. Similarly, within the factory, qualities associated with older, male artisans create the central narrative around which work identities are constructed. Thus these men are seen as most mature, most fully human at the workplace. Younger male workers and the part-time women workers have less claim to full-fledged maturity and legitimacy within that context.

Further than this, we can examine the ways different people struggle over the meanings of identity in different arenas of life. Much of *Crafting Selves* concentrates on the differing constructions of collective identities in the Satō factory: how people envision their belonging—or lack thereof—to encompassing entities like "company" and "family." These interpretations may vary from situation to situation, as events and the stakes people have in those events change. In examining disputes and conflicts in the factory, for instance, I found that workers sometimes invoked a discourse of rights, claiming paternalistic benefits as their just due, while owners might define the same benefit—a company trip, for

example—as their benevolent "gift" to workers. The familial idiom provided my part-time co-workers with tools for critique as well, however,
for they often criticized the owner for being *inadequately* familial, for
narrowly defining "company as family" in terms of his own family's interests instead of thinking of the benefit of the company—including the
workers—as a whole.

It is important to realize that conflicts, ambiguities, and multiplicities
in interpretation, are not simply associated with different positionings in
society—though of course this is a critically important factor—but exist
within a "single" self.[17] One chapter, in particular, concentrates on the
story of the chief artisan in the factory, whose narrative of mas-
culine/artisanal identity is shaped by larger cultural meanings of
artisanship, work, and relations to nature and to the material world. Just
as important, the narrative is based on exclusions of younger men and of
women workers, reiterating in another mode power relations present in
other domains of Japanese society. Finally, the narrative itself is riven by
tension and ambiguities as historical and economic changes, and the
chief artisan's fears and internal conflicts, assail the univocity of his narrative. His story leads us toward a reconceptualization of meaning and
power, where even those who have power are themselves working at
cross-purposes to their own interests, that they, too, are caught in power
relations and in their own ways are dominated by those relations even as
they can dominate others.

The displacement of the categories of self and society, and of the "personal" and the "political," and the resulting paradoxes and multiplicities
of selves perhaps come most sharply into focus with the final chapter on
gender ideology. Women workers occupy a marginal structural position
at the Satō factory. As part-time workers, they constitute a secondary labor force, a buffer group which can be used to absorb economic dislocation. On the other hand, they are critically important members of the firm
on other levels: as eroticized mothers to the younger artisans, as erotic
objects for the older artisans, and as appreciative audiences for the central masculine story of artisanal prowess and masculinity. In enacting
themselves as women at the workplace, the women I knew asserted
claims for a more central place in the factory. And by invoking their links
to the home, they challenged the work ethic of masculine artisanal prowess so celebrated by the male artisans. Yet in so doing, they inevitably tied
themselves more closely to conventional gender ideologies, thus ensuring their structural marginality in the firm. These contradictions cannot
be attributed to some essential proclivity of Japanese women to be sub-

missive or accommodationist, or to some conspiracy of Japanese men to subjugate their women. It is rather that the narrative productions of self and the assertions of gender identity for women in the factory produced contradictory and unintended consequences. Their stories of contributing to both company and family are not celebrated culturally as are stories of craftsmen's prowess. And their invocations of gender inevitably occur within a field in which gender possesses a particular sedimented history, which presents possibilities for the construction of satisfying identities and for the subversion of those identities, just as it enforces and disciplines the production of gender. My part-time co-workers, then, showed me how the levels we call personal, institutional, economic, and political cannot be neatly separated from one another and that identities are not essential wholes, but subject-positions—shifting nodal points within often conflict-ridden fields of meaning.

A final *caveat lector:* precisely in an attempt to create a new vision of my material I engage here certain writing strategies that eschew some of the ethnographic canons of representation. The reader will find here no organizational charts of company structure, little statistical, so-called objective data, and scant linear, empirical description. With the aim of imparting a vivid sense of everyday life, I attempt to recapture dialogue and events as they occurred on the shop floor and elsewhere—words uttered by "real people." To protect the privacy of the people who appear in these pages, I have used pseudonyms, but I consider it theoretically/politically/rhetorically important to allow my co-workers to have names, to become particular beings with particular quirks and idiosyncrasies, characters readers could follow through the course of the book. The collective noun "the Japanese" is used as little as possible, and I have tried to avoid generalized statements using abstract individuals, such as "the Japanese woman is. . . ." The problems of suppressing differences within identities do not disappear in this rhetorical move, for other collective identities surface at other levels: women, men, artisans, Shitamachi dwellers, indeed, the "I" itself. But I will try to problematize those collective identities and remain mindful of the differences and the inevitable exclusions on which they are based, even as I deploy the terms.

The structure of the book reflects certain tensions in its simultaneous resistance to and preservation of the narrative conventions of ethnography. The first part, "Settings," is the most "traditional," with its invocation of the setting trope and the sketches of what Donna Haraway has called the "narrative field" within which my period of work at the Satōs' took place. In chapter 2, I seek to broadly outline the political, economic, and historical context, describing the location of the Satō factory as a small, family-owned firm and the resonances those designations had for people in the ward of Tokyo where I lived. Chapter 3 focuses on an extraordinary experience at an ethics training retreat where the Satō workers were sent to become better human beings and better servants of the company. It provides me a way to introduce the recurring themes of work, family, identity, and power as they were articulated in a vivid and highly elaborated form.

The next part, "Family as Company, Company as Family," begins with a consideration ("Circles of Attachment") of the living meanings of family for the people I knew, intertwining vignettes and dialogue with an exposition of the literature on "the Japanese household." "Adding the Family Flavor," the chapter that follows, deals with the Satōs' attempts to create a "family" atmosphere in the factory and with the ironies, fissures, and unintended consequences such an attempt produced—given the malleability of the idiom, its constitutive history, and the ruptures inevitable in any deployment of meaning. Issues of "resistance" come to the fore in "Company as Family?" which centers on workers' complaints and reactions to their shifting positioning in the company and on the ways they both challenged and reproduced idioms of "company as family" in their "resistance." The ironic twists of meaning they give to the "company as family" idiom lead us to a consideration of narratives of "resistance" in the social science literature and point us toward a different way of conceptualizing "resistance" to a "hegemony." Those concerned with a poststructuralist politics might find this chapter of particular interest.

While the section on "company as family" deals with the problematic construction of collective identities, the final section centers on the equally problematic construction of gendered work identities on a level that would be conventionally labelled "individual." I tell the stories of the chief male artisan and the female part-time workers in order to highlight notions of identity as enactment and rhetorical assertion, to show that "even" individual identities are contextually constructed within fields of power and meaning and cannot be easily separated from specific situations, from culturally specific narrative conventions, or from abstractions we label history, politics, and economics. Identity here is not a unified essence, but a mobile site of contradiction and disunity, a node where various discourses temporarily intersect in particular ways.

My writing, then, is deployed strategically, to expand notions of what counts as ethnography and what counts as theoretical, and to problematize conventional views of identity and the ethnographic canon, even though those conventions can never be entirely transcended. Through vignettes, I introduce themes of work, family, company, community, and identity—concerns important to the people I knew—and through the analysis of these specific events and "experiences," I try to unravel the complexities of the lives of those I describe. I also employ different styles and voices, interweaving them and locating myself and my friends and co-workers in shifting, moving fields of discourse. Though the distinction between "theory" and "immediacy, experience and description" can never be entirely erased, it will be questioned, disrupted, and displaced—undermining itself through reflexive passages such as this one. I hope to blur the boundaries between rhetoric and theory, personal and political, self and society through an account which constructs the multiple ways the "experiences" of my friends and co-workers exceed, resist, yet in some form inevitably, ironically, reproduce the culturally specific forms and metaphors that shape their lives and to which they themselves give meaning.[18]

Because I argue that "style" and "theory" are inseparable in the process of writing, let me end with my reasons for choosing *Crafting Selves* as a title. It distills into two words a number of the points I will argue throughout the book. First, work and personhood are inextricable from one another. In transforming the material world, my informants also transformed themselves. Secondly, identity is not a static *object,* but a creative *process;* hence crafting selves is an ongoing—indeed a lifelong—occupation. Third, crafting selves implies a concept of agency: that human beings create, construct, work on, and enact their identities, sometimes creatively challenging the limits of the cultural constraints which constitute both what we call selves and the ways those selves can be crafted. Finally, as I have argued, perhaps we should not speak of "the self" as a global entity, but of selves *in the plural.* Perhaps then we can come to appreciate both the insistent rhythms of common cultural idioms, and the many ways they reverberate through people's lives.

2   *Industries, Communities, Identities*

In the first chapter, the reader encountered the neighborhood and the people I knew via visual impressions mediated through the eye/I of the anthropologist. In this chapter we reencounter the same neighborhood in a meeting no less mediated through the ethnographer, but this time the members of the Satō company and my co-workers should emerge more clearly on their own terms, through their articulation of their placement within the context of Japanese industry and divisions we might call "class." The issues of complex, multiple selves, power, and reflexivity resurface, to be played out in another register. Instead of addressing issues of multiplicity, contextuality, and ambiguity through the ethnographer's fragmented and multiple selves, or analyzing the disciplinary production of multiple selves through language, here I highlight my co-workers and neighbors' own shifting facets of their collective identities as they construct themselves within matrices of power. What did my co-workers and neighbors think about themselves as workers in small business? As members of a "class"? As residents of Shitamachi, the "low city" (cf. Seidensticker 1983) or "downtown" section of Tokyo, or even more specifically, as residents of a particular ward in Shitamachi? And how do other Japanese in turn define people like my neighbors? Here I seek to situate the Satō company and its members within larger contexts and to begin to address the specificities of how they go about crafting selves. Working in small industry was a meaningful facet of my co-workers' and neighbors' identities, but these meanings were shaped by constraints we might call cultural, historical, and political/economic.

The Industrial Context, Firm Size, and Identity

My choice to live and work with people who were involved in small factories and businesses was made in a spirit of revisionist criticism of prevailing representations of Japan. At that particular historical moment, in the late 1970s and early 1980s, and continuing on until the present, scholarly and popular attention has centered on the Japanese main-stream. Regnant images of Japan, Inc., fostered in a milieu of increasing Japanese economic preeminence, stressed familiar themes of lifetime employment, harmony, homogeneity, diligence, and a "Confucian ethic," said to be characteristic of all workers in Japanese industry and generally characteristic of Japanese society. The alarmist literature decrying the loss of American economic hegemony led to a spate of works seeking to unlock the secrets of "the Japanese way"—in such works as *The Art of Japanese Management* (Pascale and Athos 1981), *Theory Z* (Ouchi 1982), *Japan as Number One* (Vogel 1979). Decoding these secrets and imple-menting them in the United States would enable America to regain its "proper" place at the top of the global economic hierarchy. But these in-sights into the "Japanese way" were based almost entirely on large industry, on elite government bureaucracies, and on the lives of Organi-zation Men in elite firms. Though such studies are necessary and important in delineating a hegemony within Japan, to equate "Japan" with this infinitesimal, though powerful, sector is a problematic concep-tual slippage.

In fact, large firms are by no means the largest employers of Japanese workers, nor is the story of large firms the only important story to be told. Most of my interviewees and neighbors worked in companies labelled *chū-shō kigyō,* small and medium-sized enterprises, a specific, culturally salient category in Japanese society. *Chū-shō kigyō* are defined as those firms in manufacturing having fewer than 300 employees, or those in the wholesale and retail trades having fewer than 50 employees. In 1978, the year when this study began, 99.4% of all firms in Japan fell into this cate-gory, and they employed 75.8% of Japan's workers (Chū-shō kigyō chō 1978, 54). These numbers have remained fairly constant; in 1984 small and medium enterprises employed 81% of the labor force and con-stituted 99% of businesses (Ministry of International Trade and Industry 1984, 113). To begin to sketch out a more complete picture of Japan will require serious scrutiny of people who work in these smaller businesses and all those who are outside the elite mainstream.

In carrying out analyses of the "other side" of Japan, it is equally important to avoid easy accusations of exploitation and domination. An-other strand in the literature on postwar Japanese society amplifies the difficult working conditions that obtain in small industry, the margin-ality of women workers, the political conservatism of the petite bourgeoisie, and the plight of minority groups such as the Burakumin.[1] Again, this is part of the story. But popularized accounts of Japanese industry that adopt this point of view—television documentaries notable among them—have sometimes attributed Japanese economic success to the existence of such exploitation, contrasting the Japanese system to a more "just" American system. One might point instead to culturally and historically specific articulations of capitalism, and the ways exploitative practices exist in a plethora of ways in the contemporary United States as well as in Japan. When the accusatory finger is directed only toward Japan, "exploitation" becomes another name for "unfair practices," and such accusations become one more weapon in the so-called trade wars.

Hoping to avoid these extreme ends of a continuum, I seek here to follow out the ambiguities and ambivalences in my informants' identities as workers in small enterprises and as residents of a particular area in Tokyo. Neither thoroughly oppressed and exploited nor serenely happy in their exclusion from hegemonic ideals, the people I knew constructed complex, multiple, ambivalent senses of themselves. And in order to understand those ambivalences, we must first turn to my informants' problematic location as workers in small industry and in particular, as residents of a ward in Tokyo associated with small factories and shops.

The "Dual Structure"

As the company presidents (*shachō*) of small firms, my co-workers, and my neighbors showed me, the cleavage between small and medium industry on the one hand, and large industry on the other, is far more than a purely economic distinction, for it calls up disparate images of lifestyle, stability, and cultural worth. The category *chū-shō kigyō* is itself defined negatively, in opposition to *daikigyō,* or large enterprise, as that which lacks everything the large enterprises possess. The upper sector of the so-called dual or two-tiered structure (*ni-jū kōzō*) is presumed to be large, stable, well-financed, productive, and technologically innovative, the leaders in their respective industries. They have larger numbers of workers and greater access to capital. Moreover, the standing of such companies is reinforced through association with prestigious financial institutions (Suzuki 1969, 3) and with top-rated educational institutions, whereby large firms do business with the big banks and recruit most heavily from famous universities. This in turn enhances the prestige of the latter organizations, in a circular process (Clark 1979, 71–72). The lower sector occupied by small and medium firms is the obverse side of the coin: here one finds lower profits and wages, substandard working conditions, and keen economic competition. These enterprises have little access to financing from major banks, nor do they recruit from famous universities. On every scale, according to the cultural image, the small and medium firm is found lacking.

This symbolic bifurcation clearly oversimplifies the matter. Small and medium enterprises constitute a large, diverse group, collapsing into a single category businesses that are prosperous and viable with those on the verge of bankruptcy; the small, specialized shop offering "traditional" objects of consumption for a specialized market with the subcontractors linked to the largest, most technologically advanced industrial manufacturers. (See Patrick and Rohlen 1987, for a detailed picture of the political economic situation of small enterprises.) Other analysts such as Rodney Clark have proposed the rather more accurate phrase "industrial gradation:" a ranking of firms based on size, productivity, and prestige. In fact, the small and large firms simply represent two ends of a continuum rather than completely opposed terms. Indeed, many observers have noted that the striking characteristic of the Japanese economy is the relationship between the size of industry and wages/productivity: "There are always gaps between best and worst practice in any economy, but the correlation with *scale* seems to be much closer in Japan, and the persistence, indeed the enhancing, of these differentials was regarded as one of Japan's most serious industrial problems" (Broadbridge 1966, 65).[2]

An argument could be made that there is nothing intrinsically wrong with a two-tiered economy, provided one also believes that both sectors are healthy and viable. Inevitably, there may be differences between small and large firms in any economy. Yet the magnitude of these differences and their implications for people's lives and livelihoods lead one to think that the differences in the Japanese case bear critical scrutiny. Take, for example, the issue of job security. Commitment to lifelong employment is primarily a feature of life in large companies. An argument could be made that so-called permanent employment can exist precisely because there are people and companies in less secure positions who absorb economic shocks. First of all, only the permanent employees—usually the young, better-educated males—are the beneficiaries of lifelong employment. Keeping on a permanent labor force, which is guaranteed substantial benefits, creates a high fixed expense. As I will argue in the chapter on women and part-time work, during periods of economic difficulty companies prefer not to fire their regular employees as a way of cushioning their losses. Instead they pass the burden to smaller firms and to temporary and part-time workers.[3] For example, in the immediate post-war period, subcontracting relations between small and large firms increased under circumstances which were highly disadvantageous to the small firms. During difficult times, the large contractors simply stop ordering from the smaller subcontractors, and/or delay payments. As a result, the subcontractors, not the parent firms, suffer from any economic downturn. Sometimes they are forced into bankruptcy (Nakamura 1981, 175). Subcontractors and part-time workers—who have shown a striking growth in number in the postwar period—provide the floating labor force necessary to the preservation of benefits and security for full-time (usually male) workers in large firms.[4]

Scholarly debates about the dual structure aside, I wish to stress here that the distinction between small and large firms is a *culturally* meaningful one, recognized as such by the government and by Japanese people themselves. For my friends, neighbors, and co-workers, these distinctions among firms are laden with symbolic, cultural, and moral value. Education, personality, and family structure, among other things are—at least according to stereotype—different among these different segments of society. As Rodney Clark put it:

> It does not occur to British or American people that because a company is small, then it and therefore its employees are necessarily in an inferior position; and if its employees are in an inferior position then they must be of poor quality, because otherwise they would have achieved greater things. . . . What bank would lend cheaply to a smaller company, and what customer would order from one, in preference to a much larger rival, when all the world knows that small companies are unstable and poorly managed by uninspiring people? (1979, 72–73).

One must ask how the people I knew constructed their senses of identity in the face of this wider context of economic and moral inequality.

Small Enterprise and the Construction of Identities

The question of firm size and its implications for the ways people crafted themselves within this power-imbued industrial context were especially salient in Arakawa, the ward of Tokyo where I lived and worked. My initial impressions of the neighborhood as a place of small enterprises filled with people at work, turned out to be on the mark. In this ward of Tokyo, 95.5% of all enterprises had fewer than 20 workers. Of the enterprises located in this area in 1978, the year I first arrived in Japan, 38.6% were in the wholesale and retail trades; 37.3% in manufacturing; and 13% in the service industry. When one looks at the number of people employed in

53

each industry, the rank order changes somewhat: 44.5% work in manufacturing; 27% in wholesale and retail; 10.3% in the service industry, and 7% in construction.

Arakawa ward is very much the home of small, family-owned factories. The rate of bankruptcy is high. The economic bureau in the ward office devotes much of its time to offering consultation and assistance for people suffering economic hardship. They run workshops on a variety of topics: taxes, management techniques, finding new parent companies for subcontractors, among other services. Financing is available through the ward for those people who have gone bankrupt, and for those who are trying to start up a new business, for workers who need assistance, and for managers who are suffering the aftereffects of the oil shock—a sizeable number, apparently, considering the frequency with which these workshops and financing programs are offered. Because of its efforts to help the firms in the area, the ward administration has a reasonably good relationship with the community. In my interviews and talks with countless people who lived and worked in Arakawa, a consistent theme was the difficulty making ends meet. Everyone had to work hard to survive; everyone would have appreciated a little extra in order to "live a better life." As the *sensei* from the local cram school put it, "Most people are making it, but just barely. For all of us, some money would be a lifesaver."

People in the neighborhood often distinguished between small and large companies. During my interviews, for instance, people would often respond to my research topic by saying, yes, in Japan, there is too much of a gap between small and large businesses. In the factory, my co-workers echoed these remarks, commenting that the differences between small and large firms was just too great (*sa ga arisugitchau*). When Itō-san, a young artisan, quit his job at the Satō factory for more lucrative employment with a subcontractor for Mitsubishi, he made sure he paid us a visit to boast about his new job and his vastly improved wages and working conditions. He casually dropped the fact that one of his neighbors in his apartment building was one of Japan's favorite middle-aged crooners, and of course, his stock rose even more. When Ohara-san, the head artisan, commented that Itō's change of jobs "must be like going from hell to heaven," he acknowledged those differences in company size and prestige and therefore in employees' work situations. Other co-workers invoked the distinctions between small and large firms in other ways. Itakura-san, a part-time worker, had a son who had bitterly experienced the cultural realities linking education and firm size. In high school, the young Itakura was not of a scholarly bent, but he possessed a prodigious talent for things mechanical. He chose to attend a technical school—more academic institutions were clearly out of his reach—and after graduation, he found a job that fulfilled his and his family's most cherished dreams: a position as an engineer in a large, nationally-known electronics firm. After a few years, however, it became obvious that Itakura's degree from a "second-rate" institution was a barrier to career advancement, creating a promotional ceiling beyond which he could not ascend. Rather than sit back and watch while his less skilled co-workers continued to climb the promotional ladder, he eventually quit in disgust and found a job in a smaller firm closer to his home. He speaks with anger about the prejudices of the large firm, where competence was outweighed by the "correct" educational credentials, yet he is obviously unhappy with his less prestigious affiliation with a lesser-known company.

Perhaps none are so eloquent about these differences, both positive and negative, as the owners of small firms. Accompanying a representative of the Subcontractors' Association[5] as he made his rounds through Arakawa, I was able to ask owners about the general situation in which they found themselves. "*Shibararete iru,*" tied down, chained to their work, was the reply that occurred time and again. Pressed by the parent company, pressed for money, pressed for time—theirs was a grueling, precarious life. Most complained about the high price of materials, the low unit price they received, the long hours, their difficulties in finding workers, and, most poignantly, their sorrow at seeing their businesses die out for lack of successors.

One man stood out for me as exemplary of the subcontractor near the bottom of the chain. He and his father were metalworkers who made, at that time, parts for video game machines. The factory was small and dark, sheets of metal and boxes of parts stacked here and there. As we sat and talked, his wife, a wan, tired-looking woman, served us the requisite cup of tea. The man's first remarks detailed the difficulties of their situation: with only two people, they had trouble completing their orders on time. Searches for employees had proved fruitless. Moreover, though the owner and his father worked at least 12-hour days, thanks to inflation and the low price per unit the parent company paid them, the profit margins grew slimmer and slimmer every year. "No such thing as a *bēsu appu* (yearly raise in base pay, standard for salaried workers) here," he said grimly, adding that there was no future in this sort of work. Even his two young sons who helped him after school had no intention of following in his footsteps. (Later, the Association consultant told me that this was because "today's young people" have no desire to work in a business where the competition with other firms is keen, the pay low, the hours long, and the work "dirty." They much preferred a "clean" office job.) Yet the same owner, when asked about the good points of his occupation, perked up immediately and began to expatiate on its compensations: "I like having my own work, making my own product on my own time. Not everyone in Japan is a retainer of a feudal lord (*kerai*)." After all, this man was a *shachō* —company president—of his own firm. His attitude in the face of obvious economic difficulty was striking. But optimism and enthusiasm aside, the *shachō*'s plight attracted murmurs of sympathy from the Association representative after we left the factory. The consultant, himself a white-collar, salaried worker, contrasted the life of the factory owner with his own, articulating his own ambivalence: "I never have to worry every day whether or not I'll make enough to survive, but I don't have the same independence as that *shachō*."

The contrast between the entrepreneurial/artisanal way of life and the life of the white-collar worker arose in many other interviews, of which one other example bears mention. An owner of a firm with 10 employees contrasted his way of life to that of the white-collar worker in large companies. His second son chose to work in a trading company rather than to help out his father. "It's better to be in a trading company," said the owner. "You don't have to suffer; you don't get squeezed. All those big businesses do well, and we little guys get stomped on." Small firms were at a technological disadvantage in comparison to large ones. Worried, he sought advice from the consultant from the Subcontractors' Association. What sort of machine should he buy? The race would be won in this business (plastic and metal parts), he was afraid, by the people who had the most advanced machines—ones he might not be able to afford. Still, working in small firms had its rewards. The best thing was to "get out there and fight, on your own, to make a quality product." For this *shachō*, an artisanal pride in using your own skill to make a fine object compensated at least partially for his competitive, pressured economic situation.

The gradations between small and large firms and the distinctions between artisan/entrepreneur and white-collar worker take on considerable significance as two axes along which people like the Satōs and other owners of small factories construct their identities. From their points of view, such a construction of identity is fraught with complexity and ambivalence. Owners like the two men I have described, and artisans like my male co-workers, take pride in their workmanship and in their independence. Unlike white-collar paper-pushers, they have their skills and their freedom from constant supervision. Still, when these *shachō* consider the larger scheme of things—the organization of society, the distribution of benefits and privileges, the ways their work is defined by a larger audience—their ambivalence emerges. The men I interviewed realize that, except in a few outstanding cases that prove the rule, they as employees of smaller firms are unlikely to win the same recognition and respect accorded to workers in larger firms. A sense of unfairness, occasionally of exploitation, often coexists with a celebration of their independence. And poignantly, even this statement about independence must be examined critically. As Fukuzawa-san, a maker of plastic accessories, said to me jokingly, he thought he worked longer hours as an independent than he did as a company employee. Men like Fukuzawa and the two *shachō* have no one directly supervising their work on a moment-to-moment basis. Yet, with their long hours, pressing deadlines, and the feeling of being constantly "squeezed," one wonders how much "independence" they really have.

Tensions, ambivalences, and contradictions animated the discourses of firm size and occupational life style, tensions that reflected and replayed the power relations at work in this discourse of work and identity. But perhaps just as salient was another distinction Tokyo residents would often make in their everyday lives, which proved to be a recurrent theme in the factory and the neighborhood: the culturally and regionally specific contrast between "uptown" and "downtown," a contrast that highlights distinctions based on occupation, firm size, and a semiotics of "class" and "taste".

Shitamachi and Yamanote

In Tokyo itself, the socioeconomic division between small and large firms, blue-collar and white-collar, is projected onto the realm of symbolic space. In the folk wisdom of Tokyo dwellers, the city is divided into roughly two parts. The western half is called Yamanote, the hillside or the foothills, while the eastern part is Shitamachi, literally downtown, for it lies on a plain on the lower ground near the bay. Though the boundaries are far from clear-cut, this geographical division corresponds to two different cultural images of its residents. Yamanote is the home of the bureaucrat, the professional, the white-collar worker in large, elite firms. It is the mainstream, modern ideal. Shitamachi, on the other hand, conjures up images of the merchant, the artisan, the small family business. A more "traditionally Japanese" ethos is thought to reign here.

57

These images arise in part from the hierarchical Tokugawa social structure, which placed aristocracy and the samurai over farmers, artisans,
and merchants. These social structural divisions were reflected in a symbolic cleavage of the city of Edo (Tokyo). During the Tokugawa period,
the Yamanote area was settled primarily by the aristocracy and the samurai classes, while Shitamachi was the home for the merchants and
artisans who provided services for their superiors (cf. Seidensticker
1983; Wagatsuma and DeVos 1984). Social class and geography where
thus substantially overlapping categories.

Though the rigid hierarchies no longer exist, the Yamanote/
Shitamachi distinction possesses contemporary significance. Geography
and "class" are again conflated, as two Japanese friends confirmed for me
by arguing heatedly about the applicability of the word "yuppie" to describe a Shitamachi restaurant. Both antagonists were students for
advanced degrees at Harvard, and both were from aristocratic, wealthy
families. After going back and forth, one of them shouted in exasperation: "Yuppie is *not* Shitamachi, it's Yamanote!" Implicit in this distinction
are "class," power, and lifestyle, conceptualized in terms of symbolic
space.

As a way of catching up these differences on many levels, the Ya-
manote/Shitamachi distinction constitutes part of the self-image of my
Tokyo friends, relatives, neighbors, and co-workers. They invoke the distinction not simply to describe geography, but to interpret people's
actions and to construct one aspect of their identities (cf. Dore 1958;
Smith 1960; Bestor 1985). The symbolic division of Tokyo is enacted in
differences in language and behavior, which are in turn imbued with
moral value. For example, relatives and teachers who lived in the
Yamanote area initially were taken aback that I would choose to live in
"such a strange place." Occasionally, they would show interest in the
"customs" of the merchants and artisans I knew, inquiring about matters
of etiquette and, in particular, language. They asked what pronouns men
used for self-reference, and when I replied with *ore,* the most informal
masculine form, adding that the artisans frequently used the particle *yo*
to punctuate their speech,[6] my relatives nodded knowingly and said that
this was quite masculine, but verged on the vulgar (*gehin*). What were
perceived as breaches in etiquette also occasioned comment from
Yamanote friends. For example, I had laughingly recounted an anecdote
of one of my first days on the job in the factory, when one of the artisans
asked whether I was a local high school student. "Ah," said my relative,
"that is something those people would do. It is a little rude, because it

assumes you're of lower status. He should have asked, 'What school are you going to?' instead." This relative, himself a manager of an American fast food chain in the Yamanote district and not an elite executive by any means, explained to me that, yes, this is how someone from the working class (*rōdō kaikyū*) might speak.

The dominance of Yamanote culture is evident from the fact that their language is considered standard Japanese; therefore, by definition, "making the shitamachi man a speaker of a dialect" (R. J. Smith 1960, 249). Shitamachi speakers are renowned for their inability to distinguish the syllable *hi* from *shi*. They are also supposedly less apt to use the elaborate forms more characteristic of Yamanote Japanese. My co-workers, for instance, thought that overly polite language was snobbish and pretentious. As we worked, we often listened to the radio, and people were free with their commentary on the exquisite but convoluted language the announcers used. "What does that mean?" said Yutaka-kun, laughing, when he heard one of the honorific ways of saying "eat." "I only know *kū*," that is, the male, extremely informal—and in Yamanote eyes, vulgar—form of the verb. During a chat about the changes in Tokyo since the war, Akimoto-san mentioned the Azabu district of Tokyo, now an elegant residential neighborhood. "The people who live there are a different sort altogether," she told me. "They say things like *sayō de gozaimasu*. They have nothing to do with our lives."[7] People like Akimoto-san, who lived in Shitamachi and rarely ventured to the western part of Tokyo, apparently felt uncomfortable and inept even attempting to use these linguistic forms, and in any case, they had little occasion to try.

Lest readers think these are idiosyncratic impressions based on the work of a single observer, let me relate a story that confirmed my reading of the situation in my own mind. Before actually moving to Arakawa, and throughout my entire stay there, I studied tea ceremony in the Ura Senke style with a teacher based in Arakawa.[8] Our group was asked to perform the *nodate,* outdoor tea ceremony, at the ward cultural festival (*bunkasai*), a common fall occurrence in Japan. Typically, a cultural festival might feature performances of Japanese music, poetry, and dance, and exhibitions of paintings, flower arrangements, and crafts created by local people, school children, or members of the sponsoring organization. Our teacher instructed us to advertise our performance as widely as possible to drum up an impressive audience and, not incidentally, to show up the representatives of Omote Senke, the other important school of tea who would be performing only a few yards away from us. Accordingly, I invited a friend, a sociologist who was studying upper-class families in the Yamanote area. He arrived a little early, so we decided to kill a few minutes viewing the flower arrangements and ink paintings on display in the exhibition hall. As we entered the gallery, I ran into an acquaintance, a tough, energetic woman much like all the women I knew. She descended upon us, extolling the virtues of the afternoon's coming attractions. "*Zehi irashite kudasai!*" (Come, by all means!) she said as she urged my friend to attend the tea ceremony. We thanked her and said yes, I was performing and he would be there. As we stepped into the elevator and descended to the ground floor, my friend turned to me and said, "How do you stand it?" "What?" said I, bewildered. "The language! I felt as though I were being attacked!" (*Kōgeki sareta mitai*). The staccato barrage of words had taken him by surprise. His informants, he told me, spoke in slow, elegant rhythms, in a murmur soothing to the ear. For instance, to invite us to the tea ceremony, they might have said "*Yoroshikattara, ochaseki e dōzo . . .*" (If you'd care to, please [attend our] tea ceremony . . .), a much more indirect, elliptical utterance than the vigorous directive, "*Zehi irashite kudasai*". Indeed, my friend informed me that an afternoon with these tough Shitamachi women had given him stiff shoulders (*katakori,* a culture-bound syndrome), which I found to be a kind of vindication, since it was the ailment from which I constantly suffered. The peppery, casual, no-nonsense Shitamachi language I heard and used every day contrasted sharply with the legato languor of Yamanote speech, and these differences were marks of "distinction" (Bourdieu 1984) imbued with moral value.

Cosmopolitanism and acquaintance with things Western were also markers of difference between Yamanote and Shitamachi. Yamanote friends inquired about my co-workers' knowledge of foreign loan words, surmising (accurately, as it happened) that this knowledge would be more limited than their own. For example, whenever I went to meet American friends or went shopping at the Ginza (about half an hour away by subway from the factory), I often stopped at a crêperie or at the Imperial Hotel for cheese blintzes. That blintzes might not be a familiar part of everyone's vocabulary came as no surprise, but given the (I thought) well-known chain of crêpe restaurants and the fact that were working in a confectionery factory, I thought the same would not be true for crêpes, especially in cosmopolitan Tokyo. But one day, Hamada-san began talking about an exotic new dish she had seen on TV, "something like *tamagoyaki* (a thin egg omelette)." I interjected that it sounded like a crêpe. Hamada-san looked at me strangely, the word "crêpe" obviously not registering at all—or sounding like one of my unfortunate linguistic mistakes. "Like *tamagoyaki* it was," she repeated, and proceeded to describe the batter in detail.

I remember my own surprise when I began working at the factory, as further assumptions—such as "all Japanese are comfortable eating with knives and forks"—were quickly dashed. Sakada-san, a part-time worker who dazzled us with her skill at complicated feats of wrapping confections, played up her cultural ineptitude at a fancy reception given by her husband's parent company. "At home we always use chopsticks," she said, and she graphically described her consternation in the face of a daunting array of Western silverware. In settings like these, Shitamachi people are forced to confront what Yamanote dwellers might call their lack of "cultural capital" (see Bourdieu and Passeron 1970). As Bourdieu (1984) so exhaustively demonstrated in his analysis of "taste," differences like these also encode certain differences in social position.

Even—or perhaps especially—mundane preferences like food, could provide people with vehicles for discussing Yamanote/Shitamachi distinctions. One friend, a Japanese undergraduate at Harvard, joked about my doing research in Shitamachi. "Let's go to Asakusa[9] and have some *takoyaki!*"[10] he said, grinning. I, quite fond of the stuff, took him seriously and enthusiastically agreed. "Eh?" was his shocked reply, his eyes widening in incredulity. Needless to say, we didn't go. *Okonomiyaki,* a kind of doughy pancake available with a variety of fillings, was another kind of food pronounced typical of Shitamachi. Two or more people cook it on the table in front of them, nibbling as it browns on the grill, while they talk and drink their beer or whiskey. From time to time, the tireless Mrs. Sakamoto and I used to meet at a neighborhood *okonomiyaki* place after she got off work at the family construction company. The cooperative, informal way of cooking and eating together was typical of Shitamachi, she told me. "Yamanote has some *okonomiyaki* restaurants too, but you can't expect the same friendly atmosphere you'd get in Shitamachi." *Dagashi,* cheap candy, was another "specialty" of the Shitamachi area. As though invoking the name of a faraway land, Mrs. Tanoue, the wife of my friend the woodworker, told me, "You know, they say there are no *dagashi* shops like this in Yamanote." In fact, there may be—but the *perception* that such differences exist is an intriguing social fact.

Even the ways of serving guests were supposedly quite different in the two areas of the city. The middle/upper-class aesthetic is one of scarcity, so that sweets or other snacks for guests tend to be presented singly, on an attractive serving dish. Guests are given a single cup of tea, which can later be refilled, if one is so brazen as to make such a request. If you are a woman, you should decline refills or hearty portions politely in order to avoid appearing too greedy or too hungry.[11] Someone who ate with gusto could elicit reactions of thinly veiled shock and dismay, as I learned from experience, guided both by personal proclivity and my Shitamachi bias. In Shitamachi, people would say that they preferred to be more informal. Their custom was to bring out the whole pot of tea and a whole bag of sweets or rice crackers, so that the guests could feel at home and help themselves. At the same time, their informality was a sign of their generosity and hospitality. And healthy appetites were encouraged. Mikami-san, an energetic grandmother whose family ran a nearby cardboard factory, was the living embodiment of a Shitamachi ethos, and she worked hard at creating and maintaining this persona. One way she did so was to serve up her handmade noodles to all her guests, and when I failed to slurp them noisily and enthusiastically enough, she scolded me for putting on airs. In fact, at least according to my observations, the etiquette surrounding the serving of food could vary widely in both Yamanote and Shitamachi, depending on the formality of the setting and the intimacy of one's relationship. Still, the cultural stereotypes persist. The daughter of Hirata-sensei, the wonderful elderly woman who was my guarantor, told me about a Yamanote anthropologist who came to visit their home. When she brought out the pot of tea and a dish of rice crackers, he asked, with obvious "professional" curiosity, "Oh, is this how you do things in Shitamachi?" His question, and his treatment of her hospitality as quaint and inferior custom, clearly rankled even after several years had elapsed.

Another indication of Yamanote preeminence lies in its general desirability as a place of residence. It is far more likely for a Shitamachi person who has "made good" to move to the Yamanote area than vice versa. In fact, while people can cite countless examples of the former, never have I heard of a single case of the latter. Moving "up" to the foothills is, indeed, moving up in the world. Smith (1960) tells of the various adjustments the "arriviste" will have to make in order to be fully accepted into Yamanote society. Language, dress, manner (no "wisecracking" allowed, says Smith), would all have to be altered to conform to the canons of bourgeois restraint and respectability. This only serves to further establish the dominance of Yamanote culture. Even many of the craftspeople and merchants, proud of their Shitamachi heritage, pay lip service at least to the ideals of the highly educated executive and professional classes. Many agreed that perhaps there was little future for most young people in these "traditional" Shitamachi occupations, and that these days everyone wanted "clean" work, a nice office job where they could become a *heibon na sarariman,* a conventional, average white-collar paper-pusher.

Economic and social status, then, is indexed in language, etiquette, and taste, but these differences are themselves indices of certain character dispositions, expressed in ambivalent Yamanote images about the personality of the Shitamachi dweller. Many Yamanote acquaintances expressed sympathy for the fact that I had to live in Shitamachi, because Shitamachi people had the reputation of being nosy and having no respect for privacy. My doctor and my acupuncturist, both residents of a posh section of Tokyo where many foreigners lived, attributed my physical ailments to my immersion in Shitamachi life. "You have to *ki o tsukau* all the time," said the silver-haired doctor, who would often make reference to his lengthy sojourn in the States and his degree from Case Western Reserve Medical School. "You never have any privacy." My acupuncturist, who spoke the most melodious, graceful *sayō de gozaimasu* honorific Japanese, would counsel me to watch out for my neighbors. "They are good-hearted, but sometimes too much so—they get meddlesome." Hatanaka-san, my landlady, intimated that her neighbors were easygoing and didn't worry about details (*ki ni shinai*), but that the opposite side of the same coin was a certain superficiality (*fukami ga nai*) and a lack of education or cultivation (*kyōyō ga nai*).

The ambivalence was returned in full measure. Stereotypically, Shitamachi people are said to be informal, warm-hearted, emotional, quick to anger, and quick to forgive. Hayashi-san, whose family owned a local shoe store, asserted emphatically, "Our language may be rough, but we're straightforward" (*kuchi ga warui kedo, hara ga wakaru*). She went on to contrast Shitamachi openness with Yamanote deceptiveness, hinting darkly at what went on "behind those walls" (referring to the walls surrounding the Yamanote house, which separate it from its neighbors, thus ensuring privacy), and said that you could never tell what a Yamanote person was really thinking. "They will bear grudges for years, and you'll never know it," she warned me. Another informant went so far as to blame the contemporary scandals in government and in the large corporations (at that time, Lockheed, and Nissho Iwai) on the "dirty dealings" that went on behind the Yamanote facade of politesse and respectability.

Yamanote people, I was told, were so obsessed with keeping up appearances that they would never dream of borrowing anything from a neighbor. Yokoyama-sensei of the hairdressing salon where I worked during the busy end-of-the-year season, had spent a week visiting friends who lived in a California suburb. She pronounced the place *Shitamachiteki* (Shitamachi-like). Neighbors were always dropping in to borrow sugar or laundry detergent or other everyday items. "In Yamanote," said the *sensei,* "that would be like showing weakness." You were supposed to plan ahead and be entirely self-sufficient, not depending on your neighbors to make up for your own lack of foresight. Countless people I talked to commented time and again about how Shitamachi people didn't care about appearances in this way, that they didn't have to pretend to be so perfect. They, in contrast to Yamanote people, were easygoing (*ki ni shinai*). Neighborhood relationships were, and should be, warm and informal, allowing one to reveal more of one's "inner" self (*honne;* cf. chapter 3) without excessive concern for the social proprieties (*tatemae*).

Shitamachi, in my informants' discourse, conjured up images of certain kinds of orientations toward the world, embodied in language, etiquette, and personality. This way of life is in part rooted in a distinctive Shitamachi culture that reached fruition during the Tokugawa period and early Meiji. The culture of the *chōnin,* or townsman, is now considered the source of the era's unique ethos. *Chōnin* culture was really an urban phenomenon, centered in the cities of Osaka, Kyoto, and Edo (renamed Tokyo in 1868). Vital and dynamic, in many ways it could be characterized as a culture of entertainment and momentary pleasure. As such, it was known as the *ukiyo,* the floating world. Within Edo, the realm of the *ukiyo* was Shitamachi. The pleasure quarters were here, in the Yoshiwara, and there are still famous geisha quarters in older Shitamachi areas such as Nihombashi, Fukagawa, and Asakusa. Popular entertainments of all sorts found their home here. *Sumō,* the ancient style of wrestling that even now adheres to traditional period costumes, pageantry, and splendid ritual, was centered in Edo from the end of the eighteenth century, and it still has its heart in the Ryōgoku district of Shitamachi. The *Kabuki* theater, now located in such posh locations as the National Theater and patronized largely by clients of large corporations and Yamanote folk, was one of the urbane and slightly risqué Shitamachi entertainments. Its flamboyance—splendid costumes, magnificent posturing, dazzling special effects, and often a kind of exaggerated, larger-than-life acting—embodies the showy, exuberant ethos of Shitamachi culture. Puppet plays, though perhaps reaching their highest aesthetic expression in Osaka, were another creation much enjoyed by townsmen in Edo. The most famous of them were penned by Osaka townsman Chikamatsu Monzaemon, who along with his grand historical pieces also wrote many famous domestic tragedies, *sewamono*, based on the lives of the *chōnin*. The *ukiyo* usually makes its appearance in the form of a courtesan with whom the *chōnin* falls in love. In Chikamatsu's most famous domestic tragedies, the irremediable split between the ties of *giri*, social duty, and *ninjō*, human feeling, prove overwhelming for the lovers, and in despair and resignation, they commit double suicide. *Rakugo*, a kind of humorous storytelling often based on tales from the merchant class, was another of Shitamachi's cultural legacies. Finally, perhaps the most famous contribution to Japanese culture, at least in the West, are the paintings of the floating world, the *ukiyo-e* wood-block prints. Originally a popular form of art used for illustrations, posters, and the like, it was scorned by the aristocrats and samurai as vulgar. Above all the prints show us the world of the courtesan and the pleasure quarters, sectors of society that were at least in theory off limits to the samurai. Other famous woodblock artists depict the lives of the *chōnin*: the workshops of the craftspeople, the storefronts of merchant houses, and roadside scenes of common people.[12]

Classic Shitamachi culture is based on certain aesthetic principles held dear by the connoisseur. One is that of *iki*, a slightly decadent, showy, asymmetrical stylishness. Smith calls it a combination of "refinement, tension and sensuality" (Smith 1960, 244). A fine-looking old man, white-haired perhaps, dressed in a kimono, straw hat tipped at a slightly rakish angle, would be *iki*. So would the way some geisha dress: *obi* slung low and wound slightly askew so that one side is slightly lower than another, the *kimono* dipping provocatively at the back to reveal the nape of the neck—the traditional erogenous zone. Robert J. Smith describes these qualities in the following passage:

> Only a candid and open-hearted man could live the life of *iki*, and it was considered poor style to conceive an overwhelming passion or to pursue hopeless goals or to appear obsessively interested in anything. This quality of evanescence and its allied concept of *shibumi* (astringency, but underlaid with luster or mellowness) characterized the life and personality of the man of *tsū*. Such a man was an adept, a connoisseur, an urbane individual skilled at living in stylish romantic dalliance (1960, 245).

Iki described those who lived life with style and panache.

Note that this way of life required a healthy income. Merchants were ideally hardworking and frugal, yet—in Edo at least—they should know how to enjoy their money. In fact according to stereotype, the Edokko, children of Edo, were said to spend freely, with never a thought for the morrow—a characteristic said to be passed on to their present descendants. To worry, scrimp, and save too much had no style.

As commerce expanded and the merchants' wealth grew, the *chōnin* came to occupy an increasingly contradictory position in the Tokugawa hierarchy. The Confucian doctrines espoused by samurai leaders disdained merchants as parasites living off the production of others. Money should therefore not occupy a warrior's interest, for it was "dirty." Such an attitude became increasingly anachronistic in the face of a growing commercial economy. With no significant wars to fight, too many samurai were left with idle hands. Some spent their time in the floating world, gambling, attending the theaters and the pleasure quarters, and running up tremendous debts. Agricultural production could not make up for this "underemployment" of the warrior class. As a consequence, the merchants, the most despised of classes, were in fact bankrolling many of the samurai who fell deeply into debt to the merchant houses. There were intermarriages among the families of wealthy merchants and the genteel but sometimes impoverished samurai, further blurring old class divisions.[13] Some of the lesser samurai were even reduced to menial work, such as different sorts of craft labor.

In the larger scheme of things, however, the merchant and artisan were still defined as inferior. They remained legally defenseless against capricious assertions of samurai authority (their assets and property, for instance, could be confiscated, often in the form of involuntary "contributions" to the government, known as *goyōkin*). Samurai above all still possessed the right to bear and use swords, and hence the right to kill commoners, particularly those who were not acting in proper accordance with their station. The reverse would have been unthinkable. Within this system rife with contradictions, the *chōnin* appeared to maintain a healthy skepticism and ambivalence toward their samurai superiors. Many took pride in their life and culture, satirizing in literature and art the weaknesses and the foibles of the "masters." Yet, when the Meiji revolution came, the merchant class was not in the political vanguard, and as a whole, they never mounted serious political challenges to the social order.

The distinctions between *chōnin* and samurai have been enshrined in notions of a Golden Age of Shitamachi culture. The glories of the Genroku period; a vibrantly creative world of art, literature, and theater; and the *joie de vivre* of urbane, sophisticated dandies dedicated to a life of *iki* and *tsū,* become part of a glorious Shitamachi past which is often romanticized, celebrated, and perceived through a haze of nostalgia. The financial, cultural, technological, and educational centers of Tokyo and indeed, of Japan, have moved to the foothills, and in that context, the deployment of a Shitamachi image can come to take on meanings of a "truly Japanese" Golden Age that reigned before the advent of consumer capitalism or an essence of Japaneseness that remains despite the high-tech cosmopolitanism of present-day Tokyo.

Contemporary representations of Shitamachi show us a nostalgic version of the "truly Japanese," embodied in Shitamachi life. And this life takes place in a simple, good-hearted, emotionally expressive world that echoes my neighbors' own verbal self-representations. Indeed, aside from people like the local cram school teacher, no one I knew ever invoked the Genroku period, or spoke of Shitamachi's cultural efflorescence. Rather, they cited stereotypes of informality most strongly articulated in what is perhaps the most popular contemporary depiction of Shitamachi life: the Tora-san series of feature films. So successful is this series that the Shōchiku film company brings out three eagerly awaited new episodes every year. All have basically the same plot. The lovable, naive, and pure-hearted Tora-san, an itinerant peddler and a Shitamachi archetype, appears unexpectedly at the home of his aunt and uncle, who run a *dango*[14] shop near the Taishaku temple in the Shibamata section of Shitamachi. Inevitably, Tora-san falls in love with a "Madonna"—a lovely, but always unattainable woman. He displays his emotions in a transparent way that is both touching and embarrassing to his relatives. Emotionality also erupts into brief episodes of violence, usually occasioned by snide digs from the family's next-door neighbor, the *shachō* (company president) of a small printing factory next door. Tora-san pummels the "Octopus" (so nicknamed for his bald head) or tries to strangle him, shouting imprecations of the most hilarious sort. The fight usually ends as quickly and simply as it started, with no hard feelings. Invariably, the ending is sentimental, as Tora-san realizes the hopelessness of his passion and leaves once again for his life on the road. On New Year's Day, the family receives a New Year's postcard Tora-san has sent from some far-off corner of Japan. This endlessly repeated formula is apparently endlessly compelling to many Japanese (and I count myself as one of Tora-san's greatest fans). Tora-san seems to embody the emotionality and sentimentality of Shitamachi people: their good-hearted nature; their attachment to family. Tora-san, my friends and neighbors would tell me, is pure, naive (*junjō, tanjun*) a mythical icon of Shitamachi life and, I think, a symbol of Japanese identity. He is their *honne,* the world of inner feeling and an aspect of their Japanese selves they may treasure and whose loss they may mourn. Tora-san's family becomes our family, and the very familiarity of the plot echoes the endlessly recreated yet somehow unchanging essence of "Japaneseness" Tora-san embodies. But ambivalence is always already part of the story. I would also wager that elites and professionals, even as they engage in nostalgia or smile in recognition of the familiar, might love Tora-san—but they would never really want to *be* Tora-san.

Arakawa and the Creation of a Shitamachi Identity

These images of Shitamachi all come into play within Arakawa ward, as community leaders try to construct an identity for the ward. Arakawa is certainly solidly within the eastern, Shitamachi section of Tokyo, but it has a vexed relationship to these widespread cultural representations of Shitamachi, either as repository of Genroku culture or as home of a simple, sentimental essence of Japan. Unlike older sections of Shitamachi, famous for their past cultural eminence, Arakawa cannot lay direct claim to the rich cultural legacies of the *chōnin.* During the days of the floating world, Arakawa was nothing but fields, paddies, and a hunting ground. It is the Shitamachi of the small factory—a far less glamorous image than that of the old pleasure quarters or the wealthy merchants who lived their lives with such inimitable flair. Asakusa—also a rather later addition to the old Shitamachi area—had its temples and the pleasure quarters, the Yoshiwara. Fukagawa had its *geisha, ninja,* and its practitioners of traditional arts. Nihonbashi was the center of old Shitamachi mercantile culture. Even newer areas such as Kanamachi/Shibamata have their legacy in lovable Tora-san and the engaging films that have made him such a national star.

Which is not to say that Arakawa has no city-wide reputation—but it is a less than enviable one. Arakawa is known for its high concentration of small factories (*machi kōba*). More than that, however, it has at points been known as a "city dump" (Wagatsuma and DeVos 1984, 14) and a place of symbolic pollution. The municipal sewer treatment plant is here. So is a large crematorium, associated with the pollution of death in both Buddhism and Shinto. In fact, when I announced to relatives that I would be moving to Arakawa and would begin my research there, one older man asked, with more than a hint of distaste, whether the place still smelled. At one time, he told me, the odors from the crematorium and sewage plant were unmistakable, wafting through the train as you passed through the station. To add to its heritage of symbolic pollution, Arakawa is home for a temple where the bodies of prostitutes were thrown and abandoned, and of Kotsukappara, the former execution grounds of the Tokugawa shogunate.

In the immediate postwar period, social disorganization in Arakawa was acute by Japanese standards, and the ward was known for a high rate of juvenile delinquency.[15] It even made an appearance in the *Wall Street Journal* (November 12, 1985) for its efforts at curbing severe psychological and physical hazing of junior high school students by their classmates—a problem recently gaining national attention, and by no means limited to Arakawa. To heighten its lower-class image, Arakawa borders on the Sanya district, a slum where day laborers live, renting stalls in which to sleep at night. Furthermore, a substantial number of both Koreans, a minority victimized by discrimination, and the Burakumin, the so-called untouchables of Japan, who were traditionally engaged in ritually polluting occupations such as butchering, leatherworking, and shoemaking, live in the ward.[16]

Despite Arakawa's lingering reputation as a place of social disorganization and symbolic pollution, one would be hard put these days to recognize it on the basis of these early descriptions and stereotypes. The development of the transportation system is one key factor in this transformation. Serving the ward are two municipal subway lines, one private railway line, the only remaining municipal trolley, and three branches of the National Railway System, including the most important branch, the Yamanote line, which traces the circumference of central Tokyo. The convenience of transportation to central Tokyo—it is, for example, only thirty minutes by subway to the main business districts in the Ginza and to Tokyo station—has meant a shift in the composition of the ward, to include a number of commuters who have transformed at least parts of Arakawa into a bedroom community. Moreover, due to high land prices, pollution regulations, and the complaints of residents in the area, most of the large factories have moved to more spacious and hospitable locations in Adachi ward, farther away from the central city, and in neighboring Saitama prefecture. The furniture industry, for instance, once the pride of the ward and the most famous in Tokyo, has relocated in Saitama. Only a few large concerns—an electric company, a toy factory, and a bicycle factory—remain.

The poverty with which Arakawa was once associated is less evident than in the past. The ward was famous for its low-income "longhouses" built in the early part of the century (Wagatsuma and DeVos 1984, 14); one still sees some of the old, somewhat ramshackle wooden buildings, and as I have argued, most people are living in obviously straitened circumstances. But particularly in the commercial districts and in the neighboring residential areas, the impression is one of busy commercial activity and increasing prosperity. Modern concrete *danchi,* or apartment buildings, coexist with older wooden dwellings and some modern, single-family homes. Social problems associated with poverty—particularly the economic and social discrimination against the Burakumin population—are noted periodically in the ward newsletter, and the ward has established various political action groups and educational programs to deal with discrimination. Delinquency, though still a source of concern for community leaders and educators, is on the decline.

Substantial efforts have been made to change Arakawa's association with pollution—both symbolic and otherwise. Few noxious odors emanate from local factories. The sewage treatment plant sparkles in its high-tech, hygienic modernity. In fact, during one of the years I lived in Arakawa, the municipal officials opened the grounds of the sewage plant as a beautifully landscaped park, complete with a pond dotted by stepping-stones, a playground, and a special corner serving as a kind of mini-arboretum, devoted to wild plants and flowers. The ward publicized its dazzling new showpiece in a front page article in the ward newsletter and even sponsored a contest to give the park a name. Resonant with respectability, it is now known as the Arakawa Nature Park.

Given an unsavory historical legacy, the ward administration eagerly sought to tap into a more complimentary Shitamachi heritage. They came up with several schemes to give the ward an "image up" (*imēji appu*). One idea was their campaign to select a "ward tree." The actual popular choice was the gingko tree, but in a carefully worded explanation in the ward newsletter, the chairman of the selection committee explained their rationale for choosing the cherry tree instead. In the Tokugawa period, parts of Arakawa had been a hunting ground for the *shōgun.* When he went hunting with his falcons, cherry trees lined the banks of the canals. Moreover, the woodblock artist Hiroshige had once depicted these trees in a print. Furthermore, in the Meiji period, the river banks were apparently famous for their cherry blossoms. So—despite the fact that few cherry trees still exist in the concrete, urban sprawl of present-day Arakawa—the cherry tree became a ward symbol.

Similarly, the ward was eager to recognize as "national treasures" or "important cultural properties" some of the local craftspeople and the objects they made. Happily, national criteria were redefined to include the makers of relatively utilitarian objects, and the ward office published a survey of many of the ward's finest craftsmen, including the maker of the lacquer trays who lived down the street. The slim volume was complete with black and white glossy photographs. Any other sort of cultural performance merited full media play: photos of the cultural festival, for instance, in which the anthropologist is visible as a server during the tea ceremony; wide-angle shots of an orchestra playing Beethoven's Ninth as part of the "traditional" Japanese Christmas celebration. Discovery of any cultural artifact—a pot from the Yayoi period, or a smidgen of a scroll left by an Edo-period traveler—was enough to prompt exhaustive coverage. The ward administration sought through their newsletter to highlight the positive cultural achievements of the ward in the face of an originally negative image of Arakawa as a place of disorganization and pollution. The earnestness and urgency of their attempts to claim for the ward a celebrated Shitamachi past no doubt reflect the magnitude of their status anxiety.

Ambivalent Identities

Yamanote and Shitamachi were vibrantly alive as facets of my Tokyo friends and co-workers' identities, identities fraught with ambivalence. In many ways, the bourgeois respectability of Yamanote by and large looks askance at the "vulgarity" of what it considers "declassé" Shitamachi culture. For in the eyes of an elite, a semiotics of "class" and "distinction" defines both Shitamachi men and women as a lesser "other," united by their common characteristics. Their occupations are necessary for the functioning of society, yet they were not perceived as equal. They were said to be rough in speech and action, less possessed of the polished social surface required of the respectable middle-class sensibility. Their speech was too rapid-fire and direct either to be alluringly feminine or to possess the sober weightiness of the middle-class masculine ideal. For my Yamanote friends and relatives, the people of Shitamachi embodied traditionalism, lack of education, lack of restraint, insufficient knowledge of etiquette and proper behavior, and an almost cloying closeness in

71

their social relationships. In my informants' discourse, these characteristics were linked in some loosely articulated way to a heavy concentration in the manual or mercantile trades. Like the distinction between small and medium vs. large enterprises, these perceptions are based on oppositions of highly valenced moral qualities, where the Shitamachi dwellers' associations with roughness, emotionality, and manual labor interweave "class" and geography, constituting the people of Shitamachi as inferior or at best, quaint anachronisms.

Yet as I have argued, for Yamanote dwellers, attitudes of cultural superiority coexist in tension with a romantic nostalgia and a backhanded sort of respect. Shitamachi culture and its former greatness can be acknowledged as important, even superior to present-day Yamanote culture—but it is no more. The characteristics of modern Shitamachi dwellers—their reputed informality, naiveté, and openness—are also seen in a dual light: as lesser, but also as representative of a way of life for which some people feel a yearning, an *akogare*. Tora-san can serve here as a synecdoche for all Shitamachi residents. I have seen Yamanote businessmen shed a tear at Tora-san films, sorry perhaps for the simplicity and warmth they may have lost in their corporate world. Tora-san symbolizes qualities that are considered part of the "Japanese character," qualities the Organization Man must downplay. After all, emotional volatility, inability to delay gratification, and social ineptitude in the ways of the middle-class world are not likely to carry them very far. Even if they mourn the loss of these qualities in moments of romantic nostalgia, none of them would seriously want to trade places with Tora-san or with the man who made parts for video machines—except perhaps for a short period of time.[17] For the Organization Man and the Middle-class Housewife, people who live in Shitamachi are the secret sharers in their constructions of identity. Shitamachi is both a reminder of who they are—the repositories of what is "traditionally" or "truly" Japanese—and of what they have lost. And nostalgia is possible precisely because there is a protective distancing of self from the other.

For my friends and co-workers in Arakawa, elements of ambivalence riddle their constructions of identity as Shitamachi residents and members of small companies. On the one hand, most people take a distinct pride in the Shitamachi way of being. For the people I knew in Arakawa, most of whom were long-time residents engaged in small family businesses, living in Shitamachi was a meaningful cultural construct and an integral component of their identities. Even people who knew they would live in Shitamachi only a short time—like Kitagawa-san, a young artisan who would probably return to his home in northern Japan one day—would invoke their allegiance to Shitamachi. One day as we were discussing the merits of various department stores, Kitagawa-san extolled the virtues of his favorite, in Ueno. *"Ore wa dauntaun,"* he said laughingly, in fractured English (As for me, it's "downtown"). Amongst themselves, people who live in Shitamachi can feel fierce pride in their cultural heritage, and some—like the Satōs and other merchant families on our commercial street—even cite their cultural superiority. They feel Shitamachi dwellers are more honest, more open, less pretentious. Shitamachi people do not necessarily define themselves as explicitly "subordinate" to Yamanote ideals. For example, the women I knew who were engaged in family business were community leaders and solid, prosperous, self-confident citizens, notable for their sharp tongues and tough resilience. It is hard to imagine them feeling "inferior" to anyone. Yet, even the most enthusiastic advocate of Shitamachi culture could hardly claim that theirs was the dominant ethos in the larger society. Moreover, not all residents of Shitamachi equally partake of the cultural glories of the *chōnin* and their legacies. The less exalted place of Arakawa within Shitamachi itself meant that those who lived there had to justify the "legitimacy" of their pride through efforts at appropriating and invoking a legitimating history— hence the ward administration's efforts to publicize Arakawa's past and present cultural achievements.[18] Moreover, even if my friends and neighbors feel worthy amongst themselves, that worthiness is not likely to be validated by the dominant Yamanote culture. Pride in Shitamachi can be tinged with resentment and informed by an awareness of inequality in the context of Tokyo and of Japan as a whole. A positive self-image is inevitably shaded by recognition of the greater social prestige awarded the white-collar worker and the Yamanote dweller.

Thus, both the Yamanote and the Shitamachi dwellers could construct positive senses of self through setting themselves apart from each other. The process differs slightly, however, in the two cases, the differences reflecting the distribution of power in the wider society. People in Yamanote could look at Shitamachi with nostalgia and even occasional admiration, as the locus of a culture and of certain human characteristics they had lost. This nostalgic longing was inseparable from an awareness of Shitamachi's present "inferiority" in the bureaucratic, middle-class world of present-day Tokyo. For people in Shitamachi, accentuating the difference between themselves and

Yamanote meant pride in their own way of life, but also involved an implicit acknowledgement of the dominance of the new middle-class ideal. My Shitamachi neighbors set themselves apart from their Yamanote counterparts: Shitamachi people, they would say, were warmer, more human and honest, more independent, and even, in some cases, wealthier than the relatively poorly paid bureaucrats and white-collar executives.[19] Yet in high-tech, cosmopolitan Tokyo, it is Yamanote which represents a dominant culture and a new-middle class elite. The world of Shitamachi, as my friends and co-workers constructed it, exists in a tense, fluid, and ambivalent relationship to the hegemonic Yamanote ideal.

My friends, neighbors, and co-workers located themselves in larger contexts, among which the most often invoked were distinctions based on firm size and the symbolic geography of Tokyo.[20] These, too, constitute important facets of their identities, riddled with often wrenching ambivalences: complex combinations of nostalgia, resentment, superiority, and pride. The different languages of identity (and, arguably, languages of class) are in turn inextricable from differences in power. These languages of identity and inequality lead us back to the issues of crafting selves within matrices of power, and the ambivalences, ironies, and contradictions inevitably generated thereby.

For though Yamanote and Shitamachi are defined oppositionally, clearly the oppositions are not of equal weight. Crafting selves along this axis immediately bears inscriptions of power. The stereotypes and cultural elaborations of Yamanote and Shitamachi—for the people I knew, much more vibrantly meaningful than some abstract class identity—are inseparable from power relations, even as the narrative conventions produce a rich, multifaceted discourse, alive with tension and ambivalence, within historically and culturally specific situations. To invoke Yamanote/Shitamachi distinctions is to reappropriate and re-create discourses with a resonant history, to "invent tradition," as terms with a particular historical legacy are redeployed.[21]

Gradations based on firm size, stereotypes associated with occupation, the Yamanote/Shitamachi distinction, and the specific location of Arakawa ward in relationship to these images, constitute axes along which people I knew crafted selves. Work, power, and identity emerge as themes riven by strong ambivalences and multiple meanings. I have tried to sketch out the contours of one set of tension-ridden idioms through which identities can be constructed. In the following chapter, we see how nostalgia for what counts as a truly "Japanese self" comes into play at an ethics training camp where the Satōs sent their workers. A narrative of this startling experience throws into relief the close intertwining of power and identity, as the camp attempts, through disciplines, to create a particular kind of "self." The recreation of traditions also takes on particular resonances given the high proportion of people in small business who sent their workers to the center, and the particular historical moment of increasing nationalistic pride in which our participation in the training programs took place. The camp sought to consciously impose a set of hegemonic meanings of Japanese selfhood and to transform us accordingly. But perhaps every such attempt can be only partially successful. For although its power was unforgettable, even a highly resonant, vividly articulated set of practices may never be univocal and seamless in its meaning, as success and compliance are fissured by small resistances to the doctrines themselves and to attempts to secure complete closure.

3   *Disciplined Selves*

The taxi glided silently up the hill and pulled into a wide, gravel-strewn driveway. *"Rinri Gakuen"* (Ethics School) said a discreetly displayed wooden sign. A young man with sculpted features and a crew cut, all severe angles, motioned the driver to proceed to the entrance of the building directly ahead of us. Fringed by pine trees, the dazzling white façade almost obscured the silhouette of Mt. Fuji rising above the forest. It was an impressive—if somewhat daunting—sight.

I glanced with a mixture of apprehension and exhilaration at my traveling companions from the company. It would be difficult to imagine two more disparate personalities. One, Adachi-san, looked—if possible— even more apprehensive than I. A company veteran who specialized in crafting Japanese sweets, he was the living personification of the "typical" traditional artisan: quiet, uncomfortable with people, eloquent not in words but in his artistic skill. The other, Ogawa-san, poked his head out the window, straining for a better view of the building. This was his second trip to the place, and he was clearly eager for the excitement to begin. His ebullient personality had made him one of the company's most popular employees. And, unfortunately for my best-laid plans, his energy knew no bounds. Having arisen at six that morning to catch an early train, I had fully intended to catch a few extra winks in preparation for what lay ahead. Ogawa-san, despite his previous night's carousing with one of his *senpai,* or seniors, apparently had other ideas. Every time my eyelids grew unbearably heavy, he peppered me with questions about myself and America, and in turn, he needed little prompting to pour out his life story, from life in his hometown in the country to his present position at the company in Tokyo where we all worked. An entertaining informant, but an exhausting traveling companion.

When I first began work at the confectionery factory, from time to time two or three workers would be inexplicably absent for a few days, My casual questions yielded fragmented, incredible tales of walking barefoot over rocks, of marathons and cold water baths. A little further probing linked these cryptic events with our inspirational afternoon meetings in the company. Every day after lunch we would gather and read from a pamphlet called "Education at the Workplace." One person would read aloud the short essay for the day, sharing his/her impressions, and then we would chant in unison the day's slogan ("Let's put our tools away carefully," or "Let's cooperate with each other," for example).

All this was part of an "ethics movement" the owner had heard about through his friends. He attended one of their seminars, and, taken with their teachings, sent one of his daughters to the ethics school. Before the program, she was a typical teenager: a usually cheerful young woman who had her sulky, rebellious moments, most notably when she was asked to help out with family chores. After, she was a paragon of virtue. She arose at five every morning to run two or three miles, and, before leaving for school, she even found the time to make box lunches for her younger siblings to take with them. Not surprisingly, the owner was delighted by these stunning results, and this time, he decided to send all his full-time employees to the ethics school, two or three at a time. Those of us who were female part-time workers would ordinarily not be included in this act of largesse—part-timers generally do not receive the benefits accorded to full-time workers—but because of my anthropological interests, he indulged my request to attend. For a moment, staring at the forbidding building, I regretted my anthropological enthusiasm.

Luckily, however, I stayed. The ethics center articulated a powerful, vivid doctrine of selfhood that first drew my attention to this critical discourse in Japanese life. Because the center was in the business of transforming selves, it elaborated an explicit theory of selfhood: what constitutes an ideal self; the inseparability of selves from the sites of their construction in families, companies, schools, and societies; the disciplines—culturally specific forms of pedagogy—that were deployed in order to create these ideal selves. As such, the center provided one highly specific, even extreme expression of certain cultural discourses, but as I shall argue in later chapters, the same themes—sometimes taken up differently, sometimes recapitulating what I saw and heard at the center—appeared in countless different variations in everyday life in the factory and the neighborhood. Yet, although the ethics practices drew on culturally familiar themes, I also want to draw attention to the incompleteness of their attempts to transform selves. Certainly, if people like Mr. Satō had expected their workers to be transformed, ethical training turned out to be something of a disappointment. In any attempt to construct a regime of "truth," fissures, resistances, and reappropriations of meaning may be inevitable, and success partial at best. What the ethics center allows me to do, however, is introduce, through a series of startling events, the recurring motif of this book: the historically and culturally specific, discursive production of selves in the domains of work, family, and community.

The Ethics Retreat

The Rinri (Ethics) movement arose during the dislocation of postwar occupied Japan, in response to what the founder, Maruyama Toshio, termed the deterioration of the moral fiber of the Japanese people.[1] Japan, he claimed, was becoming a country where "you could do anything, if you just had the money." Maruyama, inspired by his mission to save the best of the Japanese spirit, began to write extensively on ethical training, eventually devising a set of programs to disseminate his philosophical teachings. He died a number of years ago, but his eldest son, a graduate in philosophy from Tokyo University, succeeded to the headship of the movement.

The organization has expanded from its original humble beginnings and now boasts headquarters in a central part of Tokyo and a membership of 100,000 persons throughout the country. One teacher told me of their desire to spread their teachings abroad, and toward that end, members have established a fledgling organization in Los Angeles. The movement's defining practice is the "Morning Gathering" (*Asa no Tsudoi*), a half hour of inspirational lectures and activities held early in the morning, before members depart for work or school. In addition to attending these local meetings, many participate in programs held at the organization's educational center near Mt. Fuji. Here one finds a museum enshrining Maruyama's relics, a research center for advanced students of the movement, lodgings for teachers, counselors, and students, and the ethics training school. Standing in the shadow of Mt. Fuji, apart from the farming town at the foot of the hill and the Self Defense Force training camp farther up the plateau, the ethics organization forms its own self-contained community.

The Ethics School was founded in November of 1975. Its primary goal is to train workers in the ways of ethics, stressing the importance of putting into practice the teachings of the ethics movement in general. The school runs several different seminars, programs tailored to meet the needs of different kinds of participants. Among them are the managers' seminar (*keieisha zemi*) for owners and managers of companies; the leaders' seminar (*shihaisha zemi*) for supervisors, division chiefs and people in positions of authority; the regular employee seminar (*shain zemi*); the young lady seminar for unmarried women; the married women's seminar (*fujin zemi*); and, finally, the youth seminar, or *seinen zemi*, the most demanding and strenuous program of all. The precise content of each seminar is altered slightly to accommodate its participants, so that, for instance, the young lady seminar stresses training to be a good wife and mother and the owner/manager seminar concentrates on management problems. The basic organization of the program and the general ethics philosophy have remained largely unchanged.

I participated in the rigorous youth seminar, a six-day program for those up to forty years of age. There were twenty-six of us, including four women. Half the participants were there "on company orders," representing a variety of small and medium-sized firms (fewer than 300 employees in manufacturing; fewer than 50 in wholesale and retail), including an ironworks factory, a real estate agency, a company that designed ships, and, of course, our confectionery. The workers themselves ranged from factory employees who worked on assembly lines to university graduates in management positions. Others came on their own, on the recommendation of friends, relatives, or other acquaintances. These people usually sought solutions to specific problems. For example, of the three other women in my squad, one was a former orchestra violinist undergoing a career crisis; another a salesperson for a cosmetics company who disliked her job; the third a high school student prone to truancy.

The fees for the six-day stay were approximately ¥40,000 (U.S. $200 at an exchange rate of ¥200/dollar), while shorter seminars were a uniform ¥30,000. Individual participants must find their own funding, while employees come at company expense. Participants may attend as many times as they wish or can afford. For instance, Ogawa-san was there for a second time at his own request; another of my work companions intended to return soon. Our employer, pleased at this show of enthusiasm, gladly footed all the bills. One teacher told me of a wealthy entrepreneur who owns a famous chain of golf courses. He has returned over ten times, and his employees have come back with almost equal frequency.

The organization of hierarchy and authority also requires explanation. Teachers were full-time, paid staff who had undergone years of training in the ethics movement. They directed the center's activities and gave the lectures. *Gakusei,* students, were in their apprenticeship to become teachers. They were occasionally allowed to lecture or lead exercises.

Jishūsei, the younger counselors, were unusually dedicated or enthusiastic former participants who had been asked to return as *senpai,* seniors, to the new participants. Typically, the counselors were directly involved in our activities, spurring us on to greater heights of enthusiasm.

Perhaps the most obvious feature of life at the school was its group organization involving group responsibility. Each squad slept in the same room, ate at the same table, exercised together, and sat together in class. The position of squad leader (*hanchō*) rotated daily, giving most participants an opportunity to be in a leadership position and share responsibility. The leader's duties included accounting for all squad members at roll call, taken at the beginning of each exercise, and collecting our diaries at the end of the day. When we stood in group formation, the leader always assumed a position at the head of the line.

We participated in activities as squads, not as individuals. Group organization was especially effective as a means of compelling us to comply with school regulations. The rules seemed endless, and even minor infractions incurred penalties. For example, there were spot inspections of our bedrooms (we were instructed on *exactly* how to make our beds), toilet areas (there are slippers worn specifically in toilet areas in Japan, and the regular slippers we took off outside the toilet area had to be lined up neatly), and the bath (the plastic baskets where we kept our clothes had to be stacked carefully, not left halfway out of the shelf). At the end of every day, the teachers announced penalties by squad—no individual names were mentioned—and the resulting embarrassment was half the punishment. Tardiness and sloppiness were the chief offenses. As will become clear, it was never pleasant to have to suffer for the "slovenliness" of another, so the stress on group responsibility acted as a highly efficient self-policing mechanism. One woman in our squad was chronically late and often left her bed unmade or made improperly, so the other three of us were often reduced to covering for her—fixing her bed, for instance—so the entire group would not have to suffer for her shortcomings. It was an infernally effective means of generating consent to the rules.

In order to impart the flavor of the center and its teachings, I begin here a narrative account of the opening exercises, a typical day at the center, and special events in which we participated. Subsequently, I will explicate certain recurrent features of the center activities and doctrine, in light of the school's aims to create ideal selves. Because I am concerned to give an account of how I arrived at certain understandings, I make no attempt to disguise my reactions as an American, and I try, as far as possible, to give some indication of how other people reacted to each exercise. I hope to convey to the reader a sense of the deep and often contradictory emotional responses my fellow participants and I had to this extraordinary set of experiences: profound feelings of warmth, anger, indignation, guilt, sadness, delight, frustration, and contentment. In fact, I will argue, it was precisely this combination of strong emotion and rigid form which provides the key to the interpretation of the ethics center program and its underlying assumptions about crafting disciplined selves.

Opening Exercises

Adachi-san, Ogawa-san, and I were greeted at the door by two young women wearing name tags, who showed us where to deposit our luggage and then ushered us into a bright, modern classroom. About twenty people were seated there in silence: businessmen with gray suits, white shirts, and the sheer black socks so common in Japan; a young woman in her high school uniform; two other young women in jeans and heavy makeup; and some men nattily dressed. A few more people trickled in. I wondered what on earth we were waiting for.

Suddenly, a man sitting on a chair near the blackboard, an armband surrounding his upper left arm, leaped to his feet. He stretched out his arms and pushed down the metal buzzer in his hands, which gave out an ear-piercing ring. Many of us jumped visibly. "It is now two minutes before the hour!" he barked. "Adjust your posture!" It was such a shock that one's instinct was to immediately obey, and we all straightened up in our seats. His loud voice and jutting chin make him seem all the more intimidating. Exactly two minutes later, he leaped up again to ring the buzzer, this time to say, "The opening ceremony will now begin!" and then barked out orders to "Stand up!" "Bow!" "Sit down!"[2]

I was too stunned by this to take in many of the welcoming pleasantries offered by the head of the center. He did inform us, however, that we were divided into four squads according to the rooms where we would sleep, and so we, the women, were Squad (*Han*) Four. When he finished, the "militaristic" discipline was repeated: We were ordered to stand up, utter thanks, and exit from the room single file, turning to bow before we stepped out the door.

Getting Acquainted

On the first day, two exercises helped us get to know one another. The first was a series of games to break the ice, the second I can only describe as a kind of confessional encounter session.

"Musical chairs" or rather "musical *zabuton*" (seat cushions) was the first. We counted off into groups of "apples," "bananas," or "pears," with an "it" sitting in the middle of the circle. When she or he called out the name of a fruit, all the "apples" or "bananas" scrambled madly for another cushion, creating a flurry of frantic activity. Anyone unlucky enough to be "it" three times had to entertain us by singing. Amusingly enough, some pop stars manqué clearly made no effort to find another *zabuton,* so they could indulge their desire to perform. Ogawa-san from our company was one of these, and he gave us a rousing rendition of a Go Hiromi[3] tune. One person was clearly dying to sing, but when he launched into a juicy, sentimental folk ballad, he was so agonizingly tone deaf that all of us—even the teachers—had to bite our lips or cover our mouths to stifle our laughs.

In another game, we formed two concentric circles and walked until we were told to stop. The person facing us became our conversation partners for the moment, as we introduced ourselves and made small talk. When the teachers first explained the exercise I mentally rolled my eyes, thinking how contrived it was. To my surprise, it did turn out to be a good way to meet people, some of whom looked so aloof or intimidating that I might never have bothered to introduce myself on my own initiative.

Later that evening, we had an opportunity to reveal ourselves more intimately. We sat in small groups, forming a circle, and introduced ourselves, told our reasons for coming, and stated what we wanted to accomplish during the program. The intensity of the introductions varied widely. Predictably enough, those participants sent by their companies uttered standard phrases: "I want to experience this to the fullest," "I don't usually have time to reflect on myself and my life," "The spirit of thankfulness is something I want to learn." But others were clearly more emotionally involved. One young man who gave the initial impression of enormous competence and control, burst into tears, sobbing so convulsively that he was unable to speak for some moments. He was sickly, he said, and often rebelled against his parents. In fits of anger, he would leap into the car and take long, reckless midnight drives that once, at least, culminated in a serious accident. He caused his parents constant anguish, and he hoped that the training center could teach him the discipline to be better. Two men, one of them exceedingly serious and rigid in his demeanor, the other with a vacant look in his eyes, confessed to having had nervous breakdowns. Two of the women also broke into tears as they told their stories. Inazawa-san spoke of rebellion against her parents. She constantly fought with them. She had tried everything. This was her last chance, she said between sobs. The violinist, Hashimoto-san, had found relationships with her fellow musicians in the orchestra backbiting and eventually so unbearable that she quit in frustration. Now she was lost. What was she to do with her life? The teacher listened sympathetically to all of us, trying to point out similarities in our tales, and encouraged us to help one another.

As transparent as these exercises were, they served their purposes. After our games and confessions before each other, the tight, almost unfriendly little groups loosened. Ogawa-san had told me this would happen, and he seemed to be right. Everyone seemed more comfortable with the others, as though the cliques were giving way to a single group encompassing us all.

A Day at the Center

The program we followed was highly structured and followed a similar pattern each day. From the 5 A.M. call to rise, to the official "lights out" at 9:30 P.M., virtually every minute was accounted for. Only rarely would we have a little extra time (after meals, for instance) to play a game of ping pong or sit and chat with other participants. The "tight schedule," to quote Japanese English, is evident from the following:

5:00–5:40	Wake up, wash up
5:45–6:50	Cleaning, morning greeting, vocalization practice
6:55–7:30	Exercise, cold water ablutions
7:45–8:30	Morning meeting, lecture
8:30–9:40	Breakfast
9:40–12:20	Lectures, tours, sports, special activities
12:30–1:20	Lunch
1:20–4:30	Recreation, lectures
4:30–5:30	Bath
5:30–6:30	Dinner
6:30–9:40	Lecture, *seiza,* diary, closing ceremony, lights-out

To impart a more vivid sense of a day's rhythms and the flavor of the experience, I attempt here to take the reader with me through a typical day at the center.

Wake Up

Promptly at five each morning, the loudspeakers would blare, "Good morning, everyone! It is now 5:00. We will assemble downstairs at 5:15." Then for the next fifteen minutes as we scrambled to get dressed, wash our faces, and make our beds, the stirring strains of the theme from "Rocky" spurred us on. A counselor stood near the washroom, invariably a disgustingly cheerful person who smiled, bowed, and greeted us with "Good morning" as we dashed in to wash our faces and brush our teeth. All of us complained heartily about having to arise at that ungodly hour; in fact, one woman lay in bed moaning the first day. Despite our urgings, she arose sluggishly and dallied in her preparations, and by the time she trailed downstairs, all of us were already assembled in the lobby. True to center policy, our entire group was disciplined by having to perform 15 extra minutes of *seiza,* the meditation exercise which can cut off blood circulation in your legs. After that episode, the rest of us made certain that our recalcitrant roommate arrived downstairs on time, her moans notwithstanding.

Getting up early was in fact the subject of our first lecture. This day, we were told, comes but once. To wake up late is to lose out from the beginning. It is unnatural, and by indulging one's desire to stay in bed, it leads to selfishness, passivity, an upset of body rhythms, slovenliness, failure, and ultimately, unhappiness (*fukō*). In another breathtaking chain of causality, getting a good start on the day—jumping out of bed as soon as your eyes opened—is natural. It leads to an obedient, gentle heart (*sunao na kokoro,* the ideal disposition of the self), positive and constructive behavior, success, and happiness (*shiawase*). We were even given a demonstration of how to arise properly. The men were to leap up and kick off the covers, booming out a resounding *"Hai!"* (Yes!). Women, on the other hand, were to be less abrupt in our movements, carefully folding up the quilt and arising with a smile and a gentle, cheerful *"Hai."* The realization of ethical goals begins with concrete activities, and among these, early rising was critically important.

Seisō (Cleaning)

Cleaning is a standard ingredient of spiritual education in Japan. For example, Zen and its associated arts ideally begin every teaching session with cleaning, usually crouching on one's hands and knees and scrubbing the floor or wiping the *tatami* mats. In the tea ceremony classes I took in my neighborhood, for instance, students were charged with this responsibility before every lesson. Japanese students and teachers as a matter of course clean the floors, lockers, etc., in their schools before classes begin.

Each morning, a teacher would announce our cleaning duties for the morning. One or two students and a counselor were assigned to each task. No matter how humble or distasteful, the work should be performed with a glad heart. No job is too good for anyone. Not surprisingly, given this philosophy, cleaning the toilets and the bath and washing the floors were the most common chores. To simply perform the task was not enough, however. It was equally important to show tremendous enthusiasm, so the counselors would lead us in chants of "*Faitto!*" (Fight!) as we hosed down the toilets, emptied the tins of sanitary napkins, and scrubbed the floors.

Cleaning, in and of itself, was not objectionable to me, but I found the chanting a needless, silly waste of energy and complained to my roommates about it. To my great surprise, no one really joined me in my criticism.

Chōrei (Morning Ceremony)

After cleaning, we jogged to the statue of the founder Maruyama, facing Mt. Fuji. The head of the school led us in a rousing shout of "Good morning," and briefly lectured on some inspirational theme. Then, a tape recorder played the national anthem as counselors raised the flags of Japan and of the ethics movement. Like our company's noontime gatherings, the morning ceremony was built around the pamphlet "Education at the Workplace." Each day teachers chose one among us to share his/her impressions of an article based on personal experiences at work.

These stories were often profoundly moving. One farmer who suffered from a chronic illness told us of his problems and shortcomings. His eyes glistened with tears as he described his habit of using sickness as an excuse to lean on others (*amaeru*) and to indulge his selfishness (*wagamama*). From now on, he vowed to mend his selfish ways. Contrition and a simple eloquence animated his words. As we listened, many of us were ourselves moved to tears. Ogawa-san took "conserve energy" as his theme. He was one of the artisans entrusted with delivering our confections to the customers, and sometimes, he confessed, he would put his foot on the gas and speed recklessly to "let off steam." "I might have caused an accident," he said, ruefully. "And since the van belongs to the company and not to me, I wasn't worried about wasting gas. Now, though, I will be more careful." Hashimoto-san was equally articulate. Her job with the Philharmonic had been stormy. She argued frequently with older members of the orchestra. What was worse, she had lashed out in anger against her teacher, to the point where they were no longer on speaking terms. Her strained relations caused her to quit the Phil and even to contemplate giving up music as a career. "As soon as I get home, I am going to take the initiative and call my teacher to apologize," said Hashimoto-san, red-eyed. Her touching speech imbued the motto of the day, "Let's cooperate on the job," with new meaning for us all.

The participants were skillfully selected and their speeches were without exception articulate, moving, and, according to my informal polls, relevant to people's work experience. The teachers reinforced the speakers' emotional involvement by praising each one for honesty, for relating the theme to personal experience, and for taking the topic to heart rather than treating it simply as an intellectual exercise.

Hassei Renshū (Vocalization Practice)

Perhaps a more accurate characterization of vocalization practice would be "shouting practice." After the morning ceremony, we trotted, squad by squad, into the spacious grounds adjacent to the main building. Lining up single file, we faced a grim young counselor who shouted out *"Hai!"* to which we responded *"Hai!"* in rapid-fire succession. This complete, we formed two lines facing one another. Bowing to our partner, we exchanged "Good morning, X-san" and then "Thank you, X-san." Teachers stressed the importance of answering immediately, without a pause.

The central part of the exercise was a bit more unusual. Each of us was forced to stand in front of the group, facing Mt. Fuji, and scream at the top of our lungs, "Father! Mother! Good morning!" Other seminars more specifically tailored to one particular company require participants to shout, "I am the sun of X company! I will make X company number one in Japan!" Not a few of us demonstrated considerable embarrassment during this event, but here the school capitalized on its keen knowledge of psychology. Every word was rewarded with a shout of encouragement and appreciation from the gallery. The group applauded after each person finished. Typically, shouters would have the traces of embarrassed smiles on their faces as they bowed to the others. The squad's encouragement made an embarrassing, difficult exercise infinitely more tolerable.

Disciplined Selves

The head of the school, during an interview, revealed the aims of this exercise. Above all, it should inculcate receptiveness and a willingness to greet and appreciate others and to eliminate resistance toward responding positively toward authority. Enthusiastic replies would eventually excise the negative qualities of sullenness, resentfulness, and passivity, through the sheer energy generated by shouting. Giving thanks to our parents would deepen our ideas about filial piety, just as company seminars would heighten the feeling of being part of a company. Above all, the point was to throw all our energy into the shouting. It matters not who is loudest or longest. The lesson is to try to the utmost of your ability.

These lofty sentiments aside, shouting filial greetings at Mount Fuji elicited a good deal of satirical comment from my co-workers at the Satō factory. Suzuki and Yamamoto, the young artisans who were later known for their "uncooperative" attitudes when they themselves came to the center, would parody the exercise by crying out, in a strangled falsetto, "*Otōsan, okāsan,*" as they feigned tears and dramatically staggered around the shop floor. Adachi-san, the silent subchief in *wagashi,* offered his criticism in another mode. "*Hidoi yo*" (It's terrible), he said in distressed tones to one of the part-timers. "They make you stand up in front of everyone and shout." And Hamada-san, the part-timer, murmured sympathetically in agreement. "*Adachi-san wa shizuka da mon, ne . . .*" (Adachi-san is quiet, so . . .). The postmortem revealed resistance and skepticism not immediately evident during the exercises themselves.

Exercise/Running

We ran at least one and a half miles a day, often more, as a rehearsal for the 7.5 kilometer marathon scheduled for the next-to-last day of the program.

Teachers again emphasized spirit and perseverance. To engender the proper enthusiasm, we shouted and chanted as we ran.[4] Speed was not the issue; the key was to finish and not to give up. Moreover, exercise would enhance the mutual development of mind and body. Care for the body exhibited filial piety and gratefulness to nature, for after all, one's body was not really one's own but a gift from nature and from one's parents and ancestors. To neglect the body is to lack appreciation for the precious gift of life.

Needless to say, many of the younger sports enthusiasts welcomed this part of the day. In fact, Ogawa-san had waxed eloquent about the joys of the vigorous outdoor exercise. Those who, like myself, were of a more sedentary persuasion, were noticeably less enthusiastic.

To provide encouragement and models of physical and spiritual health, teachers or counselors usually ran with us. Invariably they were paragons of physical conditioning: compact, muscular, without an ounce of excess flesh. One, whose shaved head made him look like a Buddhist monk, used to run alongside us, barefoot. His vitality and physical prowess made him something of a minor legend at the center.

Our teachers may have seemed tireless, but we students were another story altogether. On the longer runs, our enthusiasm for chanting dimmed considerably as people grew more noticeably fatigued. Nonetheless, everyone did somehow manage to "go the distance," though not without uncomfortable aftereffects. I once spied Adachi-san, my coworker, seated on the floor of the lobby, shoes at his side, as Ogawa-san massaged his cramped feet. Blisters and plastic bandages were all-too-familiar features of our everyday lives, as were grumbling complaints from those like Adachi-san and myself, who were none too pleased with this form of enforced bodily mortification.

Misogi (Cold Water Ablution)

Misogi, or ritual ablution with cold water, has a long history in Japanese religious tradition. Shinto ascetics, for example, have been known to stand under a mountain waterfall at dawn on a cold winter's day, as part of their regime of bodily mortification and physical austerity (cf. Blacker 1975).

Our *misogi* followed a fixed pattern. We sat in rows in the lobby, adopting either the formal Japanese *seiza* posture, legs folded under us, back straight, hands folded, or the yoga lotus position. Our teacher brought in a portable tape recorder, and he played us soothing, vaguely Indian music. We listened, eyes closed, as his resonant voice told us to simply allow our minds to go blank. Eventually, each group proceeded single file to the bathing rooms, men and women separately. We were to remain silent, in order to create a contemplative, meditative atmosphere.

We removed our clothes, folding them neatly in the bins, and proceeded into the bath. It was Japanese-style: a large central tub, big enough for perhaps ten people, surrounded by a tile floor, with faucets and mirrors placed at about knee level around the circumference of the room. A stack of plastic basins occupied one corner. Counselors told us to take a basin and sit *seiza*-style in front of a faucet, kneeling on the icy tile. First, we gracefully rinsed out our basins—the movements, to me, reminiscent of the pouring of water in the tea ceremony—then filled them with cold water and set them to one side. Palms on the floor, prostrated so that our foreheads touched the ground, we repeated the following words:

> I/we[5] humbly give thanks for water, the source of life. With this pure, precious water, I will clean and purify my mind and body. Without disliking the cold, thankful for the cold, I will purify my heart.
>
> *Inochi de aru mizu ni, tsutsushinde kansha itashimasu. Kono kiyoki tōtoki no mizu de, shinshin o araikiyomemasu. Samusa o iyagarazu, samusa ni kansha shite, kokoro o kiyomemasu.*

We then took the basin of icy water and poured it down our backs. The first day we poured eighteen basinfuls in this fashion. The next day, after the first basin, we were told to enter the cold bath together, breathing deeply as we crouched down in the water, clasping our knees. The counselors, who entered with us, counted to ten—an excruciatingly slow count, I might add.

Upon emerging from the tub, we sat *seiza*-style once more and repeated the same chant, this time in the past tense. The leader dismissed us, and we silently restacked our basins neatly in the corner and filed out to dry ourselves and get dressed. We then walked silently back to the lobby and returned to our meditation.

Here I must add a digression on the place of collective bathing in Japanese culture. The friendly social relations that may take place among bathers at the public bath, say, or at a hot springs resort, can be termed *hadaka no otsukiai,* naked acquaintances or relationships. One is divested of one's social identity and can interact with others as an equal. In Japanese it is also possible to *hadaka de hanashiau,* to talk things over nakedly, saying what one truly feels, without pretense. By carrying out our cold water ablutions in the nude, we were symbolically divested of the outer trappings of our social selves. By doing so collectively, we were not only purifying our minds and bodies, but symbolically cementing our connectedness to one another.

Our *"misogi* primer" explained the aims of the exercise. It should instill in us a gratefulness to Nature, through giving thanks to the water. It should also make us aware of our bodies (through their mortification) and hence of the fact that they were gifts from Nature and from our parents. Perhaps more important, however, was its role in bringing out decisiveness, the strength of will needed to actually enter that cold bath, and hence to perform any unpleasant task. Thus, it was a symbolic cleansing away of selfishness, which in turn should teach us *sunaosa:* gentleness, meekness, obedience.

Many people told me that *misogi* was one of the day's more pleasant activities, and I had to concur. (That fact that it was June and not December undoubtedly made a significant difference as well.) Admittedly, it was agonizingly painful to pour that first basin of water or to take the plunge into the tub, and our bodies took undeniable note of the shock. The violinist turned blue at the lips, and her teeth chattered. I shivered. Yet, after this initial insult, the water felt refreshing following the morning's vigorous exercise. The cold made the skin tingle with warmth. Still, not everyone shared this view: our recalcitrant roommate was always reluctant to enter the bath and even complained that she might die from the cold. I realized I had begun to internalize the ethics teachings when I found myself thinking that her complaints really arose from a lack of resolve and weakness of character. From another point of view, one could say that our roommate was the person who provided the most resistance to the center's extreme disciplines.

(*Asa no Tsudoi*) Morning Gathering

Although this "morning meeting" is the centerpiece of the national ethics movement, it assumed less importance at the school.

After gathering in the classroom, we would raise the central text, *Happiness for the Millions* (*Bannin Kōfuku no Shiori*), straight in front of us, at eye level, and recite in unison the major ethical aphorisms. "Hardship is the gateway to happiness," "Other people are our mirrors," "Today is the best day," we would chant. Selecting one of these as a theme, a teacher or counselor would lecture for the remainder of class. The morning meetings encouraged us to *realize* the goals we had set for ourselves. In fact, teachers would exhort us daily that practice, realization (*jissen*) was the essence of the movement. According to one of their favorite aphorisms: "If you try, you will change. If you try, you will understand. If you try, you can do it." The Japanese "*Yareba kawaru. Yareba wakaru. Yareba dekiru,*" has a compelling, insistent rhythm.

If the teachers had intended the lectures to showcase their teachings, they must have been sorely disappointed. From what I observed in class, the lectures were taken least seriously of all the exercises, and they seemed to have little effect. Almost no one—except the anthropologist—took notes. Not a few of my fellow participants told me that they just didn't understand the lectures, because the subjects were too difficult and abstract. One man literally fell asleep one morning, and began to breathe heavily and then to snore, whereupon the counselors prodded him and hissed a sharp reprimand as he started and opened his eyes. To further distract our attention, by the time we entered the classroom, it was a good three hours since we had jumped out of bed, and most of us were ravenous. "I'm thinking more about breakfast than the content of the lecture," said Kurihara-san, a real estate broker.

Later in the week we were all asked to give short speeches about our impressions of the school and what we had learned so far. Teachers gave us minute instructions on the proper form to follow: bow at the proper angle, have a pleasant facial expression, use the appropriate language level. Their comments on each speech were confined almost exclusively to these matters of external form. For instance, my "best feature" was my smile, but my bow was much too perfunctory: I hadn't stood properly upright before dashing back to my seat.

The speeches, in actual content, were all variations on a theme. Almost everyone repeated certain stock phrases, stressing enthusiasm and perseverance. "*Isshokenmei gambaritai to omoimasu*" (I want to stick with it with all my might); or "*Sei ippai keiken shitai to omoimasu*" (I want to experience it to the fullest). Some were less visibly enthusiastic than others, although almost everyone paid lip service to this ideal. There were two conspicuous exceptions, two young artisans from a foundry, who both became good friends of Ogawa-san. Through their impolite language levels (using *ore*, the informal—some would say vulgar—masculine first-person pronoun), and their refusal to mouth the ethics ideals, they showed resentment of teachers' authority and skepticism about the entire program. The head of the school found their insubordination sufficiently threatening to issue a word of warning.

Meals

By this time, it was 8:30 and high time for breakfast. Each squad sat down to a different table. A female counselor stood up and told us to adjust our posture and to lightly close our eyes. Then she would "say grace:" "We give thanks for this meal, the source of life," (*Inochi no moto de aru shokuji ni, kansha itashimasu*). Finally, she would say "*Itadakimasu*" (I will humbly receive), a signal for us to dig in.

Even our food held a lesson for us. The food itself was standard Japanese fare: *miso* soup and rice, fish or meat, and various vegetables.

Cleaning our plates, even if we didn't like what was served, would prevent selfishness and lead to a grateful, gentle heart. Giving in to likes an dislikes, on the other hand, was the beginning of selfish, egocentric behavior.

After meals, all squads were responsible for cleaning and clearing their own tables. Mature adults should learn how to clean up after themselves.

Mealtimes were businesslike. We spent less than fifteen minutes actually eating and then dashed to clean up, so that there would be more time to relax, chat, play ping pong, or rest in our rooms.

Afternoons

We usually participated in a recreational activity during the afternoon, and most of these differed from day to day. Some of the most important will be described in the following section. We would have an hour for our baths, and than an hour for dinner, after which we proceeded to the main classroom for a lecture.

Seiza

This was the primary evening activity. I have already described the classic *seiza* posture in my discussion of *misogi,* the cold water ablutions. *Seiza* is the formal Japanese way of sitting on the floor. Older people, particularly women—who must be more proper in their adherence to etiquette than men—can often sustain this position for hours, but most young people, especially young men, find it uncomfortable, painful even, after just a few minutes. The circulation in the legs and feet can seem to stop completely, and it is possible to lose sensation and muscular control.

In this case, the *seiza* exercise was explicitly modeled on Zen meditation. We were told to remove our slippers and socks and line them up against one wall. Then we entered a large, empty, dimly lit room and kneeled down in rows, maintaining complete silence.

Our teacher appeared in formal Japanese dress: wearing the *hakama,* or divided skirt, and carrying a long wooden stick in his hand. With his traditional garb and shaved head, he resembled a Zen monk. The stick, as in Zen, was designed for *keisaku,* the ritual administration of blows. Should we be unable to concentrate, should we find ourselves in pain or getting sleepy, we were to ask the teacher to strike us with the stick. This we could do by silently folding the hands and bowing as if in prayer as he went by. We would then bend over, head prostrated to the ground, and the teacher would "do us the favor" of delivering two sharp blows to each side of our backs.

All of this was designed to heighten our filial piety. "Gratefulness to your parents (*oya e no kansha*) is the key to a naive heart (*sunao na kokoro*)," our teacher declaimed. "Recall the faces of your mother and father when they saw you off, recall their faces when they took care of you when you were sick." Then he turned to his portable Sony tape recorder and played us a sad, haunting melody with its sentimental lyrics:

> Mama stayed up all night to knit gloves for me.
> Though the winter wind was cold, she knitted diligently.
> News from my hometown arrives.
> I can smell the fragrance of the hearth.
> Mama spins thread all day, all day she spins.
> On the dirt floor, Papa works with the straw.
> I have to keep going too.
> How lonely the winter at home.
> I wish they had at least a radio to listen to.
> Mama's chapped hands hurt. She grinds the fresh miso.
> When the remaining snow melts, it will soon be spring.
> The fields are waiting.
> I can hear the murmur of the brook.
> I am flooded with nostalgia.

The reaction to this song was, to me, incredible. It struck some deep emotional chord in many of the participants, for to my astonishment, every counselor was in tears, and some of them were actually sobbing. Many of the participants, both men and women, cried uncontrollably. Even more astonishing, this tremendous emotional outburst occurred every night. On the second evening, we had to kneel down and shout out, "Mother, Father, please forgive me!" prompting a round of even more violent sobbing.

As the tape played its mournful tune, the lights were dimmed, enveloping us in darkness. The teacher slowly and deliberately made his way down each row. This was our opportunity to request *keisaku*. At first I had vowed to forego such bodily mortifications, but my anthropological conscience persuaded me to give it a try the second night and each night thereafter. The blows left one quite breathless, and—according to my roommates—left red marks on my skin for the remainder of our stay. Still, in later discussions, many of us agreed that it didn't seem so terrible after the first experience. It did, said one woman, make one feel more penitent. On any given night, perhaps two-thirds to three-quarters of the participants asked for the blows, and all the counselors invariably did so.

On, obligation, was our take-home lesson. The realization of our indebtedness and obligation to our parents should create feelings of appreciation and regret for our thoughtlessness. Judging from the violent emotional reactions this exercise engendered, I would say that for many it served its function beautifully. Yet cynicism was not lacking. Among those of us who had come from the Satō company, this exercise elicited all manner of scornful comments. Mr. Satō himself later commented to me that the women, in particular, were like Pavlov's dogs, automatically turning on the tears when they heard the song. I also remembered the hysterically funny demonstrations of this exercise that Kimura-san, Suzuki-san, and a few other artisans performed for the rest of us in the factory, much to our collective amusement. Though none of this cynicism was evident during the exercise itself, clearly solemn demeanor at the retreat cannot be read as total, unqualified acceptance. Resistances and parody emerged in other contexts.

Setting Goals; Diaries; Closing Ceremony

After this intense experience, we adjourned to a classroom to write in our diaries. There were entries telling whether we had arisen immediately or lingered a few moments when it was time to get up; whether we had performed one good deed for the day; and what our impressions of the day's activities had been. Every day we were supposed to set concrete goals, such as, "I will answer in a loud voice," or, "I will not be late." These we inscribed at the top of the next day's page. We then handed in the diaries to the teachers and received them back the next morning, complete with comments and suggestions. Teachers would enthusiastically reinforce any kind of positive comment about the center's teachings, explicating it further and urging us to even greater effort and enthusiasm.

Thereupon we filed into the lobby, assembling by squad for the closing ceremony. The head of the center gave a short speech. Then each person shouted out his/her name, the goal for the day, and whether or not it had been accomplished. We had to be loud and forceful; those who hesitated or spoke too softly had to repeat the exercise until they were sufficiently enthusiastic. Finally we were dismissed, and after a long, tiring day, no one challenged the curfew.

Special Events

Each day brought, in addition to this basic structure of activities, a number of special events designed to teach us key ethical concepts. Let us examine those events and teachings in more detail.

Refresh Time

"Refresh" in this case had nothing to do with our refreshment or relaxation, but with "refreshing" the floors of the school. Teachers assigned each squad to a different part of the center. We in Squad Four were in charge of the long upstairs corridor, and counselors instructed us to take rags and fall to our hands and knees to polish the floor. They were right behind us, leading a chant and scrubbing along with us. Dutifully crouching on our hands and knees, we wiped and polished, chanting all the while. At first we began with the usual "*Faitto!* and "*Wasshoi!*" but an even more intriguing chant followed: "Polish the floor! If you polish the floor, your heart too will shine! It will sparkle!" (Again, the Japanese has a rhythm and resonance lost in translation: *Yuka o migake! Yuka o migakeba, kokoro mo hikaru!*)

The floor was covered with tile and thus painfully hard. Our knees hurt, our hands and arms ached from the weight placed on them. The corridor seemed endless, and just when we reached the end, and, I thought, a welcome rest, we were told to turn around and go back over the entire corridor. At the halfway mark, all of us joined together in the lobby to learn the school song, animated by inspiring images of soaring hawks and international peace. Then, after twenty minutes, we were sent back to continue our scrubbing for another interminable fifty minutes—this time with a five-minute break.

Reactions to this exercise were fascinating. Like me, many said they focused either on their pain and discomfort or had allowed their minds to go completely blank. Most people said they felt resistance (*teikō o kanjiru*), and all found it exhausting and demanding. Hashimoto-san complained of sore arms and knees for days. Complaints aside, however, no one found the exercise especially surprising in any way. This reaction in turn surprised *me*. Others explained. Though it was an ordeal, it was simply another variation on the theme of cleaning as spiritual discipline. We had encountered it in our morning cleanings, and it occurs in other contexts in Japanese culture. Later, when I reported on this and other activities to my landlady's children, they laughed and said that it didn't sound like much compared to their high school clubs, where the discipline was much more demanding. I, on the other hand, was indignant about the extreme discomfort to which we were subjected. My fellow participants may have felt opposition or resistance to the extreme nature of the exercise, but the form in which it was cast seemed to make more cultural sense to them than it did to me.

Sagyō

In marked contrast to refresh time, *sagyō* was actually pleasant. Its goal was to teach us the value of work.

On a warm, sunny afternoon teachers led us to a small plot of tea bushes, down the hill from the school, where they gave us baskets in which to place the picked tea leaves. Silence was supposed to prevail, but the loveliness of the day and the camaraderie that had grown among us made it a pleasant social gathering. Even the counselors—who were our immediate "seniors"—chatted away, oblivious to the stern looks of the teacher in charge. Apparently sociability was the wrong lesson to learn. The teachers had had enough of our merry disregard of their exhortations, and finally they marched up and coldly reprimanded us for our lack of seriousness. They ordered us to go to the garden, pick up a trowel and a pair of gloves, and begin weeding. This time, anyone who talked would bring down upon his/her squad some dire (unnamed) penalty. The discipline took effect. Chastened, we sat silently in the rocky garden, weeding in the bright sunshine. After the allotted hour elapsed, we lined up, washed our hands, laid our trowels down in neat piles, and silently filed inside to take our baths.

At the beginning of *sagyō* we were given a mimeographed sheet explaining the goals of the exercise. We were to throw everything into work, with no extraneous thoughts. From this we could learn vitality, perseverance, and the full use of our abilities. The actual content of work might vary dramatically, but whatever the task, work itself should give us great joy. Above all, we should strive to avoid idleness, for that leads to evil thoughts. We should attempt to take the initiative in our work and not wait to be told what to do. Instead we should see what needed to be done and do it. Work is not a matter of speed, quantity, or skill, but of perseverance. We should thank our parents for giving us life and the opportunity to work. At the workplace, we should obey orders cheerfully. If we had "juniors" under us, we should look after them; if we were "juniors" we should treat our "seniors" with respect.

Clearly, this was the ethics movement's portrait of the ideal employee: obedient yet enthusiastic and persevering, ready to take the initiative and to attend to any task, no matter what it might be; cooperative; never idle; loyal; and pleasant. Later in this chapter I will comment more extensively on the movement's goals.

These claims were not made explicitly during the exercise, however. Among all the events, this one was pleasant, since it allowed us the opportunity to be outside and to talk and joke with each other, but otherwise it was not especially memorable or striking. Many participants spoke of the tea picking as fun (*tanoshii*), "although I wouldn't want to do it every day" said a ship designer. If its aim was to make us into ideal employees, *sagyō* seemed sadly ineffective.

On no Sōgen (The Field of Obligation)

Whereas Ogawa-san may have found refresh time the worst ordeal, for me *on no sōgen* far surpassed even that discomfort. I had heard chilling horror stories about this exercise from other company employees. The teachers in later interviews told me that, indeed, the field of obligation and the marathon were the two central events of the entire program.

It was a pitch-black evening. We were assembled in the lobby and our teacher told us to remove our socks, roll up our pants above the knee and sit, *seiza*-style, on the hard linoleum of the lobby. Our eyes were closed to the dim light as the teacher lectured us about the pain we were about to experience. "The pain," he said, "will make you grateful for material things: shoes, that cover your feet, clothes, all material objects. Most of all you should know that the pain you will feel is only one-thousandth of the pain your mother felt in bearing you." Then he read us a graphic passage about the agonies of childbirth, grisly enough to discourage anyone from ever having children. We were to give thanks for the gift of life, and thus realize the immensity of the obligation we owed our parents. This was the field of *on*.

Silently and in single file, we walked barefoot about a quarter of a mile to the school athletic field. The teacher instructed us not to look down as we walked. This was no easy task, for the path was strewn with coarse gravel and rocks, and each step brought new stabs of pain. Now and again someone would gasp as she or he stepped on a sharp rock. As I walked, I remembered one young artisan at the factory, Kurokawa-kun, who warned me, "Kondō-san, it really hurts. You might cry." Iida-san, one of the part-timers, had quickly replied, "Kondō-san won't cry—she's not like you," a remark that elicited laughter and teasing, since Kurokawa—always the butt of jokes in the factory—had in fact cried during this part of the exercise. Remembering this exchange, I resolved not to cry out—no easy task. The quarter mile seemed interminable. I was certain my feet would be shredded to ribbons. Actually I was moved to anger, not to tears: the whole exercise seemed ridiculously extreme, silly, and painful. I cursed my decision to come to the center, even my decision to become an anthropologist!

At long last we reached the field, but if we had thought this would bring sweet relief, we were sadly mistaken. We lined up on one side of the field and sat, *seiza*-style, on the fine gravel. With each passing minute, the body weight pressed one's legs ever more deeply into the rocks. Every bump, every jagged edge, dug into the skin. "Concentrate on your breathing!" our teacher shouted. And, pain aside, it was a strangely affecting scene: all of us in a single, straight line, our teacher facing us across the field rimmed with black pine trees, the only light from the full moon above.

"Think of the pain your mothers felt in bearing you!" boomed out a voice from across the field. And then the melancholy strains of " 'Kāsan" (Mom), that old familiar tune, wafted our way. As usual, there was sobbing aplenty, and tonight everyone requested *keisaku*. Some people told me afterwards that the blows took their minds off the pain in their legs (I was also of this persuasion), while others stressed their sincere penitence. After twenty minutes or so, we walked silently back to the hall, washed and dried our feet, and sat down once again on the linoleum of the lobby. The teacher then exhorted us about how easy, pleasant even, this *seiza* felt compared to sitting on the rocks. In our ingratitude and softness, we had even complained about the hardness of the linoleum! We should be grateful and realize that pain and hardship were only relative matters. Cultivating endurance and a humble attitude would help us overcome any difficulty.

Later comparison of my reactions with others' revealed my place on the extreme end of a continuum. Only a few echoed my indignant response to the pain. "How can this really accomplish its purpose?" asked one skeptic. I frankly expressed surprise that we had escaped unscathed; not a single rock had pierced the skin. Staunch defenders such as Hashimoto-san argued for the teacher's point of view. Without a doubt, the floor was much more tolerable after sitting on the gravel, so perhaps pain was relative, after all. My highly skeptical reactions seemed again to be atypical. Clearly, this exercise held deep significance for many, a sig-

Disciplined Selves

nificance most eloquently expressed in the convulsive sobs of the many who cried so piteously as we knelt on the rocks. Yet, as the parodies of *seiza* and this exercise showed me, the results were far less stunning for many of the artisans at the Satō factory.

Basic Practice

Our lessons in filial piety continued the following day, in a rehearsal of our speeches to our parents that we would deliver when we arrived home from the center.

Though it was a bright, sunny afternoon, the curtains in the *seiza* room were drawn, creating a quiet, solemn mood. One by one, we knelt at the front of the room—facing the windows so that the others were not directly in our line of sight—and composed a speech to our parents, using the following pattern:

1. Greeting parents, by bowing formally with hands on the ground, forehead to the floor, and announcing our return.
2. Telling parents where we had gone.
3. Explaining what the program was like, what we had learned, especially about filial piety, and how—if at all—the school had changed our attitudes about ourselves and our families.
4. Thanking parents for everything they have done, using concrete examples.
5. Apologizing for all the trouble we have caused and promising to improve in the future.

I was initially skeptical. How could this exercise generate anything more than embarrassment? But for most participants, the ethics teachings seemed to take on personal meaning at this point. To listen to the confessions, the room was full of selfish and egotistical people. Even the most rebellious young men who had been sent on company orders seemed to take this exercise seriously. One of the foundry workers, labeled "insolent" by the teachers, tearfully poured out his emotions. He had been a sickly child, and he remembered how tenderly his mother had cared for him during times of illness. Like others, he promised to appreciate all she had done for him and to be less selfish in the future.

A few who had come on company orders demonstrated their personal involvement for the first time. Misono-san, a real estate agent, was a big, jolly fellow, always telling jokes and delighting in making others laugh. He was older than many of us, in his middle thirties, and he seemed to have an ironic, sophisticated view of the world. Up to that point his attitude toward the exercises had been formally correct in every way, but a bit detached, as though he were observing the proceedings with a distant eye. Misono-san addressed his mother in his remarks, and, to my great surprise, broke into sobs. He confessed to his mother that he had spent most of his life being ashamed of her. She lived in the working-class ward of Tokyo where my company was located, and he—now a prosperous, solidly middle-class citizen—had been embarrassed by her less-than-fashionable address and her uncouth ways. "I will be a better son," he vowed. "Thank you for everything you've done for me." Afterwards, he seemed lost in thought for a long time.

Coming toward the end of our stay, basic practice was our first opportunity to synthesize the ethics teachings and to reflect seriously about their applications to our everyday lives. It was, for me as well as for some other participants, the first time I felt more of a participant than an observer. The darkness of the room, where only our silhouettes were visible, gave us anonymity and made these barings of the soul easier. That everyone else confessed so emotionally no doubt encouraged others to follow suit. From all appearances, the teachings were beginning to take effect.

The Marathon

By any standard, however, the highlight of the seminar was the 7.5 kilometer marathon. all the women in my group had been dreading its approach. Every morning the first words spoken were, "I hope it rains on the day of the marathon," and then, "I wonder if they'll make us run, even if it rains." To our dismay, the day of the marathon dawned sunny and bright. To "prepare" us for the afternoon's ordeal, we had to run two miles during the morning.

After lunch we were ushered into the classroom. The head of the school lectured us in stirring tones about the marathon and its purpose:

> The marathon is a competition with yourself. It doesn't matter whether you come in first place; it doesn't matter how fast you run. What matters is that you run to the best of your ability. A person who is last, but runs with all his might, is better than someone who comes in first, but doesn't try his hardest.

He also reassured us that anyone could finish. People with heart conditions, even a woman eight months pregnant, had completed the course. All we had to do was keep going, stick with it.

A few calisthenics to warm up and stretch, and then we were off. The course traced a large circle, taking us down dirt roads and hills past the training ground of the Self Defense Force, through the woods and onto the country highway into town, then back up the paved road leading to the center. Most of the young men had been looking forward to the race, and they sped off into the distance, leaving others to run more slowly in groups. After perhaps the first third of the course, the traffic thinned considerably, as people began to run individually, each at his/her own pace.

Certainly there was no lack of encouragement. One of the teachers drove by slowly in the school van, which was adorned with the motto "One good deed every day." His two little daughters—neither could have been more than six years old—leaned out the window to shout "Fight!" The counselors stationed at the various crossroads cheered us on with cries of "Fight!" and "Stick to it!" (*Gambare!*), and a few teachers ran with us, staying beside some of the slower people to spur them on. The townspeople, obviously accustomed to all of this, joined the chorus by holding up their fists and shouting out "Fight!" as we jogged by. One little boy even "gave me five" as I passed him on the highway.

The first half or three-quarters of the course was almost pleasant. At one's own pace, the distance did not seem unreasonable. The scenery was superb, the air fresh and fragrant, and I was thoroughly enjoying the country sights: horses in their paddocks, switching their tails lazily; soft light filtering through the leaves, the special light Japanese call *komorebi*; a wooden bridge crossing a clear, shimmering stream. As time wore on, however, I began to concentrate on the simple act of putting one foot in front of the next. At this point, the charms of the passing scenery paled considerably, except as an occasional distraction from my pain and discomfort.

Finally, we approached the hill, the last quarter mile to the center. It was a steep incline, and I was tempted to stop and walk. A few others, I noticed, ran quickly for awhile, then walked for a bit before they resumed their quick pace. I tried to adhere literally to the school's "Japanese" way of doing things: sticking to it, plodding along slowly, but always running, no matter what the pace. For a brief moment, I did succumb to temptation and slowed to a walk. To my surprise, this pace was even more difficult to sustain, as though my body had built up a certain rhythm of forward movement. Perhaps there was something to this perseverance notion after all. I immediately switched back into a job, huffing and puffing up the hill, and somehow even summoned up the energy to turn on a burst of speed at the end.

101

My reaction was apparently not uncommon. I was amazed that I, too, had come to at least partially assimilate the ethics teachings, relying on endurance to carry me through to the end. Comparing notes with some of my companions who had been equally apprehensive, I found their amazement at their accomplishments to be as great as my own. All the women agreed that in the end, it came down to a matter of individual will. One woman said in wonderment, "Perhaps it's true—you can do it if you try." A few men told me they enjoyed the feeling of putting all their energy into something. Ogawa-san had come in first place, but he repeated to me the same phrases we had heard in our lecture. The point was to run to the best of your ability and to stick it out until the end. He was happy I had finished (apparently this had been the source of some worry for him) and afterwards, on returning to the company, he spread the word that I was a *gambariya,* a person who sticks with it—an expression of considerable praise.

The marathon was, from all appearances, highly successful. Most of us did in fact seem more receptive to the notions that: (1) you can do it if you try; (2) life is not a competition with others, but a battle with yourself; and (3) the road to success is through consistent, constant effort.

The Play and the Farewell Party

The marathon had no sooner ended than the hectic last-minute preparations for the play and farewell party began. Each squad chose a play to stage; the best performance would win a prize.

The protagonists in our folktale were three men sent to the Underworld. Through cooperation with each other they make themselves so bothersome to Emma Daiō, Guardian of the Underworld, that he lets all three escape and return to their lives on earth. Omachi-san, the cosmetics salesperson, was the carpenter who hammered down the needles on Needle Mountain. Emma Daiō, angered by our ingenuity, then threw us into a pot of boiling water, and the high school student played the priest who, through his incantations, cooled it down. Now completely enraged, Emma Daiō wanted to be rid of these infuriating creatures once and for all, so we found ourselves in Emma Daiō's stomach. I was the doctor who gave him a laxative to "expel" us.

Our thespian adventure meant we had considerable dialogue to memorize (poor Hashimoto-san, who played Emma Daiō, stayed up late the night before, practicing lines). After the marathon, our squad bathed quickly and ran upstairs to put the finishing touches on our costumes and rehearse our lines. Dinner was equally perfunctory: we wolfed down our meals to give ourselves a few extra minutes of rehearsal time.

Soon the long-awaited performances began. We drew lots to determine the order of our performances, and to our dismay, we were last. We sat, nervously fidgeting, as the other three groups put on their plays. The performances were all exuberant, humorous versions of fairy tales or, in one case, the Stanley-Livingstone expedition to Africa. Each in some way satirized the regulations at the school: "Fifteen extra minutes of *seiza!*" decreed one despotic king, as his subject was taken away, kicking and screaming. Others poked fun at shouting practice or imitated one of the teachers. Our own rendering of the play was heavy parody, laced with a dose of enthusiastic overacting. The head of the school and one of the teachers acted as judges, and they took all the teasing in stride, laughing in a good-natured way at all the jokes.

The performances were followed by a songfest, when we relaxed and sang for about half an hour. Then, the head of the school stood up to announce the prize winners: Squad Four—us! Our group was in a state of mild shock. I was sure our performances could never measure up to the other hilarious acts. One counselor whispered to us knowingly, "*Isshokenmei yatta kara, ne*" (It's because you gave it all you had). I shook my head. Even at that level, the school took its opportunity to emphasize themes of enthusiasm, energy, and throwing yourself completely into the task at hand.

The party culminated in a sing-along. We linked arms to form a circle, swaying back and forth as we sang a traditional Japanese farewell song to the tune of "Auld Lang Syne." The lights were dimmed, and as we swayed from side to side, one of the teachers punctuated our singing with shouts of "It's beautiful!" In retrospect, I realized how skillfully conceived it was: the marathon as the ultimate individualistic endeavor, where individual will was tested, and then the return to community, fostering a sense of camaraderie, teamwork, and feelings of warmth, intimacy, and connection to others.

In fact, the warm feelings persisted until it was time for lights-out. People talked with one another, some animated, others wistful at the prospect of leaving friends they had made. We hurriedly exchanged addresses. All of us in our squad were reluctant to go to sleep, and we stayed up past lights-out to talk, vowing to visit one another after we left on the morrow. Though only six short days had passed, most of us felt we had made some good friends, and we were sorry the session was coming to a close.

The Final Day

The final day marked our re-entry into the "world outside." For the first time our routine changed radically. We did no exercise, and *misogi* was our first activity of the day. We cleaned our rooms and changed back into our regular clothes from the jogging outfits we had worn throughout our stay. More than anything, the change of clothes symbolized our return to the outer world, as we assumed at least the shells of our old identities. Differences re-emerged: we were again businessmen, students, workers.

The teachers gave us their final words of exhortation: to put into practice all we had learned at the center. Without this realization in practice, their efforts and ours would have been in vain. To close, I was asked to read in English, from the Perls poem popular in the sixties, familiar from the posters and greeting cards of the era: "I do my thing, and you do your thing, and if by chance we find each other, it's beautiful."[6] At the end, a teacher led us in a chant of "It's beautiful! It's beautiful!" repeated again and again. It was a rousing end to an unforgettable experience.

Theories of Selfhood: The Dialectic of Form and Feeling

The efficacy of the center's programs, I will argue, lay in specific notions of selfhood and pedagogy that pivoted around dualisms expressing the recurrent themes of form and feeling, social and emotional, outside and inside. Building on culturally specific themes of selves defined in webs of relationships, the teaching at the center formalized and exaggerated these themes.

First, ethics doctrines assumed the existence of human sentience and virtually boundless energy. According to lectures, the energy was *ki*, "the movement of the spirit from moment to moment" (Doi 1973, 97), a central concept in any discussion of Japanese selfhood.[7] As Rohlen points out, *ki* is breath or vital force shared with the air (indeed, the characters for "empty *ki*" can mean "air") and with other living beings, and the task is to "hold" *ki* in the proper way (Rohlen 1978, 135). In ethics center parlance, we were to harness 100 percent of our *kiryoku* (power of *ki*). Exercises were designed to generate enthusiasm in order to draw upon the resources of this energy: shouting, running, and so on in order to "burn" our *ki*. In fact, teachers exhorted us to "100 percent combustion" of our *ki*, for if properly harnessed and "fired up," it would be an endless source of *shūchūryoku,* the powers of concentration.

The most relevant term in our discussion of the center's theories of

Disciplined Selves

selfhood, however, is *kokoro,* the heart, the seat of feeling and thought. To improve and polish the *kokoro* was our goal. The *kokoro* partakes of the energies of *ki.* These emotions and energies cannot be left on their own, to focus on themselves, lest the *kokoro* become intent on the expression of its own selfish desires, with no thought for others. Indulgence and laxity would allow us to slip into the state of *wagamama,* selfishness, the root of all negativity in human life. One must find means to polish the *kokoro,* to heighten its sensitivity, to shape it into *magokoro,* a sincere heart, or *sunao na kokoro,* a naive, receptive, sensitive heart.

The concept of *sunao na kokoro* directs the energies of *ki* and *kokoro* toward constructing selves in human relationship. In its ethics incarnation, *sunao na kokoro* is a heart accepting of things as they are, without resistance or questioning. It is a heart sensitive not to its own desires, but to the needs of others. This sensitivity should be willing and self-generated, for ideally the desires of the *kokoro* and those of society should run parallel. The moral force of the ideal of *sunao na kokoro* emerges still more clearly in contrast to its opposite: *hinekureta,* i.e., twisted, eccentric, crochety, perverse, and prejudiced. These are the characteristics of someone who is self-indulgently anti-social, who allows egocentric quirks to disturb smooth social relations. Were people made aware of their social connectedness, they would also realize the inappropriateness of such selfish behaviors.

The realization of *sunao na kokoro* can only occur, therefore, in human society and in a specific nexus of relationships. The most important of these was our relationship with our parents. The ability to feel the burden of *on,* obligation, to our parents who gave us life, was the center's most central teaching. Shouting practice, the *seiza* and *on no sōgen* exercises, *misogi:* all of these should foster feelings of obligation to our parents. Proper realization of *on* would lay the foundation for rewarding relationships in all spheres of social life. In order to fully harness the energies of our *ki* and *kokoro,* we must try to repay our obligations by extending ourselves for the sake of others (*hito no tame ni tsukusu*).

The realization of *on* and the spirit of *sunao na kokoro* should carry over into our everyday lives through the adoption of three key attitudes. The first is *meirō,* cheerfulness and brightness. No matter what the difficulty, you should always try to be cheery and optimistic. A pleasant demeanor is a fundamental responsibility in a human world. Second are the values of *aiwa,* love and harmony. If people would care for each other and try to cooperate, we could possess the foundations for living in

105

harmony. Third is the belief that we should put these attitudes into practice by working joyfully, throwing our full energy into work. Working gladly includes an affirmative attitude toward the content of the work itself, but equally crucial is a cheerful, cooperative attitude toward others at the workplace. Each injunction infuses life-in-human-relationship with profound emotional significance, a way to craft ideal selves.

Indeed, the notion of happiness is unthinkable without others. We must live in harmony, in a community where people are sensitive to each other's desires and wishes. To make people in our lives happy is to create happiness for them and for us. A basic law of human life is that other people are our mirrors (*Hito wa wagakagami*). Whatever a person does will inevitably be reflected in the behavior of others. Accordingly, cheerful greetings and smiles will serve to smooth social relationships and in so doing, create happiness for all concerned. Conversely, expressing negative emotions will only engender a similar response in people around us. Through realizing our obligations to others, we can simultaneously savor the joys of human relationship. Happiness means the connection of self to other selves.

Theories of Pedagogy

Thus, the goal of the ethics program was to create a gentle, yet positive and energetic self, sensitive to and connected with others. The center tried to effect such a transformation by imposing on the *kokoro* a variety of strict disciplines. A teacher explained to me the rationale behind the exercises: *katachi de hairu,* to enter through the form. Do this and the *kokoro* will eventually follow. The process of true learning begins with a model, a form, repeated until perfectly executed. Without this form, there can be no transformation of the *kokoro*.

Like the Zen arts[8] and other methods of learning and self-cultivation, one first learns through imitation. Stereotyped movements are repeated endlessly; for example, as a student of tea ceremony, one begins with seemingly simple tasks such as how to walk properly, how to fold a tea napkin, how to wipe the tea utensils. Unlike similar movements in everyday life, these are precisely defined, to be executed "just so." Later these learned actions are orchestrated into a ceremony that is the epitome of "natural," disciplined grace (cf. Kondo 1985). The martial arts, also arts of "the way" (*dō*), practice their *kata,* patterned movements, until the movements are inscribed in muscle memory. In a sense, for these arts, content is secondary to repetition of form.

Similarly, rigid discipline shaped the outer form of our actions at the retreat. No detail was too minor to escape attention: beds were to be made in one particular way; bows taken at a particular angle. The emphasis on neatness and punctuality reiterated the same message in different registers. I specifically questioned the head of the school about the matter of greetings. Teachers always insisted that we answer exactly according to pattern; no variation was permitted even if the content of the sentences remained the same. This, I was told, was to elicit compliance. Repeating greetings verbatim would ideally break down resistance and selfishness, and participants would learn to respond automatically to the teachers' greetings. Variation for the sake of uniqueness and difference is thus not important; rather, adhering to the proper form is accorded primacy, for it tempers the selfishness of the *kokoro*. Whereas archetypal Americans might find weakness of will in this conformity, the ethics center (and many other institutions in Japanese society) would find weakness of will in failure to conform and properly discharge social duties.

This conception of pedagogy tacks back and forth between what might seem like familiar dualisms—for example, surface/depth levels of the "self." Yet the moral weight is placed not on some sense of the "self" as inviolable essence, separate from "society," but on the construction of disciplined selves through relationship with others and through forms we might find coercive. Both the Zen arts and the ethics center realize that tension may exist between these levels. But it is by first keeping the rules which define the form, even if one's understanding is incomplete or one disagrees with them, that a sincere attitude is eventually born. Thus, my employer who expressed skepticism about the efficacy of the exercises in filial piety or participants who later satirized the exercises had nonetheless taken an important first step by conforming to the rules in the formal context of the seminar. At some level, as long as one is outwardly true to the form, it is not important what one feels at the "depths" of one's being. Both at the center and in everyday Japanese life, there is a legitimate place for confession of weakness, satire, and irony, but only in the appropriate contexts. For example, we were allowed our structured opportunity to take an ironic stance vis-à-vis our own experience during the play, where we could parody the ethics center exercises.

Clearly, this involves a notion of sincerity quite different from an American definition of the term. Sincerity, *magokoro,* becomes sensitivity to social context and to the demands of social roles—not dogged adherence to an "authentic," inner self to which one must be true, regardless of the situation or the consequences for others. One's *honne,* "real feelings," or *ura,* back or verso, always exists, sometimes in a state of tension, even opposition to the *tatemae* or *omote*—outer, social surface. Yet, if one begins with the imitation and execution of proper forms, the levels work with, not against, one another, thus creating a *sunao na kokoro.*

In such a theory of selfhood, bodily movement and physical appearance may be considered indices of—or synonymous with—the dispositions of the *kokoro.* This, some would argue, is true not only for programs such as the ethics school, but for Japanese society in general. Rohlen (1978) comments on this phenomenon:

> There is no more powerful symbol of the perfected inner life than that of outward composure. . . . To be neat, proper, and orderly—whether in housekeeping, factory routines, personal relations, or daily ceremonies—is to possess the necessary will, energy, and attention. Japanese social order is buttressed by the idea that orderliness is an expression of something far more important—the character of those being orderly (p. 136).

Physical action can in fact be perceived as isomorphic with spiritual change. For example, polishing the floor was explicitly equated with polishing the *kokoro:* "If you polish the floor, your heart too will shine." At mealtimes and before every lecture, and especially during the exercises of *misogi* and *seiza,* we were told to adjust our posture, for having the proper posture was the equivalent to having a proper attitude; "fixing" (*naosu, tadasu*) the posture was equivalent to adjusting the *kokoro.* In *misogi,* purifying the body was equated with purifying the *kokoro.* Inner and outer are not divided and opposed; indeed, there is no inner/outer division invoked here.

The ethics center recognizes the severity of its disciplines. Arising at dawn, sitting on rocks, and running marathons are fully acknowledged to be demanding tasks. Yet *kurō,* hardship, has a paradoxically salutary effect. Hardship draws on the inner reserves of energy, allowing one to tap their potential to the fullest. At the center, in fact, one of the central doctrines was "Hardship is the gateway to happiness" (*Kunan wa kōfuku no mon*). Hardship gave the *kokoro* the chance to mobilize its resources to get one through difficult times. When the full energy of the *kokoro* is thrown into a task, one can withstand the greatest difficulties. Thus undergoing hardship and surviving it were keys to a *sunao na kokoro* and to a happy life.

In Japanese society generally, hardship is considered one pathway to mature selfhood. At the factory where I worked, apprentices were to undergo a period of *kurō,* receiving paltry wages and laboring long hours in a place outside the indulgence of the natal home. This would remove traces of selfishness, making the apprentices into skilled craftsmen and mature adults. Without undergoing suffering, one was condemned to remain childlike. Women with whom I worked in the factory commented about a cocky young artisan that, *"kurō ga tarinai"*—he hasn't suffered enough, or that, *"kurō saseta hō ga ii,"* he should be made to suffer. The implication was that hardship would temper his youthful immaturity.

One can survive such hardship by drawing upon one's energy and enthusiasm. In the wider society, throwing one's all into a task is thus considered intrinsically good. In everyday Japanese conversation, people ideally perform their social roles—mothering, studying, working—*isshokenmei ni,* with all their heart and soul, or *sei ippai,* with all their might, to the utmost. At an institute dedicated to self-cultivation, such inspirational phrases were even more common. Both teachers and participants invoked these expressions regularly to describe their attitudes and the way they would like to experience or have others experience the activities and teachings.

Yet enthusiasm alone will not suffice. You must also see things through to the end, and as a result endurance and perseverance are among the most frequently cited virtues in Japanese society (cf. Lanham 1979). At the ethics center, at the workplace, at home, and at school, people extol the virtues of *nintai*—endurance; *doryoku*—effort; and *gaman*—endurance. Perhaps the most popular expressions of encouragement are forms of the verb *gambaru,* to keep at it, stick to it. As the marathon taught us, it is the trying that is the good in and of itself. The actual result is secondary. It is no surprise, then, that the marathon was the climax of the youth seminar. The emphasis was on finishing the race and running to the best of one's ability, rather than on one's place in the competition vis-à-vis others. Learning to stick to a task, no matter how difficult or unpleasant, thus strengthens the *kokoro.*

To summarize, the ethics center's ideal self is a *sunao na kokoro,* a gentle, sensitive heart. Responsive to social demands, sensitive to social context, it is a heart capable of appreciating the obligations and joys of living in human society. In order to realize this *sunao na kokoro,* the pedagogies galvanized emotional energies while subjecting the participants to strict systems of disciplines and punishments. It was an exemplary instance of a disciplinary production of subjects.

Japanese Selves and the Ethics Doctrines

The pristine beauty, rigid discipline, and profoundly felt emotions of the ethics retreat were features of a world set apart from the chaotic bustle of everyday life. The center built on general ideologies of selfhood by exaggerating and systematizing them into specific, highly elaborated theories and a series of vivid, concrete experiences.

The ethics center and the wider culture are separated by a cleavage between "the ritual and the mundane" (Crapanzano 1980), the extraordinary and the ordinary. The precise manner of demarcation differs significantly across and within cultures, as well as over time, but minimally one could point to some degree of formalization and exegesis as signposts of the extraordinary (ibid.). Tambiah defines the ritual domain more exhaustively, as characterized by the following features: "formality (conventionality), stereotypy (rigidity), condensation (fusion), and redundancy (repetition)" (1979, 119). The center makes full use of these symbolic features of ritual, and its symbolic efficacy rests on the distinction between the extraordinary and the ordinary.

The center presents a coherent, packaged image of the world and of human beings, taking tired platitudes and common sense assumptions and systematizing them. Given that the center is in the business of transforming selves, this process of rationalization in turn enables the center to offer structured solutions to problems in a manner consistent with its imaged world. As Swidler argues in her exposition of rationality in the work of Max Weber: "An integrated view of the world creates a whole framework within which people experience reality, and it thereby influences their actions" (1977, 37). The ethics center provided such an integrated framework.

The doctrines would not have their compelling power, however, without a certain degree of familiarity. They drew upon deeply held moral values and cultural themes. I have mentioned the Zen arts, but one can also find similarities to morals education in the schools (Lanham 1979); indigenous psychotherapies (Reynolds 1980); other company training programs (Rohlen 1974); school clubs, and so on. Here, comments from my fellow workers who attended the seminar are telling. Some were skeptical. "*Kawaru mon ka*" (No way we'll change), sneered Yamada before he went, but his response upon returning, a thoughtful "*Son wa shinai*" (I didn't lose anything by it), though lukewarm at best, was far from his sarcastic condemnations before the trip. Considering his "insubordinate" behavior and his beating by the teacher, his comments were especially moderate in tone. A few became devotees. Kitano-san sought out a local chapter of the movement so he could attend "morning meetings." Kōno-san provoked smiles from the part-timers when he came back, with is deafening "Good morning" greetings. "*Tanjun, to iu ka . . .*" (Should we say . . . simple?) whispered Akimoto-san, a part-timer. Though few people's lives were transformed ("'Oh, so this sort of thing exists,' is about the extent of it," said one of the older artisans), most thought the seminar was a good thing. And even the sharpest criticism did not take issue with the specific ideals themselves. Rather, "it was just common sense." In other words, why go through all the trouble to learn what everyone should already know?

This "trouble" was the source of the center's distinctiveness. It relied on vivid, exaggerated experiences to teach us more abstract principles. If enthusiasm and energy are important, then chant during cleaning and running. If hardship polishes the self, then sit on jagged rocks and plunge into icy baths. If filial piety is the key to happiness in other social relationships, then scream greetings at your mother and father, and sob with guilt, remembering your complete dependency on them. In everyday life, few would dispute the importance of enthusiasm, hardship, or respect for one's parents. But through codified precepts and through heightened experience, the center allows participants to live out these commonsensical platitudes.

Indeed, the genius of the ethics center lies in its recognition of itself as a ritual experience.[9] With this recognition, it creates a space for the expression of disbelief. First, it assumes that people will feel resistance initially. Its unusual, even bizarre, exercises in fact encourage disbelief. It is precisely because of this resistance and disbelief that participants may come to embrace the key ethics center precepts. That is, as participants experience their own powers to change under extreme conditions, they may begin to question their initial resistance and begin to believe in their own powers for self-transformation. For example, few could have been more skeptical than I. Yet by the end, the ability to withstand such strict discipline and mental and physical hardship became a source of wonderment and even pride to me and my roommates. By allowing for and even encouraging a limited degree of resistance, the center was paradoxically able to transcend it in many cases.

Secondly, the center protected itself by marking off an appropriate context for the expression of resistance and disbelief. In the play, for example, teachers left room for an ironic stance. By acknowledging the extreme nature of the ritual experience, the teachers established a safe distance between themselves and any complete, unthinking acceptance of their doctrines. Such an acceptance would have been terrifying, an erasure of individual consciousness. It would have created a programmed automaton, not an ideal self. Rituals in their formality and conventionality promote a kind of distancing of individuals from these public social forms (Tambiah 1979, 124). In a sense, the play was a formally sanctioned arena where we could acknowledge the ritual status of the ethics center experience. The dramatic form allowed for the publicly recognized inclusion of irony and resistance. Even these could be given public expression in the appropriate situations without causing devastating damage. Satire and parody could be accommodated—as long as these expressions of resistance were limited to the appropriate contexts.

The Politics of Creating Selves

The discussion of resistance leads us to consider the issue of power and its deployment in the disciplinary production of selves at the ethics retreat. The notion of a relationally constructed self can mean in practice that a subordinate must conform to the expectations of a superior. The existence of a *honne,* an emotional core of sentience, protects a subordinate; limited expression of this *honne* can be allowed in specific contexts such as our satirical skits, but the larger structure of power relationships is never seriously challenged. When it is, punishment is swift. Two of my co-workers, who attended an ethics seminar some weeks after I had returned from the retreat, consistently arrived late to the morning assemblies. On the last day, they also appeared late, in rumpled clothing and with their hands thrust deep in their pockets, as was their habit. The teacher—our leader in the Zen meditation exercises—apparently made an example of the two young men, declaiming that he was disappointed in the workers from the Satō company, who were so disrespectful of the rules at the center and who clearly had learned absolutely nothing from their stay. When his tirade ended, he struck both artisans.

By exaggerating certain cultural forms and assumptions, then, the ethics center creates a profoundly conservative, even coercive, program. And this coercion came both from without and from within, as self-imposed discipline. Take the striking degree of self-mortification required. To become better, happier persons, and certainly to become better workers, we were forced to subject ourselves to pain. Activities familiar from other cultural settings thus were exaggerated in the extreme. Rather than performing the usual seated meditation on *tatami* mats, we sat on hard linoleum, then on gravel. Rather than simply cleaning the floor once, we had to chant as we polished the floor endlessly. This was justified on the grounds that hardship and pain enabled us to reach mature selfhood, but one cannot ignore the conservative political implications of such an ideology. Selves had to be mortified to "fit in" with society; there was no attempt to transform that society or its structures.

The political implications of ethics-center ideology are especially clear when we link selves to the workplace. The center's integrated framework of meaning embeds selves in the domains of work and family. We were offered a picture of the world in which bonds of care and loyalty would connect selves to families and to companies.[10] In both families and companies, we were to realize our indebtedness to our "superiors," attempting to repay them by enthusiastically carrying out our prescribed roles as dutiful sons and daughters and as loyal, diligent workers. In work we connected ourselves to others through laboring for a common goal. Moreover, the discipline and hardship of work was to polish our hearts, rendering them less self-centered. In mastering our work, we became more mature human beings. Selfhood and work were as one. From the point of view of management, such doctrines provide a ready rationale for asking workers to take on even the most tedious and menial jobs, for invested with sufficient concentration and enthusiasm, even cleaning toilets and scrubbing floors could be exercises in self-cultivation. By extension, long hours and poor working conditions can be seen as hardships to be borne, not challenged, for such hardships serve to polish the self.

By playing on these notions of selfhood and by locating selves in work and family, the ethics center reiterates familiar themes echoed in so-called paternalistic managerial ideologies (Bennett and Ishino 1963; Kondo 1982; Fruin 1983; Wagatsuma and DeVos 1984). The notion of "company as family" is especially resonant in the face-to-face paternalistic atmosphere of a small family business. Confronted with what they view as a less "traditional" and more "selfish" labor force ignorant of the deep emotions of obligation and loyalty owed to employers, owners such as Mr. Satō would have much to gain should their workers ingest this ideology whole. The center's ideal worker was disciplined, punctual, loyal, neat, hardworking, responsible, self-motivated, respectful, and enthusiastic. From the managerial point of view, the ethics center and similar programs are designed to produce diligent, loyal workers.

That the ethics retreat drew at least half its participants from the small/medium-sized business sector attests to the perceived need on the part of managers to revive this "traditional" discourse of managerial familialism in the face of a labor shortage and an historical moment of perceived Westernization where today's young people are seen as increasingly individualistic. Thus the ethics center draws on deeply held values, asserted at a particular moment in history. It reinforces a particular kind of worker/management relation within a particular economic situation in order to recapture an idealized past of benevolent paternalism and worker loyalty.

In short, the ethics retreat introduces the key theme of the disciplinary production of selves in the domains of work, family, and community we will follow through the lives of my co-workers. It does so, however, in an intensified, highly elaborated form. By rationalizing readily available common sense assumptions in Japanese culture, it offers participants an integrated framework for solving their problems. It does this by intensifying, exaggerating, and systematizing such assumptions and by using devices of tension and paradox to create eventual resolution. However, this discourse of self-transformation must be placed within a larger historical and political context. Ideologies of selfhood are not innocent with respect to power relationships, a factor little acknowledged in most studies of "the person" or "the self." Selves are produced through specific disciplines and transgressions elicit particular punishments, just as the ethics doctrines offer particular, compelling, and satisfying pathways to self-fulfillment.

I must also stress that the apparent seamlessness of the ethics center's doctrines and practices is only apparent. The small resistances, the parodies, and the ineffectiveness of the center in completely fulfilling its programme cannot be dismissed. Especially telling in this regard is the fact that Mr. Satō himself thought the success of the center to be limited. He said to me, "Most of the young guys just want to be outdoors and get some exercise. They haven't really understood." He considered his sole success to be the case of Akita-san, the chief of the Western pâtisserie division. Before Akita-san's experience at the retreat, his family used to sit down at the table and immediately begin eating. After returning, Akita-san had made it a point to say, "*Itadakimasu,*" the conventional greeting one utters before a meal, and he has taught his little daughters to do the same. For Satō himself, the center has had some effect. He initiates more half-price sales as thanks to his customers, a decision that has increased his business. This is no mean result. But these positive effects of the retreat also coexist with parody, dismissal, and resistance at some levels, despite success and acceptance at others. No regime of truth is completely encompassing, as my co-workers at the Satō factory showed me in the complexity and diversity of their reactions.

This complexity and the simultaneously creative and coercive power of culturally specific discourses are perhaps nowhere more evident in the everyday lives of my friends, neighbors, and co-workers than in the compelling, emotion-laden arena of family. Love and power intertwine, creating wrenching existential dilemmas and possibilities for fulfillment and satisfaction—dilemmas and possibilities producing certain kinds of selves. For the family, too, is a site where selves are crafted.

Part

2

Family as Company,
Company as Family

4   *Circles of Attachment*

Masao, a young high school student, walked in my door with a troubled expression on his face. It was time for our weekly lesson in English conversation, my way of doing a favor for his family. Masao was usually enthusiastic and engaging, but this time he seemed preoccupied. After the hour ended, I casually asked him how things were going. "Would you mind if I spoke with you for a few minutes?" he said, his voice worried and urgent. I nodded assent, wondering what the problem could be.

The following week, he said, he would have to choose the division of the university to which he would apply.[1] His real love was art, and he desperately wanted to be an art teacher. Should he pursue his own career interests, or apply to the business division and prepare to take over his family's shoe store? In other circumstances, he would have had no hesitation in applying to the liberal arts division. But matters were not so simple. His father wanted him to take over the business, and although his mother told him to do whatever he wanted, he could tell that she secretly hoped he would follow in his father's footsteps.

Family history weighed on him heavily. Masao's grandfather had founded the shop in the days when the main street was little more than a dirt road where horses would plod along, pulling carts behind them. Fresh from the cold, snowy regions in the north country, the grandfather had apprenticed himself to a cobbler near Ueno, eventually becoming one of the master's most able and trusted journeymen. After many years of hardship and privation, he selected this outlying ward of Tokyo and became one of the first merchants to open up shop on what is now a lively commercial thoroughfare. Eventually he was able to act as patron to two apprentices of his own. And commensurate with his community standing, he became the first president of the local merchants' association. The success story was complete when the eldest son, young Masao's father, took over the enterprise in the late fifties. Under his aegis, the firm ceased to make shoes and became a purely retail outlet, enlarging its

119

floor space and expanding its business. My pupil was the present owner's only child.

"On the one hand," said Masao, "I know that lots of teachers can't make enough money to live on." The market for teachers was glutted, as was the market for artists. But the family business, despite all the pressure, seemed no less precarious economically. There was too much competition from the big stores, and people just weren't buying the way they used to. He hated the grueling schedule his parents kept, taking no vacations, working six days a week, staying open on holidays hoping to take advantage of the holiday crowds. Even then, they barely managed to get by financially. "I envy the children of *sararīman*,"[2] he said. They can take their vacations. Home and work are clearly separated. Life is more predictable. Even the most average (*hei hei bon bon na,* an *absolutely* average) *sararīman* can count on that much. Still, he said, his father wanted him to take over the business, carry on the family name and occupation, keep their ties with the merchants' association, and bring them back to real prosperity. In a voice choked with emotion, he said that it would be a shame for his grandfather's hardships and his father's hard work to go to waste. It would be a shame for the enterprise to die, after a mere two generations (*ni dai kagiri*).

"I am sorry to bother you with this," he said. "But I go to a boys' high school, and my classmates aren't very sympathetic (*omoiyari ga nai*). And teachers like Kinpachi-sensei[3] just don't exist—that's a fantasy." I murmured what I hoped were consoling words, but I frankly felt completely inadequate to advise the young man, so torn by this agonizing existential dilemma. Although nothing was resolved by our conversation, he went home saying he felt better for having talked with someone. I was left feeling stunned, for the fact that he would approach me, a foreigner to whom he was not particularly close, attested to the magnitude of his problems.

How could one so young anguish so over this decision? What gives families and family firms such power to shape people's lives? To further understand the source of Masao's dilemma and the power of the family firm it is necessary to appreciate the importance of *ie,* the family as the weight of history and obligation, and of *uchi,* the family as a center of emotional attachment. It requires, above all, an understanding of the *living* meanings of family: how personhood and mature self-fulfillment can be woven into the fabric of family duty and family continuity. Young Masao was at a point in his life when the conflict between family duty and self-realization seemed particularly acute. For him, the tension seemed almost intolerable. For Masao and for the other people I knew engaged in family business, notions of family not only shaped thought and behavior, but were deeply, poignantly felt.

Households: *Ie* as Obligation

My theoretical stakes in this chapter are positioned within debates familiar to scholars of Japan. Here, I want to argue with analysts of Japan who see the inevitable convergence of Japanese life with its Western counterparts, a convergence based on a collapsing of "modernity" with Westernization and technological development. What I found alive and well among the people I knew who are engaged in small family businesses is the so-called traditional *ie*, or household—a development of fairly recent vintage and an entity which no longer has legal existence, since it was dismantled in the postwar Constitution. Of course, as Masao showed me, adherence to these deeply meaningful cultural constructions is not achieved without ambivalence, and signal changes may indeed be in the air. But those of us who have worked in family businesses—large or small—could never argue that the *ie* is defunct.[4] What I have to say could be considered characteristic of the Japanese households engaged in small family enterprises and of all families with some sort of substantial cultural/economic capital at stake. In this chapter, then, I explicate the assumptions underlying this culturally specific notion of household, set out some of the relevant literature on the subject and provide underpinnings for the following chapters, which discuss the malleability of the familial idiom as it is deployed in the Satō company, within a specific historical context. The emphasis on continuity in everyday life despite dramatic historical changes sets the stage for later chapters that dissect these claims for an unproblematic continuity and closure. Precisely because of a constitutive history that defines households as highly organized, task-performance units based on work, and as sites of identity formation which enjoin their members' loyalty and love, "company as family" becomes a readily available idiom for people like the Satōs to deploy within their family enterprise.

The Japanese term *ie* is designated by a character which can mean the physical building of the house or the household line (Kitaoji 1971). Etymologically it carries the meanings of "hearth," signifying people who belonged to the same domestic group (Chie Nakane 1983, 259).

In anthropology families are usually thought of as kinship groups linked by relationships of descent—in the sense of biological relationship—from some common ancestor. Our American notions of kinship as biological relationship and jural ties (cf. Schneider 1968) profoundly influence our analytic frameworks and have been the source of much controversy in the literature on the *ie*.[5] Rather than a kinship unit based on ties of descent, however, *ie*[6] are perhaps best understood as *corporate groups* that hold property (for example, land, a reputation, an art, or "cultural capital") in perpetuity. They are units of production and/or consumption, encompassing the roles of corporation/enterprise/household. Equally important, *ie* can serve primary religious functions, such as those of ancestor worship and worship of tutelary deities (*ujigami*). *Ie* also provide the primary form of social welfare in Japan, including care of the aged and the infirm.[7] Pelzel (1970) succinctly describes the *ie* as a "task performance unit." Bachnik (1983, 179) emphasizes its enterprise and socioreligious functions, arguing convincingly that *ie* should be analyzed as such and not as kin-based domestic groups. Nakane captures the key elements of life in an *ie* as: "a personalized relation to a corporate group based on work, in which the major aspects of social and economic life are involved" (1983, 260). The core of this corporate group may indeed be composed of people related biologically, but this need not be the case.

One interesting illustration of this point emerges from etymological evidence in the research of Japanese anthropologists and folklore scholars. Yanagida (1957) commented on the original usage of the terms *oya*, parent, and *ko*, child, as indicating superior and subordinate statuses within a labor organization. The *oya*, as head of the group, assumed a role of responsibility and protection for the *ko*. The group subsumed ritual, economic, political, and social functions. The biological parents and children were indicated with linguistically marked terms as "birth parents" (*umi no oya*) and "birth children" (*umi no ko*) (Yanagida 1957, 114). Thus, biological relatedness was only one special attribute of a much broader category of "parents" and "children."

As is the case in other kinds of corporations, *ie* organization is based on a set of *positions* rather than a set of kinship relations (Kitaoji 1971; Bachnik 1983). In any given generation, there can be only two holders of permanent positions in the *ie*, a married couple.[8] They are, so to speak, trustees of the corporation, who will take care of the family property and fortunes during the period of their tenure. They should do their best to ensure the survival and, ideally, the increasing prosperity of their *ie*, which they can then hand over to their own successors.

Joining an *ie* means belonging to an institution that links one to the past and projects one into the future. All the past generations of successors are included as members in perpetuity, even in death.[9] These household ancestors are commemorated at New Year's, at the summer Obon festival for the dead, and during the vernal and autumnal equinoxes. Households with Buddhist altars or shrines will usually give the dead offerings of rice, water, incense, and other foods, often on a daily basis. Such rites link *ie* members to the past, and offer the living comfort that they too will live on after death. Continuing the *ie* carries on the legacy of these ancestors and creates a legacy for one's descendants. In belonging to an *ie,* a single generation's contribution will be but a brief moment in time, a small part of a much larger, enduring corporation which existed before you were born and will continue when you die.

Your household of birth, however, may not be the household you join as a permanent member. The size of the *ie* in any generation is limited to two and only two successors. No matter how many children there may be, only *one* can be a successor along with his/her spouse. Those who are not designated successors to these permanent positions are not, therefore, permanent members of the *ie* and must set up their own households, usually at the time of marriage. This is strikingly different from more truly patrilineal systems, such as the Chinese, where the ideal is an extended family of parents, several brothers, and their wives and children, living together in a family compound. In contrast, in Japan the nonpermanent members of an *ie* must leave at the time of marriage, and consequently one rarely sees two married couples of the same generation living in the household, except in extraordinary circumstances (e.g., economic need, inability to find housing, etc.).

Sometimes, as we shall see in the next chapter, these nonpermanent members are conceived as branches of the main household. The permanent members receive the lion's share of the inheritance, as well as primary responsibility for caring for the aged parents and for commemorating the ancestors. The junior, temporary members generally receive some kind of assistance as their form of inheritance, often in the form of monetary aid and/or education. Sometimes they are set up in the family enterprise (*kagyō*), as junior branches. Their new families may be called *bunke,* branch households of the main house (*honke*). While the *honke* provides leadership, a center of ritual celebration, and economic aid and resources for the junior branches, the *bunke* owes the *honke* labor service and certain ritual obligations. When this economic relationship of mutual dependence and obligation exists along with a main house/-branch house structure, the larger form of *ie* organization has been labeled a *dōzoku*. (Cf. Nakane 1967, 82–123, for an illuminating discussion on the nature of *dōzoku* organization.)[10]

The difference between *ie* and true kinship-based groups emerges more clearly when we consider this critical issue of succession; that is, succession to a *position* in an organization, rather than inheritance, which implies the partition of property and goods. Because the *ie* is a corporate group established, at least ideally, in perpetuity, the overriding concern is how to ensure the *continuity* of the *ie* over time. Thus, two permanent *ie* members must be recruited in each generation. *Kinship, in the sense of blood relationship, is only one of these recruitment mechanisms.* The person(s) who take over the *ie* may in fact be totally unrelated by blood. Ideally, people would prefer not to take this latter course, but they may choose to do so if the continuity of the *ie* is sufficiently critical to them.

The *ie* has often been characterized as a system of primogeniture: succession by the eldest son. This is not a rule, however, but a *preference.* Article 970 of the Meiji Civil Code of 1898 (itself a document forged through various factional and ideological struggles) wrote into law a system of preferences in which near relatives took precedence over far; males over females; legitimate children (even female) over illegitimate children; and older children over younger (Sebald 1934, 227). Under ideal circumstances, this meant succession by the eldest son. However, this practice was by no means uniform in all parts of Japan at all points in history (cf., e.g., Ishihara 1981). In some areas ultimogeniture, succession by the youngest son, was the dominant form, and there were other patterns of succession, including some forms in which women were successors (Hayami 1983). Indeed, the Meiji Civil Code's system of preferences could be seen as the adoption of *samurai* practices as the legal norm for the entire society (Hamabata, forthcoming). As we shall later see, this system of preferences was not instantly and uniformly accepted, but eventually the ideology of the Civil Code became sufficiently widespread to penetrate folk ideology, so that when informants discuss the *ie* or the "Japanese family system" (*nihon no kazoku seido*), primogeniture is almost invariably mentioned. Moreover, the preference for primogeniture still affects people's life trajectories. For example, among many of my co-workers at the factory, the eldest son was raised with the expectation that he would be the successor, a process so "natural" that many of my informants said that their decision to take over the headship just happened, "*nan to naku*"—somehow.

Perhaps one could best characterize the system of succession as one of ranked preferences which can be modified according to economic and social conditions: the presence of appropriate successors; their competence; the relationships with other households one may want to create through marriage, and so on. Within this system, recruitment priorities are arranged along a number of axes: (1) householdship over housewifeship; (2) biological kin over non-kin (items 1 and 2 both from Kitaoji 1971, 1048); and, I would add, (3) competence over incompetence (cf. Pelzel 1970, Kitaoji 1971, Bachnik 1983, Kondo 1982). Note that this creates flexibility and tension within the system, for all the preferential features may not be possessed by a single person. In general, *ie* continuity takes precedence over considerations of blood relationship, for it is conceivable that blood-related kin can be passed over for an unrelated person who demonstrates competence at the family trade— perhaps a trusted apprentice (cf. Pelzel 1970; Bachnik 1983; Kondo 1982). The important issue, then, is the *perpetuation* of the *ie* itself. The *way* it is done is a secondary matter.

Bachnik sees the critical point of succession as the time of marriage. She stresses the notion of *two*-person strategies of recruitment, arranged in the following order of desirability: (1) man from in-group, woman from out-group, the usual version of "marriage;" (2) woman from in-group, man from out-group, the so-called adopted bridegroom or *muko yōshi;* (3) both man and woman from out-group, so-called *fūfu yōshi,* adoption of a married couple (1983). In all cases, the member from the outside is in an initially disadvantageous position, for she or he must become accustomed to the ways of a new household. Over the years, however, this position is strengthened, for structurally the outsider who marries into the household is more meaningful and important than the blood-related sibling or child who marries out and thus becomes a member of another household. Again, we see the overriding importance of the household and its continuity over blood ties.

The forms of so-called adoptive marriage highlight this drive for *ie* continuity. Unlike in the United States, for example, where adoption generally takes place at a young age, in Japan "adoption" usually occurs in adulthood, as a form of *marriage*. Indeed, the second most common form of marriage/succession is bringing in a man, from the outside, who marries into the family and takes over the family name and, usually, the family business. The *muko yōshi,* adopted bridegroom, is in a position structurally equivalent to that of the new bride. He must be incorporated as a new member from the outside, accepting what is likely to be a lower status than if he were the successor in his household of birth. An oft-quoted maxim warns men against becoming a *muko yōshi* as long as they have three *go* of rice. Yet adoptions are not at all uncommon, and most families can point to several within a few generations. This was brought home to me when I first began interviewing at family firms in my immediate neighborhood. Of ten household enterprises within a two-block radius of my apartment, only one adhered to the classic pattern of in-marrying bride living with the husband's parents. There were two *muko yōshi,* one *fūfu yōshi* (where both husband and wife are adopted, as described below), and the rest were neolocal households where the wife took the husband's name, but the couple lived separately from the husband's parents. The *yōshi* in the neighborhood were cast to type, however. They were second or third sons—i.e., not slated to succeed to headships in their own households of birth. And both had what my landlady called *yōshi* personalities: gentle and self-effacing, for they, like a new bride, had to be punctilious in their relations with members of the new household. In fact, my own relatives in Aichi prefecture provided me with a textbook case. In my grandfather's generation, all the boys had left home, for Tokyo or Kobe or America, to make their fortunes. The youngest daughter, the only one left in the household, married a *yōshi.* And her daughter followed suit. This daughter, a tall, stocky woman, entertained me and my Tokyo relatives in the parlor, while her short, slender husband served the tea and cakes.

The difference between the incorporation of a *yōshi* and that of a bride is one of gender, and since males are given higher status than women, *yōshi* may be treated more carefully than their female counterparts. It is also true that some of my informants, thinking of the difficulty in finding *muko yōshi* these days, are grateful to their sons-in-law and hence treat them with more care. Hamabata (1983) also notes that at least among some families, the daughters also consider receiving a *yōshi* an inferior form of marriage, depriving them of the chance to become an *oyomesan* of another household. In some urban households, another pattern is emerging in which the husband lives with the wife's family but keeps his own name. Structurally, this differs in striking ways from the classic *yōshi* situation, for by not taking on the bride's surname, the husband is essentially not a permanent member of her household, despite the residential arrangements. Still, the primacy of the *ie* over individual desires means that *muko yōshi* remains a viable strategy for continuing the *ie.* Given that only one son could conceivably be a successor in any given *ie* in any given generation, nonsuccessor sons eventually leave to establish their own branch households or go out to other households as *yōshi.* Nakane estimated the proportion of *yōshi* in some villages in the sixties to be as high as one-third of household heads (Nakane 1967, 67).

The final form of marriage is *fūfu yōshi,* adoption of both husband and wife. This can occur through fosterage, when either boy or girl is adopted at a young age. Eventually she or he will marry and carry on the household line. It can also occur near adulthood, when the couple is brought in to succeed. In my neighborhood, the little shop across the street was one such example. The woman who ran the shop was from a large family in the agricultural north of Japan. Her Tokyo relatives, distant cousins, were an older couple with no children. With the prospect of the business dying out and no one to care for them in their old age, they brought their teenage kinswoman to Tokyo to live with them and help take over the family business. A few years later, she married, bringing in a *muko yōshi.* He works in a machine shop in a neighboring ward, while she minds the store. Her adopted parents both died some years ago. She has no regrets, she says, about becoming successor to her relatives' household enterprise. It is hard work, but so was the farm—and Tokyo has so much to offer.

In this discussion of marriage and succession strategies, one can see the simultaneous exigency and flexibility of the *ie* system. On the one hand, its structural requirements are unyielding. In order to continue an *ie* over generations, one must without fail find two successors. Furthermore, the number of successors is always two and only two. All other members of the *ie* must establish their own households. We see here that the *ie* system's imperatives demand that individuals shape themselves to fit into this structure; the organization does not expand to fit the individuals, as it might in a Chinese patrilineal system. On the other hand, given these organizational imperatives, the *ie* system offers a *range* of alternatives for people to use in filling the positions. All other things being equal, the oldest son would inherit and bring in a bride from the outside. But if he is incompetent, or if he leaves, or if there is no eldest son, a daughter can bring in a *yōshi,* or the older couple could conceivably adopt two unrelated persons to carry on the household line. Unlike classic lineal descent systems, this system holds merit to be of considerable importance, and an incompetent son may well be passed over for a more capable person unrelated by blood. The value of "achievement" over "ascription" is clear: *ie* continuity and the good of the *ie* as a whole should take precedence over the ascribed category of kinship as blood relationship.

When an *ie* faces a transition between generations, one final alternative exists: extinction. Occasionally the decision to allow the *ie* to die out will be matter-of-fact, an issue arousing little emotional concern. Perhaps more often, especially for those contemplating the fate of an enterprise with a long history, such a decision will not be taken lightly. Economic factors, among others, are likely to weigh heavily in the choice. Certainly for young Masao, the economic precariousness of the *ie*-enterprise was a cause for concern and an important factor in his decision. In my immediate neighborhood, I saw many economic casualties of the *ie* system, people whose enterprises could not attract successors for lack of financial viability.

Mr. Tanoue, the skilled craftsman who made wooden trays, was one such example. He worked in a small room off one corner of his house, his lanky frame settled on the floor as he planed wood, measured boards, carved wooden nails, and pounded rice into the paste he used for his trays. I would visit him periodically, tapping on the sliding door of his workroom, which was open except in the coldest weather. Sometimes he would call when he was making something unusual: a container for hot water to dilute the soup for noodles or a holder for toothpicks. When he had a large order to fill, he would sometimes be invisible, hidden by the stack of wooden trays reaching from floor to ceiling of his tiny, sunlit workroom.

Mr. Tanoue was a third-generation *kijiyasan,* woodworker, already in his early sixties. No successor for him was in sight, a fact he called his greatest regret about his work. His daughter, a tall, gracious woman, had married a white-collar executive recently transferred to a provincial city. The husband had not taken the family name, nor had he taken over the enterprise, so the Tanoues were coming to an end with this generation. Mr. Tanoue mourned the situation, but he was now resigned to it. Of the five remaining *kijiyasan* in Tokyo, only one had a successor, he told me, and even that "young master" was in his forties. Now, there was too much competition from the shoddily made, mass-produced trays from Nagano prefecture. Young artisans made inferior merchandise to profit from the recent *mingei* (folk art) boom. In contrast, Mr. Tanoue sold only to professionals. He took orders from a middleman, the people who lacquered the trays, and they in turn sold the finished lacquerware to *soba* (Japanese noodle) shops. Only the most elegant, expensive *soba* shops would buy the sturdily built handcrafted trays; now people only went for convenience—"they just use things and throw them away," he complained. "Young people see artisans like me and they think, 'no matter how hard you work, it doesn't amount to anything.' They prefer to work in companies." The craftsmen were in a trade which, in all likelihood, was destined for extinction.

The Tanoues and numerous other craftsmen engaged in artistic traditional crafts often expressed regret that their lifestyle no longer seemed to attract successors to what they believed to be an honorable occupation. To them, this was a fact to be mourned. But in structural terms, extinction is always a possible choice for a household facing a transition between generations. Economic alternatives may offer greater opportunities outside the household enterprise, and sometimes the chance for greater income and social mobility will prove more compelling than the drive for *ie* continuity.

The Fukuzawas furnish an example. In our discussions during my visits to the Fukuzawa household, the eventual fate of the *ie*-enterprise excited little concern. Mrs. Fukuzawa, a good friend of my landlady, was an athletic, slender woman who radiated energy when she talked. Her husband was a gentle man who ran a one-man press operation in a workroom to the side of his house.

On one visit, I asked Mr. Fukuzawa to show me his work. We slid open a door off to the side of a hallway and descended into a small, dark workroom. A large press machine loomed in the dim light, dominating the space. Buckets of warm water held plastic sheets to soften them before they went to the presses. From these sheets, Mr. Fukuzawa stamped out accessories for women and children, in a rich variety of shapes: Snoopy and other characters from "Peanuts," leaves, squares for belt buckles, anchors, tiny animals. From there, they went to the *kenma,* a machine which resembled a large, revolving barrel. It rounded off the corners of the pieces and gave them a smooth finish. Mr. Fukuzawa added final touches by hand, carving out the veins in the leaves, drilling holes for Snoopy's eyes. Large blue baskets, stacked here and there, gathered the finished products. From the Fukuzawa workshop, they would go to yet another factory to be painted, only then to be returned to the main company who had placed the original orders.

Mr. Fukuzawa was a second son. He had entered the press trade only in the last few years, rather by accident. Until his early forties, he had worked in a shoe factory, but the chemicals—PVC, he thinks—began to be a health hazard. Eventually he could scarcely stand the smell and feared for his health, so he quit his job at the company. His brother, who lived a few doors away, made the molds used to cut the plastic sheets. With this brother's help, Mr. Fukuzawa changed trades. He converted a room of his house into a workshop, and occasionally collaborated with his brother in designing new molds. Unlike Mr. Tanoue, then, he was a newcomer to his enterprise. Also unlike Mr. Tanoue, Fukuzawa was prospering. The Japanese public was wild for the plastic Snoopy and Hello Kitty figures, and he was deluged with orders, enough to keep the presses thumping from morning till night, six days a week.

Especially striking was his enthusiasm for what initially appeared to be a monotonous, mechanical job. Contrary to my expectations (based no doubt, on a "mental" worker's conscious or unconscious devaluation of manual work), he spoke animatedly about the pleasures of work: always trying to do things more quickly, more cleanly. Mrs. Fukuzawa also spoke with pride about her husband: he was always thinking, devising new methods to improve productivity. Because it was his *own* enterprise, his satisfaction was even greater—although he always ended up working more on his own than he would have if he were an employee at some company, he laughed.

Despite his prosperity, Mr. Fukuzawa had little desire to groom his son to follow in his footsteps. If the son did, fine; if he didn't, that was also fine. In fact, succession was highly unlikely, for Mrs. Fukuzawa confided that her son looked down on her husband's occupation. Nor were either of the young daughters likely to grow up to marry a *muko yōshi* who would take over the firm. All the children were aiming for middle-class success. All were academically talented students at good schools, and Mr. Fukuzawa was working hard to pay their tuition. This was no mean feat, for two children attended competitive junior high schools attached to famous private universities. The third child was enrolled in a public high school linked to an elite national university, where tuition costs were minimal. Mainstream success as a professional or an executive was the son's goal. As women, the girls faced greater difficulties if they pursued careers, but at the very least, their parents expected them to marry well-educated, white-collar workers. For the sake of social mobility, the Fukuzawa *ie*-enterprise would die out—without regrets.

Thus, we have seen several alternatives to the problem of succession. A son, preferably the eldest, may succeed, bringing in a wife. A daughter may marry a *yōshi*. The family may adopt both a man and a woman, in the *fūfu yōshi* pattern. And if circumstances make these undesirable choices, the *ie* may be allowed to die out. This decision may be greeted with a variety of reactions. Sometimes, there is no appropriate successor, and the end of the *ie*-line is cause for much regret. At other times, when social mobility and economic opportunities look especially desirable, the extinction of the *ie* may cause little concern. And sometimes, as in young Masao's case, there is pressure to take over a faltering *ie*-enterprise in order to *make* it viable.

At this point, one can begin to sense the urgency of Masao's dilemma. The *ie* is not simply a kinship unit based on blood relationship, but a corporate group based on social and economic ties. Thus, the *ie,* the household line, and the *kagyō,* the family enterprise, are of critical moral, social, and emotional importance. They should ideally be carried on in perpetuity, so much so that many alternatives exist to ensure that the household will not die out. The responsibility facing young Masao was thus a daunting one. As the only son and the only child, he carried the weight of history on his shoulders. He had no siblings who might act as successors. Conceivably the parents could try to recruit an unrelated successor to both household and enterprise, but since the shop was manned only by husband, wife, and one or two part-time employees, *fūfu yōshi* was not a serious possibility. To give over the enterprise to an unrelated person they would have had to find someone who knew the business and who could be expected to sufficiently dedicate himself to the future prosperity of the *kagyō.* Since there was no such person, the decision rested entirely with Masao. Though his family's enterprise was not economically healthy, his parents still wanted him to succeed. It was his duty to improve the family fortunes. If he chose to be a teacher, the hard work of grandfather and father would come to an end, two generations of effort expended for naught. It would be a burden of guilt difficult to bear.

This burden is particularly acute because it carries with it implicit moral values about personal rectitude and maturity. For the parents with a *kagyō* to pass on, subordinating one's individual desires to that of the household enterprise takes on the character of moral virtue. Pursuing one's own plans and disregarding the duties toward the household smacks of selfish immaturity. Knowing this, Masao was facing a choice between two alternatives, neither of which was completely satisfactory. Should he carry on the family business and thwart his career plans as an art teacher? If he did, he risked self-betrayal. Yet if he did not, could he live with the unspoken moral judgments about his selfishness? Masao was at a point in his life where the cleavage between individual desire and duty to the *kagyō*—itself infused with tremendous emotional meaning—was especially sharp. And whatever his choice, it would inevitably be nuanced by tension and ambivalence.

Marriage and Succession: The Weight of Obligation

For young men like Masao, the dilemma of succession may present itself as they face their college applications. For many, however, the crucial moment of truth is at the time of marriage. What sort of spouse will one marry? What are the expectations surrounding marriage? For people in household enterprises, there are critical questions, for as I have argued, marriage within the *ie* system is above all a mechanism for ensuring the continuity of the *ie*. Again, considerations of the *ie* should be given preference over individuals' selfish desires, and where considerable *ie* resources are at stake (in the form of property, money, or "cultural capital") this tendency will likely be intensified.[11] Individual preference need not be entirely ignored, but it should be a secondary consideration. The continuity and prosperity of the *ie* should be of utmost importance.[12] Someone who can work well in the family enterprise and who can get along with other family members may be more valued than a person who pleases the spouse alone. If desire and obligation are in conflict, it is duty that should precede desire.[13]

What does this mean for the people who marry under such circumstances? At times, it means living with an emotionally arid, even repugnant, relationship, as I found when talking to my landlady's mother-in-law. A lively woman born in the later years of the Meiji period, she could always be counted on for joyously amusing conversation. Invariably she regaled us with tales of her marriage to her late husband, dropping one-liners that left us helpless with laughter.

The *obāchan* (diminutive for "grandmother") had been the eldest of three daughters. As she approached the age of twenty—legal adulthood and prime marriageable age for a woman, in those days—her parents pressured her to find a husband as soon as possible, for until she was "out of the way," her younger sisters would also find it difficult to marry. Worried relatives arranged a meeting with a prospective bridegroom, an event the *obāchan* still bemoans. "You weren't even supposed to look at him directly, so I thought he was taller and more handsome than he turned out to be! I was tricked!" Almost any evening in front of the television set would prompt similar comments. Eyeing one or another of the actors, she would sigh, "In my next life, I'm going to find a tall, handsome husband—just like X-san," depending upon whom she chose as her favorite that evening. Her comments sent us all into gales of uncontrollable laughter. "*Obāchan* is at it again," we would chuckle as we wiped tears of mirth from our eyes.

Suffice it to say that she married her husband after meeting him only once.[14] From what the *obāchan* told me, the two of them never really did like each other much. He was a real "Meiji man," a tyrant, she claims. Exacting in his demands, he would even insist on seeing her housekeeping accounts to make sure that they were in order. In Japan, where women are usually in charge of the household budgets, this can be perceived as a real encroachment on a wife's sphere of influence. Still, she fulfilled her duties as a wife beautifully. She bore him a son, took care of the house, cooked, cleaned, sewed, and managed the finances even when times were rough. "Every morning," she said, "I would see him off at the door, help him on with his shoes, and bow down to say, '*Itte irrasshaimase.*'"[15] In other words, she was an exemplary housewife. But as soon as he stepped out the door, she would hiss, *sotto voce,* "*Kuso jiji!*" (Shitty old man!) Even now, she says she doesn't open up the little Buddhist altar she keeps in her bedroom, at least not very often. Her husband's picture is there, and every day one should give the dead offerings of incense, rice, and their favorite foods. "I don't want to remember," she laughs.

I recall the first time I heard their stories. Despite my extensive reading about the structure of the Japanese family system, I was a bit shocked. Desiccated descriptions of social structure had done little to prepare me for the human consequences of that structure, and I found myself reacting in terms of my typically American assumptions about love and marriage. Should she really be saying these things about her dead husband? Didn't she love him at all? How could she bear being married to someone she "didn't really like"? But after I came to know a number of older women in the neighborhood, it became clear to me that the *obāchan* was far from an unusual case. Many of them were widows, and all vehemently asserted their intentions never to remarry. "What? And have to take care of a man again?" was typical of their responses. For all these women, life began anew after their husbands' deaths and after their children reached adulthood. They blossomed. Free from the responsibilities of family, they could do as they pleased: chat, shop for *kimono,* make shrine pilgrimages, visit famous parks to view the flowers of the season, and spend time with their own friends.

For these women, marriage conjured up images of duty, responsibility, family honor, and persevering in the face of hardship. Marriage as a form of succession ensured continuity of the *ie*-line. They had not expected emotional fulfillment in their relationships with their spouses, although it would have been a pleasant bonus. Emotional satisfaction would come with their children, with members of their own natal households, and in widowhood, as they enjoyed their friends. After many years of hardship, they could take pride in knowing they had carried out their duties and survived the demands of an exigent system. Now, they had earned the leisure and the pleasures that widowhood could bring.

The difficulties these women faced are built into their structural positions in their households. All had married in the preferred way, where the woman is recruited from another *ie* and comes to live with her husband and his parents, who are still likely to be heads of household. Initially, she is in the lowest permanent position in the household, and it is her duty to shoulder most of the domestic responsibilities. She must learn the ways of the new household (*kafū*) and accept the tutelage of a not-always-welcoming mother-in-law, who may at some level resent the newcomer and act as a demanding taskmaster. Structurally, she presents a threat to the mother-in-law as competitor for the son's support and affection, and Japanese culture abounds in tales, both true and apocryphal, about such mother-in-law/daughter-in-law conflicts.[16] Moreover, she cannot necessarily count on her natal family for complete support and sympathy, for once married, she is a full-fledged member of another household and is treated as such.[17]

In such a system, the relationship between spouses is downplayed in favor of the household as a whole. The bride is considered in a sense the bride of the *household,* whose duty it is to serve all household members (especially the present head of household), not simply her husband. The emphasis, once again, is on the continuity of the *ie* through time, so that the horizontal links between husband and wife or among siblings take a back seat to the vertical links among the generations. I learned of this in poignant detail when I spoke with the bride of the household where I was living for the summer. She and her husband were no longer living with his parents, less a result of her lobbying than of the household's interest in directional divination. The young couple's horoscopes and auspicious directions for the year dictated a move to an area to the southwest of the parents' home. When I first spoke with her in her new residence, I was surprised at her frankness about her position and her eager curiosity to learn about American families.

Knowing that I knew her father-in-law, she began to tell me about her trials and tribulations. As the *oyomesan,* the bride, she had the responsibility for the cooking and cleaning for the entire family. Though the mother-in-law helped, the senior generation was relatively free to go about company business and to participate in volunteer activities. At the time, the young wife was also studying typing, which forced her to keep a grueling schedule. She studied late at night, awoke before dawn to prepare breakfast, did all the cleaning and laundry, went to class, and rushed home by four so she could shop for the evening meal and have dinner on the table by the time everyone else came home.

One morning, some months into her marriage, she decided to fix herself coffee and toast for breakfast. The family was engaged in the construction industry and the men, in particular, had heavy work to do, so they ate hearty Japanese fare, complete with rice, fish, vegetables, and green tea. The bride, from a more Westernized family, preferred something lighter, she explained. So she prepared one of the usual breakfasts for the rest of the family and fixed herself some toast and coffee. The otōsan, head of the household, glowered at her as she sat nibbling on her toast. Finally he simply blew up. Who did she think she was, making herself something different to eat? She was the bride of the household and it was her duty to learn the ways of *their* household! She should forget her selfish ways and eat what they were eating! Furthermore, her duty was not to please herself or her husband first, but to first serve the *head* of the household! "I cried and cried," she says, and tears still well in her eyes as she tells the story. The otōsan, then in his fifties, is considered a man with traditional ideas, but such stories are not uncommon among oyomesan, "even" now.

The message is clear: the bride must try to forget the habits she learned while growing up in another household and learn the ways of her new, permanent household. She must in a sense "kill herself," as the Buddhist term goes, in order to cast herself in a mold acceptable to the members of her present household. As in Masao's case, the requirements of duty are associated with mature adulthood. Recognition as a fully participating member of the household comes when you have reshaped yourself according to its roles and duties. Resistance or rebellion within this framework can be considered a sign of immaturity and selfishness, even moral weakness.[18] Even a seemingly trivial choice—opting for a different breakfast food—can be such a sign. Moreover, upon reflection, the oyomesan seemed to consider such treatment harsh, but she deemed the sentiment basically appropriate. An oyomesan does have to fit into the ways of her new household. And, she says, though the otōsan may be traditional, he is also a thoughtful, caring person in many ways, demonstrably concerned for her health and welfare. Despite the strictures of household membership, maturity is linked to the fulfillment of household obligation.

Though the life of an *oyomesan* can be hard, sticking it out (to *gambaru*) should eventually bring its compensations. Since the newly incorporated member—in this case the bride—does become a full member of the household in structural terms, her status is likely to rise steadily with time. The designated successor (*atotori*) and the bride will eventually become heads of household, who may have their own sons- or daughters-in-law to take over the most troublesome tasks. The mother (*okāsan*) of the household under discussion is a fine example. As the eldest child of a box manufacturer, she was saddled with onerous chores at an early age. She helped her mother take care of her younger siblings, and even while she was attending college she cooked for the twenty-odd employees who ate with the family every day. Like her daughter-in-law, the only hours she had available for her studies were late at night, after everyone else had gone to bed. When she married Mr. Sakamoto, she was spared potential conflicts with her mother-in-law, for he was a second son from the northern provinces, come to Tokyo to make his fortune. They in fact set up business in a district of Tokyo where her natal family lived, and many of her relatives joined in the new construction/plumbing business. Still, the beginning years were hard times. Mrs. Sakamoto studied for a plumber's license and was just as ready as her husband to go out on call to fix a customer's leaky faucet. She took care of the books, raised her family, and helped out in the family business. Because she is such a tough, energetic woman, it is no surprise to the outside observer that she could manage on all fronts. Now, her children married and the business on its feet and prospering, she can enjoy the fruits of her labors. She no longer need shoulder primary responsibility for all household chores: they have hired help, and the *oyomesan* does most of the work. Business accounts are also taken care of by a hired bookkeeper. Now she can throw herself into the community projects she loves: flower arranging, volunteer work, ward committees, and ward politics. Dedication to the family business and the fulfillment of one's duties to the household can have their eventual payoff, over the long term. Satisfaction for a "job well done" and the increased authority that comes with age and position combine to make life for Mrs. Sakamoto rewarding indeed.[19] Despite the trials of the new Sakamoto bride, over the years she, too, will come to enjoy a higher, more advantageous position in the household.

With Masao and with Minako-san, the Sakamoto bride, the strictures of obligation to the *ie* are especially evident. Such deeply felt conflicts can occur at any point in the life course, but they emerge most forcefully when the issue of succession is still under negotiation, as in Masao's case, or when the structural change from one household to another is still recent, as in Minako's. Yet—not unlike the ethics center—Japanese culture allows for this resistance. It is *expected*, part of a culturally familiar script. Eventually, perseverance in fulfilling one's duty to the *ie* will temper one's resistance and provide a source of satisfaction. The elder Mrs. Sakamoto is one example. Her years of hardship have now brought its rewards. She is as busy as ever, but now she can afford to sit back just a little and delegate some of her responsibilities. She can spend more time with her beloved flower arranging. The widows in my neighborhood have traced out similar life trajectories. After discharging decades of duty to their demanding husbands and their families, they could luxuriate in new-found leisure and freedom. But it is my employers, the Yokoyamas and the Satōs, who have truly lived out ideal cultural scenarios. For them, desire and duty became one.

Two Ideals

Once again it was my landlady who alerted me to the critical issues surrounding the family. We were having tea one day when she remarked that she had been so surprised, years ago, when her friend Sadako announced her engagement to an apprentice in the Yokoyama's family beauty salon. "The two of us used to go out together with our boyfriends," said my landlady, "and Sadako was always so popular. I was a little taken aback when she told me, but she said that she wanted to carry on the family business, and he seemed like he would make a good, reliable husband."

Mrs. Yokoyama, now in her early forties, is lovely and vivacious. One can easily imagine that she had her pick of handsome boyfriends. What made her select someone she considered dependable, but rather dull? Why was the household enterprise so important? How could she so calculatingly sacrifice personal happiness, even for the sake of the *ie* and the business? These questions flashed through my mind as I listened to my landlady's stories.

The Yokoyamas had been in the business of hairdressing for generations. Mrs. Yokoyama's mother in fact still runs the main shop, located next door to the family home. The father died many years ago, but he was an adopted bridegroom, the second son of a family of barbers. Upon marrying into the Yokoyama *ie*, he changed his surname and succeeded to the headship of the wife's household. This couple had two children, both daughters. Once again the family was left with no potential male successor. The eldest daughter decided that she in fact wanted to be a hairdresser and take over the shop. Eventually she chose to marry one of the shop apprentices who was willing to take on the Yokoyama surname and continue to work in the family enterprise. She says quite frankly that at the outset she was not particularly in love with him, but chose him because he fit the requirements of a reliable, hardworking husband who would be good for the business. Now, each person—the grandmother, the husband, and the wife—heads a separate branch of the enterprise, and they are planning yet another branch in a neighboring section of the ward. The only child, a son, wants to take over the business when he comes of age. He is a student at a junior high school famous for its art and design classes, and he plans to spend a few years working at a cosmetics company before taking over the salons.

Further talks with Mrs. Yokoyama clarified some of my questions about the pressures of succession and family continuity vs. individual desire. She told me that, after they had been together many years, her love for her husband had grown. The experience of living and working together had made them closer, comfortable with each other in an easy intimacy based on mutual respect. Their case embodies a cultural ideal. With the *obāchan* and Masao, the emotional costs of fulfilling one's obligations to the *ie* are painfully clear. But the Yokoyamas have created a solution which fuses emotional warmth with family duty.

The owner of the Satō confectionery had a similar tale to tell. Like the Yokoyamas, the Satōs were longtime residents of the neighborhood; in fact the present owner was the fourth Satō to head the family enterprise. The firm history reads like an ideal script. The present owner's grandfather left the family farm in the north country to come to Tokyo at the turn of the century. He apprenticed himself to a famous maker of *senbei*, rice crackers, near one of the famous shrines in the Asakusa area of Tokyo. Many years of apprenticeship finally won him a chance to separate from his master, and in 1921 he set up his own shop in a neighboring district, a process known as *noren wake*, dividing the shop curtain.[20] His eldest son worked alongside him, eventually taking over the business. In this generation, the family added *wagashi*, Japanese sweets, to their repertoire. The eldest son, grandson of the founder and the present owner's eldest brother, took over most of the management duties in the mid 1950s. But tragedy struck in 1957, when the present owner was nineteen. The father, retired head of household, suddenly died, and later the same year his successor succumbed to cancer. At the time, young Yoshio was enrolled in electronics school, hoping eventually to become a pilot. As the youngest sibling, he was the only one who had not left home, the only one not yet established in a career. With the death of his father and of his eldest brother, the successor, his responsibilities were clear. He quit electronics and entered a trade school to learn the art of creating *yōgashi,* Western pâtisserie. While his mother, another brother who made *senbei,* and the company's employees held down the fort, he studied for a year and then returned to take over the business. In 1960 the two brothers had a falling out, and they divided the family property. The older brother started up a shop selling his deliciously crisp *senbei,* and it became a local sensation. So successful are they that the store opens for only an hour and a half each day, from 3:00 to 4:30. When the brother's wife runs to unlock the doors, a long line of housewives has already formed, and by 4:00 the day's supply of *senbei* is usually gone.

Young Yoshio was left with the confectionery, what he termed "an unhealthy enterprise." But he didn't want to "lose" in comparison to his successful brothers or vis-à-vis other shops in the neighborhood. At the time there were five relatives and five employees working in the shop and the factory. In order to diversify and to tap into a new market, he added *yōgashi,* Western pâtisserie, to the more familiar *wagashi,* Japanese cakes. He wanted to make the shop known for its quality products, using only the best ingredients: no additives or preservatives. His hard work and ingenuity eventually paid off. Orders increased, and the number of employees grew steadily. In the late seventies and early eighties, the firm employed thirty full-time employees in the factory, three full-timers in the shop, twelve part-timers, and an assortment of high school students who came after school or during the busy holiday season. In 1979 they moved into a beautiful new factory/residential complex, a strikingly modern, three-story building which houses the factory on the first two floors, the family residence on the third. They have realized a cultural ideal, where each generation adds something new, constantly augmenting the prosperity of the *ie.*

The Satōs are exemplary in yet another way. In 1963, the owner married. His bride hailed from the north country village where the Satō grandfather had lived, and where Satō descendants still cultivate the land. The young Mrs. Satō is a tall, strong-looking woman: "like country people, *gatchiri shite iru* (sturdy), not like Tokyoites who look so unreliable," said my landlady, herself Tokyo born and bred. It was, in a sense, a backhanded compliment, a way of saying that Mrs. Satō was neither stunning nor vivacious. She *is,* however, warm, dependable, a hard worker, and a fine mother. My landlady had once boldly asked Mr. Satō, her grade school classmate, why he had chosen a woman like that. "I needed some-one who would fit into the family . . . because my mother is the way she is," was his reply. Again, consideration for the household as a whole was the primary concern.

The needs of the household and the personality of the elder Mrs. Satō were particularly important in this case. So far my narrative has concen-trated on the male line of succession, but Mrs. Satō the elder was instrumental in holding the enterprise together with her incredible dy-namism and hard work. And she was a woman with a definite style. Many locals remember how heartily she used to boom out, "*Irrasshaimase!*" to customers, or how she could scold unruly children (my landlady among them) for their misbehavior. In her younger days, she managed the shop, cooked for the workers, and did the housework for the family. Now, she does the family cooking, freeing the young Mrs. Satō to work almost full-time in the shop. They cooperate in making the confectionery a suc-cessful enterprise. The young wife plays her role beautifully, and she fits in well—no easy task, given the tireless example of her feisty mother-in-law. She has proved her mettle by working in the shop, overseeing the young female shop workers, helping in the factory during the busy sea-son, keeping the books, and doing most of the housework for her family. Her commitment to the *ie* is symbolized in her hard work and dedica-tion. And again, it is the *ie* to which she contributes. She is far more than simply the wife of an individual man.

Still, one cannot discount the importance of the relationship between the spouses. Over the years, the Satōs have had four children and they seem to have a warm, comfortable relationship—at least, so it seemed when I traveled with the Satōs and their children to the wife's natal home. They appear to pull together, they demonstrate concern for one another, and they have developed, like the Yokoyamas, an enviable mutuality and complementarity in their relationships. The years of working together have drawn them closer to one another.

This glimpse of marriage and succession in some of my informants' lives can only begin to suggest the human dimensions of the *ie* system. In this section, I have highlighted the demands of *ie* as obligation: the cor-porate nature of the household and the drive for household continuity. In human terms, I have called the demands of structure an emphasis on form over feeling, duty over individual desire. The examples I cited are those in which satisfaction arises through the fulfillment of duty, and maturity is defined as the execution of duty. Here we see the coercive *and* creative effects of cultural discourses, as they generate realities and shape individual lives through stringent sets of constraints. Simultaneously, discourses on *ie* create definitions of proper human conduct and mature personhood, providing the pathways to fulfilling these life trajectories and offering specific kinds of punishments for transgressions.

Yet can the *ie* remain so powerful a force through obligation alone? Can coercion offer us the most convincing explanation for Masao's powerful emotions? In the following section I turn to another aspect of household organization: the *uchi*, the household as a circle of attachment and a locus of identity.

Circles of Attachment: *Uchi* as Feeling

The term *uchi* describes a located perspective: the in-group, the "us" facing outward to the world. It is the *ie* or other group to which one belongs. While the notion of *ie* highlights continuity, generation after succeeding generation, *uchi* focuses on the household in close-up, as a center of belonging and attachment. *Uchi* defines who you are, through shaping language, the use of space, and social interaction. It instantly implies the drawing of boundaries between us and them, self and other. *Uchi* means "inside;" like *ie,* this inside is not necessarily limited to the family or even to the household. Depending on the context, it can be any in-group: *ie,* company, school, club, or nation, although here I will confine my remarks primarily to the level of the household/enterprise.

Uchi cannot be understood in isolation; it immediately calls to mind other terms against which it is set—much as *tatemae,* social surface, calls to mind *honne,* real feeling; and *omote,* the formal, front side evokes *ura,* the intimate, the verso. One common term with which *uchi* is paired is *soto,* outside. *Soto* can mean everything outside the physical structure of the house. In symbolic terms, *soto* means the public world, while *uchi* is the world of informality, casual behavior, and relaxation. *Soto* is where one must be attentive to social relationships, cultivating one's *tatemae,* whereas in the *uchi* one is free to express one's *honne.* Crossing the boundaries from *uchi* to *soto* can involve a complete readjustment of behavior: posture becomes more proper and disciplined, language levels are potentially raised (depending on the status of the addressee), and dress is expected to be more proper, less casual.

Another pair of terms, *uchi* and *yoso,* places *uchi* against the background of its relation with other households or groups. *Yoso* literally means "another place," and this other place is usually another household. *Yoso-yuki* (*yoso*-going) clothing is one's Sunday best; *yoso-yuki* manners are one's most formal manners. Both *uchi/yoso* and *uchi/soto* highlight the social and symbolic aspects of *ie* membership. Rather than a unit of biological kinship, the *uchi* is the center of participatory belonging, the center from which one can create relationships with the outside world.

This center of emotional attachment is symbolized in linguistic expressions common in everyday speech, which serve to draw the boundaries between *soto* and *uchi*. For example, when one leaves the *uchi,* one says *"Itte kimasu,"* (I) will go and come back.[21] The *uchi* is the group from which one leaves to take part in the *soto* world, but it is also where one returns. The person or persons remaining in the *uchi* will reply with *"Itte irasshai"* (Please go and come back). When someone returns to the *uchi,* even from a walk in the neighborhood, he or she should announce the return with *"Tadaima"* (Just this moment), a shortened version of the phrase *"Tadaima kaerimashita"* (I have just this moment returned home). The person who is in the house replies, *"Okaeri nasai,"* (come home, or welcome home). In all cases, the point of orientation is always the in-group, the *uchi*. Leaving or returning to the group must be marked by an announcement. It would be inappropriate and strangely cold to announce one's arrival in any other way, such as *"Ohayō gozaimasu"* (Good morning) or *"Gomen kudasai"* (Excuse me), for these greetings are used when one visits *another uchi*. The same is true for expressions such as *"Ogenki desu ka?"* (How are you?), which expresses concern about a person's health, or *"Dochira e?"* (Where are you going?).[22] Both phrases would sound ludicrous addressed to members of one's *uchi*. It would be as though you knew so little about your own intimates that you actually had to *ask* them about their health or their destination. In short, the inner/outer distinction is built into language use, and in uttering the most common greetings every day, Japanese people create and recreate the boundaries of the *uchi*.

Another way of distinguishing in-group from out-group is in the use of what Bachnik (1982, 12–14) calls noun suffixes, such as -sama, -san, -kun, -chan, in order of politeness and distance.[23] These are generally used vis-à-vis members of another group, as terms of both reference and address. It is rude for an outsider to *omit* the noun suffix when addressing a member of another *uchi*. Two incidents vividly illustrated this for me. One came from the Sakamoto bride, Minako-san. She complained to me one day about the rudeness of one of the Sakamoto uncles, who insisted on addressing her as "Minako." In fact, when he wanted her attention, he would call out, "Oi, Minako." Both words were offensive in her eyes. *Oi* is an extremely informal male interjection a patriarchal husband might use to call his wife. The omission of -san as a term of address was also a gross breach of etiquette, for she did not consider the uncle a member of her *uchi*. He apparently thought otherwise.

A related incident with the Sakamotos showed me again how linguistic markers are used to bound the in-group. I had just moved in with the elder Sakamotos, when the married daughter came to visit with her two young children, a boy of five, and a young daughter barely able to toddle. I was enjoying getting to know this lively woman and her engaging children. One day the mother and I watched as the boy played with his sister, and chanted her first name—Kaori—as she toddled about the room. Charmed by the little girl's tentative efforts at walking, I joined in with a "Kaori." The little boy turned to glare at me. "You shouldn't say that. That's rude. You should say 'Kaori-chan.' You're not one of us." I was embarrassed by my gaffe, and stunned by his vehemence. Most of all, I realized that in-group/out-group distinctions must be of enormous cultural importance, for here was a child of five who had already mastered the process of drawing linguistic distinctions between *uchi* and *yoso*. The mother stepped in to smooth things over. "But Dōrin (diplomatically omitting the san from my first name as well) is living here. She's like *uchi*" (*Uchi mitai na mon da*). He was not convinced, however, and almost cried, claiming that it wasn't so. I sat in embarrassed silence and eventually tried to change the subject.

What both examples point out is the great importance attached to in-group/out-group affiliation. Language reflects the boundaries between in- and out-groups, but it also can be used to redefine situations and people as relatively in or relatively out. Second, people may have varying understandings of in-group/out-group affiliation, as did the uncle and Minako-san, the former apparently assuming that any member of the larger Sakamoto clan could be treated as an *uchi* member. Third, the boundaries between in-group and out-group are fraught with emotional significance, as both Minako-san's reaction and the response of the young boy clearly indicate. Finally, this linguistic marking of boundaries is considered sufficiently important for a child to master it at an early age.

Boundaries between *uchi* and *soto* are also created through the symbolic use of space. *Uchi* can refer simply to the physical structure of the house. Within the house, members can indulge in informal, relatively uncensored behavior, speak in more intimate language levels, and wear casual clothes.[24] But matters are more complex: the house itself is divided into varying degrees of *uchi*-ness, so to speak.[25] For example, the house is likely to have a front door and a back door, the *omote-guchi* and the *ura-guchi*. One is the public entrance, where visitors enter the house; the other is usually the kitchen door, where good friends and delivery people come. Formal guests would never arrive through the back door; to do so would be unthinkably rude.

Likewise, the rooms of the house itself can be classified into varying degrees of *soto* and *uchi*. If the family is wealthy enough, they will have a guest room, usually floored with *tatami* mats, for receiving formal guests. These rooms embody the Zen aesthetic for which Japan is famous: austerity, simplicity, clean lines. A recessed alcove, or *tokonoma,* will display art objects, scrolls, or flower arrangements. My landlady's house was one example. Their *tatami* room occupied the central space in the house, and formal guests were always received there. As in many such households, the *tatami* room doubled as the master bedroom at night, when the couple rolled out their *futon*. In sharp contrast to the austere aesthetic of the *zashiki,* the formal parlor, are the rooms where the family does most of its actual living: the kitchen and the *chanoma,* the tea-drinking room. Both are likely to be cluttered and lived-in. In older houses, the kitchen will probably be small, dark, uninviting, crowded with utensils, food, and appliances. The *chanoma* usually has a low table around which the family sits, and more often than not, this is where you will find the television, providing the background accompaniment to dinner conservation. It gives the impression of a messy, but comfortable, intimacy. The demarcation between formal and informal parts of the house was perhaps clearest in the Sakamoto's residence. The kitchen, toilet, bathroom, and *chanoma* were all in one wing of the house, which one approached via an entrance opening onto their garage. The more formal *tatami* room/master bedroom was in the other wing of the house, and guests arrived at the main entrance on a path of rounded, unevenly placed stones, such as one might find in a formal tea garden. Formal guests are unlikely to have access to the more *uchi* or *ura* parts of the house, and indeed, one can measure one's progress in getting to know a Japanese family by where one is allowed to go in the house; i.e., how far into the *uchi* one is allowed to penetrate.

Correlated with this spatial continuum of intimacy and distance are the behavioral and linguistic markers we have already discussed. That is, a guest received in the *zashiki,* formal parlor, will be addressed in polite language levels, and everyone involved will at least initially adopt the

144

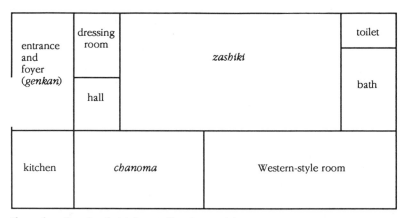

entrance and foyer (*genkan*)	dressing room	*zashiki*		toilet
	hall			bath
kitchen	*chanoma*		Western-style room	

Floor plan of my landlady's house (first floor only)

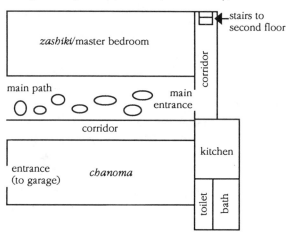

Floor plan of the Sakamoto house (first floor only)

more disciplined, formal sitting posture and a more modulated, controlled facial expression. Conversely, conversations in the kitchen or the *chanoma* are likely to be livelier, more informal, and not as attentive to the niceties of language and etiquette.[26] Thus, spatial, linguistic, and behavioral symbolism make the continuum between *uchi* and *soto* a social reality for the members of an *uchi*.

Uchi also provides a located perspective from which its members interact with members of other *uchi*. Again, linguistic evidence provides us with common examples from everyday life. When people "give" or "receive" in Japanese, they have an array of different choices from which to select. Roughly in descending order of politeness (and out-group to in-group), we have the following verbs in their informal forms (ending in -u instead of -masu):

Give
sashiageru (giving to out-group)
ageru (giving to out- or in-group)
yaru (informal, giving to in-group)

Receive
itadaku (humble, receiving from out-group)
kudasaru (humble, receiving from out-group)
morau (medium-polite, receiving from out- or in-group)
kureru (informal, receiving from in-group)

The choice of a particular verb makes a statement about the relationship between the giver and the recipient. For example, *sashiageru* is an honorific and implies giving something to a member of an out-group, especially someone of higher status. *Kureru* means someone is giving to you or your *uchi,* and implies that the giver is in a relationship of informality and intimacy with you. You could use this verb to indicate that a close friend or a family member gave something to you, for instance.[27]

Furthermore, giving and receiving verbs apply not only to objects, but to actions as well. In English, we rarely specify the *direction* of actions unless absolutely necessary, i.e., if someone has done something specifically *for* or *to* me. Actions are complete in themselves. In Japanese, people use the giving and receiving verbs countless times a day to express the direction of an action either toward or away from the speaker or the speaker's *uchi,* and they do so in contexts in which we would not conceive of using the same terms. The underlying principle seems to be that human behavior is not seen in a vacuum, as atomistic action. People's actions instead link them to their *uchi* and to other groups.

The indefatigable Mrs. Sakamoto gave me a memorable lesson in these principles. She lectured me on the use of her favorite phrase, which sounds excessively convoluted in English translation: *sasete itadakimasu,* I (or my group) humbly receive your allowing me to do (something). This, she said, was infinitely preferable to the simpler phrase, *shimasu,* to do, precisely because *shimasu* indicates an impersonal action. *Sasete itadakimasu,* on the other hand, implies that you are able to act due to the benevolence of others. In simply *acting,* you are linked to others in relations of obligation and connectedness. Using the phrase *sasete itadakimasu* should instill in the speaker a feeling of humility and gratefulness, for no one can get along in life without the help of other human beings.

Clearly, people use language to reflect and to create relationships with-in and among *uchi*. Mrs. Sakamoto's favorite saying was one example. I encountered countless others when I began to work in the factory. Even in the absence of extremely close emotional relationships, members of a work group may use informal language to *create* a feeling of *shitashimi*, intimacy, within the *uchi*—in this case, the work group. At the factory, the most polite receiving verb people used was the formal form of *kureru*, i.e., *kuremasu*. A more polite tone would have imparted an impression of distance and snobbishness. The choice of verbs, then, both makes a statement about a relationship and creates an emotional tone which shapes a relationship. For example, when a foreman at the company wanted a middle-aged part-timer to perform a task, he would often say, "*Obāchan, yatte kureru?*" Auntie (using the informal suffix, chan), will you do it for me? "*Yaru yo!*" (Yeah, I'll do it), she might sing out in return, using equally informal language. In these cases, the informality of the giving/receiving verbs and noun suffixes fostered a feeling that we were all members of the same *uchi*. Conversely, there is no more chilling or more sardonic way to quarrel in Japanese than to suddenly become icily polite with people you know well. Using *sashiageru* when you usually use the verb *ageru* can be a devastatingly effective weapon, precisely be-cause it places one's intimate friends or relations into the category of outsider.

Jane Bachnik cogently summarizes the significance of the linguistic term *uchi*:

> The word most commonly used for "house" in everyday lan-guage, *uchi*, if unmodified, refers to *me, my* (or *our* "household"); as well as I, me, my group (we or us). *Uchi* can be qualified by a modifier (or set of modifiers) to refer to another group (*sono uchi* "that house;" *Watanabe san no uchi* "Watanabe's house"). For address I use the terms *otaku*, "your house;" "you." . . . *Uchi* is in some senses the counterpart of the English 'I,' but *uchi* also has the basic sense of my group (mean-ing my primary group). . . . *uchi* is also the zero-point of the speaker's discourse (1982, 14–15).

As the zero-point of discourse, *uchi* locates selves, providing a place from which to encounter the world. And because it is the zero-point of dis-course, it is virtually impossible to create an utterance without somehow taking into account the in-group/out-group distinction. We see, then, how language locates utterances within a social field. By speaking, one inevitably speaks as a person embedded within a particular *uchi*. One is never an isolated individual.

Soto and *uchi* are also modes of emotional orientation and action. Within the *uchi,* relationships, especially with one's mother, are likely to be warm and intense. *Uchi* is where one can let one's hair down, a refuge to which one can retreat. This sense of emotional closeness is fostered by a number of factors at work in childhood socialization.

The first is a structural tension inherent in patrilineal, patrilocal societies.[28] As Margery Wolf pointed out in her classic *Women and the Family in Rural Taiwan,* women who go to live in their husbands' households are left with little or no emotional support save for their own children. A brittle bond between the spouses—in which the man is likely to be closely tied to his own mother, rather than to the stranger, the new bride—leaves women with few alternatives. They must turn to their children in order to love and be loved.[29]

Fostering this intimacy between mother and child are a host of socialization practices in which interdependence and the fusion of selves are recurrent themes. For example, body contact between mothers and their children is fostered through extended periods of nursing—usually around one year, but this can be extended to two or three, depending on a variety of factors (Lebra 1976, 141). Mothers and children tend to bathe together, sleep together—probably until the birth of the next child (E. F. Vogel 1963, 231; Caudill and Plath 1966)—and generally remain in close body contact through the preferred form of transporting a baby: *onbu,* strapping a baby onto the back (Lebra 1976, 141). These varying practices pivot around a common assumption, "that the psychological boundaries between the two (mother and her newborn infant) are indistinct. That is, the baby is felt to be an extension of the mother rather than an autonomous being, as is the perception in the United States" (R. J. Smith 1983b, 71).

Ideal typical mothers are represented in film, novels, television, and other media as selfless, sacrificing, and totally giving. Through sacrifice and total dedication to their children's welfare (which in turn provides the mother's primary source of self-esteem and validation), they can create strong emotional bonds based on feelings of dependency and fusion, the other side of which is the manipulation of guilt. This martyrdom on the child's behalf is the mother's best disciplinary weapon. By reminding the child of all she has done for her/him, or simply by suffering in silence, she teaches the child to internalize her desires and to act accordingly. George DeVos explains the dynamic more fully:

Mothers tend to "suffer" their children rather than to forbid or inhibit their behavior by using verbal chastisement or even physical punishment. The child, while this form of discipline is going on, learns gradually the vulnerability of the loved one and that control of an offender is exercised not by doing anything to the offender but by self-control. The offender becomes frightened by his awesome capacity to injure the person he loves. Deviant behavior can inflict injury which is irreversible upon the very person on whom one has learned to depend so deeply. One's own behavior can lead to the illness or injury of another by damaging the beloved's sense of self and role.

In a positive sense, the mother expresses the capacity for self-exhaustion on behalf of her child but in so doing creates an awesome sense in the child that aggressive behavior is destructive" (1985, 155).

If the mother's implicit message had to do with the importance of the *ie*-enterprise, one can begin to see how difficult such pressures might be to resist. The drive for continuity is bound up, not only with the pressures of *ie,* obligation, but feelings activated in children as members of an *uchi:* dependence on the mother and the resulting feelings of guilt.

The creation of a safe, secure atmosphere within the *uchi* is another part of a mother's work. This in turn reinforces the cleavage between the dangerous or unpredictable outside and the safe, warm inside. Vogel (1963) links the constant contact between mother and child, where the mother is always nearby to care for the child's needs, with the child's dependence on the mother's presence. He cites a number of examples where children exhibit fear of abandonment by their mothers, including a distinctive mode of disciplining the unruly: not by keeping them *inside* the house, but by *locking them out.* Exclusion from the *uchi* is the worst possible punishment. Among my own relatives, I saw similar examples. When my second cousin wanted her daughter, little Ruri-chan, to behave, she had only to calmly invoke the garbagemen, who would come to take Ruri-chan away. "Take me away?" Ruri-chan would say, her round eyes widening. "Take me away?" she would repeat softly. No further words were required.

Takeo Doi, in his classic work on the emotion of *amae,* dependency, elaborates on the distinction between *uchi* and *soto,* linking the expression of dependency needs to the in-group. As we have seen, only within the *uchi* (be it family, company, or school) can one express one's *honne* and one's desire for indulgence. In one's inner circle there is no need to cultivate the *tatemae* or worry about consequences of one's actions toward others. There is no need to hold back one's desires. Indeed, in Doi's terms, *enryo*, restraint or holding back, is "the gauge for distinguishing between inner and outer" (1973, 40). In the *soto* world, people must take care not to offend others. "One holds back with the idea that one must not presume too much (*amaeru*) on the other's good will. The fear is at work, in other words, that unless one holds back, one will be thought impertinent and disliked accordingly" (ibid., 39). He distinguishes three "concentric circles" of relationships: the insiders, with whom one can express one's desire for *amae;* the "meaningful" outsiders, with whom one must *enryo;* and the strangers (*tanin*) whom one does not know and therefore to whom one need not *enryo.* In all cases, the distinction between inside and outside, *uchi* and *soto,* is crucial in determining one's mode of behavior and one's form of emotional expression.

Hisa Kumagai (1981) extends Doi's framework, and in so doing, further elucidates the nature of the link between emotional expression and inside/outside. She shows that *amae* is only half the story; that in order for a person to seek indulgence, someone else has to give it (in Japanese, *amaeru* and *amayakasu,* respectively). One party expresses selfish desires, while the other *holds back* her or his self, in order to allow the other party to express those desires. Within the family, these positions usually correspond to the roles of child and parent. When a mother suffers in silence, or demonstrates that she will allow her child's inappropriate behavior out of her love for the child, she further reinforces the boundaries between *uchi* and *soto.* Only within the *uchi* will children be allowed to act in such an outrageous way.

Outside the family, one may also have to seek indulgence, through making requests of others. In these cases, one must *tanomu,* request favors of another (such as the request that I teach English to my benefactor's pupil). Its corresponding term is Doi's *enryo,* to withhold oneself, to hold back—the analogue, in the *soto* realm, of *amayakasu.* The correspondence would be as follows:

	Expression of self	Withholding of self
Uchi	*Amaeru*	*Amayakasu*
Soto	*Tanomu*	*Enryo*

In short, although similar emotional orientations may occur in both inside and outside realms, the expression of those orientations will be quite different, depending on whether one is dealing with insiders or outsiders.

This contextualization of behavior, say analysts such as Doi (1978) and Nakane (1970), accounts for actions that may initially puzzle the Western analyst. The *Uchi Benkei* syndrome is one such well-known phenomenon, in which the perfectly polite and proper young boy (or girl) becomes a terror at home. Among some of the children I knew, this was far from uncommon. One little girl, for instance, would constantly pout and demand sweets and toys while at home; outside, she was the model of propriety. Doi and Nakane both link the inside/outside continuum to the ability of some Japanese to act with complete lack of concern toward strangers, or the tendency of some Japanese tourists to behave wildly when abroad. In both cases, they are not bound by the need to *enryo,* for the stranger is a socially meaningless person, and usual social norms do not apply.

The tendency to classify behavior as relatively *uchi* or relatively *soto* provided me with a key to a puzzle confronting me when I took a brief trip home at the end of the summer. I was still living with the Sakamotos, and the young successor and his wife came home with me. They were guests, to be sure, but they also identified themselves with me, as intimates. They called my parents *otōsan* and *okāsan,* father and mother, vicariously placing themselves in my position—something one might do with a good friend and her family. The husband and wife chose very different modes of defining inside and outside behavior, however. The wife was a model guest, acting with perfect *enryo*. She claimed to enjoy our hospitality and was never demanding in her requests of us. Her husband was quite the opposite. Apparently, he defined the situation as more of an *uchi* context, no doubt in part because I had come to live in their household. Consequently, he felt free to make what in our eyes were breathtakingly assertive demands. Accompanying my mother to the supermarket, he would point to his or his wife's favorite foods and ask that my mother buy them. He opened my father's closet, found a belt he liked, and asked if he could take it home. ("No," was my father's reply.) He came upon some of my brother's old games and models in the closet, and asked if he could take *them* home. He wanted a Harley-Davidson motorcycle in the worst sort of way, and we spent many a day going from dealer to dealer, comparing prices and shipping costs. Certainly, a guest should be catered to, and he was entitled to make some requests about where to go and what to see. Nonetheless, I was completely taken aback by his uncensored demands. Where was the stereotypically polite Japanese guest? Perhaps he thought that all Americans were aggressive and demanding—although I had not been so as a guest in their house. Perhaps he was abandoning all restraint in another culture, a possibility suggested by Doi. But we were not in the category of complete outsiders. The wife provided the most plausible clues, when she began to tease her husband about being a "big baby." The answer, I think, lies in the definitions of *uchi* and *soto* behavior. In a way, the son was defining our family as a place that was relatively *uchi,* in which he would be allowed to ask for indulgence. He was entitled to play the part of a demanding child.

Soto and *uchi* are thus contextually defined. They are not fixed, kinship-based entities. They depend to a large extent on the "other" against which they are set, and there can be room for individual play and choice. The husband and the wife each made different choices, negotiating somewhat different relations with our family. That is, making those choices is *constitutive* of different kinds of relationships and different degrees of intimacy and distance, inside and outside. But of course, the range of choices is highly restricted, constituted in advance, and so constructed as to permit a certain amount of play and perhaps subversion and change at the margins.

Finally, belonging or choosing to belong to an *uchi* involves a whole package of decisions about language, behavior, and social interaction. Belonging means active participation, not passive membership. One must prove in action one's loyalty to the *ie.* With intimacy come emotional expression *and* the imperative to perform. I came to realize the consequences of belonging to an *uchi* during a visit with the Sakamotos. I spent the weekend with the young couple who were now living in the main house, while the elder Sakamotos had moved to a nearby prefecture to start up a branch shop there. During the weekend, they had a distinguished visitor, a Zen priest the bride had known in her work in the government bureaucracy. He was a jaunty fellow given to wearing berets, a marvelous raconteur. In the presence of this guest, I could also have acted as a guest, waiting to be served, or I could have thrown in my lot with the women and helped with the hectic behind the scenes preparations of what would clearly be a sumptuous meal. Several factors affected my decision. I was younger, less distinguished, and more familiar with the Sakamotos than was the priest. Equally important, I had heard murmurings that perhaps the three of us might go and visit the *sensei* and his family in their beautiful seacoast town during the New Year's holidays. (This we eventually did, and they treated us royally.) Given these circumstances, my choice was clear. I opted for a relatively *uchi* mode of behavior. I stayed mostly in the kitchen, arranging food and warming bottles of *sake*. We scurried back and forth endless times between kitchen and parlor, putting food on the table, making sure the guest always had a warm bottle of *sake,* pouring it if the son were being neglectful, clearing the plates.[30] Long after the men had finished their meal—in fact, as they began to be boisterously inebriated—we were finally able to sit down. *Uchi* means belonging, but in choosing to belong, one also chooses to actively participate.[31]

At this juncture we can begin to fathom the power of *ie* and *uchi. Uchi* locates selves. It in effect defines who you are, how you speak, and how you act towards others. And by speaking, acting, and using space, Japanese people recreate and redefine the boundaries of *uchi. Ie* and *uchi,* the household line and the *uchi* as a center of emotional warmth and personal identity, create a symbolic whole with tremendous power. No wonder it produces such an impact on young men like Masao. Not only does the decision about succession summon up the obligations to ancestors and prospective descendants, it galvanizes deeply felt emotions of belonging and participating. It may also call up profound feelings of guilt. Countless times a day, Japanese people must use their *uchi* as their zero-point of discourse. Countless times a day, they recreate the boundaries of *uchi* as their locus of identity. Both creative and coercive, such insistent symbolisms cannot easily be resisted.

Yet people do resist, and things do change. In the coming generations of successors, we see both significant continuities and possible incipient transformations. As we will see, different members of a family enterprise held quite different ideas about succession and about familial duties. What sorts of struggles over the meanings of family took place in my informants' lives? Are resistance and desire for change merely part of a cultural script, to be eventually encompassed by the demands of the *ie?* Or are real, if not radical, changes in the offing? Two intriguing situations brought these questions to mind. The first is the case of the reluctant Sakamoto successor, our demanding guest. The second is the designated successor to the Satō confectionery, where a succession dispute lurks in the future.

It had been a few weeks since I had seen the young Sakamoto couple, and I received a call from Minako-san. Would I like to go to the exhibit of paintings on loan from the Prado? I happily arranged to meet her near the entrance of the museum.

She came up to me, gracefully dressed in flowing pleats, a straw hat shading her face. "How is Tomio-san?" I asked as we stood in line. "Fine," she replied, "as far as his health is concerned, but not so fine psychologically." Apparently this happened once a year. He became depressed about the state of the company. He slept later and later (till six, late for that family). He was frustrated by the difficult relationships at the factory, where some of the relatives were "all talk and no action," and other relatives tried to cover up for them. He was despondent at the prospect of having to carry on the company. "That special, shining quality (*kira kira shita mono*) has disappeared," she said. "His *faitto* has disappeared. And when that happens for a man—it's the end." When she first met him, he radiated energy and enthusiasm. He had wanted to be a politician, and with his capabilities, his charm and good looks, it was easy to see how he might well make a go of it. But the difficulties of working in the firm were getting him down.

Their trip to America had also opened their eyes. The very different attitude toward succession in America they found especially striking. Minako-san explained to me that she considered the pressure to succeed to the family business an "egoism" on the parents' part. "They think their children are their possessions (*mono*)," she said, "so they have the right to dictate their children's lives. I think life is just too short to live out someone else's dream," she said passionately. "I think people should be allowed to do what they want to do." Then, laughing, she admitted her words were confirmation of her so-called negative influence on her husband. By telling him such things she was holding him back (pulling on his leg, as the Japanese expression goes). She was working against the *ie* as a whole, encouraging him in his selfish behavior. As an *oyomesan,* she should push him to give 120 percent, but she limited him to only 70 percent. "We laugh and joke about what a bad *oyomesan* I am," she smiled. After the exhibit, a long lunch in the dining room of the Mitsukoshi Department Store enabled her to explain more fully the difficult relationships among the uncles, cousins, and grandmothers. It gave me some inkling of the depth of the problems Tomio-san would inherit if he stayed in the family business. It was a prospect he did not relish.

Minako-san was also under pressure to spend more time at the business, doing the books and acting as receptionist. She minced no words about her intentions. She had absolutely no desire to spend much time there. If Tomio-san's position was difficult, hers was at least equally so, for she was viewed with suspicion and some hostility by a few of the family members. The Sakamoto company was a place she preferred to avoid.

Her dream was to return to her job in the national office for social welfare, a prestigious government position, but her parents-in-law were dead set against the idea.

To me, Tomio-san's dilemma recapitulated Masao's to a great extent. But Tomio-san's was in a sense even more extreme, because he had chosen to enter the family enterprise and had found the atmosphere to be difficult, even intolerable at times. One could view his dilemma as a natural phase in successorship, built into the *ie* system, where resistance is overcome by years of perseverance. Moreover, extinction of the *ie*-enterprise is always a structural possibility, although clearly in this case it was not viewed as desirable. On the other hand, one can see important shifts from the so-called traditional *ie* model. One key factor is the position of Minako-san, who was confident and sure of herself, having worked in a post of national prominence for some years. She had married late and had a good idea of her own desires for her life. The *ie*-enterprise did not fit in with those plans. A second is the wider availability of competing models for family life. Their visit to America and their curiosity about "the American family" was of course one example, but Japanese middle-class ideals now more closely approximate American notions of nuclear family, though by no means are they identical. With successors like Tomio-san and Minako-san, it is possible that a greater number of *ie*-enterprises may choose the path of extinction. Yet I must stress that this is far from a foregone conclusion. For this couple, *ie* continuity and obligation to the enterprise were imbued with moral and emotional meanings, and as such shaped their lives. It may be that for Tomio-san, his resistance is a phase which will be overcome over the years. Duty and desire may strain against one another now, but they may yet fuse.

The last I heard, Tomio-san was still in the family enterprise. Minako-san had gone back to work, not for the family firm or for the national bureaucracy, but for a local government agency.

The case of Hiroshi-san, the successor to the Satō confectionery, highlights what one might call a relatively individualistic orientation, and foreshadows possible future changes. His dreams and his vision of the enterprise differ significantly from those of his uncle, the present company president (*shachō*).

In my interview with him, Hiroshi-san seemed determined to prove that Japanese family firms were as advanced or rational as their American counterparts. He stressed his differences from the typical Japanese of stereotype, who lived to work. He liked to have fun, he said as he showed me his voluminous record collection and state-of-the-art sound system. In fact, that very evening, he and his cousin were going to a Jackson Browne concert. He had studied business and economics at the university, and his goal was to get the firm on more solid financial ground. "The company and household budgets still aren't completely separate," he said ruefully. He wanted to do something about that, to rationalize operations. Most of all, he wanted to ease the burden on the *okāsan,* Mrs. Satō. Indeed, as I entered his room for the interview, I noticed her on her hands and knees, scrubbing the kitchen floor.[32] "She works all the time," he said, "like the typical Japanese."

Hiroshi-san had just been made *tenchō,* head of the shop, a few months ago. "When someone first called me *tenchō* I turned around to see who they were talking to," he laughed. But now he was accustomed to the change in status, and spoke articulately about his job and its difficulties. What I found striking in his responses was the degree to which, disclaimers aside, he subscribed to familiar notions of *ie* continuity and the imperative to make the enterprise prosper. "I can't really say this while the *shachō* is still around," he said conspiratorially, but whenever he became *shachō,* he wanted to add a space where customers could sit down and have some pastry and coffee. Something elegant and nicely appointed, with an open, American feeling, he said. His aim was to introduce the people of this more conservative district of Tokyo to different pastries, to get them to try new and unusual things. In fact, marketing a new product was the most gratifying aspect of the job, he told me, and here in Shitamachi, it was a distinct challenge. At first, people tended to be suspicious. The cherry tarts looked like *umeboshi* (salted, pickled plums), they would say, and the blueberry tarts looked like they had raisins on top. The biggest problem had been marketing cheesecake, for the rich, cheesy taste is not appreciated in a country not known for its love of dairy products. They tried ever more delicate recipes and devised all manner of advertisements and promotional sales to entice people to buy the new product. At almost two dollars for a tiny slice, it was no bargain, but their efforts finally succeeded. Hiroshi-san counts this as one of his most satisfying triumphs. His aim, he said, was to create a pâtisserie/café where Shitamachi people could enjoy pastries in an environment equal to the well-established shops of the Ginza or the trendier Aoyama or Roppongi. He continued to speak with animation and enthusiasm. Clearly, Hiroshi-san subscribed to deep-seated assumptions about obligation to carry on the *ie,* an obligation bound up with his own personal identity. He wanted to put his distinctive stamp on the enterprise during his tenure as *shachō*.

We went on to discuss his daily schedule: up at 7:45 to make it into the shop by 8:10 for a 9:00 opening. For the first half hour he was by himself, doing the cleaning, putting out the pastries in the display cases. The first shift of full-time workers showed up at 8:40 and went until 6:00; the second worked from 11:00 until 8:30. The part-timers arrive at 9:00 and stay until 1:00. The shop itself is open from 9:00 A.M. until 8:00 P.M.. Hiroshi-san oversees operations all day. Apart from an hour for lunch and half an hour for dinner, he took no breaks, and he worked these hours six days a week. Perhaps the hours will be less demanding in the future, but the shop has been suffering from a shortage of employees for some years now, and the situation shows few signs of improving. Moreover, if the *shachō* is an example, Hiroshi-san's time commitment may only increase with the years.

Indeed, his chief complaint was that he had so little time of his own. He attended a weekly management seminar, but the shop kept him so busy that he rarely had the time to study. He should come home and devote two hours a night to his books, he said, but then, "my own time would disappear, wouldn't it?" He again stressed his differences from the Japanese who found their *ikigai,* their *raison d'être,* in work. His *ikigai,* he emphasized, was in leisure and consumption. He wanted to spend his money on a nice house, nice clothes, and good records. And he would like to pursue his interest in sports: volleyball, basketball, baseball, and tennis. Unfortunately, in order to enjoy these sports, you need more than one person, and all his friends have their day of rest on Sunday, one of the shop's busiest days. He also liked to play music, and was a electric bass player of some repute. Hiroshi-san's desire for more leisure and more consumption does in fact seem to be a change from the attitudes of the present owner, who is thoroughly immersed in business and business-related activities. Yet, although one could label his attitudes and desires more hedonistic, in practice he was thus far reproducing the same pattern of hard work he saw in the *shachō* and the *shachō*'s wife. For him, the dedication to work was in part necessary, but it did not fully encompass his sense of self. The "behavior" of hard work was still evident, but its meaning has clearly undergone a change in Hiroshi-san's case. Commitment to expanding the *ie*-enterprise was still strong, and so was his enthusiasm and gratification with each success. But the constant pace of work was also likely to prove more frustrating for him than it might for the present *shachō*.

A third interesting potential shift seemed likely if he took over the en-

'terprise. By personal proclivity, he had absolutely no interest in the community and business associations so important to the *shachō*. From what I could gather, the shop's attractive displays and delicious *okashi* were part of the firm's success, but the social component—making contacts and creating a visible presence in the business associations—also served to enhance that success. Hiroshi-san seemed unimpressed by the whole issue of community involvement. "No," he said, waving his hand in a dismissive way. "I have no interest in such things. That's for the *shachō*." Were that the case, the social position of the family and firm might become quite different within the context of the community and the ward at large, where the present *shachō* was considered an up-and-coming leader and one of the community's outstanding citizens. In a similar vein, Hiroshi-san had little interest in planning the parties and trips that were such an important feature of life during the tenure of this *shachō*. Parties were OK, he said, but what he disliked was the coercion: "'Sing!' They always tell you," he said with distaste. Were the parties to decrease in number or disappear altogether, the atmosphere at the company would indeed change dramatically.

Hiroshi-san's ideal lifestyle, then, both traced out familiar themes and introduced potential far-reaching changes. He enacted his dedication to the *ie*-enterprise, working hard and taking responsibility for a quality product. He was involved in creating new products to sell, in order to expand their stock. He had dreams for the future, for making the enterprise grow. And in all this, his sense of identity was deeply involved. But clearly, changes were in the offing. He wanted to further rationalize management, and he disparaged the "half-baked" financial arrangements in the company, where household and shop accounts were not clearly separated. This, too, he saw as part of a drive to expand and improve the family fortunes. More revealing are his desires for consumption and leisure, for in this light the meaning of work will be quite different for him than it was for the older generation. And finally, his more individualistic perspective may lead to a change in the firm's standing in the community and the way it is viewed within the context of local business associations. Such a change might even have an impact on the firm's prosperity.

Perhaps unknown to Hiroshi-san are other potential problems which may present themselves in the future, as I learned by talking with the present *shachō*. He worries about Hiroshi-san's attitudes, well aware of their differences and the potential implications of Hiroshi-san's lack of sociability for future business. For example, he bemoaned the fact that

Hiroshi-san had few close friends and seldom enjoyed going drinking. Hiroshi-san was friendly with only one of the artisans from the factory and kept his distance from the others. And apparently he didn't mix much with the other young merchants on the street, showing little interest in the merchants' association. Such personality traits were unfathomable to the *shachō,* a quintessentially gregarious merchant who enjoyed socializing. He was worried, too, about the impact this more individualistic, introspective approach might have on the business, for the essence of commerce was dealing with people. Though the *shachō* himself did not allude to the fact, others—both friends of the *shachō* and workers in the factory—told me that they saw a succession dispute brewing. The young Satō son, the *shachō*'s third child, was in his mid-teens, and he had apparently expressed interest in the firm. If the present *shachō*'s dissatisfaction with Hiroshi-san continued, an interesting—if painful—dispute might occur, fought out on the grounds of merit and degrees of *uchi*-ness. If Hiroshi-san was an *uchi* member, he was still not as *uchi* as the *shachō*-san's own son. At last report, however, everything was still as it was when I left. A few years down the road should prove decisive in settling the succession issue for this coming generation, thus steering the future course of Satō Shōten.

Why, then was Masao so torn and distraught? What makes the *ie*-enterprise such a powerful force? We have found that the *ie* as obligation to the household line and *uchi* as a center of emotional attachment provide a meaningful symbolic framework for its members. Hamabata (forthcoming) calls them axes of (male) authority and (female) intimacy, love and power. As such, they are living realities which locate you in history and position you vis-à-vis other households. *Ie* and *uchi* structure language, behavior, space, and feeling. They are laden with profoundly felt emotional and moral values. They form a culturally approved arena of self-realization in which to forge an identity. They circumscribe a circle of attachment and belonging, and they require participation, loyalty, and hard work from those who belong. *Ie* and *uchi* define a world and give its members a place in that world. In belonging to an *uchi* and participating in an *ie,* people create selves.

Yet *ie* and *uchi* cannot mean the same things to all people. Crosscutting forces of gender; age; position in the family structure; point in the life course; and economic viability, among others, shape the perspectives of its members. Differences in perspective create conditions for conflict and for change. Masao-san, Minako-san, Obāchan, Tomio-san and

Hiroshi-san, show us some of the multiple definitions of *ie* and *uchi,* and the ways struggles over their meanings continue in individual lives.[33] As living, productive discourses *ie* and *uchi* mobilize resources, people, and powerful feelings in a multiplicity of registers. For people engaged in family enterprise, *ie* and *uchi* create and constrain, providing the arena in which to enact compelling dramas of guilt, pride, happiness, jealousy, competition, frustration, scorn, despair, and resignation.[34] As long as this is so, *ie* and *uchi* will be constitutive of my informants' realities, a site of the play of the simultaneously creative and coercive effects of meaning. The *ie* and *uchi* are sites, in short, for the disciplinary production of selves.

To this point, we see this interplay primarily in the phenomenological realities of individuals' everyday lives. This explication of the meanings of family—*ie* and *uchi*—sets the background for the enactments of family and conflicts in meanings of family. But within what historical matrix do these conflicts occur? What happens to the meanings of family when they are deployed in another setting: the factory? In the following chapter I show how these meanings are constituted in dynamic processes of historical change and through everyday practices in the specific context of the Satō factory.

5 *Adding the Family Flavor*

We have seen that the constraints of duty to the family line—if you will, the coercive, hierarchical aspects of *ie*-structure—and the *ie* as a circle of emotional warmth and locus of identity, are still compelling realities for the families I knew, perhaps especially for families engaged in a family enterprise. But what of the notion of *"company* as family", so loudly trumpeted in postwar studies of Japanese industry? Countless tomes tell us that the "company as family" idiom is pervasive in Japan, shaping workers' lives and creating disciplined, loyal employees who strive to achieve group goals. Management practices such as lifetime employment, payment of wages by seniority, and quality circles—so goes the familiar explanation—reinforce the family feeling, for a Japanese company is a community of people who share a common destiny (*unmei kyōdōtai*). But how does a capitalist organization designed to maximize profit mobilize and deploy this idiom? What contradictions and tensions are generated thereby, and what are the historical and cultural matrices within which those tensions are generated? How compelling *is* the metaphor of "company as family," for whom, and in what ways? What political stakes are involved? How are these meaningful idioms invoked, challenged, reproduced, reappropriated, and redeployed in a context of power relations? And what tensions and excesses of meaning animate its deployment? In this chapter and the next, I lay out the complexities of the discursive strategies surrounding the notion of *uchi no kaisha* (our company), in the Satō confectionery. My approach highlights the strategic appropriations, political deployments, ironic twists, and subtle nuances in the peregrinations of an idiom, as it creates and constrains people's lives within the Satō factory and without (cf. Foucault 1979, 1980).

I begin by sketching in broad strokes the ways the relations between family and firm have been shaped in large sweeps of history, politics, and economics. The Satō company's attempts to add the family flavor, through trips, benefits, gifts, and recruitment practices, took place within a narrative field shaped by legal codes, the constructing of a national identity, and the growth of capitalism—in short, forces shaping the relations possible between family and company in Japan. These stories provide the ground for the figure of everyday life in the Satō factory, where we will follow out the ways different actors appropriate "company as family," and reveal the ironies and multiplicities of meaning in any deployment of this supple idiom.

Merchants and Artisans: The Familial Embrace

Large-scale changes in Japanese history and the Japanese economy have shifted the relationships between firm and family relationships, which are constantly in flux, historically mediated, adjusted, and readjusted on a daily basis in multiple ways. The basically linear narrative I offer describes major shifts over long periods of time, a movement from an *ie* structure that embraces working participants—apprentices—as full-fledged members, to one in which the separation between family and workers assumes greater importance, and "company as family" becomes metaphorical and open to particularly interesting contradictions, though it remains a vibrant social reality.

The first part of the story deals with large commercial household confederations (*dōzoku,* in social scientese) which, in Kyoto in the Tokugawa period, were known as *noren uchi,* within the shop curtain.[1] The structure was that of the *dōzoku* I have described in chapter 4, in which the directorship of the *noren uchi* resided in the *honke,* or main household, which acted as the federation's ritual/economic center. Merchants distinguished between two types of subordinate, or branch households: *bunke*—branch households headed by blood-related kin, and *bekke*—households headed by non-kin, usually former apprentices and clerks. All members of the *noren uchi* could hang their common banner, the *noren,* outside their door, marking them as members of the same *kagyō,* or *ie*-enterprise.[2]

I have already stressed the extent to which so-called biological kinship counts for relatively little in Japan, when compared with the importance of "blood" in, for example, Chinese, Korean, or American kinship. But in the pre–twentieth century *ie* confederations like the *noren uchi,* these tendencies were strikingly apparent; indeed, one could argue that the distinguishing feature of *ie*-confederations in this period was precisely the degree to which non-kin were truly full-fledged—if junior—members of the *noren uchi.* Kin and non-kin households were distinguished, to be sure, but this was only one axis of difference among many: age, gender, the important distinction between successors and nonsuccessors, to name but a few. Merchant households, Nakano argues, were especially receptive to non-kin members, for merchants were not dependent on land as their chief resource. Consequently, the boundaries of the household enterprise were flexible, able to expand to accommodate more new members than might have been the case in an agricultural household (Nakano 1966, 29). As cities grew and people left the countryside to find work in burgeoning urban centers, merchant households were able to find a ready supply of labor through people not related to the *honke* by blood. In fact, by Nakano's count of merchant households in the Kyoto-Osaka region, "roughly one-third of the members of a 'typical' urban *ie* had no kin connection" (ibid., 18).

As *ie,* commercial *ie*-confederations were hierarchically organized systems of work and task performance (cf. Chapter 4) which incorporated new members into the *noren uchi* through a culturally specific form of apprenticeship. The key distinction determining the life of an apprentice was whether or not he qualified as potential head of a *bekke,* non-kin branch household. The young male apprentices who were potential *bekke* heads were known as *detchi,* and they joined the household usually at the age of ten (Takeuchi 1960, 96), though the range went from around eight to about seventeen (Nakano 1966, 20). In a tale of apprenticeship that remains familiar to the present day, *detchi* began their learning by doing odd jobs such as running errands and doing housework; certainly at this beginning stage, they were not entrusted with any tasks that bore centrally on the management of the shop. For their pains they were given room, board, clothing, and a minimal allowance (Hazama 1969, 8). The *genpuku* ceremony, marking a boy's accession into socially recognized adulthood, signaled a new stage in an apprentice's life, when apprentices could begin to learn the trade in earnest. After approximately ten years of service the *detchi* became a *tedai,* ready to take on more central tasks of managing the shop.[3] If the *tedai* continued to prove himself through years of faithful service, he might be granted the status of *bantō,* head clerk, the chief position of power and responsibility among shop employees.

According to the ideal typical career scenario in commercial *ie,* the master would reward the loyal *bantō* by setting him up in a branch household, a process known as "dividing the shop curtain" (*noren wake*). Heads of these new *bekke* usually married later and thus separated from the main house later[4] than did their counterparts who were related by blood to the main house. In both cases, however, the master provided branch households with the capital and the goods to set up shop, and gave them introductions to the merchant guilds, or *ka-bunakama,* thus providing them with some initial guarantees of cooperation and goodwill from their fellow merchants. In return, the branch households owed their *honke* significant—indeed, unrepayable—obligations. The *bunke* and *bekke* were to donate their labor whenever the *honke* would so request, and they were compelled to discharge appropriate ritual obligations—memorializing the ancestors during the appropriate holidays and death anniversaries, giving gifts, attending important *ie* ceremonies, and so on. These ritual obligations should not be dismissed as secondary to the more obviously economic obligations to offer aid in the form of labor or capital. Hazama (1969, 9) points to these relations of obligation and dependence between masters and their former apprentices as the key dynamic in merchant household confederations. Within these hierarchically organized relations, non-kin apprentices could find their place as full-fledged members of a *noren uchi.*

This was not true for all apprentices, however. The articulation of enterprise and family was markedly different for a second major category of apprentice, the *chūnen,* middle years, who came to work in the household enterprise after they had reached social adulthood—that is, after they had undergone the rite of passage, the *genpuku* initiation. These *chūnen* had neither the long-term training of the *detchi,* nor, one assumes, could they therefore earn, in the ordinary course of events, the trust of the masters in the same way as a *detchi* might. Except in extraordinary cases, when the *chūnen* did prove their loyalty and abilities and when the main house was exceptionally prosperous, the *chūnen* were not allowed to become heads of branch households.[5]

In merchant households, then, the key division among members was between those who qualified as potential full-fledged members of the *noren uchi* upon reaching adulthood (in other words, those who came in at an early age as *detchi* and proved their loyalty to the household enterprise through years of faithful service, as well as those who were related by blood to the heads of the *honke*), and those who did not (the servants and those who came in after adulthood, who did not, therefore, prove their dedication to the household). Succession practices linked the forging of mature personhood with work and with service to the household, for only those who had disciplined themselves through work, creating themselves within the matrix of a *particular* merchant *ie-*confederation, were qualified to become full-fledged members of that confederation. Transposed into a slightly different key, the same themes emerge among artisans.

Artisanal households pivoted around the hierarchical relations between the master—the *oyakata,* or parent figure—and the *totei,* the apprentice; less emphasis seems to be given larger confederations like the *noren uchi.* Usually, the apprentices were unrelated outsiders, but they lived in the master's household and spent a fixed period learning the trade—acquiring their skills, polishing their "arm," as the saying goes. Contracts specified the length of service, though this period differed at different historical moments[6] and among different trades.[7] Guilds, or *kabunakama,* set forth these guidelines governing the relations between master and apprentice.

The process of becoming an apprentice required attestations to one's character from proper guarantors, and if those met the master's approval, then the apprentice could enter the master's house for a few days in a process called *memie,* a probationary period designed to ensure the approval of both parties involved. If both were satisfied, the master handed over part of the apprentice's "salary" and received in return a certificate of guarantee, or *ukejo,* from the official guarantor, or *hōkōnin,* of the young apprentice. Part of the contract generally specified the apprentice's due: room, board, work clothing, and two three-day vacations a year (during the middle of the summer and at the end of the year, when the apprentices were allowed to return to their natal homes). After the contracted period of service—usually ten years—had elapsed, the artisans often donated a year or more of free labor to the master, a custom called *ongaeshi bōkō,* returning obligation, or *orei bōkō,* service in gratitude (Yoshida 1976, 271). Toward the end of the Tokugawa period, this period of service decreased substantially in response to a greater demand for factory workers (Gordon 1985, 22).[8]

Conditions were often demanding and difficult, and some young boys ran away. Masters then possessed the power to blacklist the runaways through the guild, in all likelihood preventing these boys from finding another job. Presuming the apprentice remained, however, he learned techniques primarily through watching what others did at the workshop (*minarai*) and began to gain proficiency in the skills of the trade.[9] After completing his period of service, he was a journeyman who could then serve out other periods with other masters in order to learn different techniques. Indeed, as is the case for artisans in other parts of the world (cf. e.g, Sewell 1980), artisans in Japan highly valued the independence

Family as Company, Company as Family

and the knowledge acquired by going from workshop to workshop to learn new techniques and polish their skills. Eventually, the journeymen hoped to become masters and set up or inherit their own workshops (cf. Gordon 1985, 22).

Relationships in the artisanal world were also hierarchically organized, based on relations of mutual obligation. The apprentices and journeymen were cast in an older brother / younger brother idiom and arrayed in a hierarchy, but especially for those artisans who traveled extensively to polish their skills, the fixed length of service at any one master's workshop worked to attenuate the enduring bonds of loyalty and obligation owed to any particular master (Hazama 1969, 8). Mobility and independence were prized, yet, ideally at any rate, there was a special relationship between an artisan and his first master (Gordon 1985, 22). This first workplace was where the apprentices forged their identities as artisans, and the masters owed them both the education in techniques of the trade, and moral education as members of society (Endō 1978, 85).

Moving Toward Kinship

Two major developments occurred at the end of the Tokugawa and in the Meiji Period that centrally affected the *dōzoku* system. One was the growth of capitalism, and the other was the codification of household structure in the Meiji Civil Code.

The first development, the emergence of a growing capitalist economy, created several far-reaching changes in the *ie*-enterprises. Perhaps the most obvious was the increasing use of wage labor and a concomitant change in the relationships between masters and apprentices. In the larger merchant households, a system of commuting salaried workers began to be used in conjunction with older forms. Smaller firms tended to adhere to the more established system, where economic aid was only a part of a much more complex set of relationships between *honke* and their *bunke* and *bekke*. The less prosperous enterprises might find it difficult to compete with the attractions of the salary system in the larger enterprises. And certain shops might use what Nakano calls a "mixed mode" of employment, where the new salaried commuters worked alongside the "resident *tedai* who got half-pay and could expect to become *bekke*-heads; and . . . *bekke*-heads who worked as commuting clerks. The first of these clerks were employed on the basis of the employer-employee relationship, the second clerks were in the *ie*-head and

166

non-kin member relationship, and the third and last clerks were in *honke*-head and *bekke*-head relationship" (Nakano 1966, 85).

In the large merchant households, another critical development occurred: an increasing separation between the commercial and the kinship aspects of the *ie*. It was most clearly symbolized in the physical split of the household building into the *mise,* the shop, and the *oku,* the interior, the residence where the househead and his wife lived. The *mise* included the lodging quarters for the *detchi* and *tedai* (ibid., 125). The division sometimes became even more pronounced, either when the *honke* head moved to a separate residence altogether, converting the former shop/residence into a purely commercial space, or when he established the shop in another location, taking over the entire building as a residence for himself and his family. In both cases, the *honke* head himself became a commuter to the shop (ibid.).

Along with the physical separation came an increasing rationalization of management. For example, household accounts came to be kept separately from the shop's capital. Moreover, the creation of new shops began to take precedence over the creation of new *bekke,* so that instead of creating both simultaneously, as had been the custom, the main shop and its managers would create a branch shop first, and only then send members of the *bunke* or *bekke* to manage these shops. As Nakano states: "When the *honke*'s own house came to be distant in location, finance, and management from its shop, it was the main shop (not the house) that would establish a branch shop and then appoint a branch house to take care of it. Thus, the branch shops in a large, bureaucratized enterprise became differentiated from the branch houses that ran them. Branch house members might no longer reside at the shop but live elsewhere and commute to the shop daily" (ibid, 59).

In the largest enterprises, this reached a point where live-in apprentices were no longer included as real members of the *ie,* nor were their "branch houses" part of the larger *dōzoku* or *noren uchi* organization. They were part of a *dōzoku*-like organization of main shop and branch shops, working there as commuters (Nakano 1966: 129). But this was quite a different status from being incorporated into the master's family as a real member of the *ie,* and it tended to make the relationship between the master and the apprentices/clerks much more a superior/subordinate tie based largely on economic considerations.

In terms of *noren uchi/dōzoku* organization, then, the growth of the capitalist economy and the increasing separation of shop from residence created a changed *dōzoku* system in which kinship as biological relationship, far from growing weaker, actually increased in importance. More and more, there came to be a separation between those who "shared the same last name" (*dōmyō*) and those who did not, with the key roles of ownership and membership in the *dōzoku* restricted to these blood-related people. The apprentices and clerks could still play important roles as managers of *dōzoku* property—indeed, they were recruited and trained to do so, as members of the *dōzoku* themselves sometimes distanced themselves from management. They could still potentially marry into the *honke* family through the process of *muko yōshi*, but their incorporation into the *dōzoku* as full-fledged members was becoming increasingly rare.

The worlds of artisans also changed considerably under the impact of capitalism. The *goyō shokunin*, the suppliers of goods to the aristocracy and the samurai classes, existed largely in the cities or castle towns of the Tokugawa period, and their fates were tied closely to the fate of the upper classes. Not having been able to expand beyond this narrow circle of demand to develop on their own, these suppliers to the *samurai* were largely unable to compete in the new, competitive capitalist markets. Sumiya argues that the artisanal guild structure was riven with contradictions from the middle of the Tokugawa period, giving rise to new types of artisans. As he describes the situation: because the numbers of *oyakata kabu*, master's shares or stock, were fixed and because there were no inter-urban guild networks regulating journeymen, there was a fixed number of masters and a host of journeymen who were unregulated and mobile. Some artisans even hired out by the day, and there were those who did not even possess their own tools of the trade, usually the symbol of artisanal identity. Though he has his own agenda—seeing precursors of wage labor in artisanal forms of work—Sumiya argues convincingly that at the beginning of the Meiji period, increasing numbers of masters began to view the apprenticeship system as a means of extracting cheap labor. Family feeling became further attenuated when a new form, commuting apprentices, appeared, whose relationship to the masters more closely resembled that of employee to employer (Sumiya 1955, 45). Again, Sumiya's story is one of the increasing differentiation of economics and wage labor from other domains of life as capitalism began to flourish in the Japanese context.

In both merchant and artisan households, then, there was a movement toward kinship, but in different ways. In the merchant households, the key was the separation between *mise* and *oku*, shop and residence. Again, management became more rationalized and restricted to kinspeople. *Bantō* and other apprentices were no longer incorporated into the *dōzoku,* unless they came in through marriage. Among artisans, one sees a relationship of paternal benevolence and artisanal loyalty attenuated by, on the one hand, the growth of capitalism, and on the other, the unregulated nature of the guild system, so that journeymen in some ways began to resemble wage laborers. Though among artisans the familial idiom was always crosscut by artisanal ideals of mobility and independence, the direction of change points toward a further attenuation of this familial model. We will see that the familial idiom is resurrected and redeployed in large factories, however, especially after 1918.[10]

The Meiji Civil Code

These changes in the organization of the large merchant *dōzoku* were reinforced during the Meiji era (1868–1912), with the promulgation of the new Meiji Civil Code (Minpo). Part of a complex relationship with Western powers and, in fact, designed with the aid of a Frenchman, Boissonade, the Meiji Civil Code enshrined in law a model of *ie* influenced by Western conceptions of family and by the *ie* of the samurai class, from whom the law's designers were drawn.

Nakano succinctly summarizes the critical changes. One was that ownership of the *ie* was now in the hands of the househead and not in the hands of the *ie* itself. The househead became owner of the *ie* property rather than a mere trustee. The Meiji Civil Code also set up a system of parameters for choosing successors, which gave preference to the eldest son, although it allowed for flexibility within the system. This flexibility depended upon the satisfaction of certain preferential criteria: (1) near kinspeople over distant; (2) legitimate over illegitimate; (3) older over younger; and (4) male over female (Meiji Civil Code, Article 970, cited in Bachnik 1983, 72). Finally, membership in the *ie* was reserved for those "with the same surname," usually those who were related by blood or marriage. Apprentices, clerks, or other resident servants could no longer be given the status of full-fledged members of the *ie,* unless they married in. The Meiji Civil Code thus raised to the level of law the prevailing practices in samurai and wealthy merchant households, where the preference for succession by primogeniture and the almost exclusive restriction of *ie* membership to blood-related kin were the norm (Nakano 1966, 74; Hamabata 1983, forthcoming). It also relegated women to a subordinate position according to the neo-Confucian ideals prevalent among members of the samurai class. These samurai ideals were enshrined as the norm for the rest of the society, whose ideas of kinship, marriage and "women's place" were anything but uniform (R. J. Smith 1983a, 73; Hamabata, forthcoming).

Legal strictures and the practices of everyday life can, of course, occupy quite different spheres of social reality, and the Meiji Civil Code in no way produced sudden changes in household structure or practices of marriage, divorce, and kinship. As late as the 1930s, the villagers of Suye, described in Smith and Wiswell (1982), seemed to have what one might call a casual attitude toward these matters of love, marriage, and *ie*-structure. Premarital sexuality, divorce, and infidelity made Suye a lively place, to say the least. Take, for example, the casual attitude toward divorce and remarriage. Wiswell, quoted in Smith (1983), writes of a woman named Mrs. Maeno:

> Today I met Mrs. Maeno. She told me that one of their six children died. Before marrying Maeno, she said with a smile, she had two husbands. The first marriage lasted only six months because she could not stand her mother-in-law's constant criticism, so she left. Her second marriage lasted only a month. She disliked the man and made her bed separately. This third marriage was contracted sight unseen. It is working out fine. (p. 79).

There were even some extraordinary cases, such as "old lady Tanno."

> She is said to be exceptionally hard to get along with. There is no other like her in Suye. She was once married to someone in Kawaze, but left him and her infant daughter. (The girl eventually married and died without ever seeing her mother again.) Then she married at least ten different men, eventually ending up with Tanno. They say she stays with him because he is so quiet (ibid.).

Indeed, the divorce rate was actually quite high at the turn of the century (3.39 per thousand in 1892). During the period 1882–1897, just before the Meiji Civil Code took effect, the divorce rate in Japan was in fact higher than those of the United States, Denmark, Sweden, the USSR, and Great Britain (F. Kumagai 1983, 87). The frequency of divorce decreased at a slow but steady rate from the turn of the century to 1964 (when it was 0.74 per thousand) (ibid., 85). Scholars have attempted to explain these changes in various ways. General agreement seems to exist that marriage and divorce were easy to obtain before the institution of the Meiji Civil Code. Afterwards, people had to register both marriages and divorces, making the process more cumbersome. In addition, divorce seems to have been more prevalent among the rural populations and the "lower classes" (read people of nonsamurai origins and those not possessed of wealth). Still, old lady Tanno and Mrs. Maeno aside, the rate of divorce did decrease over the years, partially as a result of the Civil Code, the more cumbersome practices of registration, the dissemination of neo-Confucian ideology in the schools, and the adoption of a more "proper" Confucian morality. In a turnabout of our generation gap, the younger generation in Suye were far more conservative in their sexual conduct and in matters of marriage and divorce than were their mothers or, most certainly, their grandmothers.

The discrepancy between the Code and general practice was particularly evident in three provisions. (Cf. Nakane 1967, 17, for a fuller discussion of these discrepancies.) First, the investing of the head of the household with property rights and rights of authority over household members was at variance with practice and *ie* ideals. Although they now possessed these legal rights, most *ie*-heads continued to act as trustees of the corporate *ie,* rather than as individual owners of property, an attitude I found prevalent among my informants as well.

Secondly, the Civil Code emphasized a categorization of relatives called *shinzoku,* based on patrilineal and ego-centered principles of kinship, which had—and still have—little to do with actual inter-household relations. Nakane explains:

> Goshintō (Five Categories of Relatives graded according to their closeness to ego) . . . had its legal importance in terms of indicating a distance between relatives, rather than of delineating a set of relatives as a group. . . . The Goshintō was originally produced in the seventh century when the first firm state government was established in Japan. As a model, the mourning grades of the Chinese royal family of the T'ang dynasty were followed, with some modification" (1967, 39).

Unlike customary practice, where there is little distinction between husband's or wife's relatives, cognates or affines (see, e.g., Bachnik 1978), the Goshintō accorded a low fifth-ranking place to the wife's parents and sister's husband (ibid.), both key one-step links in *ie* ideology and practice. However, the Meiji Civil Code provisions on *shinzoku* "had hardly any effect; although they had been aware of the terms *shinzoku* and Goshintō, the majority of the rural population had no very clear recognition of relatives in terms of the Five Categories" (ibid., 40). They continued, one surmises, to act on the basis of relationships among households.

Third, the Civil Code limited *bunke* to "all households of sons or brothers regardless of the economic arrangement made by the parental

household" (ibid., 84). A *dōzoku,* we will recall, must combine economic and ceremonial exchange with the main/branch house structure.
If such is not the case, the group is far less likely to take on a corporate
character (ibid.). Thus the Civil Code emphasized genealogical relationship rather than the economic and social character of the corporate *ie.*

Household-Company-State: Contested Meanings

Thus both the introduction of the Meiji Civil Code and, in merchant
households, the separation between shop and family, tended to restrict
family membership to kinspeople only. Now, trusted employees could
be treated "like" family, but they could not "be" family, unless they married in. It is only at this point, Nakano argues, that so-called fictive kinship
and enterprise familialism became possible. Before, members of *bekke*
were full-fledged members of the larger *ie*-organization. Now, however,
bekke grew fewer, and employees were outsiders treated like family in
cases where the employer wished to demonstrate benevolence.

Yet it was precisely at this historical moment that the meanings of family were invoked in the industrial workplace. During the early part of this
century, managers in large enterprises in heavy industry energetically articulated explicit ideologies of paternalism, resurrecting the "beautiful
customs" of "traditional" Japan in response to labor unrest (Gordon
1985; Fruin 1983). Labor unions would be unnecessary and disruptive,
for the paternalistic care of the employer for the employee—who in turn
owed the employer gratitude, and diligent, loyal service—obviated the
need for such unions. Increasingly, in a complex process described by
Gordon (1985), large companies in heavy industry, in response to their
"ill-disciplined" artisanal labor force, with its legacy of mobility and independence, began to adopt policies of pay and social welfare practices
that encouraged longer-term employment and commitment. The metaphor of company as family was used by managers to assert more direct
control over their work force, wresting power from the labor boss contractors who had been intermediaries. Most strikingly, companies
extolled the beauty of familialism, where managers care for loyal and
hardworking subordinates, in order to combat the 1911 factory law. The
metaphor opened itself to multiple appropriations, however, as propo-
nents of the law also invoked the ideology of familial management,
arguing that the "beautiful customs" of familialism would work in tandem with regulatory legislation (Gordon 1985, 68). Mark Fruin (1983)

also shows how the Kikkoman family firm articulated an explicitly familial ideology in the wake of the Great Strike of 1927–28, extolling the virtues of the "spirit of industry" (*sangyō damashī*) and the common goals uniting managers and workers. "Company as family" is not simply a management ruse, however. Gordon stresses that workers also couched their claims to full membership and belonging to the firm in an idiom of familialism, and T. C. Smith also demonstrates workers' appropriations of the familial idiom, which emphasize their "right to benevolence" (1988). Through these complex negotiations among managers, the government, and workers, what we now call the Japanese employment system was forged.

The turn of the century was also a period when the meanings of family were at issue, the subjects of public debate and concern. The theories of *kokutai,* the state as a household with the emperor as its head, were marshalled and deployed in multiple contexts and enshrined most notably in the Imperial Rescript on Education of 1890 (Gluck 1985). This "concentric circle" (Ishida 1984) theory of society, in which family was encompassed and reproduced at the levels of school, company, and the state—each similar in structure, each a template for the others—proved compelling and ubiquitous. (See also Arichi 1974; Kawashima 1950; Satō 1980; Isono and Isono 1958.) Gluck argues that the agricultural *ie* had dominated the social landscape in rural areas, but was under siege from changes: the tendency of rural migrants-to-cities to live in conjugal units, severed from property and indeed, from propriety, and secondly, the apparently increasing numbers of owner/farmers who were leaving the land or were otherwise forced to abandon the established *ie*-structure (1985, 187–88). It was in this context that the values of familialism were reappropriated and reasserted: "As the traditional rural *ie* seemed to be disappearing, the connection between family and nation was increasingly stressed and the concept of the family-state evolved as much in the name of the family as of the state" (ibid., 188).

The debates on the meanings of *ie* and the Meiji Civil Code could also be viewed as an attempt to create a hegemonic vision of family based on old, samurai values in the face of upper-class dismay at the varied and often casual practices of kinship among commoners. Hamabata, in a lively and insightful historical narrative of changes in *ie* structure, sets out the "bewildering array" of customs confronting the ministry officials faced with the task of writing the Civil Code (Hamabata, 1983 and forthcoming). Scholars of the period seemed to agree that the Confucian and neo-Confucian emphases on loyalty and filiality, the vision of family embodied in the code, were indeed characteristic of a samurai family which had already "crumbled" (Arichi 1974). Policymakers' debates centered around the fate of this "antiquated" *ie.* Some men argued that it should be jettisoned so that the code should reflect commoners' customs, while the victorious faction wanted to revive and recreate "tradition," to uplift the benighted practices of the common people. Thus the Code revived an already anachronistic family structure which, even in its heyday, characterized only the elite.

The deployment of the "company as family" idiom in the early part of the century, then, took place in a field of meanings where "family" was already an intensely contested terrain.

Postwar Changes

After the end of World War II and the promulgation of a new Civil Code under the direction of Occupation authorities, the legal structure of the Japanese *ie* was dismantled. That is, the new Civil Code made equal inheritance the law, and thus abolished the preference for primogeniture. The head of the household was stripped of patriarchal authority. Women were given the right to initiate divorce. Legally, the *ie* no longer exists as a corporate group which holds property in perpetuity. The household can now more properly be called a "family" in the kinship sense, at least from a legal point of view.

As we have seen, however, the *ie* and *uchi* are still resonant idioms in the lives of the people I knew. Once again, the rift between legal code and customary practice is deep. Moreover, it is during the postwar period that the metaphor of "company as family" is most resonant in large firms, for it is at this point when the "Japanese employment system"—characterized by welfare paternalism, promotion by seniority, so-called lifetime employment, and worker identification with the firm—becomes a social reality. (Cf. Gordon 1985; see also Abegglen 1958 for a classic description of this employment system.) The *ie,* as we have seen, has been an arena of contest, its meanings forged in debates that surface with vigor in a multiplicity of contexts from the Tokugawa period to the present. And perhaps the household is such a highly charged, meaningful metaphor precisely because of its fluidity, its openness to appropriation from many quarters.

Moreover, the *ie* provides a ready template for social groupings in general. It pivots around a hierarchical structure of power and authority; it creates a feeling of belonging and emotional warmth; it links this belonging to task performance—that is, to work, and to merit, rather than to mere passive belonging; it is a zero-point of discourse, constitutive of identity. A company, a school, the state can all be potentially seen as organizations that require of their members acknowledgement of relations of authority, feelings of belonging, and meritorious work. Yet, when the metaphor is stated in these bald terms, its ambiguities are apparent. Only an analysis of the *particular* ways these features are articulated in particular contexts can reveal their subtleties and ironies. In previous chapters we have sketched out some of the ways *ie* and *uchi* remain compelling, resonant idioms for the people I knew. And we have seen that these meanings are not static or univocal. At this point, let us return to the Satō factory to see what a finely grained analysis of everyday life might tell us about the peregrinations of this key idiom in the lives of the people I knew.

The Satō Company: Company as Family?

Just as there have been contests over the meanings of company and family over the course of Japanese history, so there are conflicts enacted on the level of everyday life in a particular setting. Like the *ie,* the Satō company was an organized, hierarchically structured entity which involves many aspects of its employees' lives. It provides an internally differentiated structure of power and authority, and it serves as a circle of emotional attachment and a nodal point of identity.

Japanese history and culture imbue the Satō company with familial meanings it might not otherwise have in another cultural setting, making the *uchi no kaisha* metaphor especially apt. Take, for example, the structural organization of the company. Perhaps the most obvious cleavage between workers is the distinction between permanent and temporary (or so-called part-time) employees. Both the male artisans and the young women who work full-time in the shop are permanent or full-time employees, entitled to all the benefits I shall presently describe. Part-timers, my co-workers, are structurally marginal, and their rights, duties, and privileges in the company are more attenuated and ambiguous. Bachnik (1983, 177), for example, draws a parallel between the structurally temporary members of a household, who must eventually leave one day to establish their own branch households, and the temporary members of a company. In both cases, temporary members receive fewer benefits than their permanent counterparts, and their senses of belonging and commitment would likely be muted. Given this position within a culturally specific matrix, the distinction between temporary and permanent employees in Japan takes on a significance surpassing its usual meanings in the West (see, e.g., Beechey and Perkins 1987). Because the *ie* is basically an enterprise/work organization rather than a unit of kinship (Bachnik 1983), the *ie* and the company can act as templates for one another in ways not possible in cultures where "household" has a different sedimented history.

Still, company is not quite family, at least not all of the time. The Satō factory was in fact in a peculiar and delicate position vis-à-vis its deployment. First, it was a firm with a good thirty full-time employees, a problematic size. It was somewhat too large for "familial" face-to-face interactions on a constant basis. In the old days, in fact until the 1960s, both the Satō family and their workers lived together under a single roof. Everyone took their meals together, and employers and employees alike speak of this as the *kazokuteki* or family-like, phase of the firm's history. The company was smaller then, with just a handful of artisans and two young women who worked in the shop. "Company as family" had an immediacy then it does not now possess. Owners and workers no longer live together, nor do they take their meals together. Though Satō was never really a master working alongside his apprentices, workers who have been with the company for a long time say that he used to be much more of a personal presence on the shop floor. No longer is this the case. Mr. Satō's activities with the merchants' association, his plans to expand the number of stores, and his business dealings with suppliers and customers, keep him away from the factory most of the time. He is a businessman above all. Moreover, in order to keep workers on their guard and under surveillance, he has installed cameras on the shop floor. From their offices, the owners can now view what goes on in the entire factory, if they so choose. Certainly this creates major contradictions when the Satōs invoke the "company as family" idiom in this setting of suspicion and surveillance, contradictions that will be more closely examined in the next chapter.

Other transitions and contradictions are part of the firm's history. The late seventies and early eighties were a time when Japanese identity was again becoming a source of pride, when Japan's economic success was being consolidated and traditional arts, for instance, were regaining a certain cachet among young people. When, at least sporadically and in some quarters, "Japanese" values were being celebrated, the *shachō*'s enthusiasm for the ethics retreat (the school itself founded in 1975) made historical sense. This revival and reinvention of tradition, however, collided with other important discourses, including most prominently that of so-called rational economic management. For example, the *shachō* had aspirations to expand, which he has successfully accomplished, but in order to prepare his way, he had hired a management consultant to help him streamline operations. As I found out from Hiroshi-san, however, the company and household accounts are still not completely separate, an arrangement Hiroshi-san, with his training in management science, finds "half-baked". As we shall see in more detail in the next chapter, the collision of different discourses makes for both wrenching and creative tensions.

Perhaps the embodiment of these contradictions is the spatial symbolism of the Satō factory. A startling white, in glittering contrast to the general grayness of the neighborhood, the three-story building houses Japanese confections on the first floor, Western pâtisserie and the company dining hall on the second, and the Satō residence on the third. On the one hand, the Satō residence is contiguous with the factory, and company and family are in one sense indivisible. Yet in another sense company space and family space are clearly demarcated, despite their close proximity to each other, and the *shachō* and his family occupy the highest positions in the company. Mr. Satō himself is the center and key decision maker on most counts. In that sense, there is no doubt who is most *uchi* in the company. Moreover, the building has no place for workers except as workers. Either they live in the company dormitory, a good fifteen-minute walk from the factory, or they rent their own houses or apartments.

Consequently, in many instances, there is a sharp demarcation between the *shachō* and his family on the one hand, and the employees on the other. It is a demarcation played out in spatial symbolism, the payment of wages, the accordance of respect and deference, and working conditions. It is difficult to always maintain the guise of harmonious familial relations when you have installed cameras on the shop floor to check up on your workers. In another sense, though, the "company as family" metaphor must embrace all workers at least some of the time, and the Satō family attempts to "impart the family flavor" (*kazoku no aji o tsukeru*) through a variety of institutional and informal practices. Certainly this is done with an eye toward making work life more pleasant, in accordance with accepted custom, but it is intended to promote efficiency and productivity as well. And this efficiency and productivity, though it bears some rewards for the workers, will primarily benefit the *shachō* and his family.

These contradictions animate the "company as family" discourse in the Satō company, providing ground for irony, ambiguity, and resistance. Perhaps it is because the idiom is in many ways so compelling and yet so problematic that it must be asserted and reasserted in multiple registers of experience. In the rest of the chapter, I examine the principal ways the Satōs try to add the family flavor to life at the company, and describe to what extent and at what levels their attempts can be said to work.

In Loco Parentis

The Satōs' involvement with their employees often begins with the re- cruitment process. All the younger full-time employees came to the company through personal ties, which Mr. Satō was very careful to culti- vate and exploit to their fullest. Indeed, he spent a good deal of his time traveling in the northern prefectures, where the Satō family had its roots and where relatives still farm in a village near the Japan Sea. He main- tained close ties with teachers in the area, and on occasion his networking paid off in the form of a prospective employee his teacher friends would recommend to him. Yutaka-kun, whose ambivalent rela- tionship with the firm I will later discuss, and Kon-chan, who was slightly learning impaired, were two of these. Both were likely to spend most or all of their lives as Satō employees. There were also a number of full-time male artisans who had entered on five- and six-year contracts in order to learn the trade before they returned to their own family confectioneries as successors to the business. These young men usually came to the com- pany via some mutual acquaintance—a sugar salesman, for example. Whatever their route of entry, they could be sure that Mr. Satō took time to get to know them and their families. "If there's any trouble," Satō ex- plained to me," and they want to quit and go home, I know their family situation. I can say, 'But then you'll have to deal with thus and so,' and that usually does the trick." So Satō's counsel was meant on the one hand to offer solace and advice to his employees, but it was also designed to en- sure the stability of his labor force.

A ceremonial dinner introduced new employees to the company. The appearance of a newcomer always provoked curiosity on everyone's part, and the morning after the dinner, the factory was abuzz with spec- ulation. Umezawa-san's case was especially memorable. His pompadour, reminiscent of the ducktail haircuts of the fifties, "makes him look like one of the *bōsōzoku,* motorcycle gangs," said one of the older artisans, laughing. Another commented on the white suit and black shirt Umezawa-san had chosen for his "debut". "Looks just like a gangster, doesn't he? Wonder how long this one will last." In fact, the part-timers' predictions turned out to be fairly accurate. "Less than a year," went one guess. "A few months," was another. In fact Umezawa-san stayed only a few months, dissatisfied with the long hours, the low pay, and the minimal number of holidays or vacations. Eventually he went back to his home prefecture, a few hours from Tokyo by train, to work with his brother-in-law, an auto parts dealer.

Living arrangements were also part of the company's in loco parentis care, a common feature among most of the small companies where I conducted interviews. At the Satōs, for instance, the unmarried male and female full-time employees were housed in company dormitories. While institutional-looking, the housing was no worse than the average dorm room, and had space for a set of bunk beds and the usual bedroom furnishings. Workers might spend their off hours in the large common room, watching television or playing with pinball machines, and if they got home too late to use the public baths, a large communal bath was available in the dorm. Room and board were subsidized (workers took their meals at the company lunch room, on the second floor of the factory), and cost about ¥9000 a month, approximately $45 at the contemporary exchange rate.

The Satō factory was by no means unusual in instituting these practices. A nearby factory that made cardboard boxes housed their employees in apartments they rented especially for the artisans. The doyenne of the factory was famous for her homemade noodles, which she often fed to her employees—and to the visiting foreign anthropologist.

But it was an incident at the beauty salon where I worked that showed me how seriously many owners took their *oya gawari*—in loco parentis—roles. After our end-of-the-year party at a bar in Ueno, a lively commercial district some distance away from our neighborhood, the eight of us faced the prospect of getting ourselves home in our semi-drunken state. The *sensei* hailed two taxis for us, and we clambered in. I was in the car with the chief—a divorced woman with a young child—and with two other hairdressers. "We never get a chance to talk," said the chief. "Would you like to stop for coffee?" Coming from our supervisor, it was a quasi-obligatory request, or so it seemed to me at the time, so of course we assented. After about an hour or so of party post mortem and unwinding from the raucous festivities, we went our separate ways: the chief to her apartment, I to mine, the young hairdressers to their company flats adjoining the *sensei's* house. The next day, at our morning meeting, the *sensei* was furious. "I stayed up waiting until all of you got home! If you had just thought to call . . . I worried myself sick! And besides, what is a mother of a young child doing out so late at night?" she said angrily, as she turned her wrath on the chief. "You have responsibility for the child, just like I have responsibility for these girls!" In loco parentis meant the responsibility of worrying over the whereabouts of the employees—especially in the case of women—and the corresponding responsibility, on the part of the employees, to comply with "parental" expectations.

The company also served as surrogate family in its involvement with important personal events in their employees' lives. The Satōs, for instance, kept a list of people's birthdays, including those of the part-time workers, and when the auspicious day arrived, Mr. Satō would ceremoniously present the birthday boy or girl with a gift: a handsome leather belt, for the men, and a double-stranded pearl necklace and matching pearl earrings, for the women. Gifts were much more lavish if the employee happened to come of age (twenty in Japan) while she or he was a Satō employee. At the formal New Year's party, where we stiffly sat through a multicourse Chinese banquet at a famous Tokyo hotel, the new *shakaijin* (members of society) came up on stage to receive from Mr. Satō a more generous gift: an entire new suit and a new pair of shoes for the young men, a wristwatch for the young women.

Marriage was an especially important occasion for company involvement. Like many bosses in companies of all sizes (cf., e.g., Rohlen 1974), the Satōs acted as ritual go-betweens in most of their employees' marriages.[11] In fact, by the time I started work in their factory, the Satōs had already been go-betweens for ten employees, when Mr. Satō was just in his early forties. An adult is supposed to serve in this capacity at least thrice in a lifetime, goes an old saying, but the Satōs and other employers with smaller businesses no doubt found themselves acting as go-betweens for as many as forty or fifty employees over the course of the years.

During my stint as a part-timer, I caught a glimpse of the action from the sidelines when one day an unfamiliar young man came to the factory door.

"Ah, congratulations!" exclaimed Ohara-san, the chief artisan, heartily. Other artisans—especially one of the young men who was apparently from the same home town as this stranger—and the *shachō* greeted him warmly. Through their ribald joking, it became clear that the young man was about to be married.

"Kitahara-san," whispered one of the part-timers to me. "He used to work here a few years ago, before he went back to his parents' place in Iwate. His father died last year." While he was working for the Satōs, Kitahara-san had met a local Tokyo woman, the daughter of a merchant who sold luggage and leather goods on our busy shopping street. He was in town for the *yuinō*, engagement ceremony, and the *shachō* was acting as *nakōdo*, go-between.

"It'll be rough for the *oyomesan* (bride), 'cause she was born and raised in Tokyo. Wonder how she'll manage, going out to the country with him," Itakura-san, one of the part-timers, murmured in a concerned tone.

"Oh well," sighed Nomura-san, herself raised on a farm. "It can't be helped."

"I'm jealous," laughed Ohara-san, the chief artisan. "I'd love to be young again."

The next week, on the date of the wedding, our factory was virtually deserted, as most of the artisans and the Satō family were in Iwate, in the north country, for two days of wedding celebrations.

The company can participate in the auspicious events in their employees' lives, and it can extend a consoling hand to employees and their families even in death. During the heavy, oppressively muggy Tokyo summer, one of the elderly women who looked after the company dorms suddenly and unexpectedly collapsed of a heart attack. Miyake-san had been a childless widow, bereft of relatives who might have provided her with a respectable funeral. Mr. Satō then assumed the considerable expense of giving her both a funeral and a proper cremation. "He's so *sewazuki* (helpful and kind)," said my landlady, one of his old friends from grade school. "Just like something he would do." In other circumstances, when employees did have families who would sponsor the funeral, companies usually provided flowers or a standing flower wreath (*hanawa*). And they would make sure to donate a healthy amount of incense money (*kōden*), money that Japanese and Japanese Americans give to the bereaved family in order to help defray funeral costs.

From the recruitment process through death, then, the Satō company touches the lives of its members.

So Does It Work?

The Satōs went through considerable effort and expense in order to impart the feeling of *uchi no kaisha*. In addition to their participation in employees' key life crises, they held several company outings and parties during the course of the year I spent there. The Satōs' relative prosperity enabled them to stage more of these events than most small companies in the ward could ever have dreamed of; an end-of-the-year party, perhaps held at a local drinking establishment, was about all the smaller firms could afford. We, the workers, were quite aware of these discrepancies among companies, and we knew that we were the beneficiaries of the Satōs' prosperity. In some ways, then, frequent outings promoted good relations between the Satōs and their employees. But do they really succeed in imparting the flavor of "company as family"? For whom, when, and at what level of consciousness? Are all deployments of the idiom equally successful? To sketch the outlines of an answer and to do at least minimal justice to its complexities, I invite the reader to come with me to two company events: the annual company trip, and a "potato digging" outing for the part-timers and their children. In the former, complaints and disgruntled participants seemed the order of the day; in the latter, the participants seemed pleased and grateful for their special outing. In each case, however, I hope to underscore the ambiguities, limitations, and complexities of any appropriation or deployment of meaning, showing the ironies at work in seemingly successful or unsuccessful invocations of "company as family."

The Employees' Trip: *Shain Ryokō*

Sporadically over the course of my first few months with the Satōs, I would hear tales from past company trips. So-and-so was so funny when he got drunk, or so-and-so got sick on the plane. The year before, all the employees were flown to Okinawa for what seemed from all reports to be a fun-filled four-day vacation on the beach. The young artisans pulled out photographs from the drawers in their work tables, of themselves in bathing suits, striking muscle man poses. "Why don't you take some of these home, Kondō-san," urged Yamamoto-san, the subchief in Western sweets, as he smiled broadly. "You can show everyone how handsome Japanese men are." After we all laughed and joked for a while, discussion turned to the upcoming company trip. I had missed my chance, unfortunately, to be whisked away to a sybaritic paradise, for the Satōs alternated distant trips with local ones, and this year's would be to Hakone, a hot springs resort in the mountains not far from Tokyo. My interviews at small companies turned up the name of this place with relentless regularity as the favorite site for company outings. It was nearby, perfect for the usual two-day, one-night outing, relatively inexpensive, and beautiful—so they said. At least, I thought, I would have the opportunity to investigate what went on during company trips.

On the appointed morning in the middle of June, I arrived at the factory promptly at 8:20. On my landlady's advice, I wore a summer-weight suit, when my original instincts had guided me toward more casual wear. Glancing at my co-workers, I silently thanked Hatanaka-san for her perspicacity. Though some of the men were casually dressed, all the women were turned out, in diaphanous blouses, jewelry, frills, and high heels. Clearly this was a more momentous occasion than I had bargained for.

Nor had I—or most of the others—bargained for the strenuous travel ahead of us. Forty-five minutes of fighting rush hour traffic on one of Tokyo's busiest electric train lines left us at labyrinthine Shinjuku Station, where we boarded the more comfortable and less crowded Odakyu Line. There, at least, we were able to sit and talk with each other, and I sat with voluble Ogawa-san and his "Tokyo mother," Hamada-san. He had succeeded in maintaining contact with the young high school student who was in my group at the ethics retreat, and he proceeded to tell me about the troubles that she evidently poured out to him over the phone on a nightly basis.

In the meanwhile, a great deal of drinking and bantering went on—the usual for outings like this. Ohara-san's constant companion on the trip was a small flask of whiskey, which he brought out on the train—at about 9:30 in the morning. "*Inochi no moto,*" (the source of life) he said, taking a swig and then offering the flask to his companions.

It took us a good two hours to reach Yumoto. Soon after, at Odawara, our breakfasts made it onto the train, which we all downed hungrily. This meal had to tide us over for quite awhile, for after we debarked from the train, we waited for what seemed an interminable interval for the bus to come. "Country buses!" growled the *shachō,* and many of us milled about or sat on our bags. One of the artisans showed me his mini-Walkman, which was then still something of a novelty, and I marveled at its crisp sound.

Finally the bus arrived, and we rode up the mountain on a narrow, curving highway. A small incident occurred when the bus driver accused three of our group of not paying their fares. They had simply put in their tickets as they got on the bus, instead of waiting until they got off, as was the country practice. The bus driver, angered, almost shut the door on one of the artisans, locking him in, until the *shachō* exploded and banged on the door. "*Shikkari shirō!*" (Get your act together!) the *shachō* yelled as the bus screeched down the hill.

I was surprised that we would get off the bus at this particular spot. There seemed to be nothing to speak of for miles around, except the mountain highway, pine trees, and an uncomfortably hot sun. "We have to walk," said one of the artisans. "It's a two-hour walk, down to the lake." I looked at my co-workers in amazement. Had I known this, I would hardly have worn high-heeled sandals. The other part-timers looked equally ill prepared. Still, we had no alternative but to walk along the rocky, steep "old highway" or *kyūkaidō,* where *daimyō*[12] and their retainers used to travel—except the *daimyō,* at least, probably rode in comfort in their palanquins. As we hobbled and teetered down the steep incline, hopping from rock to rock, you could hear the loud complaints. "This isn't a company trip—this is hiking!" grumbled Itakura-san, looking pained in her spike heels.

"*Gambatte*—keep going, Kondō-san! Think of it as the ethics retreat," said Akita-san, the Western sweets division chief.

"What? This is *worse* than the ethics retreat," exclaimed another artisan.

Teramura-san, one of the part-timers, declared this whole idea to be the result of the *shachō's* recent obsession with the ethics movement. "We've never had to walk this much before," she pronounced emphatically.

The parallels with the retreat were well taken, for the two-hour hike did bring to mind walking barefoot over the gravel-strewn path. Somehow, though, we managed to survive the ordeal. Congregating at a coffee house overlooking the deep cobalt blue of the lake, we ate another snack, happily quenched our thirst on the sodas and beer offered us, and allowed the pain in our throbbing feet to subside.

Our travels were not yet over, but at least the next leg of the journey was enlivened by a bit of whimsy. We boarded a pseudo-pirate ship, complete with painted statue of a (Western) pirate, and took in the sights as we enjoyed the breezes from the lake. I was especially popular as people's worst exhibitionistic tendencies surfaced in the face of my camera, which left me little time to do anything but snap photographs. The trip across the lake was all too short. From there, we transferred to the ropeway up the mountain. A group of young artisans wanted their pictures taken with the mountains as background, so I went with them in the small, precariously swinging gondola car. We complained of the humidity and the heat, of how cramped the little cars were, of how exhausted we felt. "The *shachō,* inside (*naishin wa*), is probably really thinking how tired he is, and what a mistake it was to walk that far," Suzuki-san opined. The time we didn't spend complaining was directed toward speculation on the depth of the ravine below us, and what our chances of survival might be if our gondola took the plunge. I was relieved, to put it mildly, when we reached solid ground.

From this point near the mountain top, we had to board a rail car to our final destination. If we expected succor and rest, we were again disappointed, for we mistakenly got off at the wrong stop—meaning that we had to climb uphill for some undetermined distance in order to reach the inn. I was beginning to feel as though this were a Japanese version of Pilgrim's Progress, and we were now in the Slough of Despond. A good four hours had elapsed since our lakeside luncheon, and by this time tempers were short indeed. My co-workers hurled accusations at each other, vying to blame others for the mistake. People argued sporadically about where exactly this inn might be. After trudging up the hill for a couple of miles, we eventually found it: the Emerald Club, which by this time looked like Paradise.

We had an hour or so to rest and to dress for dinner. The rigors of the journey soon became a mere memory, as people soaked blissfully in the hot springs baths or, in the case of my roomates, the young women who worked full-time in the shop, spent the better part of the hour painstakingly reapplying their makeup. Identically clad in our *yukata,* summer robes provided by the inn, we made our way downstairs to the dining room. There we found a sumptuous banquet laid out before us: beautifully arranged combinations of vinegared vegetables, cracked crab, and the freshest seasonal fish. The only open seats were next to some men I had never seen before. "Am I at the wrong table?" I thought for a moment. But during the introductions, the man seated next to me was called the "vice-president of the Satō firm," and in fact he turned out to be the company electrician and Satō-san's best friend. (Later in the summer, I ended up going on *his* company's company trip, which Satō-san was instrumental in organizing.) He and Satō had gone to the ethics retreat together. This man, Matsuda-san, won me over when he asked whether I was from Iwate-prefecture, since so many of the Satō employees seemed to come from there. It was great fun to see him register complete shock when I told him I was American.

As soon as all of us took our seats, the festivities began. Like most *en-*

kai, parties of this kind, the idea was to create a feeling of intimacy by having us participate in entertaining each other. The new members of the company, for instance, were enjoined to sing a song. Then, as was the custom in the company, Mr. Satō held a drawing, and everyone was guaranteed to win a little prize of some kind. At a summer "beer garden" party, I had won a tube of medicine for athlete's foot, but this time, I had better luck: a split of champagne. Instead of singing, which was the normal mode of performance expected at parties, the *shachō* did magic tricks, a talent he had cultivated in place of singing. ("I'm completely tone-deaf," he confided to me one day.) Those who enjoyed singing, sang. And we played games where everyone had to get involved, successfully creating a feeling of togetherness and mutual participation. The party broke up on this note of *shitashimi,* intimacy. The *shachō* announced that there would be a continuation of the party in Room 510— *mah-jongg,* most likely—primarily a lure for the *shachō* and his friends.

With my roommates, I went downstairs again, to find most of the younger artisans playing video games. A jukebox occupied one corner of the room, and the young men found music to their liking, songs from "Saturday Night Fever." We all danced merrily for quite some time, until the heat and humidity forced us to stop. Around eleven, the downstairs crew decided either to retire or to go up and play *mah-jongg.* I had had enough excitement and went up to our room. On the way, we met Hamada-san and Teramura-san coming from the baths. "This is our third time since we got here," they confessed, smiling. As we retired, I found myself to be the only one who chose to sleep on the bed; the rest of the people were on the floor in their *futon.* "On a bed, I'm always afraid I'll fall off," murmured Sugawara-san before we dozed off.

The next morning, we actually had some time for sightseeing. We quickly toured a local museum and then took a train to the famous sculpture gardens, where we strolled about in leisurely fashion. Grumbling broke out when we discovered that we were supposed to walk several miles more, uphill all the way, to a restaurant on a hilltop. "This is *really* a hiking trip. Good thing that Sakada-san didn't come, with her high blood pressure and her varicose veins," said Iida-san in exasperation.

Perhaps our exercise made lunch—vegetables and meat grilled on racks in the middle of the table—seemed especially delicious. This was also our chance to buy *omiyage,* souvenirs, for the people back home. To my astonishment, the part-timers accumulated armloads of gifts. "For my neighbors. They buy for us, "explained Itakura-san, who had just shelled out tens of thousands of yen. "Besides, it's just a little something to express your feeling." Thus laden with *omiyage,* we took a bus and a taxi back to the station, and waited for what seemed to be an eternity for the train back to Tokyo. The heat, the walking, the late night revelry, had apparently taken their toll. *"Egao wa nai, ne"* (No smiling faces), commented the usually irrepressible Ogawa-san, himself looking fatigued and a bit glum.

We arrived, finally, back at the company, where Ohara-san and the *shachō* offered us some closing words, telling us how enjoyable they had found the trip, and thanking us for our efforts (*gokurōsama*). Managers and workers bowed to each other, and then we finally disbanded.

I realized in retrospect that somehow I had expected a marked change in people's openness to one another as a result of the trip. The following morning and in the weeks and months to come, I was to be sorely disappointed, for no such dramatic transformation occurred. The next day, if anything, was full of tension and minor irritation, for we had to restock the shop completely with fresh goods while we were still tired from our hectic travels. Conversations and tempers were especially short. Had I been Mr. Satō, I am not all at certain that I would have been satisfied with the results of this "gesture of beneficence," for the results of the trip were mixed at best, neither an unmitigated success nor a complete failure. Workers complained vociferously about the hiking, in particular. Yet most people seemed to enjoy certain moments: the participatory game-playing in the company party, the lavish banquet, the pleasures of the hot springs baths, the dancing. Teramura-san perhaps said it best when she came into the factory the morning after, groaning and complaining about how sore her leg muscles were, and grumbling that it had been ridiculous to be forced to hike so far. *"De mo, tanoshikatta,"* she said to me. (It was still fun.) At the very least, it was a chance to get away from everyday routine to a pleasant setting for a day or two.

It is important to underscore the ambivalence involved, however. Most of the complaints tended to center around the excessive walking we had done, declaring that it hadn't been a proper company trip, but hiking— i.e., some other genre of outing. The part-timers, for instance, compared this year's marathon walks to the pleasures of last year's fun in the sun on the Okinawan beaches. The underlying assumption was that the *shachō* had not adequately considered the employees' desires; he had not adequately cared for them. For the *shachō,* it was hardly an ideal return on his investment in familial care. Oddly, however, despite the lukewarm or at least erratic enthusiasm most participants exhibited for our Hakone excursion, the trip could not be labeled a failure at another level. For the complaints about the trip stayed completely within, and reproduced the legitimacy of, the idiom of "company as family." As we shall see more strikingly in the next chapter, workers often criticized the *shachō* for being *inadequately* familial.

The company trip, that staple of work life in all except the smallest companies, enacted many of the ambivalences and ironies in the Satōs attempts to add the family floor. But even in the most seemingly successful enactments of familial benefits and outings, other tensions and ambivalences come into play. For no mode of discourse can be all encompassing, and idioms are taken up quite differently by different people.

Potato Digging

At five minutes to seven in the morning, I walked up to the entrance of the factory. Already a large group—mostly women and children—was milling about in desultory fashion, more people arriving with each passing minute. Mr. Satō was in fine form, joking with the children, and he began to call roll, passing out a cloth sack to each youngster. Of the fifty or so people, the only ones I recognized were Mrs. Akita, wife of the *yōgashi* chief, one of the new part-timers in *yōgashi,* and Mrs. Matsuda, whose husband was the electrician who was Mr. Satō's best friend. Yasuko-chan, Satō's nine-year-old daughter and the next-to-youngest in the family, eventually came out to join us as we were about to leave. Today the part-timers and their young children at the Satō company were bound on a potato digging trip to the country.

We boarded a large, luxurious tour bus, complete with plush seats, public address system, and a young, uniformed, white-gloved guide. Two microphones gave both the guide and the guests a chance to sing, tell riddles, or otherwise provide entertainment on the hour-and-a-half drive to the country. Mr. Satō began with introductions. The sea of unknown women's and children's faces began to acquire names and identities. Many turned out to be suppliers and service people associated with the firm. The fruit seller was there; so were the wife and children of the printer who printed designs on the elaborate boxes we used to package our sweets. The woman sitting next to me with her young daughter was a former employee whose family company now catered the lunches for the Satō company dining hall. Most important, Mr. and Mrs. Matsuda, the electricians, and their employees were out in full force, for we were bound to Mr. Matsuda's relatives' farm for our expedition.

After an hour and a half of conversation with Mori-san, the *bentō* (lunchbox) caterer, who looked back with nostalgia on her days as a worker in the Satō shop, and halfway listening to the seemingly endless stream of groan-eliciting riddles Mr. Satō or the guide would tell, I was glad when we pulled up to a large hall, where townspeople held their formal meetings and gatherings. A one-kilometer walk led us to the potato and *daikon* (giant radish) fields. Bearing our sacks and putting on gardeners' gloves, we descended on three rows of *sato imo*, the round, white potato with a delicately flavored, slightly viscous flesh. We cleared the dirt away from the roots with our gloved hands, and then, to the children's delight, the clusters of potatoes and then the long, tubular *daikon* yielded easily, enabling the youngsters to pull the roots from the earth. They shouted and laughed as we stuffed our sacks with booty and loaded the vegetables onto a small station wagon. In the time remaining before lunch, Satō-san organized foot races. He seemed to thoroughly enjoy playing with the children, joking and teasing one or another—lifting up Masanori-kun, the young son of one of the part-timers, and then pretending to bury him in the ground, throwing the smaller ones into the air as they squealed in delight and excitement.

Eventually, all of us set out on foot to return to the village hall, where we were served the local specialty: hand-cut noodles, made from scratch. We then walked to a local shrine for a performance of *okagura,* the sacred dance of the gods, an unusual treat. Townspeople spread out mats for us, and we passed around *musubi,* rice balls, and shared cups of *sake*. People watched, munched, joked, laughed, and generally seemed to enjoy the proceedings until we were summoned back to the bus at three in the afternoon.

The bus ride home had none of the formal stiffness that had made the constant patter from the guide and from the *shachō* so necessary during the morning. A day's outing together had dissipated the feelings of unfamiliarity among us, and I ended up chatting animatedly with the people sitting near me. As was customary at most Satō outings, there was a drawing for prizes. The best one, a stuffed toy in the form of a monkey with velcro hands, who "wouldn't fall" (called *ochinai kun,* the guy who won't fall), went to nine-year-old Masanori, son of Maebara-san, one of the part-timers who worked in the shop, who seized upon it with great glee, pushing his sister away when she tried to touch it. Her tears brought reproaches from Maebara-san, who told Masanori that he wasn't acting like an older brother or "like a man". Eventually, these remonstrations took effect, and he maganimously allowed his sister to play with the toy.

Having at least temporarily resolved this mini-crisis, Maebara-san and another part-timer from the shop turned their attention to me, engaging me in conversation about my research and obligingly answering my queries. Both had been with the Satōs for about half a year. Maebara-san called her work *tanoshii,* pleasant, fun. "The people are nice," added Teramura-san. "Most companies don't do this sort of thing—you know, trips and all—for their part-timers." "In fact," Maebara-san laughed, "my father-in-law says that this job sounds like heaven, we're treated so well." Both women commented that it was unusual for part-timers to be included in company outings at all, much less outings of such relatively lavish proportions, designed especially for them.

The bus finally pulled up in front of the shop, disgorging us with our bulging sacks of vegetables: tired, but, judging from most people's reactions, pleasantly so. A pleasant end to a pleasant outing.

The potato-digging trip provides us with one example of a relatively effective deployment of company as family, which is nonetheless riddled with ambiguities. On one level, and for a number of participants, it was a highly effective exercise. Indeed, one could argue that for the Satōs, it was a brilliant stroke on many levels. First, it redounded to their credit as *sewazuki*—helpful, caring—employers, in the eyes of a larger community. Almost no other firm in our neighborhood offered, or could afford to offer, such benefits to its part-timers, and employees like Maebara-san and Teramura-san were seemingly grateful. Second, there was about it an element of conspicuous consumption—not only were the Satōs *sewazuki,* they were prosperous enough to be. Third, it enabled the Satōs to maximize, reinforce, and draw upon their enterprise networks. The former employees who were now suppliers, the present-day suppliers, and the Matsudas—the friend/supplier who arranged the trip—were all, now, drawn more deeply into relations of reciprocity with the Satōs, through their participation in this trip. Finally, the outing did seem to have a positive impact on the employees' morale, to judge from the talks I had with the part-timers and with other women. They did indeed seem to feel lucky to be working at the Satōs'—though of course, in their conversations with me, whom they did not yet know well and who was associated in their minds with the *shachō,* they could hardly be expected to express their complaints.

The introduction of the interactive context of these utterances leads us to ask about the larger effectiveness of this discursive strategy. As in any deployment of power, fissures and cleavages are inevitable, and the reach of the "company as family" notion, at least as enacted in this example, was limited to the part-timers from the shop. My co-workers in the factory maintained a humorously critical distance from the whole affair. Some of the older women were from rural backgrounds, and for them potato digging was of limited interest. "What? I did plenty of that when I was growing up on the farm," said Nomura-san. "Potato digging!" said another. "I'd rather stay right here in the factory." These sentiments, combined with a sense of obligation to their co-workers during a busy season, prevented them from going, and helped them maintain the distance which erupted in their snorts of scorn and ironic humor. Still, even these women would be forced to admit that most companies in our ward of Tokyo could not begin to offer such benefits to its employees. The irony is mixed with a certain grudging acknowledgement of the Satōs' efforts, at any rate, to do well by their employees. So, for all concerned, meanings are shaded by ambivalence. Even a seemingly successful trip like the potato-digging expedition could be successful only to limited degrees, and for certain people. The Satōs, who gained most from the success of the trip, also gained (unbeknownst to them) the scorn of some of their employees. And those employees who criticized the Satōs for this creative appropriation of "company as family," had to give them credit for at least trying. "Company as family", then, is deployed in a variety of ways vis-à-vis workers in the Satō factory, and it is riddled with contradictions and ambivalences, even as it remains a powerful and compelling metaphor.

The Company Networks: *Yoso*

I have already mentioned two occasions when I was befuddled by unfamiliar faces at Satō company gatherings, faces which eventually turned out to belong to former employees and/or to suppliers of the company. On the company trip, there was a whole coterie of such men; on the trip to dig potatoes, I met Mori-san, who catered the lunches for the company. She had talked on for over an hour about her life at the Satōs, in the days when it was really *kazokuteki,* like family. The employees had lived on the second floor over the shop, and so did the young Mr. and Mrs. Satō, who had only recently taken charge of company operations. Everyone took meals together, and Mrs. Satō, Mori-san, and another co-worker took turns preparing meals. At that point, the present shop manager, Mr. Satōs nephew, was still in grade school. "In those days," Mori-san said, "it was hard work, but it was fun in its own way. Nowadays, things are easier, but then, working gave you better preparation for running a household. We learned how to cook and clean, since we had to make meals for everyone and do all the cleaning in the shop after work was over." From working in the Satō factory, Mori-san had "gone as a bride," as the saying goes, to a household that made prepared lunches. When we look at the Satō company and its relations with other firms, familial metaphors again come into play, as social, familial, and economic strands intertwine.

But it was at the annual New Year's celebration when the importance of the company and its networks—business ties cast in a social and familial idiom—crystallized for me. Attired in our fashionable best, we were treated to a lavish banquet in a fine hotel. What astonished me, however, is how few people I knew in the crowd of over 100. Aside from my co-workers, there was only a scattering of familiar faces: the egg salesman, the boxmaker, of course Matsuda-san the electrician, and the presidents of the local merchant association and the ward Rotary Club. My anthropological curiosity piqued, I made inquiries about the identities of the others, who turned out to be other merchants, customers, suppliers, or former employees of the Satō company. Often, as in the case of Mori-san, these categories overlapped. It was clear that these events were designed to add the family flavor in yet another register: that of *uchi* and *yoso,* inside and outside, the company and its networks.

Like the household, the company is inextricable from its relations with other firms. This is true in terms of a company's positioning—size, market share, capital—vis-à-vis firms in the same industry, what Clark (1979) terms "the society of industry." But it is especially clear that for the Satō company and its business universe, social/familial idioms create the matrix within which so-called economic links are forged.

Perhaps the most striking example of this enactment of social/familial idioms was the active involvement of suppliers in the life of Satō Shoten. The Satō firm loomed large for them, as an important customer, but the weight of history was also a key factor. All had been associated with Satō for at least the beginning years of Mr. Satō's tenure as head of the company. Many had been suppliers since Mr. Satō's grandfather's generation—i.e., since the firm had been founded. Indeed, the suppliers—including the boxmaker, the electrician, the sugar supplier, the egg and dairy man, the printer, and the maker of liners for the metal trays we used in the factory—formed their own "club" around Satō Shōten, which they dubbed the Satō-kai, the Satō Club. They would hold meetings sporadically, and once a year, they traveled together in their version of a company trip. As I have already described, the suppliers were compelled to participate in a number of company activities, including the trip to Hakone and the potato-digging expedition.

A summer "beer garden" party held on the roof of the Satō's factory, complete with huge kegs of draught beer and a meal of summer delicacies, showed me both the pleasurable and the obligatory, coercive aspects of such a relationship. The Satōs gave the party in honor of record summer sales. The cool weather meant that more people would eat baked goods than might ordinarily be the case; this, coupled with the managing and marketing strategies of the new shop manager, Hiroshi-san, was credited with the unprecedented success: sales of ¥8,000,000 ($40,000) during the Obon¹³ season alone. After these announcements, the suppliers stood up and congratulated the company on their successes, and then the singing commenced. Many of the suppliers were gifted singers. I remember vividly the man who owned the printing shop, for his earnest attempt to give a stirring rendition of a sentimental folk ballad, despite his evident nervousness. My landlady, who sat next to me at the festivities, whispered to me, "Some of the Satō-kai members have taken singing lessons for years. Probably they all rehearse lots of *min'yō* (folk songs) just for parties like this." The suppliers, then, were *obligated* to make merry and to be at their entertaining best.

Ritual obligations assume other forms which are equally important aspects of maintaining social and economic ties among firms. During the New Year, for example, the suppliers go from customer to customer to offer their New Year's greetings, bearing small New Year's gifts (*nenga*): often a towel or handkerchiefs with the company name and logo. Ochūgen and Oseibō, the middle- and end-of-the-year gift-giving seasons, constitute other occasions for taking care of social and business ties. Suppliers—or, in the case of a large corporation, the subordinates of a particular boss—will give presents to their "superiors". Practical items like soap, salad oil, soy sauce, and *sake* are popular, and people often receive too much for even a sizeable family to use in a reasonable period of time. The Satōs had a brilliant idea when they recycled their gifts during the annual New Year's party, giving their Oseibō presents away during the customary drawing. "Please excuse us for doing this," the *shachō* announced. "If you get the same gift you gave us, please don't be offended."

193

A final way the suppliers cultivated their social/business relations with customers was to give them *omiyage,* the souvenirs people buy for friends, relatives, and people at work. The force of obligations and the need to cast them in this particular idiom takes on powerful immediacy and meaning when you have seen a man—in this case, Mr. Sakamoto, who owned a construction firm—just returned from a pilgrimage, driving madly to several houses to deliver *omiyage* to people who had "been of help to our business." In fact, for Mr. Sakamoto and for suppliers of the Satō company, economic success was closely tied to their relationships with their major "parent" or client firms. Thus, their livelihoods were heavily dependent on the quality of those relationships, and so singing lessons, obligatory merriment, gift-giving, and company outings were in some ways as important as quality control and other more clearly economic activities. Business relationships must be cast in a quasi-familial,[14] social idiom.

The Merchants' Association

Relationships among firms also took place in other arenas, where the companies are not linked by any direct economic transaction. The merchants' association, those people who owned businesses in the main commercial district of my neighborhood, also espoused an explicitly social/familial ethos in their group.

The merchants' association was, nonetheless, centered primarily around issues of common economic concern. Several committees divided key tasks and responsibilities, including advertising, financing, and planning special events. Headship of the committees and the presidency of the association rotated among the various business people (most of them were men; the *sensei* of the beauty salon where I worked was, as far as I know, the only woman in the association). Members discussed matters of common interest at association meetings; for example, the association designated Tuesdays as the official "day of rest" on the street. Sometimes meetings were used to disseminate information about management practices. Perhaps most important, it served as a lobby for the merchants' interests; most recently, for example, the merchants banded together to prevent a large department store from moving into the area.

Special events and outings are also part of the merchants' association and its work. They plan street-wide sales events two or three times yearly, and once a year, there is a festive, all-day celebration, with extensive half-price sales, a sizeable parade—in which the merchants march, wearing summer kimono bearing the logo of their association—and musical concerts, with Japanese folk music, the juicily sentimental *enka*,[15] and rock bands for the young people. The merchants sponsor a singing contest and donate prizes for the winner. Moreover, like many groups in Japan, including companies, the merchants hold end-of-the-year parties and plan joint excursions, including one overnight trip during the summer (often, as it happens, to Hakone), and occasional expeditions to the theater, which I would hear about in detail when the merchants' wives came into the beauty salon where I worked.

The association also mobilizes support for its members, should one of them fall ill or die. The owner of the local tea store went into the hospital for brain surgery, and the other merchants were sure to visit him, bearing gifts and their good wishes for his recovery. Mr. Satō actually made an announcement in the factory, asking those who had known the stricken fellow to accompany the Satōs to the hospital that day. "I'll give you the time off with pay," he told us. And a few people—the older artisans, mostly—did in fact go. A death among the association members elicits similar forms of support. The association donates the flower wreaths, makes the ritual monetary contributions to the family, and provides assistance in preparing food, acting as receptionists for the funeral (the amount of *kōden,* incense money, is recorded in a notebook, so that the family can reciprocate appropriately), and so on.[16] Membership in such a group, then, should involve active participation and responsibility, from planning and executing the various outings, sales, and special events, to attending meetings, to walking from store to store to consult or ask for donations. The reward, in the end, is that one should be able to count on the support of the group.

When I talked with merchants about the association, their language always stressed harmonious cooperation, warmth, and familylike support. The *shachō,* who was a major force in the organization, would expatiate on the "Shitamachi spirit" that animated the organization. The attitude, he said, was to *te o tsunaide, ikite iku,* to join hands and more forward in life, a vision of solidarity and communal warmth.

Those who chose not to participate in these organizations, however, revealed the limitations of this utopian image. Two persons in particular were a source of irritation. One shopowner was acknowledged by all concerned to be egocentric and downright unpleasant in his dealings with others. He had nothing to do with the other merchants, and they returned his lack of regard, speaking of him in the most derogatory terms as someone who "can't understand the importance of human relationships." They pronounced him selfish, one of the most damning comments one could utter in that context—indeed, in most contexts in Japan. A second deviant case was a man who, though ostensibly an active participant in the organization, somehow *never* managed to do his share of the work. When association members came to call, his wife would always tell them that he was busy with customers. "But when you ask him to play golf," said one merchant sarcastically," he's never too busy." As far as I knew, the disapproval of others remained on the level of indirectly expressed complaints, and it would be my educated guess that the association members would be willing to tolerate considerable deviance from their ideals of warmth and participation—but that once the limits were reached, retribution would be swift and thorough, a kind of *mura hachibu,* or total exclusion from the association and its resources.

Patron and Client, Parent and Child

Business and social relationships echoed one another in other contexts as well. For Mr. Satō, his contacts with mentors—parent figures—at the Rotary Club were an important aspect of his business and social life; he in turn adopted this role vis-à-vis other merchants.

Membership in the Rotary Club in this ward of Tokyo was an index of a company's commercial prosperity. Satō often spoke about how his membership in Rotary and his contact with other Rotarians had helped him. It was at their suggestion, for instance, that he had decided to hire a management consultant to help him maximize his profits. It was also via another Rotary member that Satō first heard about the ethics retreat, and its fame spread quickly through the group. And without Rotary, Satō never would have become such a believer in geomancy, Chinese directional divination, which he consulted before any important business decision. For example, he made sure to choose the most auspicious day for his ground-breaking ceremony and for the opening of the new factory, and more than once he invoked geomancy and astrology to talk to me about his children's future, expressing his concern, for example, that his eldest daughter not marry too young, because her stars guaranteed that if she married before age 25, she would have to marry again.[17] Links with Rotarians, then, provided the Satō company with pathways to various sorts of knowledge, and lifted the company from its immediate local context, drawing the Satōs into larger networks at the ward level.

Mr. Satō also adopted the role of patron/parent toward other merchants in the neighborhood. Certainly he had a profound impact on

Matsuda, the electrician, bringing Matsuda with him to the ethics retreat and helping plan the Matsudas' first company trip. But perhaps the most obvious example was Satō's relationship with Nakagawa-san, who ran a *sushi* restaurant around the corner from the confectionery. Satō had gone to the opening of the shop and was dismayed at the service and quality of the food. "Listen, you," he reportedly told Nakagawa-san, "I'm going to come back one more time. And if the *sushi* isn't fresher and the service a little snappier, I'm *never* coming back." Nakagawa-san, smarting at these remarks, was happy to place himself under Satō-san's tutelage. Now, several years later, the Nakagawa *sushiya* is prospering, and during all my visits, it served up delicious *sushi* in a simply designed, aesthetically pleasing shop—and the service was informal and attentive. In fact, for my going-away party, Mr. Satō hired out the place and brought me and some of his closest friends—people who had known each other from grade school—to the *sushiya* for a late-night feast. As he deftly shaped the fingers of rice and topped them with the freshest raw fish, Nakagawa-san regaled me with tales of his ineptitude at business dealings before his encounters with his mentor. The Satōs, then, created and recreated parent/child, tutor/tutee relationships of care and obligation in their relationships with other firms.

The Familial Idiom

Tracing out the contested, various, and ambiguous relationship of adding the family flavor to company life in the Satō confectionery leads us, finally, to consider the implications for the deployments of meaning within particular cultural and historical matrices. The meanings of company and family have been sites of important historical struggles over meaning, where larger changes in political economy, especially the growth of capitalism; the forging of a "Japanese" identity in the face of Western expansionism; attempts to reinvent tradition and secure the hegemony of a samurai class; and the outcome of World War II and the Western-style constitution imposed by the Occupation forces, all circumscribe and create the cultural and historical horizons within which company and family can be constituted in the present moment in the Satō company. Within this larger setting, the Satōs attempt to add the family flavor to life in the company, by providing certain benefits and sponsoring special events which, they hope, will promote loyal service to the firm. Familial idioms, and the resonance of company with household networks, also shape relationships with other firms, including suppliers; within the merchants' association; and in patron/client relationships among individual merchants.

The situation of Satō Shōten points toward larger lessons about Japanese firms, however. Though a firm in a contemporary capitalist economy cannot remain unaware of profit, money, and capital, and still remain in business, the cultural and historical matrices of meaning—for example, notions of work as participation and service to a larger group—and the specific situation of the Satō company as a family firm, highlight the salience of the "company as family" idiom. In their world, economic ties, narrowly defined, could never begin to encompass the richness and layers of meaning that animate work life for the Satōs, their employees, their suppliers, and other companies who form part of their network. Economic ties, for them, are far more than merely contractual, entailing intense involvement in group outings, ritual obligations, and strong bonds of loyalty, gratitude, and commitment. Company is economic enterprise, a center of belonging and attachment, and a zero-point from which the Satōs can enter into relationships with other companies. In these ways, company and family are readily exchangeable templates for one another.

Yet, in company as in family, the assertions of solidarity and warmth are in each case inseparable from the jural, disciplinary, and obligatory strands in this discourse. Contradictions and tensions arise as discourses of harmony and care clash or intertwine with other available discourses, such as that of rational economic management. In the face of this multiplicity of available discourses, within a particular historical and cultural matrix, the Satōs *assert* and enact "company as family." Inevitably, these rhetorical assertions are incompletely realized, riddled with tensions and contradictions. Those tensions and contradictions are even more clearly visible when we take up these topics from the points of view of the workers in the Satō factory, and ask how the strategic deployments of the "company as family" idiom are taken up or resisted on the shop floor.

6   *Company as Family?*

After a day off, I returned to the Satō factory and entered a room already alive with activity. Ohara-san, the chief artisan, sent me to help Hamada-san, one of the other female part-time workers (*pāto*) with preparing *an-mitsu,* a combination of fruit, bean paste, gelatin cubes, and honey. We were expected to make hundreds of these and other sweets today, as part of the half-price sale the owner, Satō-san, was offering the public. In the midst of cutting gelatin cubes, I queried, "Are they doing a special sale for us, too?"

"Oh, well, yesterday," said Hamada-san conspiratorially, "the *shachō*[1] brought down some *leftovers* of the new products, like sour cherry tarts. They were *mechakucha*—a mess! Then the *shachō* offered to sell this '2000 yen value' for only 500 yen. Not *one* of us bought any. After all, they were all turned over and broken up. Who would want anything like that?"

By this time Nomura-san had joined us, and she was equally vehement. "What we want is something you can give as a gift, something that will keep! Western sweets aren't even pretty in boxes, and they spoil right away, especially in the summer. All we can do is take them home to eat, and who can eat that much?"

"I'll bet there's no sale for the employees. There are things you want and things you don't want, and even if those tarts were free, I wouldn't take any!"

My co-workers' agitated faces, their frowns, and the fierce tones of justified anger in their voices, were unforgettable.

The memory of this incident set the tone for the entire day, and provoked heated discussions of working conditions. Ohara-san, the chief artisan, brought up the case of Itō-san, a young man who had recently quit the Satōs to take a job in a factory subcontracting to Mitsubishi Heavy Industry. "It must be like going from hell to heaven," he observed. Itakura-san, a woman in her fifties and the oldest part-timer, expanded on Ohara-san's remark, explaining to me how Itō can now wake up at 8:00, since he lives close to work. At the Satō factory, in contrast, workers

199

who wanted breakfast had to arrive at 7:00 A.M. for a 7:30 starting time. At Itō's new, cushy job, the work week is limited to five days, overtime is never more than two hours a day, and workers get double pay if they have to work on holidays. All this was unheard of in the Satō factory, where people worked six days a week, and overtime regularly surpassed two hours a day.

The conversation turned to wages, and Itakura-san told me that at the Satō factory, all the *erai* (great) people, the company officers, received no overtime pay.[2] She pointed out that all the artisans kept impressively long hours: even during the slack seasons they worked from 7:30 in the morning until 6:00 or 7:00 at night. "People talk about how hard the Japanese work," the part-timers laughed, "but Ohara-san is a special case. He works about twice the hours of the average person—sometimes even three times the hours—look at the month of March! The artisans work until midnight and get up at two in the morning."

"Plus, no matter how long I work," Ohara-san lamented, "the money is the same. And since the 'officers' have to pay for their own meals, it seems like any extra money goes to food." Screwing up his face, he said he had once refused to become "chief of the factory" (*Ichido kotowatta n da yo, ne*). But somehow, before he knew it (*itsu no ma ni ka*), there he was, a company officer who could no longer receive overtime pay.

"Maybe," I ventured, "it would be better to do without some of the things like company trips and have the *shachō* raise salaries," an opinion I had heard from some workers in other companies.

"Are you kidding?" said Nomura-san with great vehemence. "Every company in Japan has a company trip. A company trip is only natural (*tōzen*). They have to give us at least that much."

Itakura-san, spurred on by the chief artisan's plaintive narrative, launched into a philippic against the company, the structure of Japanese society, and the corruption of Japanese politicians. She began with the heated observation, "Kondō-san, your mother and father are Japanese, but a 'pure' American would never understand what Ohara-san is saying. America is a free country, where you can cry if you feel like crying, laugh if you're happy. But Japan's different. Ohara-san is quiet and gentle, and he's so long-suffering (*shinbō ga ii*) that he just takes it."

Another part-timer chimed in. "The factory can't get along without Ohara-san."

"Oh no," he demurred modestly, "everyone can manage just fine."

"But look, nobody can do the special orders except for Ohara-san. And still he's like a slave, to put it mildly."

200

Company as Family?

Itakura-san was becoming more and more vituperative in her condemnations of the *shachō*. "One of these days, I'm just going to explode, and tell him there are lots of confectioneries in Tokyo, and he'd damn well better watch it. If any inspectors come by, I can tell them about all the violations of the Labor Standards Law—like using kids under eighteen to do all those hours of overtime!"

The part-timers turned their attention from the *shachō* to politics.

"What we need are men like the Meiji politicians. They were selfless; they thought about the welfare of the whole country. The LDP[3] is no good; they're just for the big companies. In Japan, there's too much of a difference between the big companies and the small ones. The big companies are in fine shape; they can give their people lots of vacations, lots of bonuses, lots of benefits. And here we are."

"You know," said Itakura-san, "I was talking to a guy who'd worked here a few years ago. He said that it *used* to be like family here (*kazokuteki*), but then the *shachō* hired a management consultant who charged huge fees, and now the *shachō* just does as he's told. The consultant doesn't think about the workers; all he thinks about are profits! Money is a dirty thing, isn't it (*Okane wa kitanai mon da, ne*). Now, I don't think the *shachō* is a bad person— everybody has good and bad points—but sometimes he's really nice, and sometimes he's dishonest (*zurui*)."

"What about a union?" I asked.

Laughing, Itakura-san replied, "We'd probably get fired. There's only one president around here!" (*Daitōryō wa hitori da kara.*)

Finally, the conversation returned to its starting point, the half-price sale.

"It was so hilarious yesterday! You should have seen the *shachō*'s face! He couldn't believe we didn't want to buy anything."

The part-timers then began to seek creative solutions. "What would happen," said Nomura-san, "if one day we all decided not to come to work?"

"The factory couldn't get along without us," replied another part-timer.

Hamada-san conceived a plan that included a prominent role for the foreign researcher. "Kondō-san, maybe *you* should ask the *shachō* when he'll have a half-price sale for us. I wonder what he'd say then."

"Maybe he'd sell the sweets to you half-price, we could all give you our orders, and then we could come to pick them up at your landlady's place. You'd be the most popular girl in town."

201

"If he says he's not going to sell anything to you half-price, then you can tell him, 'Well, then I'll just go someplace else.' "

We were all convulsed in laughter by this time, and I was seriously mulling over the idea of carrying out their plan—but, given the situation, I felt I could hardly jeopardize my relations with the *shachō* after all his generosity to me. Even more important was my relationship with my landlady, a good friend and exemplary informant, who had provided me with the introductions to the firm. Creating trouble in the factory would have called her reputation into question as my guarantor. Nonetheless, in retrospect I wish I had, feigning innocence, asked the *shachō* about the sale. But familial expectations of loyalty in return for benevolence seemed to work vis-à-vis foreign researchers as well as native Japanese—at least in this instance.

Uchi No Kaisha: Contested Meanings

Thus far, I have treated the discourse on *uchi no kaisha*—our company—at the Satō factory in terms of management's ambivalent and incomplete attempts to add the family flavor. In this chapter we see things from the workers' perspectives. Not only do different actors appropriate the notion of company as family differently, they do so differently in different contexts and for disparate political ends. By paying careful attention, then, to the ways the boundaries of *uchi no kaisha* are drawn, we can see how workers can give a particular spin to the meanings of such an idiom, wresting it from the *shachō* and turning it to their advantage, yet creating ironies and contradictions for themselves in so doing. The discourse on *uchi no kaisha* also interwines and sometimes strains against other significant idioms and metaphors animating work life in the factory, and the clash of discourses often creates tension and contradiction. Certainly, different idioms are used to various purposes and are invoked—most centrally for this inquiry—in order to draw and redraw the boundaries of *uchi.* How *uchi* and *soto* are defined, who is placed in relatively *uchi* or *soto* contexts, and when and how people struggle over those decisions, are thus key questions we must ask when we look at life in the Satō company. Workers' identifications with the company are also mediated by the *uchi/soto* idiom, but these identifications are contextually asserted and shaded by ambivalence. These complexities should, in the end, call into question a schema of "hegemony" countered by "authentic resistance," instead drawing attention to the multiplicities, open-endedness, and contradictions that inevitably accompany the craft-

Company as Family?

ing of identities and lives within a matrix of power and meaning. This should further underline the point that hegemonies are never simply put in place, but are always contested and therefore must always be reasserted. And neither "hegemony" nor "resistance" is a simple, unproblematic category; both are alive with changing, multiple meanings and subverted by unintended consequences.

Company As Family in the Satō Factory

In any family firm which hires "outside" employees, the notion of *uchi no kaisha* is of necessity fluid and ambiguous. In the Satō company, these ambiguities are readily apparent. Satō and his family occupy the highest positions in the company, and Mr. Satō himself is the center and key decision-maker on most counts. In that sense, there is no doubt who is most *uchi* in the company. In many instances, there is a sharp demarcation between the *shachō* and his family, and the employees, a demarcation played out in spatial symbolism, in the payment of wages, in the according of respect and deference, and in working conditions. It is difficult always to maintain the guise of harmonious familial relations when, for example, you have installed cameras on the shop floor to check up on your workers. In another sense, though, the "company as family" metaphor must embrace all workers at least *some* of the time, and the Satō family attempts to impart the family flavor (*kazoku no aji o tsukeru*) through a variety of institutional and informal practices. Certainly this is done in order to make work life more pleasant in accordance with meaningful, accepted cultural practices, but it also is intended to make work more efficient and productive, a situation primarily benefitting the *shachō* and his family. Workers, on the other hand, look to *uchi no kaisha,* the company as a whole, to act as a source of care and respect for their position and their needs. Finally, as we shall see, both *shachō* and workers define *uchi* as an informal, familial space where one's *honne,* inner feelings, or *ura,* informal side, can be expressed. But the lines of demarcation are differently drawn in each case, with workers, in particular, constituting *uchi* as the work group where complaints against the company can be aired with impunity. For the *shachō,* the whole company can indeed act as his *uchi,* for ordinarily, subordinates must tolerate his outbursts of emotion. The boundaries of *uchi,* then, are contextually defined, replaying and maintaining the tension between authority and solidarity.

Within this narrative field, riven by the contradictions implicit in the notion of company as family, the Satō family can nonetheless be effective in imparting a family flavor, securing workers' loyalty, and promoting identification with the firm. But as we have seen in the incident of the half-price sale, these practices are not carried through in every context. Fixing close attention on certain revealing incidents on the shop floor will allow us to follow out the twists in meaning which provide workers with the arms they can use to criticize the *shachō*'s behavior. Finally, I will argue that the creation of *uchi* and *soto* spheres provides culturally specific means for structuring protest and resistance, channeling the reappropriations and redeployments of meaning in ways that rearrange, but do not yet fundamentally threaten, the power of Satō's readings of the idiom.

Strategic Deployments: *Uchi Soto* and *Uchi no Kaisha*

Unraveling the implications of the morning's interaction leads us to several observations about the workers' sense of *uchi no kaisha,* their appropriations of the idiom, its intertwinings with other critical discourses, and the expression of discontent and resistance in particular *uchi* contexts.

First, the workers reappropriated the familial idiom of *kazoku* and *uchi* in order to mine its critical potential, and in so doing, created boundaries and definitions for the *uchi*. Itakura-san, for instance, invoked one sense of *uchi* as the company which truly cared for its employees, when she linked the golden age of the Satō company to days when it was "really" *kazokuteki,* like family. The present disregard of the Labor Standards Law, the long hours and low wages, and the lack of regard for the part-timers' desires for a half-price sale, were ascribed, in her analysis, to Satō's departure from the truly familylike past. The new, more uncaring and exploitative practices she linked to the recent hiring of the management consultant, whose concern was merely for profits and not for the workers. She defines purely economic rationality as an evil in human terms, for it erases human dignity and defines *uchi* too narrowly, as the *shachō*'s family. For her, money was a dirty thing, an embodiment of the ways human relationships were made into commodities for Satō's profit. *Uchi no kaisha,* as defined by the management consultant and by the *shachō,* thus became *uchi* as the Satō family, not the company as a whole. Itakura-san's sense of *uchi no kaisha,* on the contrary, is more expansive, embracing both full- and part-time workers. Moreover, she de-emphasizes the long-suffering loyalty workers supposedly owe their employers in exchange for the favor of being employed. Rather, employers should care more selflessly for their workers, thinking of the workers' needs with concern and empathy. Itakura-san's deployment of the *uchi no kai-sha* notion provides her, then, with a richly nuanced critique of what she—or those who share her political views—might call petty capitalist accumulation.

The discourse on *uchi no kaisha* worked in complicated ways in tandem with other critical discourses. One was a sophisticated leftist political analysis, embraced by a few of the older, female part-timers like Itakura-san. In her biting indictments of Japanese society and Japanese politics, she invoked the days of the Meiji Restoration, when, she argues, politicians worked selflessly for the good of the country. This Itakura-san contrasted with her comments about the LDP and its connections to big business and corrupt politicians. Again, familialism seemed to represent a "traditional Japan" when properly familial attitudes were held by owners and managers, who would think not of their career advancement or their profits, but of the good of the whole. *Uchi,* in this scenario and in its critical redeployment in complaints about working conditions, again meant the *whole* company.

In an interesting rearrangement of meaning, the part-timers reappropriated one of the key practices associated with imparting a family flavor—that is, the company trip—and claimed it as a right. Certainly no owner I ever interviewed took this perspective on the matter; in their view, they were giving the employees a wonderful outing as a culturally appropriate demonstration of their kindness and largesse. In return, they expected loyal service and regard from their employees. Sometimes the owners' expectations were disappointed, and they could be deeply affected by "disloyalty," as was the *sensei* of the hairdressing salon where I worked for a month or two. She was wounded when an employee "coldly quit" just after a company trip to Hawaii. Clearly, the relationship meant far more to her than it did to her employee, for the breach of this relationship summoned up deeply meaningful, morally charged feelings about loyalty, obligation, and care. To her, this "callous" behavior was symptomatic of the "dry" contractual relationships today's young people seemed to prefer. Itakura-san, Nomura-san and others (none of them young people) took an opposing stance on the issue of so-called familial obligation to an employer. They emphatically declared it to be only proper and natural that they should, just like other workers in Japan, have their company trip. "That much *has* to be coming to us," was their assessment. (*Sono gurai wa denakuchā.*) No romantic sense of *uchi no kaisha* softened their incisive and determined insistence on their rights to certain benefits.

The part-timers' informal, ad hoc remedy for their proximate complaint—the lack of a half-price sale—revealed other ways in which *uchi* was defined: as the company work group and the informal context in which discontents could be aired. The part-timers' solution was to call on me, a foreigner and a researcher, who could in some sense mediate between *uchi* and the public sphere. My position as guest, less subject to the complete authority of the *shachō,* gave me a potential critical voice that might have been heard outside the confines of the *uchi,* the company work group.

It is important to note that the part-timers did take opportunities to register their disapproval of the *shachō* and his disrespectful treatment. Their refusal to buy the broken-up cherry tarts should not be discounted as an effective act of criticism, for according to their descriptions, the *shachō* was clearly surprised and taken aback by their actions. My co-workers insisted upon their dignity, refusing to accede to the *shachō's* definition of his offer as a favor to them, which invoked the company as a caring *uchi.* Their refusal was especially effective because it enacted their disapproval in a way that would not entail the ultimate risk of dismissal. Such a strategy reminds us again of the high stakes involved in any act of protest in a more public, formal, *soto* sphere, for union organizing and collective protests were likely to lead to "getting it in the neck" (*kubi ni naru*), as the eloquent Japanese expression goes. The *shachō* had the power to impose his reality on others and to enforce his definitions of that reality, and workers who contested his deployments of meaning risked their jobs in so doing. As Itakura-san stated so pithily, "There's only one president here."

What counts as *uchi,* and for whom, are thus matters subject to political struggles. This "politics of classification" (Stark 1986) shows how different actors can reclaim and redeploy certain idioms in ways they perceive to be just and justifiable (see also Joan Scott 1988). The part-timers, especially, can reappropriate the idiom and subvert the *shachō's* readings. But it is also clear that the *shachō's* attempts to define the meanings of *uchi* could be effective, for he had the material means at his disposal to enforce those meanings. And his definitions of *uchi* were sometimes profoundly exclusionary, albeit laced with contradictions.

Company as Family?

Wages and Working Conditions: Whose *Uchi* is it?

As the furor surrounding the incident of the half-price sale demonstrated, the battleground most fraught with significance seemed to be that of wages and working conditions, where the lines drawn between *uchi* and *soto* revealed the contradictions and tensions in the notion of *uchi no kaisha*.

The day after the half-price sale incident, the topic of salaries arose.

"Think about it," said Itakura-san. "We get a raise of ¥20 a year. Over ten years, that's only ¥200." (This was about $1.00 at the exchange rate of the time.)

"Itō-kun is lucky," said another part-timer. "Over five years here, and his salary went up by only ¥5000 ($25)! The base pay here is only ¥87,000 ($435)—of course, there's overtime you can add onto that, but to earn ¥10,000 ($50), you've got to work pretty hard!"

"Anyway," said Nomura-san, "they take out money for food and for shoes and for rent and for savings, so all the guys have left is about ¥30,000 ($150) or ¥40,000 to spend for themselves."

"It's hard work, standing over that hot grill all day!"

Even the timing of payments came under fire. Itakura-san compared the Satō company unfavorably with larger firms that gave out bonuses at the end of November, so people could use them to buy the ritual end-of-the-year gifts (*Oseibō*). "Here," she said with considerable irritation in her voice, "they don't give out bonuses until the end of December."

This talk of money provided the prelude for the scene to follow. As he was wont to do, the *shachō* sauntered in to survey the afternoon goings-on in the factory. Apparently he did not find things to his liking, for his face darkened, and he bellowed, "Look at all this mess! Why don't you people clean things up?" And, as usual, he dashed out in a huff.

Also as usual, he left an uproar in his wake. Yutaka-kun growled, "We're only getting paid to make *okashi,* not to do the cleaning."

"You really do feel like telling him off," said Nomura-san, in assent.

Itakura-san pronounced in her severe way that the *shachō* should simply decide how much cleaning had to be done in a particular day and have people do it before or after work.

Nomura-san protested, "Most companies have someone who specializes in cleaning."

And I, thinking of the dustballs accumulating in the corners of my six-mat *tatami* room, added, "Plus, there's no end to cleaning." (*Sōji wa kiri ga nai shi.*)

207

Money and the monetary idiom provided perhaps the clearest demarcation between owners and workers, the owner's *uchi* and the metaphorical *uchi* of the company as family. The paltry wages of the part-timers, the low salaries of the young artisans, and the lack of overtime provided the chief artisans, were subjects of extended commentary, as we have seen. Such "injustices" highlight the most exclusionary definitions of *uchi no kaisha,* where clearly it is the *shachō* and his family who are most centrally benefiting from the workers' labors. One morning, for example, the *shachō* repeatedly rang the bell of the dumbwaiter, signalling his impatience as he waited for the goods from the second floor to reach him. Kitano-san, a young artisan, commented wryly, "It's hard for the *shachō,* isn't it—making all that money." (*Shachō wa mōkatte, taihen desu ne.*) Money symbolized above all things the division between owner and worker, between *uchi* as owner's family and *uchi* as the whole company.

Working conditions and workers' control over the work process constituted a similar field of contention, where demarcations were drawn between the owner, who knew little about actual operations on the shop floor, and the workers, presumably his inferiors, who were possessors of this knowledge. One day, Teramura-san, who worked on the grill (her former co-worker was Itō-san, the young man who had recently taken the job with the Mitsubishi subcontractors) had to stay at home because of her painful menstrual cramps.[4] Because Itō was gone and the factory was generally short-handed, the *shachō* had no choice but to take over some of the baking himself. Standing over the hot machine all day was apparently no easy task for him, which he duly reported to Teramura-san when she came back. "*Taihen deshita*—it was terrible!" he said in wonder. After he left, she said scornfully to us, "It's *his* family's factory; you'd think he'd do this once in a while." (*Tama ni yareba ii no ni.*)

A similar complaint was lodged by Hamada-san, when the *shachō* made a new capital investment in a packaging machine. In order to make room for the bulky apparatus, the part-timers' work space had been rearranged in ways that made our work more difficult. No one had bothered to consult us on the matter, and Hamada-san was irritated all day, constantly mentioning how *yarizurai* (hard to do, hard to work with) the machine was, how inconvenient she found the new spatial arrangements, and—the final straw—how implements we used every day were not in their usual places. The can opener had disappeared, and she finally shouted out in frustration, "Why do people who don't know anything put things away in places where we can't find them?" Here again, we were presented with the contradiction of the *shachō,* whose *uchi* would presumably benefit from the workers knowledge and expertise, knowing little or nothing about the work process. To add insult to injury, he had not even bothered to consult the workers about matters on which they were expert.

In these examples, the divisions between *uchi* and *soto* were clear, centering around the issues of money, ownership of the firm, and control over the work process. The entire firm was Satō's *uchi*. Workers pointed out the contradictions underlying this drawing of the *uchi* boundary, however, when they contrasted the ownership of the firm to his actual knowledge about everyday work practices. Despite the fact that it was the *shachō's uchi,* he knew very little about what the workers went through every day, and as a consequence, he failed to adequately appreciate their contributions. Indeed, he was surprised, when he substituted for Teramura-san, at how hard the work in fact was. Satō's failure to fully acknowledge his workers was symbolized for them in a variety of ways, including the payment of low wages and failure to consult them about decisions bearing directly on their work. He made no move to draw workers into a more expansive *uchi no kaisha* by according them visible respect for their knowledge and expertise. When the *shachō* drew the *uchi* boundary narrowly, as *his* family alone, he provided workers with tools of critique as he also, in so doing, reinforced his power base and effectively excluded workers.

Similar tensions and ironies are at play in the *shachō's* other enactments of *uchi no kaisha;* they are most strikingly visible in his exercise of authority. At times he did treat the entire company as his *uchi,* and his actions both defined the meanings of *uchi,* strengthening his control, and simultaneously subverted, even as they advanced, his purposes.

Owner as *Oni*

In any work organization, the exercise of authority is a critically important issue. *Ie* structure, at least formally, is constituted through a chain of hierarchical command that buttresses the authority and legitimacy of the *shachō* and, secondarily, of his wife. In *uchi* contexts, Satō-san sometimes asserted that authority on seemingly personal whim, thus keeping workers off guard and reserving for himself a kind of privileged, arbitrary authority, bearing "family resemblances" to the constitution of authority in other so-called paternalistic systems (cf. Genovese 1974, Sider 1986). These moments also sharply drew the lines between *uchi* and *soto,* reinforcing the construction of the *shachō* as the central *uchi* figure.

The most startling examples were associated with new technologies of power and surveillance: the camera and the microphone. On the shop floor, cameras—much like the ones in American banks—surveyed our day-to-day activities. The Satōs could turn on the monitor in their office at any time. For us workers, this meant that we never knew when a transgression might bring down the wrath of The Voice. One morning, out of nowhere, it boomed, "Good morning, everyone! As I told you yesterday, uniforms are to be put out today for cleaning. Two of you haven't yet done so. If the uniforms are not downstairs by noontime, I'll have to dock the pay of the offending parties." The icily polite Japanese (e.g., *kinō mōshiageta yō ni*) barked out at an excruciatingly high decibel level was a sure sign that Satō was holding back his anger. We all exchanged alarmed glances, and a part-time whispered to me that she thought Kitano-san, one of the young artisans, had been one of those at fault. Needless to say, he slipped out of the workroom early, to take his dirty uniforms downstairs.

Satō's explosive temper could be loosed in situations where his anger was, in some ways, due to his own lack of foresight. Yet even these eruptions served to buttress his authority. One day, as we were going about our everyday routine, he burst in, his face livid, his chest heaving. "What's the matter with all of you? Today a customer came into the store and said she'd called the factory to find out how much something cost, and somebody told her it was 130 yen. Then she went to the shop and found out it was really 150 yen. She asked me, 'What kind of company is it, where the workers don't even know the prices of the things they're making?' All of you should know *exactly* how much everything costs! Where do you think your salary is coming from?! Get your act together!" (*Shikkari shite kure yo!*). And he dashed out as suddenly as he had dashed in.

Left dumbfounded and open-mouthed for a few minutes, we didn't take long to start in.

"What does the guy think? If he wants us to quote prices, he should give us a price list and put it up by the phone!" said Nomura-san, one of the part-timers.

A young artisan muttered in anger about the *shachō*'s last phrase, "Where do you think your salary is coming from?" "That's what he really wanted to say, so that's why he yelled at us," Yutaka-kun opined.

Itakura-san, the politically savvy older part-timer, also decried the *shachō*'s egregious behavior. "It's all we can do to just make the stuff and get it to the shop. How can he expect us to know the *price* of everything too?"

Company as Family?

Quickly the subject turned to judgments about the *shachō*'s personal character. *Okorippoi,* hot-tempered, was the conclusion.

"Outside (*soto wa*), he seems like a nice guy. But he always takes it out on us," said Mori-san, a part-timer. She then cracked, "Maybe the stress was just building up and he had to let it out. He must feel a lot better now!"

Hamada-san, who seemed to get on beautifully with the *shachō,* surprised me with her observation, "It's because the *shachō*'s hobby is to mistreat people." (*Hito o ijimeru no wa shumi da kara.*)

The workers contrasted Satō's gracious demeanor outside the company in formal, public situations, where he appeared to be the personification of benevolent care, with his unpredictable behavior toward his employees in the confines and privacy of *uchi no kaisha.* Clearly, *uchi* was a place where the *shachō,* too, could express his *honne,* inner feelings, and his more powerful position gave him a socially recognized platform for the uncensored expression of his anger.

Even the shop manager, who was the Satō's nephew and the designated successor to the firm, recognized the *shachō*'s explosive ire. One day I went into the store to buy sweets, and Hiroshi-san asked whether I had been at work that day. "No," I said, "I had to do some interviews." "Well," he said, "the *shachō* was like this," as he held up his two index fingers, one on either side of his head: the sign of the *oni,* the horned demon.

All of these demonstrations of temper would seem to work against the legitimacy of his authority, as they indeed did to an extent. Workers were clearly outraged by his arbitrariness and "unfair" outbursts. Yet there was another sense in which this authority could be used to bolster his control over people as he kept them off balance and tied workers' complaints to his personal characteristics, requiring them to "read his moods"—a common occurrence in unequal power relationships (cf. J. B. Miller 1976; Kanter 1977). Mr. Satō himself seemed to think that whenever he did get angry, it was justified, and he apparently took pride in the power of his anger. On my birthday in July, he held a joint dinner party for me and for his daughter Natsuko. During the course of the evening, I found out that his birthday was at the end of June, making us fellow Cancerians according to the Western zodiac. "We Cancerians," Satō-san said to me with a satisfied air," are usually quiet (*otonashii*), but when we're angry, you'd better watch out!"

Coercive power was the message of Satō-san's intrusions over the loudspeaker and the angry barrage of words he directed toward his employees. In the *soto* world of other companies and the merchant association, he could reap the benefits of his "familial" care and concern for his employees, and in all fairness, it appeared to be quite genuine. But in an *uchi* setting, the arbitrary exercise of authority left us with the uncertainty of never knowing *quite when* we were being watched or *quite how* the *shachō* might react. This was especially clear in our vulnerability to his changes in mood—which were, after all, striking—from the jovial, ruddy-faced Satō-san who joked around with us; to the cold, impassive man who one day handed out pay envelopes ("It would make you feel better if he at least said, 'Thanks for your trouble,'" said the part-timers); to the shouting, livid face wracked by spasms of anger. This meant in effect that authority was personalized and made "familial," linked to personal caprice and character (his hot temper) as much as it was tied to his structural position—a situation possible in any household. Personalized exercise of authority within the *uchi* worked paradoxically to undermine the *shachō*'s legitimacy as it provides workers with the tools of critique. At the same time, it enabled power to resurface in a personal, familial, arbitrary way which resonated with, as it worked against, his structural position as head of the company. Workers' complaints, perhaps like the complaints of family members vis-à-vis a household head, were also personalized and scattered, crystallizing only temporarily in isolated incidents. They could thwart the *shachō*'s plans to unload his unwanted sweets on them by refusing his offer, and by doing so, they managed to startle him momentarily. Perhaps their refusal even made him reflect on his actions. But more sustained, public confrontation was considerably more difficult. The isolated nature of the protests, combined with the personal nature of the complaints—arising, as they did, from the very character of the *shachō*—discouraged and defused potential, formally expressed opposition, either via the single voice of an intermediary or the collective voice of a work stoppage.

Irony and Multiplicity

Though the boundaries of *uchi no kaisha* created an arena for the exercise of authority and the generative play of power (Foucault 1979, 1980), giving rise to a plethora of creative practices and often creating warm feelings of solidarity and commitment, the contests over the boundaries and the precise meaning of *uchi* were everyday matters at the Satō company. *Uchi no kaisha,* far from possessing some essential, referential core, was appropriated and transformed by various actors in a multiplicity of creative ways.

1. For some of the part-timers, *uchi no kaisha* symbolized a return to a golden age when employers were truly familial and caring, where *uchi no kaisha* meant the whole company. For owners, *uchi no kaisha* could mean the whole company, but they emphasized the obligations of loyalty and hard work *owed* them in exchange for their largesse.

2. In other contexts, *uchi* meant the owner's family—and here, in contrast to the familial idiom, workers invoked the cold, selfish idiom of economic rationality. Money was a "dirty thing," and the management consultants who worked for profit were working for the owner's *uchi,* not *uchi no kaisha.* Wages and working conditions symbolized the contradictions in the deployment of this sense of *uchi no kaisha,* for the persons who were most *uchi* in fact seemed to know least about the work process in the factory, and revealed their lack of respect for workers by awarding low wages, berating them unjustly, conducting sporadic surveillance of shop floor activities, and failing to improve, indeed exacerbating, already difficult working conditions. The greatest contradiction in the *uchi no kaisha* idiom lay in the *shachō's* ability to fire people for whatever reason he pleased, a coercive power that provided the unspoken backdrop to everyday life in the factory.

3. For both *shachō* and workers, *uchi* was an informal context where complaints and emotions could be expressed with impunity, and where public exposure was unlikely. For workers, the most *uchi* of contexts at the workplace was the work group, where complaints could be voiced more fully, away from the dampening presence of the *shachō.* For the *shachō,* the entire company was his *uchi,* a place where his explosions of anger had to be tolerated.

In the end, however, we are left with contradictions and ironies. Though workers subvert the *shachō's* readings of *uchi* in their creative redeployments and reappropriations, sometimes registering protest by resisting his expectations—as they did when they refused to buy the tarts—they are still not able to subvert in ways that would concretely affect the shape of their lives or the life of the *shachō. Uchi* and *soto* thus, finally, create the contexts which culturally mediate the expression of so-called resistance. Until somehow they are able to confront the *shachō* outside the *uchi* context, using perhaps an "official" voice like the one I might have provided, or banding together collectively to confront him in a more public, *soto* arena, the subversive play of power occurs primarily in one place: *uchi* as work group. And though they creatively and subversively transform the meaning of *uchi no kaisha,* giving it a sharp, critical edge, their invocation of the familial idiom also legitimizes and reproduces it as a culturally meaningful arena of political contest. Equally ironically, the *shachō* can maximize his personalized imposition of authority within the *uchi no kaisha* in ways which simultaneously undermine and buttress his power.

Uchi/Soto and Artisanal Identities

One further level of complexity attracts our critical scrutiny. I have already intimated that, in the *shachō*'s absence, the atmosphere on the shop floor was informal, and my co-workers rarely seemed to curb their thoughts. Complaints, jokes, and roughhousing enlivened everyday routine on the shop floor.

Wages and delegation of authority created prime targets for my co-workers. For the male artisans, in particular, the sometimes superhuman efforts they were to make for holidays and special orders drew all manner of complaints. But even these complaints were contextually specific and nuanced with ambivalence. For even as the demands of their jobs were made tools of criticism, the hardships also became a testimony to the artisans' skill and endurance, a way to temper themselves as artisans. And no matter how much they complained within the confines of the factory walls, when the artisans stepped into the *soto* world, they acted as representatives of the company.

It was a busy day in March, and when we part-timers in the Western sweets division arrived for work, we were startled to see stacks of shortcakes and decoration cakes arranged on the work tables, awaiting our finishing touches. From the stubbly beards and the dull look in their eyes, we could tell that for the artisans it had been a morning for *hayade,* coming out early. Everyone looked too tired to talk much. One or two young artisans had red noses, and their loud sniffles punctuated our otherwise quiet morning.

At ten o'clock, Suzuki-san glanced at the clock and groaned histrionically, "*Ore, kijun hō o yabutteru!*" (I'm breaking the Labor Standards Law!).

"*Are?*" (What?) I gasped. Suzuki-san was given to overstatement and playful antics, but this time he sounded more serious than usual.

"Yeah," confirmed Yamada-san. "We've been up since two. Took those cardboards sheets over there and slept on the tables."

All of us part-timers clucked sympathetically. I marveled at the artisans' ability to perform any work at all, under the circumstances. Conversation

214

centered around physical needs and ailments. Suzuki coughed, and moaned, "It's the flu. It's really the flu." When no one looked up except for me, we exchanged significant glances, and he said of the others, "*Tsumetai, ne*" (They're cold, aren't they). Yamada, also one given to histrionics, staggered around the work tables, almost falling to the floor. "*Kutabiretaaaaa . . .*" (Tiiired . . .). And Kitano, who looked red and uncomfortable, groaned, "I have a fever." At one point, he took a small bottle of brandy—usually used as flavoring for some of the cakes—tilted it up, and drank the contents in a single gulp. "Good for colds," he said as he managed a weak grin.

At noon, the artisans raced off for the dining room and wolfed down their lunches in order to have a few extra moments of rest. We usually took an hour for lunch, and the custom was for the part-timers to eat at home. When we returned at one, the workroom was dark, and we tiptoed in to find sleeping bodies curled up in whatever space would accommodate them: on top of the flour sacks, on the tables, on the concrete floors. Matsumoto-san, chief of the baking division, stirred as we came in, and he groggily stood up and turned on the lights. "Wake up. Time to get back to work." Slowly, the men roused themselves, and work gradually resumed its usual pace. When we part-timers left around six, the artisans were still there, in for another stint that would last until midnight. For a solid week, they managed to continue this grueling two A.M. to midnight work schedule in order to fill the staggering number of special orders and provide the large volume of confections people buy as gifts during the various March holidays, among them *Ohigan*, the vernal equinox, an important time for commemorating the dead.

The young, male artisans were quite aware of the unusual and indeed exploitative character of these working conditions. Suzuki-san, in his exclamation about the Labor Standards Law, demonstrated his understanding and awareness of his legal rights. But despite this awareness, no one seemed inclined to stop working so hard. Matsumoto-san summarized one reason for their commitment. "The *shachō* should hire more workers. But it's harder and harder to find help these days." Artisans like Matsumoto, who were, admittedly, managers, could sympathize with the *shachō*'s plight, the labor shortage that plagued all small businesses. And all of the artisans seemed committed to the company, at least sufficiently to do their share to help the company get out its orders on time. Whatever their complaints, they acted together to produce fresh goods for *uchi no kaisha*.

But it was Yutaka-kun, an artisan in *wagashi,* who revealed the complexities of the artisans' relationship to the company. After a dinner lecture by an ethics teacher who had come to visit the company, he invited me for a cup of coffee at the artisans' favorite coffee house, "Pony". We played video games and read comic books for awhile, and then Yutaka-kun started to tell me about himself and about work. He, like most of the Satō employees, was from the North, and he had entered the company through recommendations from his teacher, who was an old friend of Mr. Satō. At twenty-three, Yutaka-kun had already been working for the Satōs for seven years. It didn't take long before he launched into a litany of complaints. The physical labor was too demanding, the hours were ridiculously long, and you always had to watch how you acted in front of the bosses. He laughed scornfully at his co-workers, "You see how everybody complained about the ethics retreat, but when they came back, they always go and say 'thank you, I learned a lot,' to the *shachō*." Yutaka-kun's tirade went on for some time, and I murmured sympathetically, pleased that he would be so frank.

Suddenly, he changed his tune. "But I'm glad I work there. People say if you can work there you can work anywhere." I stared at him in amazement. He continued to elaborate this point of view: that they were so busy was really due to the prosperity of the company. No other confectionery in the entire ward, said he, produced such a range of confections in such massive volume as did the Satōs'. "Look at Itoya[5]—all they have are a few *ohagi*[6] for the equinoxes." Working at the Satō confectionery, then, was a real education in the craft. In fact, it was true that the artisans seemed to prefer the demanding schedules of holidays and the fall-through-spring seasons to the slack period during the summer. "Nothing to do," the men would grumble as they paced the floor or made work for themselves— folding boxes and the like. "I'm bored," Yamada-san would howl, staggering around the work tables. The long working hours and taxing conditions, though a source of complaint, were proofs of the artisans' strength, fortitude, and endurance—the virtues the ethics retreat extolled so memorably. And not incidentally, this same fortitude acted as a testament to their masculine toughness.

Pride in their work also exhibited itself in other ways that demonstrated the artisans' identifications with *uchi no kaisha*. One free Tuesday, the *shachō* assigned the young artisans to make the rounds of confectioneries in the elegant, cosmopolitan Ginza. They were to compare prices, taste, quality, and merchandising, to get a sense of their competition. I had always been surprised that the Satō confectionery would charge the hefty prices they did for their wares, considering the economic situation of the ward. A box of sweets from the Satōs cost quite as much as those from any famous store in the Ginza, Nihonbashi, Aoyama or Roppongi. When I mentioned the Satōs' high prices, Yamada said proudly, "That's because Satō uses only the best ingredients, no preservatives. Our *okashi* stand up to any we tasted the other day."

At this, Ohara-san, the chief artisan, concurred. "I'm always surprised that the Japanese go for name brands all the time. Look at X-ya. Their *yōkan* is no better than ours. The same sugar, the same red beans." He shook his head. "And our *yōkan* is even more delicately flavored." Ohara-san's comparison implied an identification with the company, pride in the products, and an awareness that his artisanal identity was at least in part defined by affiliation with the Satō company, whatever his personal feelings of identification might be. For even though the artisans considered their products to be as fine as any made in Tokyo, they were not accorded the respect and recognition of workers in the better-known confectioneries. And whatever their complaints might be within the confines of the company, the artisans both defined themselves in terms of, and were defined *by,* their affiliation with *uchi no kaisha.*

This affiliation became clear to me one day when my landlady, Hatanaka-san, and I went to the ward bazaar, where merchants from various parts of Arakawa set up small booths to hawk their wares. We took in a performance by a local high school band, and afterwards wandered down row after row of stalls to examine the merchandise. I knew that the Satōs would be represented, but I was surprised to see the artisan who was manning the booth. There, polite and subdued, his body possessing the closure and disciplined grace of Japanese formal posture, was Suzuki-san. The same young man who would stagger around the floor, groaning about his cold and his exhaustion, the same person who engaged in roughhousing and physical antics with his co-workers, including episodes where the guys would kick and punch each other, the same person who never issued an utterance without using the most informal, "macho" Japanese, was now a model of propriety. He was a perfect representative for the company: gracious, soft-spoken, respectful. In this formal, outside, *soto* context, of course, not a hint of criticism of the company would pass his lips.

Crossing the boundary between *uchi* and *soto* structures comportment, marking shifts in behavior and language. By acting in appropriately upright and formal ways in the appropriate context, Suzuki-san enacted his belonging to *uchi no kaisha*—his usual vociferous complaints and criticisms notwithstanding. *Uchi no kaisha* could serve as a demarcated space within which intimacy, informality, and one's *honne,* inner feelings, including complaints, were allowed. And at certain levels (pride in their work, pride in the prosperity of the Satō firm) *uchi no kaisha* also compelled the loyalties of the male artisans. But whether or not the artisans personally identified with the company, *uchi no kaisha* was an inevitable determinant of their identities as defined by others in Japanese society. *Uchi no kaisha* both channeled resistance into bounded contexts and acted as an encompassing feature of identity.

Resistance?

For the people I knew in the factory, the deployment of the notion of *uchi no kaisha* was laced with contradiction, irony, and compromise. No single meaning, no single effect, could be isolated in its pristine abstraction. Workers could invoke *uchi no kaisha* subversively, yet in so doing they also reproduced and legitimized the idiom. The *shachō* could explode at us, but in so doing he both reinforced his authority and supplied his workers with materials for critique. And different discourses could collide and intertwine: while the *shachō* might deploy the *uchi no kaisha* idiom, characterizing company benefits as gifts which attested to his sterling character, workers called upon a discourse of rights, insisting that such "gifts" were simply *owed* them. When the *shachō* marshalled the language of economic rationality and profit-seeking by following his management consultant's suggestions, workers parried with their appropriation of the *uchi no kaisha* idiom, criticizing the *shachō* for being *inadequately* familial. Such conflicts could reveal the fissures in the discourse of *uchi no kaisha*; a family feeling fostered in certain contexts could be undercut by practices highlighting the cleavage between the *shachō* and his family and their employees. On the other hand, when we consider the matter of artisanal identities, workers criticize the company at one level and take pride in belonging to *uchi no kaisha* at another, as testament to their fortitude, masculinity, and skill. And whatever their ambivalent identifications with the company, they found themselves, willy-nilly, identified by others as members of *uchi no kaisha* within the context of the larger society. Given these kinds of complexities—the contradictions, nuances, and multiplicities engendered by any act or appropriation of meaning—how can one account for the lives of my co-workers within the narratives of "resistance" provided in the social science literature? Can the richness of their experiences be adequately captured by those frameworks, and if not, what theoretical moves are necessary so that we can begin to do justice to their lives?

This account of mundane interactions on the shop floor takes its place within a burgeoning literature which focuses on the agency of human actors, and, increasingly, on the small, everyday acts of resistance to hegemonic ideologies. Practices heretofore unnoticed or dismissed by grand theory as mere accommodation, false consciousness, or reformism, assume a new political weight.[7] This efflorescence of literature on resistance opens exciting new areas of inquiry and leads us to consider "unlikely" places to look for resistance and protest. The particular strategies my co-workers used, the proliferations in meaning of the *uchi no kaisha* idiom, and the unintended consequences of resistance at the workplace, point us toward two key questions: How far does a focus on resistance take us analytically? What assumptions about agency, power, and human action underlie notions of resistance?

Keeping in mind the subtleties, multiplicities, and ironies animating the deployment of *uchi no kaisha* in the Satō factory makes us aware of the difficulties with employing the notion of resistance as an analytic tool. These difficulties appear in exemplary form in several works which operate within a metaphysics of closure and presence, presuming that human lives can be seen in terms of neat, closed, monolithic, internally coherent categories. These analyses should give us clues that perhaps articulating the problematic of power in terms of resistance may in fact be asking the wrong question.

Keeping his focus on the quotidian, a theme animating the new resistance literature, James Scott, in *Weapons of the Weak* (1985), creates a vivid portrayal of peasant resistance in Malaysia. His account argues for an actor-centered, meaning-centered account of everyday acts of resistance, emphasizing the refusal of "the poor" to accept definitions of reality imposed from above. Most central to our inquiry, he shows the ways Malaysian peasants appeal to a particular, culturally shared idiom of human decency to criticize the actions of the rich. Scott rightfully takes to task those who would limit the definition of resistance to formalized, organized acts, dependent upon some transcendent principle.

Still, Scott operates with certain problematic notions of categorization and human agency. The first has to do with the polarization of Malaysian peasant society into two dichotomous groups, the rich and the poor. This binary distinction is all too reminiscent of class analyses pitting owner against worker in an uncomplicated, universal class struggle. The cultural significance of the rich/poor distinction within the Malaysian context is never spelled out fully, and the invocation of a simple binary immediately incurs suspicion, given the complications that explode binary oppositions in other cultural settings. For instance, the owner/worker distinction in the Satō company was salient only in certain specific situations, when the contradictions within the *uchi no kaisha* idiom were thrown into relief, as when the *shachō* demonstrated his woeful ignorance of the work process, despite his ownership of the firm. Even then, people tended to invoke the culturally specific and more complicated notion of the owner as *shachō*, head of the company, emphasizing that they were all members of the *same* company, arranged along a hierarchy with the *shachō* at the apex. This sense of cultural particularity never emerges in Scott's analysis, despite his explicit arguments for a culturally specific theorizing of resistance. Nor does he take into account the shifts in positioning that can occur between categories of rich and poor, so that, depending on context, ironies and contradictions might undermine and yet reproduce those distinctions.

The *shachō* and my co-workers showed me the complexities of human agency in our everyday interactions on the shop floor. People were capable of invoking the *uchi no kaisha* idiom in a subversive way at one level and legitimating it at another. This sense of multiplicity, contradiction, and tension is lacking in the notions of agency and authenticity underlying Scott's theoretical schema. His actors are resisters who, if they comply, do so because of repression, fear of repression, the "muddying of class waters"[8] by multiple social identities, and the "dull compulsion of economic relations" (pp. 243–47). In power-laden situations, when the poor face the rich, Scott argues that, especially for the poor, the "full transcript" of the interaction is masked (p. 286).

The notion that one must try to gain access to more informal contexts, to find out what the poor "really" think, is of course an important one. Without such a notion, for example, I could never have begun to discover what workers said and did when they spoke amongst themselves. But the notion of a transcript—that there is simply some sort of discursive account, more or less hidden, depending on contextually specific power relations—takes on problematic meanings when one considers the kind of self or individual who supposedly authors such an account.[9] Scott's individual who hides the transcript still retains the character of a whole, consciously intentional subject who holds well-formulated, uncontradictory opinions apart from the imposed values of the dominant ideology.

220

The "less authentic" side which comes into play in situations of unequal power is simply a kind of mask, donned for expediency's sake. Nowhere do we find that people like my co-workers can be caught in contradictions, that they simultaneously resist and reproduce, challenging and reappropriating meanings as they also undermine those challenges. That people inevitably participate in their own oppressions, buying into hegemonic ideologies even as they struggle against those oppressions and those ideologies—a familiar fact of life to women, people of color, colonized and formerly colonized people—is a poignant and paradoxical facet of human life given short shrift in Scott's schema.

My experiences at the Satō factory taught me that the nature of those oppressions, the arenas in which resistance can be expressed, indeed the very definitions of resistance are *culturally* mediated. For example, in everyday practices on the shop floor, *uchi/soto* boundaries outline a contested terrain, but also serve as culturally appropriate spaces within which so-called resistance could surface. Within the factory, meaning and power are coextensive; this intertwining of meaning and power creates sets of institutions and disciplinary practices: from the structure of the company, to the designation of the people who work there as different kinds of selves—*shachō*, artisans, part-timers, to everyday interactions such as those I have described in this book (Foucault 1979). Power/meaning *creates* selves at the workplace, and consequently, no one can be "without" power. Scott's view of agency, on the contrary, presumes power to be merely repressive, a mechanism applied from above and outside, a substance some people possess and some people do not, which prevents the expression of authentic resistance.

In short, the subtleties, ironic twists, and wrenching yet creative contradictions running through my co-workers' lives cannot be accommodated in Scott's world of resistance. The world of the Satō factory is complex and ironic, where no single category, meaning, motivation, or aspect of selfhood can be sifted out from its shifting placement in matrices of power. Multiplicities, tensions, and layerings of meaning undercut simple resistance at every turn. But as my co-workers showed me, the factory is also a ludic space, open to creative possibilities for subversion (Rosaldo 1987; Butler 1988a). For Scott, the world is a simpler place. His rhetoric is animated by a wish for clean-cut, clearly defined categories that can exhaustively account for the world, but since reality is "messier" than that, Scott is *resigned* to making do with the messiness. Itakura-san, Nomura-san, Yutaka-kun, Suzuki-san—even the *shachō*—would find this alien territory indeed.

221

They would find the terrain of resistance described by Paul Willis, in *Learning to Labour* (1977), somewhat more congenial. Here, it is not so much the lack of contradiction and irony that vexes, but the lack of creative opportunities for subversion and the complete closure of the world Willis describes that might puzzle my co-workers.

Willis focuses on the "lads" of Hammertown Boys, an English high school in an industrial city in the English Midlands. As a phenomenologically vivid ethnography which sets personal experiences within a larger political economic frame, the book has been called "the most comprehensive meditation on a trend of experimentation that seeks to adapt the writing of ethnography to take into account larger issues of political economy and broader vistas of representation" (Marcus 1986, 177). Willis puts an ironic spin on his analysis by showing how the lads, in their subjectively apprehended moments of greatest authenticity,[10] effectively disqualify themselves from acquiring the educational credentials deemed necessary for upward mobility and thus seal their fates as members of the working class. By challenging authority, playing truant, and disrupting classrooms, the lads feel affirmed and free in their oppositional stance; yet ironically, this is the moment of their greatest determination by the social order. Their rejection of middle-class values and the forces that would make them into disciplined members of the middle-class essentially consigns them to working-class lives. In this important theoretical move, Willis implicitly questions the notion of "authentic resistance," or a freely choosing individual, whole and uncomplicated.

However, Willis rests his analysis on certain unexamined assumptions which merit critical scrutiny. His intriguing contribution is to argue that resistance as well as accommodation leads to the reproduction of class relations. But on closer inspection, the society he constructs possesses the predictability of a well-oiled—if somewhat complicated—reproduction machine. No matter what people do, they manage to reproduce the capitalist system. The model of society imaged here is essentially a more sophisticated version of functionalism in which the "perverse" consequences of an act (cf. Hirshman 1989) ensure the reproduction of social relations within a closed system. Possibilities for multiplicities and playful subversions, on the one hand, or for open-ended, multiple discursive/political fields whose direction can never be predicted in advance, on the other, apparently have no place in his schema (Butler 1988a, 1989). Nowhere within such a theoretical frame could we take account of the shifting proliferations of meaning of the *uchi no kaisha* idiom, nor could we account for the collisions of this discourse with other discourses. For example, workers claim the company trip as a *right,* invoking a language of law and morality especially significant in the post-Occupation period, while the *shachō* defines the trip as a gift, part of his attempt to add the family flavor to company life. The confrontations of these discourses, through the creation of disjuncture and cleavage, are also productive of change and open new possibilities for appropriating and deploying meaning. This openness and multiplicity, then, so much part of everyday life in the factory, finds no sympathetic resonance in Willis.

If Scott premises his analysis on a particular notion of the self and power, and Willis posits a closed system driven by an infernally effective, if complicated, engine of reproduction, Louise Lamphere's (1987) historical and anthropological study of women factory workers in a Rhode Island town reveals the difficulties with positing resistance as an unproblematized category of human action. Her book offers a complex, multistranded analysis, interweaving issues of political economy, class, gender, and ethnicity as they interlace in a particular setting and over time. Based on participant observation fieldwork in a garment factory and on archival materials, Lamphere gives us richly detailed stories of women's "work culture" and their strategies of resistance on the shop floor.

What are those strategies? For Lamphere, her women co-workers' actions can be neatly sorted out into three basic categories: resistance, coping, and consent. Resistance can take the form of various overt or covert acts, from outright strikes and rebellion to less obvious strategies such as socializing new workers to the intricacies of the piece-rate system, to practices creating senses of solidarity among women, such as their efforts to "humanize the workplace" by holding baby showers, showing family photographs, and otherwise "bringing the family to work." Coping indicates the ways workers and families adjust to the larger, perceived social environment. Consent is glossed as "acquiescence to a husband's authority or to management policy either because it seems 'right' or because there seems to be no alternative" (p. 338). Certainly, it seems worth distinguishing among different sorts of actions and different degrees of resistance, but there is no indication here that the very act of distinguishing aspects of behavior also suppresses important differences and contradictions *within* the categories one elects to distinguish. The division of social practices into three groups also implies they are mutually exclusive and temporally and contextually separate, whereas one could equally well argue that people consent, cope, and resist at different levels of consciousness at a *single point in time* and that social practices can therefore be vexed and complicated, irreducible to three crisply distinct categories. Where within this scheme could we place my co-workers, who invoke the *uchi no kaisha* idiom in subversive ways, yet feel compelled to express that subversion only in certain contexts? And what of the possibilities for both consent at a certain level and resistance at another, as in the case of the young, male artisans who both criticized and identified with the company? Or what of the *shachō,* whose exercise of authority, *at a single point in time,* has paradoxical consequences, both consolidating and undermining his power?

Rather than relying on notions of a whole subject who can authentically resist power, on a notion of power as simply repressive, and therefore on the assumption that there exists a place beyond power; rather than seeing resistance as a mechanism of social reproduction within a closed system; and rather than subscribing to a view of social action as divisible into neatly separable categories, I would argue for a more complex view of power and human agency. To make sense of everyday life in the Satō factory, and to begin to give some account of the fullness, the ambiguity, and the complicated nuances of the lives of the people I knew there, another kind of theoretical move is necessary. It would require seeing people as decentered, multiple selves, whose lives are shot through with contradictions and creative tensions. People like my co-workers and the *shachō* in the Satō company may rearrange power relations as they appropriate and redeploy cultural meanings, but they can never escape to a romantic place beyond power.

In a setting like the Satō factory—indeed, in any setting—it thus seems suspect to talk of a pristine space of resistance. A term like resistance, when considered in all its living complexity, seems inadequate at best, for apparent resistance is riven with ironies and contradictions, just as coping or consent may have unexpectedly subversive effects. It seems equally suspect to speak exclusively of repressive power, for as Satō-san has shown us, the strategic deployment of an idiom can always produce ruptures and cleavages, so that in most effectively defining the contours of *uchi*—by expressing his anger—Satō-san also undermines his own purposes, reinforcing the solidarity, not of *uchi no kaisha,* but of *uchi,* the work group. When he does so, however, he is not mechanically reproducing or undermining configurations of power, for these matrices of power and meaning are open-ended, with room for play, subversion, and change. At the Satō factory, no deployment of meaning has a *single* effect, rather any action produces a *multiplicity* of sometimes paradoxical and creative effects. Finally, a more complicated view of the agency and selfhood of those who resist would see people caught in contradictions, constructing new arrangements of meaning and power as they craft their lives, but never "authentically resisting" power to attain some emancipatory utopia (cf. Foucault 1979, 1980; Butler 1987a; Haraway 1989). Such an approach would not jettison the category of resistance, nor would it prevent us from distinguishing relative vectors of power.[11] Arguing that there is no utopian space beyond power does not necessarily entail political paralysis, the chaos of meaninglessness, inability to make judgments, or nihilism. Clearly, at the Satō factory, "there is only one president," and despite the many complications and subversions at work, Satō's dominance in that setting is indisputable. But perhaps our starting point for a politics of meaning should not be a monolithic category of hegemony or domination countered by a grand, utopian space of pure resistance, especially if the forms of that hegemony or resistance become foundational categories which can always be known in advance. To indulge in nostalgic desire for "authentic resistance" might blind us to the multiple, mobile points of potential resistance moving through any regime of power.[12] Rather than positing these categories as foundational and thus invoking a metaphysics of closure and presence, we might examine the unexpected, subtle, and paradoxical twists in actors' discursive strategies, following out the ways meanings are reappropriated and launched again in continuous struggles over meaning. For perhaps it is not a matter of some utopian space of resistance as such—though this notion could be invoked *strategically,* for particular purposes—but of the complicated web of contradictions and ironies which bind us and which we in turn fabricate as we live out our lives.

Part
3   *Gender and Work Identities*

7
The Aesthetics and Politics of Artisanal Identities

It was, of all places, on the annual company trip to an *onsen,* or hot springs resort, when I began to realize the significance of work as an axis of identity for people in the Satō company. It was much like other company trips: the sumptuous banquet, where men drank impressive quantities of beer and *sake,* where people were enjoined to "Sing!" to entertain the others, where we stayed up late for yet another game of *mah-jongg* or yet another dip in the sulfurous baths. The morning after, I stumbled downstairs to the communal tables in the dining room and found myself face to face with Ohara-san, the head of the *wagashi,* or Japanese sweets, division of the company. At that point, I had been working in *wagashi* for only a week or so, and Ohara-san was, quite frankly, a daunting presence. He embodied a stereotype my informants often invoked: the stern, silent, severe artisan. In the factory, he would work for hours without a word, occasionally stalking about to glower at his subordinates as he inspected their creations. Above all, he appeared unapproachable, and seven in the morning seemed no time to make my first try. But, summoning my courage, I asked him about our one shared experience: work. I was astonished, in the course of our conversation, to see how animated he could be. The gaunt, stiff countenance now assumed a variety of expressions: frowns as he described the hardships of his childhood and his apprenticeship; an air of pride and confidence as he spoke of his craft; a softness, even, as he poetically described the delicate, aesthetic emotions he expressed in his art. In fact, he was so loquacious (and no doubt, so happy to have such a captive audience) that we were the last ones left at the breakfast table, and I had to scramble to prepare myself for the day's outing. Long afterwards, my head still spinning, I began to recall, in bits and pieces, conversations with other artisans, who often spoke in tones of affection and respect for their craft, even for the tools and the materials they used. Ohara-san and his breakfast monologue directed me toward an investigation of the ways selves are constructed at the workplace, and in particular, toward a specifically artisanal idiom of work.

229

Meaning, Power, and Work Identities

Ohara-san's morning disquisition was a kind of self-construction in narrative, refracting motifs from a larger story of artisanal work. In particular, he drew on culturally significant notions of work as a pathway to maturity and self-realization, on the one hand, and work as aesthetic participation in the human, natural, and material worlds, on the other. His story brought to life the meaningful symbolic and experiential dimensions of work that have, in recent years, begun to attract the attention of scholars in the social sciences.[1] Focusing on the meaningful aspects of work in this Japanese artisanal milieu points us toward different ways of conceptualizing the construction of disciplined selves in work and challenges prevailing teleologies of work in industrial societies as atomistic, alienating, and divorced from nature and from the material worlds.[2]

At the same time, these creative and affirming cultural meanings, set within their contexts, are contested political terrains. A growing revisionist literature, much of it written by feminists, traces out the *political* implications of work organization, in particular, craft solidarity. Solidary communities are based on exclusion of the unskilled—and unskilled, too often, means women (cf. Phillips and Taylor 1980; Gray 1987; Berg 1987; Rule 1987; Joan Scott 1988). Celebrations of artisanal community mask the cultural and historical construction of skill: how it is that jobs are labeled skilled or unskilled in the first place, and what resonances skill might have within a particular cultural context. One must therefore attend carefully to the meaningful, experiential aspects of work and to how those meanings are implicated in a larger system of power relations. In this case, an aesthetic of self-realization and connection to the material world is jealously guarded by the full-fledged male artisans in order to legitimate their place in an organizational hierarchy, an aesthetic under challenge from younger male workers, from part-timers, and from larger political and economic changes.

Ohara-san's story was also a means of self-construction. He created himself through narrative, in his very selective life history, and he asserted a similar work identity on the shop floor, enacting himself in everyday acts and gestures, in everyday situations. I have alluded to these themes through a consideration of the artisans' complex identifications with the company, as pride, resentment, and an enacting of identity occur at different levels and in different contexts. Ohara-san's narratives and performances of selfhood allow us to continue the quest to further decenter the self, not simply seeing a "concept of self" related to other abstract domains of social life, but seeing how selves are constructed variously in specific situations, how these constructions can be fragmented by multiplicity and contradiction, and how these constructions shape, and are shaped by, relations of power.

So Ohara-san's paean to his artisanal aesthetic must be taken seriously, as deeply meaningful and suggestive of nuanced, deeply felt emotion. But it must also be set more precisely within a larger story of artisanal work and, especially, within the context of the workplace. As Jacques Rancière has argued, "Whenever workers speak in the name of work, affirm its rights or glorify its greatness, we run the risk of inferring a false picture of the collectivity they represent or of the realities that underlie their speech, unless we determine very precisely who is speaking, who is being addressed, and what the stakes are" (1986, 327).

I begin, then, with Ohara-san and his story, for he was the embodiment of "traditional" craftsmanship, and as the chief of the factory (*kōjōchō*), he served as the symbolic center of the factory workplace and keeper of the dominant discourse. In so doing, my agenda is threefold. First, I want to set Ohara-san's tale within a prevailing discourse of artisanal work as self-realization and aesthetic participation in the material world, as a testament to cultural *difference*. This first move emphasizes the generative, joyous, even romantic aspects of the production of certain aspects of work identities. Second, I want to show that the discourse on artisanal identity, when contextualized within the workplace, reveals itself as a way of creating and legitimating hierarchy, by partially excluding younger men and certainly excluding all part-time workers, almost all of whom are women. Cultural meanings are not free-floating and disembodied, but are implicated in systems of power relations. Finally, lest this remain a slightly more sophisticated version of functionalism (e.g., à la Paul Willis, 1977), I attempt to complicate the picture, asking how these meanings are challenged in everyday life on the shop floor, how the dominant discourse of artisanal identity is itself subtly shaded by ironies and ambiguities, and how, within a larger political and economic situation, Ohara-san's tale acquires new and, for him, embattled meanings.

Ohara-san, Artisanal Idioms of Work, and a Narrative Production of Self

Ohara-san, as the chief of the *wagashi* division and head of the factory, was a particularly compelling subject given my tacit anthropological "foreunderstandings" about cultural distinctiveness. First, *wagashi*, Japa-

nese confections, are themselves loaded symbols of "tradition." John
Singleton (personal communication) calls them "favorite examples of
traditional craftsmanship in Japanese TV—exemplars of a national self-
image of 'tradition'." In a sense, Ohara-san was creating himself in narrative as a kind of living stereotype of the "traditional artisan," images he
himself invoked and images imposed on him by others. Younger workers
told me that yes, he was more *kibishii,* severe, than his counterpart in
Western pâtisserie, and that working in silence (*damatte, shigoto dake o
suru*) was "typical" for an artisan. Those outside the trades, such as my
landlady and her family, nodded when I described the atmosphere in
Ohara-san's division. "*Dentōteki,*" they pronounced. A "traditional" artisan who made "traditional" Japanese confections.

One must also remember the particular circumstances of the story's
telling. As an anthropologist, I found the romantic tale of "traditional"
craftsmanship compelling, a confirmation of academic descriptions of
cultural difference. And as an American researcher, I was someone
Ohara-san could impress with what was, after all, a fairly unexceptional
life history in this artisanal milieu. Gender, too, cannot be ignored. If
work identities are infused with gendered meanings, and if creating a mature self in work is also a way of becoming a man, then telling this story
became a demonstration of masculine prowess to an appreciative female
audience—as, significantly, he sipped his Scotch and water and methodi-
cally downed four plates of *sashimi.*[3]

During our conversation, Ohara-san traced out the following outlines
of a tale.

He was born in the thirties, in the cold, poor northeast of Japan. Short-
ly after he had graduated from middle school, both of his parents died
tragically in an accident, forcing Ohara-san to quit school and find a job.
He knew it would be as an artisan, because from childhood, he loved
making things. In fact, his favorite childhood hobby was building ships in
glass bottles, the more complicated the better. An uncle, a confectioner
in a neighboring town, took pity on the orphaned Ohara-san and took
him on as an apprentice. A few years at his uncle's workshop taught him
the basics of the trade, and Ohara-san decided to move on. All of life, he
said enthusiastically, is a form of *benkyō,* learning, and each shop had its
own *yarikata,* its own way of doing things. Learning these different
yarikata kept him moving, first within the same province, and then, in his
late teens, all the way to Tokyo, to try his fortunes. There too he moved
regularly from establishment to establishment, about once a year during

his early years of apprenticeship. After his skills were honed, however, he sometimes quit sooner; once, because the level of expertise was so low (*teido ga hikui*), he walked out after a single day. The quest to pursue his craft took Ohara-san to ten or twelve different workshops—from the posh suburbs to neighboring Shizukoka prefecture to the livelier areas in Shitamachi, the old downtown. But when he got married and, especially, when his children were born, Ohara-san began to think better of his itinerant ways, and decided to settle down (*ochitsuku*) in one spot. That was twelve years ago, and he has been with the Satō establishment ever since.

Ohara-san spoke in nostalgic tones about his early period of apprenticeship, though it sounded grueling, hardly the material for nostalgic reminiscence. Because the master was showing his benevolence and largesse in teaching tyros the trade, a salary of any substance would have been unthinkable. Free room and board and a pittance of a wage sufficed. The work was demanding, beginning at dawn and lasting until late at night. Yet, according to Ohara-san, these years of preseverance were a necessary part of his training. Those who stuck it out were the truly dedicated. What enabled them to endure was a dream of becoming master craftsmen themselves and one day opening their own shops. "You have to have a goal," he stated emphatically. (*Mokuhyō o motte yaranai to, dame mitai.*)

For Ohara-san, work was his reason for living, his *ikigai*. In *geijutsu*, his art, his expertise and artistic sensibility found expression. The proper practice of his craft requires skill and a delicate sensitivity to the changes in the seasons, for *okashi* change according to seasonal rhythms. This feeling for the seasons (*kisetsukan*) he extolled as wonderful (*subarashii*), one of the greatest pleasures of his work. The more mundane tasks, making *okashi* for everyday consumption, can be done equally well by the younger men, who possess the necessary strength and stamina. The attitude of most young people today, he assured me, is very different from his own. "They're in it for the money. A craftsman's attitude today is rare."

At this point, a young artisan sat down at our table, and overhearing Ohara-san's last remark, added his confirmation. Itō-san pointed to himself as a good example: "I'm not in this line of work because I like it." Work was a way to pass the time, to make money, so that he could one day realize his dream of sailing around the world with his wealthy relatives. He had no particular commitment to the craft or to the company. In fact, Itō-san eventually quit his position at the Satō confectionery and found

233

Gender and Work Identities

another job in a machine shop that did subcontracting work for Mitsubishi Heavy Industry.

Itō-san provides a foil for Ohara-san's story, which emphasizes "traditional" notions of artisanship. Let us begin by exploring the parameters of a mature artisanal identity: first, a discourse on creative self-realization through work, by polishing the self through hardship; second, an artisanal aesthetic connecting selves to material objects and to the natural world. Later, we must more clearly situate these discourses within the particularities of the Satō factory. Clearly, Itō-san shows us that not all artisans and not all workers share in these celebrations of work. For Ohara-san's tale of aesthetic self-realization also begins to tell us how some people come to be defined, in certain contexts, as less fully human than others.

Artisanal Idioms of Work:
A Collective Story

The self-images of present-day artisans are constructed within a cultural and historical "narrative field" (cf. Haraway 1988) where the notion of craftsman or artisan is deeply meaningful symbolic territory.[4] During the institutionalized class system of the Tokugawa period (1600–1868) artisans were placed below farmers as not "of the land," but they were above merchants, as producers who could create objects rather than living from mere commerce. The industrialization of the Meiji period saw segments of the artisanal population becoming *shokkō,* factory operatives, rather than artisans. The status of these operatives slipped well below that of the merchant, and factory workers generally were considered part of lower-class society (cf. e.g., Gordon 1985; T. C. Smith 1988). These parameters have changed in the postwar period; for the people I knew, the more salient divisions—at least according to Ohara-san's story—are between *shokunin,* artisan, and *shain,* company employee. Such new distinctions are richly emblematic of the contemporary prestige of middle-class, white-collar work in well-known companies.

In the ward of Tokyo where my informants lived, the term *shokunin* was used for virtually anyone who worked with his hands, even for people who seemed to be doing assembly-line work. Lathe operators, people who operated metal presses, painters of metal parts, makers of industrial-strength soap, as well as the makers of more obviously "traditional" handicrafts, all considered themselves *shokunin.* And although middle-class executives are accorded a certain dominant social prestige, *shokunin* had their own special place as the bearers of a unique Japanese

234

"tradition." For instance, a year or two before my research began, the ward office had compiled a glossy booklet with pictures and short biographical sketches of a number of artisans in the ward, living reminders of this glorious national heritage. Having these artisans in their midst enabled the ward to make claims to its cultural legitimacy, a legitimacy constantly at issue in this largely commercial and industrial area. And for artisans, claiming their identities as craftsmen gave them access to a certain respected position in society. This is all the more true in a culture which celebrates "traditional" artisanship as a symbol of national identity, to the point of canonizing certain artisans as Living National Treasures—an honor equivalent to any accorded great artists in the West. The cultural *distinctiveness* of the following maturational scenario of Japanese artisanal and personal growth cannot be understood without this wider context, where "craftsmanship" is celebrated and elaborated as a symbol of "Japanese tradition."

Work as Maturity and Self-Realization

One important way my informants talked about the process of maturation was through the notion of *ichininmae,* literally one complete portion for one person. It can refer, among other things, to becoming a mature human being (*ichininmae no ningen*), a mature gendered being (*ichininmae no onna*—a mature woman), or in the factory setting, a mature practitioner of the trade (*ichininmae no shokunin*). This process is an arduous one. It means having to undergo hardship, *kurō,* for only in this way will the hard edges of immaturity be planed into the roundness of adulthood. *Kurō* can be found in carrying out the requirements of a social role, whether it be the role of bride, mother, or worker. The hardship of a young person in "training" for the university entrance exam can be a form of *kurō*. So can economic hardship. So can the efforts of a beginner in the Zen arts.

In a work setting like the Sato factory, however, *ichininmae* and *kurō* are implicated in a particular artisanal system of apprenticeship. In the Tokugawa period, and, according to informants, through the prewar period, the *totei seido,* apprenticeship system for artisans, as well as *detchi bōkō,* apprenticeship service in merchant households, followed general patterns, informed by more general notions of *shugyō,* perfecting a trade, paying one's dues in order to become a skilled worker and a mature person.

The most exemplary form of *kurō* takes place outside the natal home, for separation from one's circle of attachment is itself a form of suffering. The theory is that outside the home, people must monitor their behaviors more carefully, polishing their skills as social beings. Indeed, the trials of the apprentice learning the particular customs of his master's house is sometimes explicitly compared to the position of a bride (or an adopted bridegroom), who must adjust herself to the ways of her new household (Singleton, forthcoming).[5] Embodying this ethos is the phrase I first heard from my landlady: *Tanin no meshi o kutte koi,* literally, go and come back, having eaten someone else's rice. Typically, successors to merchant households, for instance, were sent away, perhaps to a larger company in a related trade in order to learn the business. For the local *sake* shop owner's son, for instance, it meant working for years in the Kikkoman soy sauce company[6] before he came back to take over the family store. The owner of the beauty salon where I worked for a month or two planned to send her son to a cosmetics firm to work for a few years before calling him back. Five of the young artisans in the Satō confectionery were there on five- or six-year contracts to learn the trade before they returned as the young masters of their own families' confectioneries. Their skills polished, their selfishness tempered, the artisans would only then be ready to shoulder the responsibilities of succession.

Up until about the 1960s, from most informants' accounts, young apprentices went as *sumikomi jūgyōin,* live-in workers. Typically, they were provided with free room and board, usually in their master's house. Everyone took their meals together. Living conditions were often difficult, intensifying the degree of hardship. As in Ohara-san's story, work is described as having been demanding, occupying nearly all one's waking hours. Holidays were infrequent: the first and the fifteenth of the month, according to the older men. Wages, too, were paltry, equivalent to pocket change and little more. Masters felt justified in maintaining these working conditions because they were graciously offering apprentices the opportunity to learn the trade. The terms of the bargain were, from this perspective, generous. In exchange for their pains and expenses they incurred, masters could expect loyalty, gratitude, and disciplined hard work from their apprentices.

Not everyone would agree on this portrayal of the system, however. Masters were supposed to be exigent in their demands, and from the point of view of the apprentices, this could sometimes slip into exploitative and abusive treatment. Mythic tales of masters' cruelties abound. Tanoue-san, himself a third-generation woodworker trained by his own father, waxed eloquent on the exploitative nature of the apprenticeship system. *"Kyokutan ni ieba, dorei mitai na mon datta n desu yo"* (To exaggerate a bit, they were like slaves), he averred. *"Ningen atsukai ja nakatta"* (They weren't treated like human beings). The master and his family, went one oft-repeated story, took sumptuous meals, complete with fish, vegetables, and steaming bowls of soft, white rice, while the apprentices huddled in the background with cold leftovers, or even worse, rice mixed with barley.[7] In *hidoi uchi,* terrible households, even the tea would be the cold leavings from the master's cup. "Ah, yes," said Mrs. Tanoue, nodding her head. "I've heard stories like that." Sometimes, the treatment would be so unbearable that the apprentice would simply try to flee. Tears starting in his eyes, face flushed and agitated, Tanoue-san related the tale of one of his father's friends, who, after months of mistreatment, attempted his escape. Penniless, wearing his master's wife's old *tabi* (split toed socks), he trudged along the railroad tracks all the way from downtown Tokyo to the countryside of neighboring Saitama prefecture before he was caught.

No one can quarrel with the emotionally wrenching nature of the stories, or the fact that some masters may have exploited their apprentices. Again, however, the stakes artisans have in telling these tales may differ considerably. As the successor to his father's artisanal workshop, Tanoue-san was trained by his father. Emphasizing the exploitative nature of the apprenticeship system was perhaps a way of justifying his own lack of experience with this particular form of hardship. Another man, a maker of umbrella handles, described with thinly veiled distaste a master who constantly berated him with the epithet *don,* stupid. On the surface, he decries the *totei seido,* apprenticeship system, as exploitative. But the condemnation is ambiguous. For an artisan's claim to special powers of endurance and fortitude—and, therefore, a special claim to maturity and toughness—is also heightened thereby.

If moving outside the home and enduring difficult living conditions were defined as culturally meaningful forms of suffering, so were the pedagogies of the workplace. Like other forms of pedagogy linked to processes of self-realization, artisans' training sometimes began with cleaning, sweeping, cooking, and other tasks having no apparent relation to their chosen trade.[8] Even when the artisans began to take a more active part in learning appropriate artisanal techniques, there might be little explicit verbal instruction from the master. Learning through observation (*minarai,* literally seeing and learning) was, and often still is, the primary mode of instruction. In more vivid terms, they were supposed to *nu-sunde oboeru,* learn through stealing, learn on the sly, for one could not necessarily count on formalized instruction.

People in the ward of Tokyo where I lived and worked still clearly believed in the salutary benefits of *kurō,* hardship, through an apprenticeship-based system of pedagogy. In the Satō company, *kurō* was also invoked as a positive good, leading people to maturity. It was most often used by the older women when discussing the foibles of the younger artisans. Once, for example, the *shachō,* company president, caught Suzuki-san, one of the younger artisans, smoking on the shop floor—a capital offense in an industry where rules of hygiene were critically important. "What will the customers think if they find cigarette ashes in their cake!" shouted the owner. Suzuki-san hung his head and listened meekly, but as soon as the owner stepped outside, the young artisan exploded, "I'll quit on that bastard!" The division chief then approached, and in tones of world-weary resignation, reprimanded him with, *"Omae ga warukatta n da yo."* (You're the one at fault.) The part-timers murmured their approval in the background. To them, Suzuki-san was still *namaiki,* fresh, cocky: he hadn't suffered enough yet (*kurō ga tarinai*), and for his own personal growth, he should be made to suffer (*kurō saseta hō ga ii*). In fact, Suzuki-san was already taking the first step, by apprenticing himself to a firm far away from the north country village where he was born, so that he could learn to be a more mature human being in the process of becoming a skilled artisan.

Prevailing notions of skill among artisans—in the present day as in earlier times—stress physical idioms of technical capability. The aim is to go beyond a purely cognitive level of learning, and to *karada de oboeru,* to learn with the body.[9] A multiplicity of idioms indicate that this is a kind of physical knowledge. An artisan's skill and technique is known as his *ude,* his arm, and to hone a skill is to polish one's arm, *ude o migaku.* Both the male artisans in the confectionery factory and the female hairdressers at the salon where I worked for a few months spoke of "attaching the technique to the body," *gijutsu o mi ni tsukeru.* For the women, their specialized knowledge and practical abilities were part of their *yomeiri dōgu,* their dowry; if they had to work to support the family or to supplement the family income, they would be able to do so. The assumption is that the technique becomes one with the person, and that once learned, this physical knowledge can never be effaced. Once committed to muscle memory, skills and techniques become a palpable part of the self. Those who have put in their years of training; those who have tempered their skills to the point where skill is "attached to the body," have also become more mature persons in the process.[10]

The portability of skill dovetailed with common ideals of traveling from workshop to workshop to learn new techniques, thus highlighting *mobility* as an integral part of artisans' self-definitions. Clearly this presents a career trajectory quite different from that of today's Organization Man or even from the merchant households, where, in order to rise in the hierarchy, apprentices had to come in at a young age and remain with the same firm. Gordon (1985) describes the difficulties of early factory owners in the Meiji period, who constantly complained of problems of labor discipline. The independent artisans hired to work in the factories were often hostile to this more regimented work setting.

The pattern of moving from workshop to workshop was a living reality for many of the older artisans, who had long histories of job mobility. Matsumoto-san, the chief of the baking division, had worked in at least ten different places, all of them in the Shitamachi section of Tokyo. He quit his various jobs for a variety of reasons: disputes over job responsibilities (too much delivery, not enough time to actually make confections) and personality conflicts with the master ("We just didn't get along") seemed the most frequently cited reasons. To find new jobs, Matsumoto-san did not have to rely on personal connections. Five years ago he simply got out of the subway, saw a sparkling, well appointed sweet shop (*Eki mae ni kirei na mise ga aru ja nai?*) and marched in to talk with the head of the factory. He had been with the Satōs ever since. His skill in the midst of a shortage of skilled artisans meant that Matsumoto-san could always find another job, and not surprisingly, he radiated confidence.

Having polished the heart and the arm through hardship, having learned new techniques at a variety of establishments, having acquired in the process a certain confidence and a pride in his work, an artisan could be described as possessing *shokunin katagi,* the artisanal spirit. Such artisans' artisans are, according to prevailing images, totally identified with their work. They are said to feel their *ikigai (raison d'être)* in the pleasure of creation. If I mentioned this quality to artisans I knew, the remark inevitably produced similar results: a modest denial, followed by a smile—which I usually read as an expression of scarcely concealed pleasure. The complete involvement in creation should far outweigh the importance of monetary gain; indeed, I found the phrase *shokunin katagi* most often invoked to describe older artisans who made objects for which there was a declining market. Far from letting this situation discourage them, they continued to produce finely crafted works. Accordingly, a true *shokunin* possessed of *shokunin katagi* should practice his craft even if the financial reward were small. This dedication to creation above all else clearly entails a lack of worldliness, and indeed, this is another commonly invoked cultural image of the artisan, as naive and pure (*tanjun*), unschooled in the ways of the world.

When I discussed artisanal work with artisans and people outside the trades, more often than not they would make some reference to a quintessential *shokunin* personality, a logical corollary of this artisanal dedication to creation. Conventional wisdom depicts artisans as taciturn, a bit rough in their manner, not quite skilled at the niceties of social interaction. Ohara-san and many of the *wagashi* artisans conformed to this image, but perhaps the most striking example was Tsukamoto-san, the subchief in *wagashi,* who quite literally hardly ever said a word. Taking this artisanal quality to a dysfunctional extreme, he was ruining his chances for marriage by his taciturnity, despite his "advanced" age (late thirties) and the best efforts of many friends and co-workers. In his last blind date[11] he was pronounced "boring" by the prospective bride.

In my interviews, the lack of social skills recurred in the guise of ineptitude at business dealings, leaving artisans prey to the easy conviviality and flowery phrases of wily merchants or the machinations of cruel masters. A common ruse (common, at least, in "traditional" times—which for my informants tended to mean the early years of the Meiji Restoration) was for a master to say he would give his apprentices the capital to start up their own shops, according to the ideal pattern. "But if the master had ten or twelve apprentices, he wasn't about to shell out money for all of them. So after ten years or so he'd say, 'I was going to set you up in business, but you did this and this and this wrong. So forget it." said Tanoue-san, the woodworker. And in the face of such deceptive (*inchiki*) masters, artisans often described themselves as *kuchi ga omoi,* having a heavy mouth, lacking skill at conversation; or *kuchikazu ga sukunai,* not saying much. Though this verbal ineptitude was talked about in some ways as a failing, in another it embodies the culturally valued trait of *fugen jikkō,* silent action. This remains a defining feature of masculinity and a highly respected trait in any person; nothing is less respected than "big talk and no action," and many have written on the high value placed on silence and verbal repose in other domains of Japanese culture.[12] Whether or not these stereotyped images are true in some empirical sense (on the basis of life histories and observations, there seems to be enough truth to sustain the stereotype), they possess a mythic reality, and these images certainly form part of the self-images of at least the older artisans I interviewed.

To become *ichininmae no shokunin,* then, involves hardship and training through an apprenticeship system. To older artisans the system may have had its exploitative side, but surviving its rigors attested to their reserves of endurance and perseverance. Selfishness is tempered through the hardships of going outside one's natal home, trying to learn until the knowledge becomes one with the body, and continually striving to find better ways to make beautiful objects. A full-fledged artisan is also a full-fledged *man*: able to make a living by his arm, or technique, tough and able to withstand long hours and deprivation, in stereotype and sometimes in actuality, a strong, silent type, the embodiment of one sort of masculinity. He thus assumes a place in a culturally meaningful social grid, as a symbol of Japanese tradition and a successful actor in a highly significant maturational scenario. For a mature artisan is a man who, in crafting fine objects, crafts a finer self.

Work and the Material World

In Ohara-san's narrative of work and life, the ultimate satisfaction was to be found in experiencing work as *ikigai,* a reason for living. This artisanal ideal, based on certain forms of learning and on a notion of maturity forged through the hardships of apprenticeship, involves another level of meaning. Self-realization through one's art arises from certain kinds of relationships between people, their tools, the material world, and nature. Ohara-san, in particular, insisted upon the links to the seasons as one of the most wonderful (*subarashii*) aspects of his work. For artisans like Ohara-san, a work aesthetic celebrating a positive engagement with tools, machines, and nature, provides another axis along which to construct a mature artisanal identity.

Work and the Seasons

The passing of the four seasons (*shiki*), like the term "island country" (*shimaguni*), almost inevitably enters the conversation when Japanese people talk about Japan's uniqueness. Certainly, even if one were oblivious to changes in climate, it would be difficult to miss the humanly fashioned seasonal markers. Like the general emphasis on aesthetics in certain arenas of everyday life, attentiveness to the passing seasons is an integral part of everyday existence and cuts across class and regional boundaries (Lebra 1976, 21).

So pervasive is this seasonal aesthetic that I can only enumerate one or two of the many ways in which it graces everyday life in Tokyo. Greetings—both verbal and written—almost invariably make some explicit reference to the season, to a far greater extent than is the case in the United States I know. The range of possible expressions is finely graded and highly elaborate. Letters, for example, use conventional seasonal greetings for the rainy season, the height of the summer heat, the lingering summer heat, the appearance of the "new green" (*shinryoku*) of the spring leaves, the brilliant fall foliage, and so on.

Clothing, too, changes seasonally, i.e., according to a conventional, humanly determined calendar, and not according to weather or temperature. One changed from winter to summer kimono, for example, on a particular day, regardless of the weather. In contemporary Tokyo, the same holds true, for example, for school children, who change from winter to summer uniforms and back again on designated, "seasonally appropriate" days. Even in seemingly technological contexts, the passage of the seasons intrudes. The heat in the subways and electric trains is turned on and off on certain fixed days, defined as hot and cold seasons.

One incident vividly illustrated to me the culturally conventional, humanly fashioned aspects of Japanese seasonality. Before I began working at the Satō factory, I was living with the Sakamotos, a family engaged in the construction business. One summer day, I was about to leave the house to visit my relatives on the other side of Tokyo. The daughter of the house stopped me as I was about to step out the door. She stared at my clothing appraisingly, making it clear that my beige skirt and long-sleeved beige blouse, sleeves rolled up to the elbows, did not meet her approval. "*Yoku nagasode de irareru wa ne*" (It's amazing you can stand wearing long sleeves), she said through pursed lips. I protested that this blouse was very light and cool, long sleeves notwithstanding. She immediately retorted that what I was feeling was quite beside the point. I should change to a short-sleeved blouse in some cool pastel, for then "when someone sees you, they'll look at you and think, 'Oh, how cool she looks!' and they will feel cooler themselves." Chastened, I went back upstairs and found an ice blue short-sleeved blouse, which seemed to pass muster. But I was astounded that I was supposed to dress, not for personal comfort, but for the sake of the comfort of *others,* in accordance with some culturally constructed notion of seasonality. So clothing, among other everyday accoutrements of social life,[13] should be selected with an eye to culturally defined seasonal appropriateness and to one's obligations to a larger audience.

242

The seasons are an intimate part of the human realm, far more than simply an objective, climatic condition. The seasons connect human beings to a culturally constructed natural world, and reinforce a connectedness among human beings. Seasons and seasonal rituals locate you in a flow of time and link you to people who are part of your past, present, and future. In Japan, the rhythms of the changing seasons punctuate the rhythms of human life.

Seasonality and the Factory

Along the busy commercial street where shoppers passed the shiny glass and metal doors of the Satō confectionery, the seasons unmistakably announced their presence. Gaily colored plastic floral decorations dangled from every lamppost of the arcade, a ubiquitous feature of most commercial areas in Tokyo: pine and plum blossoms in the winter, shocking pink cherry blossoms in spring, gracefully curving willows in the summer, the startling reds and yellows of autumn's maple leaves. But we could have measured the passage of the seasons equally well *inside* the factory without having once stepped out of doors, so closely is the confectionery business connected to the seasons.

The Japanese sweets, *wagashi,* in particular, express an appreciation for nature and for the changing seasons. Toraya, one of the most famous manufacturers of *wagashi* and purveyors to the Imperial household, describes this intimate relationship.

> The Japanese people have always highly valued the emotions evoked by the different seasons of the year. The traditional "wagashi" themselves express this delicate awareness of the four seasons. One of the main characteristics of these cakes is that they each possess their own descriptive and evocative names.

The Satō confectionery, like Toraya, made a variety of poetically labeled, seasonally appropriate cakes. "Iwashimizu," a spring issuing from the rocks, was a summer cake decorated to represent a mountain stream, the clear, pure water revealing a few scattered pebbles underneath. The harvest moon, a round, golden chestnut barely visible through its dark casing of bean jelly, was called "Gekkō," Moonlight. Full-bodied confections of winter might resemble "Snowflake": a plump, white mound of steamed dough, a snowflake pattern burned into the top. Western confections were also seasonally variable. For example, during the summer light, cool gelatins and custards were the most common fare, while in the

243

winter these were abandoned for the heavier, creamier pastries and cakes.

Seasonal rhythms pulsed through the factory via the yearly cycle of rituals and holidays, creating enormous variations in demand. The rice cakes and other auspicious symbols of the New Year changed to the cherry blossom sweets of Girls' Day; the rice cakes wrapped in oak leaves (*kashiwa mochi*) of Boys' Day shifted to the hearty *ohagi* for the equinoxes; and the year ended with decorated Christmas cakes (which, Japanese are convinced, are an American tradition) topped with plastic houses, candy canes, and Santa Claus. The seasonal rhythms also created wild fluctuations in working hours. During slack times, artisans began at 7:30 in the morning and ended work around 6:00. But on one exceptionally busy day in March—itself perhaps the busiest month, given the plethora of holidays and rituals for which sweets are given as gifts—the artisans worked until midnight, put cardboard sheets on their metal work tables to sleep, and awakened at two in the morning to put in another 22-hour day.

Ohara-san claimed a connection to the natural world and to the passage of the four seasons as an integral element in a work identity. Certainly, a sensitivity to the seasons is critical in the confectionery business and finds expression in many ways in Japanese society. A delicate aesthetic sensibility does not surprise in this milieu. But an artisanal aesthetic of work is not limited to the passing seasons; it extends to the assumptions some artisans hold about their relationships to tools, machines, and the material world.

Work: Artisans and Machines

The artisanal idiom of work depends on the interconnectedness of persons and the material world.[14] Artisans gracefully transform nature, and there can be a relationship of respect, a kind of cooperation, among human beings, their materials, and their tools. For example, Tanoue-san, the woodworker, used to talk of the *kosei,* the unique characteristics, of each piece of wood. "Traditional" artisans like Tanoue-san worked with simple, hand-held tools and a mechanical lathe, creating objects of great simplicity and beauty, objects we have come to associate with a distinctively Japanese aesthetic. In this setting, perhaps it is not surprising to find a relationship of respect and mutuality among artisans, their tools, and their materials.

Yet even in more "industrial" workplaces I found similar discourses.

Another neighbor, Mr. Fukuzawa, was a *puresuyasan,* the maker of plastic accessories, including Snoopy and Hello Kitty. His small, dark workplace and the incessant clanking of the press hardly seemed the stuff of enthusiasm or romance. On the contrary, however, he spoke animatedly about the pleasures of his work. He was always trying to work *with the machine,* to do his work more quickly, more cleanly. What seemed to me like drudgery represented to Fukuzawa-san a testament to his ingenuity and creativity. And again, the machine was not an instrument of alienation, but something with which he could cooperate in the production of a fine object.

This mutual affinity between human being and machine can be seen in even more apparently atomized, industrial contexts. Lest readers think this affinity is a function only of the size of the workplace, I quote extensively from the unpublished field notes of Matthews Hamabata, who, in his research on large family enterprises, *dōzoku gaisha,* visited a brewery that manufactured a well-known variety of Japanese liquor. This particular factory was viewed as a model for all other breweries owned by the company; from conception and design to management techniques, it was the most efficient and productive in the chain. Even here, or perhaps especially here, there is a close relationship between men— the gendered term is used intentionally—and their machines, for the machines are considered extensions of human beings. The factory drew upon its symbolic fund of "traditional craftsmanship," displaying on the walls, above the metallic glint of the machines, artisanal tools from various historical periods. Again, they consciously invoked the legacy of the craftsman, seen as creating himself in his products, as a direct precursor of the present-day artisans. The invocation seemed to work.

> The odd thing is: all three managers felt that there was a special spiritual presence in all of their machines; and they stressed over and over again that their major concern was the maintenance of their machines. . . . But it wasn't a love of machinery as machinery, but of machinery as some kind of spiritual extension of themselves: *kikai o migakeba, kokoro mo migakimasu* (if you polish the machines, you're also polishing your heart). . . . For them, machines were extensions of themselves as spiritual beings, as creators of things, things of high quality. Quality was their main goal, . . . quality over speed and productivity. At any rate, there is a connectedness between men and machines, not only between men and men; there is a constant transcending of the self to create a beautiful product, a community product (Hamabata 1981).

245

The penchant for humanizing the machine implies that human beings and machines partake of the same world, and that people are intimately identified with the process of production, for the very machines they use in creating their products—even if the product is made on an assembly line—can be thought of as parts of themselves. The quality of the product reflects on its maker. The worker has many avenues, then, for identifying with the product: through his skill, through the machine that helped produce it, and through the product itself, as a creation of both a particular individual and a larger company community. Thus machines both partake of the human world and, through their use in the work process, provide one of the ways human beings reaffirm their connectedness to one another. By cooperating in the creation of a product, the artisans Hamabata describes can reaffirm their social identities. Far from contributing to alienation, artisans like these at the brewery and Ohara-san in the confectionery factory can find satisfaction in their connectedness to nature, tools, and machines.

This notion may seem less difficult to accept when placed within a particular religious and cultural context. In Japan, Shinto spirits, *kami,* may inhabit both what we would call animate and inanimate objects. Trees, rocks, waterfalls, and other natural formations can be imbued with *kami* and are sometimes worshipped as sacred. *Kami* may also reside in the workplace and in tools that workers use. Perhaps this close interrelationship was most evident in the factory on ritual occasions. During the dedication of the new Satō factory, a Shinto ritual of purification readied the *kama,* or boiler, for its new home—for workplaces and homes are always purified by Shinto priests before business begins as usual. One of the most interesting examples occurs in the film "The Colonel Comes to Japan," by John Nathan. In one of the scenes at the opening ceremony for a new Kentucky Fried Chicken franchise, a Shinto priest in full regalia brandishes his sacred staff, purifying the shop, before the ribbon is cut and the expectant crowds pour in. The New Year provides occasion for more ritual acknowledgement of cooperation among human beings, tools, and machines. At the confectionery, the center of the factory was the *kama,* or boiler. Here one could find the New Year's display of *omochi* (rice cakes) topped by a *mikan* (mandarin orange). Artisans like Tanoue-san also make a New Year's display in their workrooms, to indicate their gratitude to their tools. Artisans give thanks to the machines for aid in the previous year, and make requests for the same benevolence in the coming year: the same New Year's greeting they would give to their bosses, their friends, and their customers. Tools and machines can, then,

246

participate in the human domain; they can even be invested with a certain spirituality or life force.

Becoming a full-fledged artisan and a full-fledged human being at the workplace means engaging with the world in a particular way, cultivating a close relationship between men—again, I use the gendered term intentionally—and the material and natural worlds. Solidarity is created between men and the world, and between men and men: those who share this engagement with tools, materials, and the seasons.

Clearly, we cannot dismiss the evident enthusiasm of the artisans as mere sham, bad faith, or false consciousness. Though we (specialists in "mental" work, accustomed to thinking of machines as instruments of drudgery and alienation) may find a combination of aesthetics, spirituality, and industrial work odd, it may not be so in every culture. Machines and tools are not necessarily harbingers of alienation, for they can also be instruments of artistic creation. The enthusiasm and poetry animating these tales demand to be taken seriously as integral components of a mature artisanal identity.

Yet locating these romantic tales in the contexts of their telling should begin to arouse our suspicions. Ohara-san was talking to a foreign researcher and a woman at that, trying to convince me of the value of his work and displaying his artisanal/masculine prowess. The brewery managers were in a similar position as representatives of an exemplary factory. Surely under these circumstances they, too, would accentuate their romantic connections to work, and their invocations of an artisanal ethos through the display of artisanal tools was certainly a reinvention and appropriation of tradition. Such stories also lead us to another series of questions: How are idioms of romantic connectedness and participation implicated in relations of power in particular situations? Do all workers share this same vision of work? And what of the potential ambiguities in even a single tale? Does even Ohara-san feel connected and fulfilled in his work all of the time? In order to address such doubts, we must return to the Satō factory.

Hierarchy, Exclusion, and an Idiom under Siege

The Satō confectionery employed 30 full-time workers, including several young men on contract to learn the trade before they went home to take over their own family confectioneries, and seven to eight part-timers, with one exception married women with school-age or grown children.[15] In this milieu of family business, there were pronounced structural and gender hierarchies in the assignment of work.

At this point, one must begin to ask how a "center" and, therefore, the "margins" come to be in the Satō company. Skilled artisans occupied the top of the hierarchy. Their greater claim on artisanal maturity through apprenticeship and their aesthetic engagement with the natural and material worlds legitimated the hierarchy. At the apex were the chiefs of the Japanese and Western sweets divisions. They knew the ins and outs of the work processes as a whole, from folding boxes to crafting the most exquisite and unusual confections. Perhaps the supreme expression of the chief artisans' superiority lay in their abilities to creatively adapt their skills in order to develop new varieties of confection. Changing consumer tastes made this constant innovation imperative: *"Jidai ni notte ikanai to"* (If you don't go along with the times), said Ohara-san, shaking his head, "you won't be able to make it." This creative component of work gave the division chiefs an opportunity to use their expertise to devise new products, and they spoke with satisfaction of seeing the new project through, from conception to execution to commercial success. Their superior skills made them indispensable to the company, and their greater experience, knowledge, and creativity provided legitimation for their superior positions in the company.

This presumably skill-based hierarchy was pervasive at the factory, the symbolic chain of command apparent at a glance. The chief stayed mostly in his own completely enclosed small work space, accessible through a glass sliding door. Everyone addressed him in relatively polite language (*desu/masu* forms). It was easy, too, to discern the relative rank of the younger artisans, for they were arranged in order of seniority at their work tables. We part-timers were usually crowded together at a single table, our circumscribed space an index of our lower status.

Perhaps the most telling differences lay in the payment of wages and benefits. Accurate information about salaries and income can be notoriously difficult to come by in Japan, particularly in the small business sector where tax evasion is a way of life. The division chiefs all received a monthly salary of undetermined amount, based on seniority and status; like all company officers, they earn no overtime pay. The younger workers were also paid a monthly salary, from which sums were deducted for housing in the company dorm (about $40 per month), food (about $10 per month), cleaning of uniforms, and so on. Obviously the company heavily subsidized their expenses. Wages depended on seniority, but generally speaking they averaged around ¥100,000 a month ($500, at the exchange rate of ¥200/dollar), with small yearly increments. The part-timers were paid by the hour, and unlike the regular employees, they received few benefits of any kind (e.g., insurance, pension plan, etc.). The hourly wage when I began working at the factory went from ¥300 to ¥420 per hour, with yearly increments of ¥20 per hour, then the equivalent of five cents per hour per year.

In the factory, hierarchy was a familiar fact of life, visible in the use of language and the arrangement of space, and recapitulated in the awarding of wages. But was hierarchy always based on skill alone?

Divisions of Labor?

In fact, daily work rhythms could be quite fluid, and consequently, the divisions of labor were not always clear. A variety of tasks were performed by both part-timers and artisans; for instance, a part-timer and a young artisan worked together making *yakigashi,* sweets baked on a large griddle. One part-timer actually did some of the same decorating jobs carried out by younger artisans: making designs on petits fours, for instance. Depending on orders, artisans could in fact spend much of their day doing work that, as the part-timers explained to me, "*dare de mo dekiru,*" anyone can do.

Consequently, the artisanal aesthetic is vibrant with meaning for only a *few* artisans, for work they do for a relatively short period of time. Older, more experienced men often perform tasks which do not make use of their artisanal skills; rather, they spend a considerable amount of time performing tasks more "properly" suited to younger artisans or to the women part-timers. Within this setting, legitimating the hierarchy of work through skill is for Ohara-san and his cronies an ambiguous enterprise. On the one hand, his superiority can be clearly demonstrated when certain kinds of tasks are required. But on the other, he must daily engage in numerous less artistic activities which do not make use of his superior skills. Indeed, a good deal of work is something "anyone can do." Under these circumstances, one way to ensure the perpetuation of hierarchy is to elaborate and celebrate the aesthetic dimension of work, thereby pointing out the lack of this delicate sensibility on the part of others.

I realized in retrospect that I was an active agent in reinforcing this hierarchy of skill. Here was a foreign researcher, from a prestigious university, no less, wide-eyed and impressed with what she saw. Ohara-san made full use of my presence. During my stint as a *pâto,* he would periodically bellow out, "Kondō-san!" and I would drop what I was doing to scurry over to behold his newest creation. In the summer, for instance, I remember how he arranged tiny blue cubes of gelatin to perfectly mimic the petals of the *ajisai,* or hydrangea. One sweet depicted a *tsukubai,* or water basin that is part of the tea ceremony garden, complete with a curving green vine and a single, small ivy leaf, again made of tinted gelatin. Ohara-san's deftness never ceased to amaze me. A few hand movements, the impress of a thumb, and the shapeless dough was suddenly transformed into a work of art. Sometimes, he would ask, "Do you know what this is?" and when I guessed right, he would say, "*Sō, sō,*" (that's right), with a pronounced air of satisfaction. On another occasion, soon after I began working in the *wagashi* division, Ohara-san removed from one of the top shelves a very real-looking artificial peony. He began to bend a leaf here, adjust a petal there. The flower was in fact edible, made principally of sugar, and the owners would sometimes take it to the shop to display in a special glass case. "This was done by *uchi no shokunin* (our company's artisan)," Mrs. Satō said proudly, on more than one occasion. These beautifully crafted objects were a profound source of pride for Ohara-san. And eliciting my exclamations was a sure way of "making his stock go up," as the expression goes, showing off his skills to everyone in the factory.

Artisanal celebrations of apprenticeship and an artisanal aesthetic thus reinforce the notion of a hierarchy based on superior skills. Yet in a milieu where those skills may find infrequent expression, artisans may try to protect their quite fragile worker identities through a series of exclusionary practices. Ohara-san's demonstrations of artisanal prowess were just one example. The most striking strategies distinguish the male artisans as a group from the female part-time workers.

Exclusionary Practices

From the outset, artisans were set off from part-timers through their training. Younger male artisans immediately embarked on a workplace trajectory based on the actual making of the confections, not merely wrapping them. Perhaps the most obvious differentiations of skill occurred when a new full-time worker was hired, or when a new worker was transferred in from another division. Immediately, he was given a place at the artisans' table, and he began with the substantive work of actually making or decorating the confections—no matter how clumsy he might be. Thus, development of an aesthetic approach to craft work and the teaching of skills to the *male* workers guarded the boundaries of this select group.

On a few vivid occasions the younger artisans received explicit instruction. One memorable day Yamada-san, the subchief of Western sweets, tried to show Kitano-san, his immediate subordinate, how to make a rose from buttercream frosting. Yamada demonstrated; Kitano tried his hand. The central core of the rose began to take shape. Then it collapsed. Three, four, even five times—and finally, a barely recognizable rose took form. "*Aa, aa, dame da na*" (Ah, it's no good. I just can't do this), Kitano-san mourned, as he stared ruefully at the tiny lump of frosting. Yet, with time and practice, he of course acquired expertise to the point where a few deft movements gave life to a perfectly shaped flower.

Similarly, in *wagashi* I was witness to a session where young artisans tried their hands at a sweet decorated with a tiny narcissus, a symbol of the New Year. The stem was made of thin strips of tinted green gelatin, the center of the narcissus from the tiniest smidgen of dough in which the pointed end of a stick, about the size of a pencil point, was inserted to make a miniscule hole. Instructed by Ohara-san's example, several young artisans stood intently, bent over the metal work tables, first rolling tiny balls of dough and then pricking them with the point of the stick. Suddenly one of them, a lively young man named Hiratsuka, stood up, threw up his hands, and shouted at the ceiling, "*Ore, konna komakai shigoto ga dame na n da yo!*" I (the vulgar or informal masculine term for "I") just can't do this detailed work! He stomped up and down the work room, "letting off steam," as we all chuckled at his antics. Finally he returned to his work station. Antics aside, one cannot fail to note that both episodes included only the male artisans. No attempt was made to teach the women, and the women themselves made no attempt to join in. We had too many trays of sweets to package. Teaching skills to the *male* workers ensured the exclusion of women from the ranks of skilled craftsmen.

Exclusionary practices could assume a verbal form. Who was an artisan, who wasn't, and what could be expected of these different categories of worker could be rendered starkly apparent. One day during a lull in his work, Ohara-san came over to help me package the large stacks of hearty *monaka*, a baked pastry shell filled with sweet bean paste. His fingers moved at least twice as fast as mine, and observing this, I blurted out, "My hands are a little slow." "Oh, that's all right," he said with a startled look. "Because you're not an artisan" (*Ii n da yo, betsu ni—shokuninsan ja nai kara*). The remark was kind and tolerant in some ways, but had a patronizing air, for my impaired competence could be excused because we occupied separate occupational categories.

One incident revealed to the part-timers the disturbingly low esteem in which we were held. Nomura-san, a woman in her fifties, walked in a little after 9:30. She began to describe her exhaustion, the reason for her later-than-usual arrival. "About this time of the week I always get tired," she said. "Housewives really get exhausted, because we have to do all the housework before we come here—then we stand on concrete floors all day, *then* we have to go back and do more work at home. If only we had two days of vacation," she said. "In only one, you just can't recover." (*Ichinichi ja, tsukare ga torenai.*) Iwata-san chimed in. "All of us have errands (*yō*), and you can't exactly sit in the house on your day off. You have to get your errands done on a day when you're still tired."

Later, after we had dispersed to do separate tasks and then came back to a central worktable, Nomura-san was fuming. Apparently one of the young artisans had overheard our conversation about our exhaustion and made a scornful remark, "But you don't even work eight hours" (*Hachi jikan hataraitē nē ja nē ka yo*). First of all, we didn't actually work eight hours, because we didn't get paid for our lunch hour, but we *did* come to work around nine and leave around five. "And besides", said Nomura-san, "that's what being a *pāto* means! We are paid cheap wages, we don't get the same bonuses and rest breaks that regular workers do, but our time is our own (*jikan ga jiyū*). . . . It's *because* we can't really work eight hours a day that we're *pāto*!" At that point, the conversation took an interesting turn. Yamada-san was almost 30 years younger than the women, and no doubt his scornful remark was even more insulting given his youth. They began to impugn Yamada-san's maturity: he was *wagamama,* selfish, and he expected the *pāto* to do everything for him, an especially damning accusation in light of his denigration of their work. The young man's logic of course recognized none of the contingencies constraining his co-workers' lives. In his eyes, the so-called less demanding, repetitive work should tire us less, and he obviously accorded little importance to the part-timers' double burden of work in the factory and at home.

The artisans, then, excluded women by identifying as a collectivity of full-time, skilled workers. As a collectivity, they could protect their identities by downplaying the many contributions of the women to the work process. Yet these women are also necessary members of the company, who in some ways constituted a threat to artisanal articulations of a skill-based hierarchy. In incidents of conflict, such as I have described, women questioned the legitimacy of this hierarchy, recognizing the valuable contributions they made to the firm and the fact that they sometimes knew more than the artisans did. Moreover, women part-timers did not fully accept the proposition that artisanal superiority was based on maturity, for some of the artisans were in fact young and, from the women's point of view, terribly immature. Perhaps it is precisely *because* of these slippages that artisans so strongly reasserted their distinctiveness.

Definitions of center and periphery were not under siege from the women alone, however. Larger changes in work organization, practices of worker apprenticeship, and the older generation's evaluation of younger artisans also created shifting definitions of center and periphery, highlighting the subtexts for Ohara-san's self-construction in artisanal work.

Embattled Idioms, Historical Change, and the Construction of Identities

In one of the more poignant moments of Ohara-san's breakfast narrative, he expatiated on the artistic (*geijutsuteki*) aspects of his work. The specialty sweets were his territory. But as far as regular sweets were concerned, the young people would one day overtake him. Some of it just takes strength. Only the *geijutsu,* the art, separated him from the younger, more resilient men. His fear of aging and his fear of waning strength were also evident in a remark he later made: "When my body gives out, they may tell me 'We don't need you any more'." (*Karada ga motanaku naru to, omē ga mo iranē kara to iwareru ka mo shirenē.*) Capitalizing on his aesthetic connection to the craft helped Ohara-san to protect his place in the company hierarchy, to reassert his in fact quite fragile work identity, and to fend off vaguely envisioned future threats from younger workers.

Ohara-san's artisanal aesthetic was becoming an embattled idiom—not just in the face of young workers or a work process that made little use of his skill—but by the organizational structure of the company itself. The character of artisanal work in the Satō confectionery was considerably different from the more truly face-to-face familialism of fifteen years past. In part because he revered "rationally" organized larger firms, the owner was no master artisan working alongside apprentices and journeymen; rather, he was the president of the enterprise (*shachō*), a prosperous businessman. Ohara-san the artisan found himself placed within an increasingly management-oriented, bureaucratic company. He was an employee with an official title in an official company hierarchy: the head of the factory (*kōjōchō*) and division head (*buchō*) of *wagashi*. In short, he was a company officer.

Like company officers in larger firms and bureaucrats in government ministries, company officers in the Satō factory could put their titles on their name cards. They received a monthly salary with no extra payment for overtime, also like executives in other settings. Moreover, Ohara-san and his immediate subordinates spent more time in formal learning about management than in studying new developments in making confections. Once a month, the owner compelled his chiefs to attend a seminar led by a management consultant. None of the officers evinced any enthusiasm for this duty. Yet even formal learning about their craft was mediated through the company. Once a year, the confectionery industry held a trade show, displaying the wares of various confectioners throughout the country, and Satō artisans attended the show as a group, "on company orders." Company rather than craft seemed to assume greater importance. And though the tendency to organize on a company or workshop basis has been pronounced throughout the history of artisanship since at least the Tokugawa period (cf. Gordon 1985), it seems clear that the prestige of larger industries has produced this particular form of company-mediated bureaucratic management.

Furthermore, few firms now offer the rigorous apprenticeships of old; this development has shifted the meanings of apprenticeship. The welfare familialism of larger industries provided the model for smaller firms like the Satōs'. No longer were young artisans in the position of supplicant learners. All received a salary plus room and board. Whereas in the past artisans and masters would take their meals together, perhaps even live in the same building, now the workers had their own company dormitory. Ohara-san viewed these developments with some regret, explaining that young men tended to identify more as *shain,* company employees, than *shokunin,* artisans.

This changing situation constituted one of the great ironies of Ohara-san's "dominance." He in one sense represented an artisanal ideal. Yet it may be an ideal on the way to becoming a mild anachronism, as definitions of self as company employee, the desire for clean work, and an avoidance of *wagashi* as too traditional seem increasingly prevalent, especially in Tokyo. A situation of labor shortage may accelerate these changes, for recruitment is the most pressing problem for the Satō company and for most other small firms. In order to compete with larger companies for factory workers, small firms have had to offer some kinds of welfare benefits simply in order to maintain their work force. Interviews at other companies in this ward of Tokyo, and a trip with the representative of the Subcontractors' Association (Shitauke Kyōkai) as he made his rounds from company to company, turned up this complaint with numbing regularity. Mr. Satō dealt with the recruitment dilemmas by spending a good deal of time cultivating ties with the Satō family homestead near the Japan Sea, and traveling to vocational schools in the North Country, places where work was scarce and where young people could be lured to Tokyo with the promise of a job and in loco parentis care. The existence of numerous benefits could only enhance the prestige of the company and the attractiveness of a job offer. Young recruits from the country were in part motivated by the desire to learn a trade through "attaching the skills to the body," but the prospect of "joining a firm" also seemed to loom large. Some younger men may view Ohara-san's love of his craft as "traditional," even admirable, but it appears that increasingly few are likely to view it as a model for their own lives.

The Aesthetics and Politics of Identity

Ohara-san's story provides a way for us to explore, finally, the complexities, ambiguities, and subtexts in any narrative of self-construction, indeed in any "concept of self." Taken seriously, his romantic tale of hardship through maturity and aesthetic engagement with the world is a testament to the meaningful aspects of his work. Clearly, work mobilizes emotion and draws upon aesthetic sensibilities, even a certain spirituality, in ways that controvert our expectations about "mere" craft or industrial work. Ohara-san's narrative undercuts teleologies of inevitable, overwhelming worker alienation in industrial settings. His work is a source of identity and pride, both in and of itself, and in the value it has for the company. An economic situation of labor shortage heightens this value. Indeed, since my stint in the factory, the Satōs have only increased their prosperity. Two new branches of their shop have opened in a neighboring prefecture just outside the Tokyo city limits. Consequently, we can expect the demand for skilled workers like Ohara-san will only increase, augmenting his sense of centrality to the organization.

Still, a construction of self in work is not innocent with respect to power. Ohara-san's story was also an active attempt to reassert his identity as a skilled artisan and to buttress his claims to legitimacy as head of the factory. Thus, artisanal celebrations of work identity are persuasive attempts to aggrandize status and legitimize practices excluding other kinds of workers, especially the so-called unskilled, from admission to the community of mature, full-fledged male artisans. Solidary worker communities, or satisfying worker identities, though compelling for certain people in certain contexts, have their less romantic sides. The aesthetics of work cannot be separated from its politics.

However, one should not therefore take my argument to be as a functionalist tale of oppression. For although an aesthetics of artisanal work excludes the unskilled, and though Phillips and Taylor have rightly pointed out that often gender, not skill, is the real issue at hand, these exclusions are not simply put in place, never to be dislodged. Definitions of artisanal work are under siege, precisely from the quarters of the excluded. For example, women part-timers sometimes accept certain aspects of artisanal claims on maturity, but they do *not* accept an absolute hierarchy based on the superiority of *all* artisans. For the younger men are precisely that: younger, less mature. In the women's hands, the *artisanal* idioms of maturity provide the tools with which part-timers can criticize the artisans for failing to live up to this ideal.[16]

Historical and economic changes also assail the univocity of Ohara-san's narrative. Mature artisanal identities based on apprenticeship and delicate aesthetic sensibilities are embattled from threatened obsolescence, increasing emphasis on hierarchical company-based forms of organization, and a division of labor in which similar tasks are performed by all categories of worker. A celebration of work identity may even more strongly assert claims to a superiority based on skill, precisely because that superiority is under siege. Ironically, Ohara-san may fear that his very claims to superiority on the basis of his artisanal spirit will one day relegate him to the status of quaint traditionalism, particularly *if* members of the younger generation do indeed identify themselves as "company employees," not "artisans." (Let me emphasize that this is not a foregone conclusion, for I am not relating a teleological tale of inexorable "modernization.") Ohara-san's story reveals a final irony. He himself has apparently abandoned one important motif in this collective story, for though he may still hold a dream of opening his own shop, he has effectively opted for a secure position in a stable company, where security outweighs desires for independence and mobility. And as I argued in the preceding chapter, in Japan in the postwar period workers are inevitably defined, at least to a significant degree, by their company affiliations. In more ways than one, Ohara-san, too, has become an Organization Man.

Artisanal identity is thus no global totality, a unitary, bounded "self." To the contrary, Ohara-san's narrative of self-construction revealed not a single "self," but different selves, alive with complexities and deeply felt, subtly nuanced, often contradictory emotions. Investigations of selfhood's cultural meanings or workers' identities must begin to sensitively explore the multiplicity of selves and the fragility of those identities.[17] Nor can selves be easily bounded off from the "non-psychological" realms of history and political economy, for people like Ohara-san create themselves within these realms, giving larger forces a human face as they interpret, challenge, change, and recreate those forces. "Self" and "society" are not mutually exclusive, clearly demarcated entities, but open and shifting, resisting closure and final definition. Finally, I argue against a view of selves as universal, substantive essences, inert in their states of being.[18] Rather, people like Ohara-san are constantly *becoming,* crafting themselves in particular, located situations for particular ends. Ohara-san spun out his identity *in narrative,* to me. His was a selective account of selfhood, which he centered exclusively around work as a way of claiming for himself certain culturally celebrated ideals of craftsmanship. When he could, he *enacted* his work identity on the shop floor, using my presence, for example, as an opportunity to assert this identity. Ohara-san's artisanal self was, in short, produced in narrative and in performance, in specific, delimited situations. Ohara-san shows us that a unitary identity must be seen as an assertion, a rhetorical figure if you will, momentary and illusory.[19] An aesthetics *and* politics of meaning would embrace a view of selves as historically located, nuanced by ironies, and contextually asserted and reasserted within shifting relations of power.

8

Uchi, *Gender, and Part-Time Work*

The discourse on male artisanal identities, seen as rhetorical assertions riven by ironies, inseparable from their historical, economic, narrative, and performative contexts, leads us, finally, to the place of women as part-time workers in the Satō company. Placing them at the end of my account is a deliberately ambiguous move. It simultaneously enacts the part-timers' central importance to the firm as the capstone of my narrative, just as it enacts their marginality, relegating them to the status of an afterthought. The positioning of my female part-time co-workers within the firm and the larger context of Japanese society provides the occasion for me to bring together the many threads of my argument, allowing us one last consideration of contests over the meaning of *uchi,* this time as an explicitly gendered domain.

Any supposedly feminist account of gender and women's status in Japan of necessity negotiates an insuperable paradox between, on the one hand, the dangers of Orientalism—reinforcing stereotypes of Western women as the most liberated, while our "poor Asian sisters" languish in submission, subjugated by their men—and on the other, the imperative to carry out a culturally specific feminist critique. The complexity and delicacy of this negotiation arose in Ohara-san's case. I argued that he is both dominating and dominated, a target for critique and a poignant figure. Undeniably, his performances of masculine prowess exclude women and younger men, but in turn, they must be seen as fragile constructions, assailed by political/economic changes and constant challenges from the shop floor. Part of his claim to legitimacy and dominance lies in cultural and labor market forces which largely reserve the domain of full-time work for males. And this dominance of men in the domain of work is celebrated and recreated in culturally specific narratives. In Ohara-san's case, his conventional, narrative production of self resonates with familiar, culturally elaborated notions of maturity and craftsmanship, even as a changing political/economic context undermines the legitimacy of those very conventions.

I will argue in this chapter that similar complexities and ironies are at work in my female co-workers' lives. They asserted their gendered identities in a highly effective, powerful way, claiming for themselves an informal space within the symbolic center of the factory. But their strategy to claim this central space and in so doing, challenge the masculine celebration of prowess and self-immolating endurance on the job, inevitably relied on the discourses at their disposal, discourses about women and their place in the *uchi.* Equally inevitably, this deployment of gendered identities possesses certain structural limits, even as it creates possibilities for fulfillment and a sense of strength. For in the larger context of Japanese culture, women's narrative productions of identity in work are not part of the central story. Their narratives are not the subjects of cultural celebration; indeed, their lives cannot be arranged into a teleological sequence of increasing mastery in work.[1] In creating gendered work identities on the shop floor, my female co-workers found themselves structurally excluded from the central masculine narrative of artisanal identity, marginalized by their position in the labor force and by multiple definitions of *uchi* as a discourse about gender, embodied in both informal practices and contests over meaning at the level of law and public policy. In turn, these exclusions cannot be understood without careful attention to their nuances and inflections through a class discourse, highlighting both the shared identities and the sharp differences among women. By performing their gendered identities on the shop floor, women marginalize themselves, on the one hand, and on the other hand strongly assert themselves, making themselves indispensable to the informal social relations at the factory and providing critical challenges to a masculine heroics that would celebrate 22-hour workdays. Their stories speak to the complex issues of possibilities for resistance to hegemonic ideologies, underlining the creative potential for multiple points of contestation, just as they underline the limits, tensions, and unintended consequences of those challenges. Because my co-workers, like all of us, must use the culturally available tools at their disposal, perhaps they—and we—will never be able completely to "dismantle the master's house."[2] But resistance need not be seen as radical rupture or apocalyptic change in order to be effective. Through the stories of my female co-workers, perhaps we can begin to discern creative possibilities for subversion amidst the ironic twists of meaning that complicate the crafting of gendered selves within fields of power.

Stories of Work

Immediate and striking as I confront my fieldnotes and memories, constructing accounts of my co-workers' work histories, is the fragmentary, almost contingent nature of the women's stories and the circumstances of their telling. No commanding, masterful performance of a coherent, familiar story took place here. And I was not constructed as admiring audience for a bravura performance à la Ohara-san. Rather, my co-workers' narratives of work were really snatches of conversation caught as we wrapped, cleaned, filled, and decorated sweets. Their narrative productions of work identity—far from single, seamless performance delivered to a rapt audience—were pervaded by a sense of fragmentation, both in the circumstances of the telling and in the narrative line, as the women simply moved from one part-time job to another, without a teleology to satisfy desires for totalizing narrative closure, a ready sense of progress, or some easily discernible way to perceive continuity. Though their stories did not culminate in a linear scenario of the ever finer polishing of skills and maturity, the women I knew did speak with a sense of pride in work—but equally striking was a sense of urgency and economic necessity. The narrative conventions shaping their work histories seem contingent and noncumulative, a series of episodes that focus less on the joys of work itself than on the general value placed on adding a bit to the family income and doing something other than sitting at home.

For example, Sakada-san provided me with a long and impressive work history that appeared as almost fragmented episodes. As we stood together at one of the metal tables and wrapped sweets with gold paper, I asked her whether she had worked anywhere before she took this job with the Satōs, where she had been for three years. She laughed, and told me she had done all kinds of work both before and after she had married her husband. "When I was single," she said, animatedly, "I used to work in a garment factory in Iidabashi.[3] It was close to Yasukuni Shrine, and about this time of year, we used to go there to see the cherry blossoms and have our flower-viewing parties." The factory, she further explained, was near K. Bunko, a famous publishing house, and she laughed as she described the lunchtime rendezvous the women at the factory would have with the young men from across the way. "The guys would hang something out their window as a signal," she said, "and then we would get our lunches, and go out and eat together on the grounds of the shrine. It was innocent, really." But apparently the *shachō* of the garment factory got wind of this, called up the head of the publishing house, and they mutually put a stop to their employees' lunchtime fun. Sakada-san spent three years sewing in the garment factory before she got married.

After that, she moved to Asakusabashi, where her husband was apprenticing to a wholesaler. "I worked all over then," she continued, and I nodded in amazement as she began to recount her many places of employment: Yokoyama, Asakusabashi, Bakurochō, and two or three other spots in Shitamachi. It was dizzying to contemplate. The hardest, she told me, was a cloisonné factory near Uguisudani. She proudly described what skilled work it was, and how hard everyone found it. "I was the only *pāto* then," she said proudly, "and I stayed for a long time. Lots of people just couldn't get the hang of it."

Even with the birth of her children, Sakada-san took only a year or so off from doing some sort of wage work. At first, she did *naishoku*—piece-work at home, which had the advantage of flexibility, even though the wages were low. You did the work when your hands were free. And since her children had reached school age, she had resumed part-time work outside the home. She has been with the Satōs for two years. Sakada-san in particular loved to make things and work with her hands: sewing, knitting, and handicrafts were her favorite hobbies. When I left the Satō factory, she brought me a doll made from a soda bottle, covered with clothing she herself had sewn. Certainly her skills at handicrafts served her well in her work. Sakada-san put us all to shame—including the artisans—when it came to complicated feats of wrapping. Sakada-san's was a story of skill, but it is a story of fragmentary skills picked up in a variety of jobs. It is the dedication to wage work that impresses, no matter what its content.

Another narrative of ceaseless activity in wage work was related by Teramura-san. One of the most generous people I knew, she would invite me out for lavish *sushi* lunches I knew she couldn't possibly afford, and she would sometimes bring me small gifts—a doll made from paper, a top, little "mementos of Japan." I was always amazed at her stamina and energy. After a nine-to-five day literally slaving over a hot burner, tending the griddle where she baked the pastry shells for many of our sweets, she took off her uniform, walked about four city blocks down the street along the municipal railway line, and donned an apron at her second place of work, a *yakitoriya*.[4] I talked to her about her long days. "Don't you get tired over there?" I asked her incredulously, my own aching feet uppermost in my mind. "Usually, I don't," she claimed. "It's only when we're not busy, and we have to just stand there that I feel really tired. Right at five it's kind of empty, but things are busy from 5:30 to 7:30 or so, because people like to stop off after work to have a drink and a bite to eat. And then the place starts to empty out around eight. Anyway, I prefer working to just sitting around at home doing nothing" (*Uchi de jīto suru yori. . . .*). In fact, it was her experience in restaurant work that emerged in her descriptions of her work history. Before she started the two jobs, about a year and a half ago, she had worked part-time at a large, fancy restaurant in a neighborhood down the road a mile or two, where she helped out during the parties and banquets. I visited Teramura-san at the *yakitoriya* a few times, and she seemed to enjoy an easy rapport with customers, engaging the regulars in teasing banter. I wondered whether the chance to talk to people was all the more appealing given the restrictions of her day job at the factory, where she was so busy at the grill she almost never had a chance to come and talk with the rest of us. And though I never was able to find out about people's income—a delicate subject in Japan—I strongly suspect that the two jobs were a financial necessity, just as they may have provided a way to "get out of the house."

Itakura-san's story differed slightly from the tales told by these women who were a good ten to twelve years her junior. Part-time work was a recent feature of her life. It was only six years ago, when her husband was very ill and in the hospital, that she knew she had to go out and earn some money. "I thought for a long time about what kind of work I should do," Itakura-san mused. "I used to be good at sewing and tailoring, but there isn't much demand for that kind of work these days, and besides, it's too hard to sew for other people. I like to knit, but you can't really make money that way. And I decided that wherever you go as a part-timer is about the same, so I came here, to the Satōs. It's clean work, and I didn't want to go to a place where there were sixty-something people. And I'm not qualified to do office jobs anymore, like I did before I was married. Anyway, working is better than sitting around the house, and moving around is good for you. It's good to work, too" (*Hataraku no mo ii deshō*). Again, the striking element here is the notion of part-time work as getting out of the house and earning some money. The content and the place of work are merely incidental.

Finally, an interesting contrast between owning a small firm and working in one animated Nomura-san's comments to me. She lived only a few blocks away from me, and we would usually walk home together at lunchtime, complaining about how our feet hurt and how we never felt rested after only one day of vacation. She often told me about her daughter, who was about my age, and sometimes, secretly, she gave me little presents of food, worried that I was all alone in a foreign country without my family nearby. In many ways, Nomura-san seemed to enjoy her part-time work, even if it was physically taxing. She had been raised on a farm, and "even if the pay is low here, at least we have fixed hours. Plus on the farm, you can't ever say, 'the work is finished'" (*Kore de ii to iu koto wa nai shi* . . .). It was especially interesting to hear about the days when she and her husband used to run a sandal-making factory. "It's a lot easier to go out and get a job working for someone else," she stated emphatically. She went on at length about their problems with employees, mostly young women from the neighborhood, some from the country. All of them worked on the sewing machines. "But they were so young," she said as she shook her head. "They used to fight about whether the radio was too loud, or what program they should listen to. The older people were better; they understand more, and they compromise, but the young kids—well, they weren't like that." Over the years, the sandal-making business grew less and less lucrative, as large producers dominated the markets, and Mr. Nomura was apparently an easygoing type of manager—*nonki,* as his wife put it. They had no one to take over the enterprise, so one day they just decided to quit. Nomura-san came to the Satō factory, while her husband now works 18-hour shifts as a toll collector on the highways.

In these stories, told on the run between tasks, narrated episodically as we walked home, begun and then cut off by the necessity to start up some new task somewhere else in our work space, we may see pattern, but the patterns do not reinscribe familiar conventions associated with maturational scenarios of increasing prowess and self-fulfillment. Ohara-san's romantic self-production through hardship and poetic connection to the seasons could not be invoked as the structuring narrative convention for these stories. But that said, how do we make sense of these tales of work? And what do the stories say about the ways these women and the other part-timers at the Satō factory performed their gendered work identities on the shop floor?

In attempting to sketch out a response that takes into account some of the complexities at work in these vignettes, I begin with the larger historical discursive field within which women's work histories are produced. And this requires, first, an examination of the production of gender in the realms of national policy, law, and the changing labor market. These discourses provide both the limits and the creative possibilities for play and change. Individual identities, I will argue, are performed, but the possible forms and elements and tropes of those performances are always created within the terms of this larger narrative field.

The Discursive Field

The context for the stories begins with the Meiji period, when the projects of modernization and Westernization—or in contemporary terms, civilization and enlightenment—arose as terms of crisis in the face of Western economic, political, and military might and the internal tensions and contradictions of the feudal regime. With the overthrow of the Tokugawa shogunate, the reinstatement of the emperor, and the creation of a *rikkensei,* constitutional system (Gluck 1985), Japanese political leaders energetically embraced the task of fundamentally recreating the Japanese state. The abolishing of the four-class feudal system—including the bestowing of surnames on commoners, the repeal of sumptuary regulations; tax reform; and the adoption of the constitution, among other epochal changes—dismantled the structures of the *bakufu.* In this atmosphere of change and ferment, the Meiji bureaucrats and politicians dedicated themselves to the forging of national unity and a national identity. It is to this image of the Meiji leaders that Itakura-san referred when she invoked the selfless politicians of the Meiji golden age.

The slogan *fukoku kyōhei,* a prosperous country and a strong military, may have embodied the new national leaders' primary goals, but social change—*bunmei kaika,* civilization and enlightenment—also assumed a critical importance. Civilization and enlightenment often meant a revision of customs and mores so that Japan might more closely resemble the Western powers, for as Sievers (1983) argues, the Meiji leaders "hoped to undermine one of the arguments supporting the unequal treaty system: the Japanese were not yet sufficiently civilized to join the West on any sort of equal contractual basis. . . . as some Japanese correctly perceived, the definition Westerners gave the word was based on extremely parochial attitudes. To the extent that Japan began to look like the nineteenth-century West, it might be considered civilized" (Sievers 1983, 8). Among the Meiji leaders' concerns were far-reaching changes in institutions like the family and a reconsideration, within that context, of the place of women in society.

A variety of proclamations and regulations sought to effect changes in women's status. In 1870, concubines were given the same legal rights as wives (ibid., 13); in 1872 prostitutes' contracts and debts were canceled (ibid.), and women were freed from indentured servitude (Hamabata forthcoming, 79). Compulsory education for both sexes was legislated (R. J. Smith 1983a), though in practice many people chose to invest in their sons rather than in their daughters. On the basis of these reforms, one might be tempted to make a case for the higher position of women in the new Meiji state. But other changes undercut these reforms, and in the end, created a system in which women's subordinate position was enshrined in law. Sievers points toward a seemingly minor proclamation forbidding women to cut their hair, as emblematic of the Meiji government's policy on the question of women's role in the new state. Short hair for men (*zangiri atama*) was a symbol of progress, signaling their willing participation in the project of modernization and Westernization. "To the extent that women cutting their hair can be viewed as a real, if spontaneous, attempt to join the progressive forces trying to create a new Japan, the government's denial of their right to do so was also a denial of their right to participate and contribute actively to that change" (Sievers 1983, 15). Many present-day Japanese, like Itakura-san, see the Meiji leaders as ardent, pragmatic yet driven by high ideals, and working selflessly for the good of the country. Still, as products of their histories and culture, they did not always work for the good of women.

Perhaps the most far-reaching of the reforms affecting women's status were various attempts to restructure the family. The first of these new laws was the Household Registry Law of 1871, which reformed the old registration law that had been based on the feudal class system. The new registration was based on place of residence rather than class, and it used the *ie* as its basic unit (Hirota 1982, 4). As Hirota succinctly argues, the Household Registration Law created and buttressed patriarchal authority precisely by designating a single head of household: the man. All rights and responsibilities fell on his shoulders, including rights to property. The document's effect was to valorize ancestors, lineal relatives, and men over descendants, collateral relatives, and women (ibid.).

Perhaps even more far-reaching was the Meiji Civil Code of 1898. It was, even at the time, a retrograde document, standing in opposition to attempts by liberals and feminists to lobby for a more progressive vision of society and family life. As Ikeda tersely puts it, in the Civil Code as in the Household Registration Law, the head of the household = *ie* (Ikeda 1982, 76). It was an attempt to resuscitate older, elite models of family and gender roles. "Women who had hoped it would contain language redressing their lowly status in the family were stunned to find instead that it sanctioned that status" (Sievers 1983, 111). Again, the male household head was invested with all property rights, which passed from one household head to another, not to the spouse. Smith states: "The code is virtually silent with regard to the position of women in the household, thereby guaranteeing the primacy of its male head and his successor in each generation" (R. J. Smith 1983a). Women were not full legal persons according to the Code; the permission of the household head was necessary in order for them to undertake legal action (Sievers, 1983; R. J. Smith 1983a). Adultery was grounds for divorce only in the wife's case. As Smith notes, wives could divorce husbands, but only in cases where the husbands had actually been legally punished for the offense (R. J. Smith 1983a). In short, the Meiji Civil Code raised to the level of national law a subordinate status for women, and it legitimated a male-centered household.

In chapter 4, I argued that the code was an attempt to revive an already anachronistic family form characteristic of the elite samurai class. Part of this samurai legacy was a Confucian ideology of women's position: for example, the classic Confucian injunctions that women follow their fathers, then their husbands, and finally their sons. But other factors interlaced with these Confucian strands of thought. Hirota traces the sources of the lawmakers' attitudes both to feudal conceptions of women's roles, on the one hand, and to the Meiji statesmen's appropriation of Western models, on the other. The framers of the Civil Code apparently searched for precedents in documents such as the Napoleonic Code and took their cues from the Napoleonic dictum that a husband's duty is to protect his wife, a wife's duty to obey her husband (Hirota 1982, 7). The role of women, however, was not simply to serve their husbands or fathers or sons, but to serve the state. "Women, described by one of the authors of the code as 'excelling even Japanese men in patriotism,' were now to be tied to a family system designed to leave them few options other than to do the state's bidding" (Sievers 1983, 111–12).

Of all the injunctions for women to do precisely that, surely none was so resonant or influential as the Education Ministry's embrace and dissemination of the notion "good wives, wise mothers"—*ryōsai kenbo*. Japanese feminist scholars such as Takamure Itsue, as well as American scholars (Sievers 1983; R. J. Smith 1983a) trace the origins of the term to Meiji intellectual and member of the Meiji Six[5] group, Nakamura Masanao. A Christian, Nakamura reportedly found his inspiration in the nineteenth-century Western cult of domesticity, adapting it to the needs and goals of the new Japanese nation. According to Nakamura, "the family was a woman's proper sphere and . . . a woman's natural vocation was the education of her children. Given the recent Tokugawa experience, the suggestion that a woman should play a major role in the home, should be educated, and (within limits) demonstrate her intelligence and competence, was revolutionary" (Sievers 1981, 604). Uno (1988) sees another point of origin for the term *ryōsai kenbo,* in the writings of Miwata Masako, a female educator and frequent contributor to the magazine *Onna Kagami,* or *Mirror for Women.* Uno speculates that *Mirror for Women* was embracing and promulgating the notion of good wives, wise mothers long before it was taken up by the Education Ministry. She cites, in particular, the statement of purpose from the journal's premier issue in 1891: "The aim of *Mirror for Women* is to develop the special nature of chaste, true Japanese girls and to nurture the world's 'good wives, wise mothers' " (Uno, 1988, 9).

Whatever the source of the slogan, the message was clear. Women were to remain in the *ie* and to faithfully execute their duties as household managers and especially as educators who instilled proper Japanese values in their children. Thus, women, in fulfilling their appropriate gender roles, placed themselves in loyal service to the state. Uno argues that this vision of women's place marked a dramatic change from the Tokugawa period, citing numerous Tokugawa primers and manuals which emphasized mothers' *incompetence* in matters of child-rearing. Mothers were not strict enough to teach their children moral virtue; rather, this should be the duty of responsible males in the family, particularly the father. Mothers could engage only in "womb education": taking care of their diets while they were pregnant, and regulating their actions and states of mind in order to produce healthy babies (ibid., 5). Consequently, as both Uno and Sievers argue, the Meiji emphasis on wise mothers gave women a role as potentially competent educators of children, even after birth—a dramatic change from the Tokugawa past. Uno draws attention to the fact that this new role did not require the complete devotion to children and children's education said to be so characteristic of Japanese (middle-class) mothers in the postwar period: "average mothers' efforts to mold children into good subjects of the emperor sufficed." (ibid., 3)

Visions of women as good wives, wise mothers, animated so-called women's education. Education ministers, after about 1895, frequently mention good wives, wise mothers in their addresses (ibid., 10). Indeed, in 1899, "the government, as it instituted regulations requiring each prefecture to support at least one high school for young women, served notice that women's education would be standardized and be aimed at creating 'good wives; wise mothers' " (Sievers 1983, 112). Nagahara cites examples of several Ministers of Education, who invoke biological differences between men and women as justification for two forms of education, each appropriate to its object. Women's education should be the equivalent of our home economics or domestic science (Nagahara 1982, 152). Consequently, both higher education and vocational education (except for traditionally feminine occupations: sewing, weaving, the arts, painting, and making artificial flowers, among other activities) were largely ignored by Education Ministry officials (Hirota, 1982, 155). Instead, women's education should foster virtues such as diligence, frugality, discipline, perseverance, and cooperation, as long as those virtues were exhibited in the service of the *ie* and of the state. Women's education, therefore, was not designed to help women contribute to the state *outside* the household context, for women's proper duty—*shokubun*—was to serve the *ie* (ibid.).

In short, though feminists, socialists, and other progressive groups had engaged in lively debate and attempts at reform in the early two decades of the Meiji period, the 1890s ushered in an era of relative conservatism and patriotism, partially as a result of the successful war with China. For women, the decade saw the promulgation of a series of conservative documents which worked to legitimate women's lower status and keep them solidly within the *uchi,* the household. In 1890, women were officially barred from engaging in political activity until 1922, and an unsuccessful attempt was made to prohibit women from attending Diet sessions (Sievers 1983, 52–53). The conservative Imperial Rescript on Education of 1890 celebrated the Confucian virtues of loyalty and filial piety, and the family as the servant of the state. Again, women's place was said to be within the family. The Civil Code of 1898 enshrined a conservative, patriarchal form of samurai family as the law of the land, a tradition quite alien to the more fluid and egalitarian family lives of most Japanese. (Cf. R. J. Smith 1983a; Smith and Wiswell, 1982). And though endowing women with new powers to educate their children, powers that may have signaled an important change from the neo-Confucian ideology of the Tokugawa period, the Meiji leaders' choices still defined women in terms of their place in the *uchi* world.

Women Workers and Japan's Industrialization

The government's emphasis on female domesticity is especially ironic in light of women's prominent role in the industrialization of Japan. Spurred by a determination to catch up to levels of technological development and economic prosperity in the West, and to thereby equalize power relationships (whose skewed nature was symbolized in the unequal treaties with Western nations) the Meiji government threw itself into the task of rapid industrialization. Heavy industry, the first priority, was almost entirely government sponsored in the early Meiji period, and the workers in these plants were men (Tsurumi 1984, 4; Gordon 1985). During the 1870s the state established manufacturing plants in light industry as well—primarily materials, machine tools, and, especially, textiles: cottons and silks (Tsurumi, ibid.). Since the 1870s, the government encouraged women to work in these new factories, either in government supported private mills—most of the textile factories were in fact privately owned—or in government-owned plants.

Women workers were essential to the success of this industrialization program. Indeed, Sievers (1983, 55) points out that between 1894 and 1912, women formed an average of 60 percent of the industrial work force in Japan. Tsurumi further breaks down these statistics: "In 1900 female workers made up 62 percent of the labour force in private factories, and ten years later women and girls were 71 percent of the workers in private plants" (Tsurumi 1984, 5). Sievers points out that in 1868, the first year of the Meiji period, silk constituted two-thirds of the nation's exports. By 1912, the last year of Meiji, Japan led the world in the export of silk. From these economic indicators, it is not difficult to discern the central importance of women workers to the Meiji state's efforts to achieve economic growth. Yet, as Sievers wryly comments, "Working in a textile mill was patriotic; short hair and involvement in politics were not" (1983, 56).

The movement of young women into the labor force in these mills shows the elasticity of the boundaries of the household, and indicates that women's *motivations* were important determinants of what might be considered women's proper place. Wage work outside the home was not incompatible with devotion to the *uchi,* for it became a demonstration of filial piety. Most of these women were young and from backgrounds of rural poverty; consequently, the money earned in mill work proved an attractive proposition to many rural families. And not only would the daughter be able to provide some income for her family, there would be one less mouth to feed.

Yet the conditions which greeted many of the young women must have seemed little better than the straitened existences they had left. Indeed, conditions in the mills are now notorious, calling up "the sad history of factory women" (*Jōkō Aishi*) and images of Nomugi Pass[6], where young girls endured bitter cold and a long trek through a treacherous mountain range in order to reach their new workplace. Once arrived, the women were forced to confront brutal working conditions: long hours—officially 12 or 13 hours a day in spinning, for example (Tsurumi 1984, 6), low pay on what was essentially a piecework system, inadequate nutrition, dangerous machinery, and sexual harassment from supervisors. Tuberculosis and beriberi often awaited the overworked mill girls (ibid., 9).

Even in view of these grueling working conditions, management often invoked metaphors of in loco parentis care, attempting to at least sporadically set up the company as family. Women did not simply accept these definitions of their situation, but responded in a variety of ways. Escape was an extreme, but often used mode of resisting intolerable work lives. Workers were hired on the contract system, but even so many chose to renege on those contracts and escape the factory. As in heavy industry, rates of turnover were high.

> Few workers lasted more than a year on the job, irrespective of what the contract stipulated; most stayed only six months or slightly longer. The runaway or "escaped" worker became a symbol of the industry's preference for recruiting new labor and using it up, rather than investing in improved working conditions and higher wages. An annual turnover rate of 50 percent was typical of Meiji textile mills, and some owners seemed to have gotten into the habit of replacing virtually their entire female work force each year (Sievers 1983, 65).

In the face of this unstable labor force, Tsurumi describes management strategies to supposedly protect the women's morals as part of their in loco parentis role. Though morals may have been part of management's concern, their strategies were obviously designed to keep the workers from running away:

> "Usually dormitories were either surrounded by eight-foot fences or connected to the plant by a bridge eight feet above the ground. On top of fences and walls were broken glass, sharpened bamboo spears, barbed wire, and other forbidding objects. To be on the safe side, management locked the boarding labourers in the dormitories when they were not working" (1984, 7).

Sharon Sievers (1983) tells us about collective forms of resistance, in which Meiji women workers in textile mills initiated strikes and slowdowns. Indeed, the first labor strike, in 1886, was held by women at the Amamiya silk mill, in response to management attempts to step up the work pace and lower wages. Through their collective actions, the women were able to wrest some concessions from management, and they thereby prevented owners from instituting even more exploitative work practices (pp. 81–82). Other strikes occurred sporadically in the decades before 1890, including the Osaka strike of 1889, where 300 workers in a cotton spinning mill were able to wrest concessions from management, resulting in higher wages for workers. Sievers calls it "one of the most successful strikes staged by women anywhere in the world before 1890" (p. 83).

Tsurumi highlights yet another form of women workers' resistance: song. To those who would argue that women workers were docile, submissive, and accepting of management paternalism, she offers searing examples of women's protests:

> In Hide geisha get thirty-five sen.
> Common prostitutes get fifteen sen.
> Spinning maids get one potato.
> (In Tsurumi 1984, 13.)

Desires to escape, hopes for the future, and ambivalent, often nostalgic memories of parents and home animate the poignant lyrics (see Tsurumi 1984, 25).

> *Song of the Living Corpses*
> My family was poor,
> At the tender age of twelve,
> I was sold to a factory.
> Yet though I work for cheap wages,
> My soul is not soiled.
> Like the lotus flower in the midst of mud,
> My heart too,
> Will one day blossom forth. . . .
>
> When I return to my room,
> The supervisor finds all manner of fault with me,
> And I feel like I'll never get on in this world.
> When next I'm paid
> I'll trick the doorkeeper and slip off to the station,
> Board the first train
> For my dear parents' home.
> Both will cry when I tell them
> How fate made me learn warping,
> Leaving nothing but skin and bone on my soul. . . .

Prison Lament
Factory work is prison work,
All it lacks are metal chains. . . .

How I wish the dormitory would be washed away, the factory
     burn down,
And the gatekeeper die of cholera!

I want wings to escape from here,
To fly as far as those distant shores. . . .
                    (Cited in Tsurumi 1984, 13–15.)

In view of these moving songs of resistance, the high rates of labor turn-over, the outbreaks of strikes and slowdowns, and the ultimate form of protest—suicide (cf. Sievers 1983, 78)—management attempts to impart a sense of "company as family" seem at best a mockery.

What did women's entry into the paid labor force mean in terms of women's place in the *uchi?* How did such a situation articulate with doctrines like *ryōsai kenbo?* First, women in merchant households and in agriculture had always worked as part of their familial roles. In the case of the young factory workers, it was assumed that the women were working for the sake of their families, for by and large they came from rural households where their extra income was more than welcome. Young women were not abandoning their households when they left for the mills; rather, they were demonstrating their filial piety by going to work in the textile mills. Their commitments to the company were assumed to be temporary: a few years at most. More than one analyst has suggested that the doctrines of *ryōsai kenbo* and a celebration of women's primary duties to the household served the interests of an industrializing economy by providing a rationale for low wages and minimally acceptable working conditions. Without necessarily accepting the functionalist implications of such a view and its attribution of a kind of omniscience to capitalist managers, minimally one could still make a case for an ideology associating women with home life as incompatible with women's attempts to be treated as full-fledged members of a company.[7] Moreover, management attempts to set themselves up in the in loco parentis role as guardians of young girls' moral virtue—however cynical or sporadic those attempts—still associated women with home and with their proper domestic, feminine roles. In sum, then, the weight of Meiji law, prevailing familial ideologies, and rationales for women's work, all combined to keep women within the *uchi* sphere, despite women's protest and resistance.

272

The Occupation and Postwar Legal Changes

As I briefly discussed in chapter 4, the Occupation forces completely dismantled the legal strictures on family embodied on the Meiji Civil Code. Pharr (1980) shows in detail how these changes were contested and effected during the seven year period of the Occupation, from 1945 to 1952. By the end of this period, Japan had acquired a new, progressive constitution which, ironically, includes an Equal Rights clause that still eludes us in the United States.

Pharr traces the debate within the Occupation forces themselves, showing us the influence of a number of women in the Civil Information and Education Section who drafted measures dealing with women's rights, including sections of the 1947 Constitution. The initial measures proposed, according to Pharr, were far more radical than those which eventually found their way into the Constitution. The higher-ranking males in the Occupation forces could agree with the CI & E women about issues such as extending suffrage to Japanese women, but other measures met with considerable resistance. Citing the reactions of Hussey, a high-ranking official in the Occupation, to more far-reaching initiatives, Pharr notes, "Hussey, as a top level official, is opposing the pressure from the women's policy subsystem to implement a measure that would place other Occupation objectives in jeopardy. . . . Since there were many areas of Occupation reform where these leaders did not hesitate to incur such risks, it may be concluded that they assigned women's rights policies a relatively low priority in the overall scheme of things" (1980, 32).

Despite the debates within the Occupation about the place of women in the new Japan, and despite male revisions and resistances to the most progressive proposals, by the end of this seven-year period, an astonishing transformation—at least legally—had occurred for Japanese women. They were extended suffrage and the right to run for political office. The Labor Standards Law, containing protective legislation, was passed and went into effect in the same year. Article 14 of the 1947 Constitution endows men and women with equal legal rights, and discrimination on the basis of sex is deemed unlawful. Article 24 gives both men and women equal rights in marriage (Itō 1982, 298). The Constitution also made compulsory education and coeducation the law in 1947, repealing separate male and female education and altering the admissions policies of those universities which had not accepted women students (ibid.). Revisions of the Civil Code made equal inheritance the law and dismantled the structures of the *ie* system—though, as we have seen, these provisions have had limited impact for the people I knew. Within the Labor Ministry, the Occupation created a Women and Minors' Bureau, which exists to this day, to "help assure the implementation of the various legal guarantees extended to women" (Pharr 1980, 25).

Of course, law and everyday practice do not necessarily mirror one another, and these thoroughgoing and dramatic changes did not, and have not, produced equally dramatic changes in everyday life. Still, the promulgation of these measures undercuts the legitimacy of the patricentric practices within the household, at least at the level of law. It provides a changed setting within which the people at the Satō factory live their lives. My co-workers were reflective about those changes. More than once, the part-timers claimed that before the War, *Onna wa uchi ni iru mon da* (Women had to stay at home). However exploitative or unpleasant they might find part-time work, it is a possible option they could never have exercised had the postwar reforms and economic changes not occurred.

Women and Work

Indeed, for Itakura-san, Iida-san, Hamada-san, Teramura-san, Nomura-san and my other female co-workers, perhaps the most significant factors shaping their choices in life have to do with the labor market and the increasing entry of *married* women into the paid labor force, usually as part-time workers.

Since the end of World War II, the growth in the numbers of female part-time workers has been remarkable. In a study of female labor force participation from 1960 to 1975, Karen Holden delineates the large trends in women's employment, demonstrating the shift away from agricultural work and unpaid work in family businesses to paid work. Older women are a critically important segment of this growth in non-agricultural employment. In terms of women's probable work histories, Holden persuasively argues that "women at every age are more likely to work. . . . Declining rates of withdrawal for each younger cohort suggest that it is increasingly common for women to have continuous labor market careers or to experience only short interruptions in their work, if they do withdraw at all" (1983, 45). Many of the older women who enter or re-enter the labor force do so as so-called part-time workers.[8]

Economist Nakamura relates the trends in the Japanese economy during the postwar period to the growth in part-time work. He begins by arguing that conditions of labor shortage arose around 1960 after an initial postwar labor surplus. This labor shortage produced a number of far-reaching effects. Smaller firms were forced to offer more advantageous wage scales and working conditions in order to attract employees. Most important for our interests, the male temporary and day laborers had to be accorded greater benefits. Companies sometimes promoted them to permanent worker status in efforts to secure for themselves a more stable labor force (1981, 169). Apparently, even these measures did not produce the desired results, for "the number of temporary workers went on declining, to the point where this labor force could no longer be expected to function as a cushion against business fluctuations" (ibid.). Enter married women as part-time workers and pieceworkers. Between 1965 and 1974, over 95% of "workers for whom the job is secondary" have been women (ibid., 170). Indeed, of women employees, the proportion of part-timers was 8.9% in 1961 (Rōdōshō 1980, 12), and "increased from 12.2% in 1970 to 19.3% in 1980, the numbers almost doubling from 1.3 million to 2.56 million" (Steven 1983, 192). The growth in part-time work is especially visible in the retail and service sectors, which in 1983 employed 35.6% and 27.8%, respectively, of female part-time/temporary employees, while 22.2% found employment in the manufacturing sector (Rōdōshō 1984, 6). Predictably enough, the part-timers are the first to feel the effects of any economic downturn. The oil shock of the early to mid-1970s put a temporary stop to the growth of the part-time labor force, as the part-timers were the proverbial "first fired" (Nakamura 1981, 171).

From the employer's point of view, part-time workers are desirable for a number of reasons. According to a 1980 survey by the Ministry of Labor, employers cited as the primary advantage the savings in wages paid to employees, as well as the flexibility of a part-time labor force in responding to fluctuations in work pace and in demand for the product or service. A second major reason for hiring part-time workers was the labor shortage, a difficulty in finding permanent workers to fill the positions. Certainly the Satō company was perpetually searching for new recruits, and the grueling hours the artisans kept during the busy seasons were testimony to the *shachō*'s difficulties in finding full-time employees. The wives of owners of small businesses, however, often invoked another reason. With part-time workers, you didn't have to *ki o tsukau* (worry about someone—and in this context, also, watch the way you act) the way you did toward full-time employees. For Ogura-san, for instance, who owned a shoe store, the ability to hire part-timers was a blessing.

275

"We used to have to cook for the workers, and we always had to watch what we said, how we acted. Now the part-timers come, we pay them their wages, and that's that."

Part-time workers can be an economic blessing to managers, but what about the workers themselves? A 1983 Labor Ministry survey explored women's attitudes toward home and work. Among their respondents, 55.2% said their ideal scenario was to find a job, stop working temporarily to marry and bear children, and then resume work a few years later. A further 19.5% said they would use marriage and children as the reason to stay home permanently; 16.6% planned to remain on the job, while only 2.2% had no desire to seek employment (Rōdōshō 1984, 40). A survey asked married women about the kind of work they would prefer, and over half (53.2%) cited part-time work, while 25.4% preferred *naishoku,* or piecework they could do at home. In other words, the married women who responded to the survey desired flexible or shorter hours and/or work they could do at home, so that their household duties would not be compromised. A 1980 Labor Ministry survey asked women about their motives for seeking part-time work. Of those surveyed, 43.8% cited a desire to add to the family's income, while 38.5% said they preferred working to staying at home (Rōdōshō 1980, 15).

In examining the overall picture of part-time work, it is clear that part-time workers tend to be older, married women, and most of them work fewer years and in smaller enterprises than does the average full-time worker. In 1983, more than half of part-time female employees (52.9%) worked in enterprises with 1–29 workers, and in fact there is a negative correlation between the size of an enterprise and the proportion of part-time or temporary workers it is likely to employ. Of 1,270,000 part-time female workers, a good three-quarters were above the age of 35. The average age of part-timers is 41.7 years, while for regular, full-time employees it was 35.2 years. Of the part-timers, 85.9% were married. Part-timers had worked 3.6 years; the length of service is increasing from year to year, but it is still considerably less than the 6.3 years worked by the average full-time female employee (Rōdōshō 1984, 54).

As we will see, my part-time co-workers seemed in many ways to welcome this opportunity to work on a part-time basis, for their primary loyalty, they felt, lay in their responsibility to their families. Part-time work gave them the flexibility they needed in order to execute these duties, and none of my co-workers seemed to yearn for opportunities to become full-time employees. Employers generally often point to these attitudes as justification for hiring part-time workers and keeping women in low-paying jobs with little hope for promotion. But, as *Agora,* a Japanese feminist journal, asked, why is it that women do *not* ask for greater employment opportunities and greater responsibilities? Might it not reflect the lack of real opportunities presented to them in the labor market and the discrimination that exists once they are on the job? In 1977, for instance, women were earning 55.8% of men's wages. Then, as now, employers in large firms tend to hire young women out of junior college, who work until marriage[9] (the preferred age of marriage—*teki reiki*—is between 24 and 26) or until the age of 30, if they do not marry. If women seem unlikely to take the hint that their time is up, managers may use the famous *kata tataki*—tap on the shoulder—suggesting that the women leave the company (cf. MacLendon 1983). This enables the company to hire younger, cheaper recruits. Given the difficulties women face when they do seek full-time employment, perhaps it is simple recognition of these realities that at least partially accounts for the attitudes of women like my co-workers.

These economic, political, and historical trends delineate the parameters within which my part-time co-workers at the Satō company lived out their lives. Women's gendered work identities are in part created at the levels of national law, public policy, economic trends, and cultural ideologies, particularly the familial ideologies linking women to the *uchi,* the home. But the meanings of women's work identities are both flexible and enmeshed in relations of power. The story I have related thus far sets forth the limits of the discourse shaping my co-workers' lives, but it cannot account for the multiple, layered, ambivalent meanings of work as it is lived out in the creation of gendered work identities on the shop floor. In order to begin to trace these complex interrelationships, let us return to the neighborhood and to the Satō factory, to the meanings that the people around me gave to their work.

Work and Its Meanings

Work, for the people I knew, possessed theme and pattern; it provided a means of participatory belonging in a meaningful organization and constituted a method of creative self-realization. Work, for the owners of the Satō confectionery, enabled them to fulfill their duties to the *ie*-line and to derive a sense of their own competence and worth. For the male artisans, work was a central aspect of their masculinity and of their maturity; for the younger artisans, in particular, identification with the Satō firm, though riddled with ambivalence, provided a significant axis around which their identities could be constructed. For the women I knew, we shall see that work was an essential aspect of their definitions of self, controverting stereotypes and expectations about the fragility of part-timers' commitments to their work. All these discourses must be set, however, within the context of the artisanal/industrial/mercantile ward where the Satō factory was situated, for the forms that the participatory belonging and self-realization could legitimately take were highly circumscribed.

Watanabe-san, a taxi driver who lived in the house in back of my landlords, the Hatanakas, neatly summarized the prevailing attitudes of the *mawari no hito,* the people around you, in the ward where I lived. When talking about his neighbors, he explained, *"Karada o ugokashite inai to, nani mo shite inai to omowaretchau,"* that is, to translate literally, if you aren't moving your body, people will think you're not doing anything.[10] Nakane (personal communication) argues that the value placed upon serene contemplation that she so noticed in India, for example, does not exist in this Shitamachi area of Tokyo. Consequently, the emphasis on physical activity is at least partially inflected through class and economic status, for if my neighbors and co-workers were *not* physically moving, they in fact might not be able to make ends meet. In this ward where work meant physical movement in shops and factories, constant, sometimes frantic activity was a feature of everyday life, a feature I attempted to evoke at the outset, through the setting trope. Though my neighbors' work can be construed as evidence of human resilience and vitality, work for many of my neighbors was also grueling, tough, and consuming of one's life. A teacher who instructed many of the neighborhood children in his after-school cram school (*juku*), told me that the people in this ward were *shigoto no aima ni ikite iru,* living their lives in the intervals between work, in the interstices of work. "It's not that they like working so much—they are suffering, but they put up with it because they have to." The emphasis on physically visible movement was apparent even in people's choices of favorite leisure activities. The same teacher, Itō-sensei, told me that the mothers of his pupils all yearned to do sports of some kind. "That, you see, is the ultimate luxury—expending energy in leisure rather than work."

Given such a grim economic scenario, lack of physical activity would mean a breach of commitment to the family, a blemish on one's moral character. A person who is not moving must be lazy and unproductive, not doing his or her part to contribute to the family budget. Physically visible movement thus becomes an index of involvement with, and proof

of commitment to, company and family. And this proof of loyalty is required of both men and women. Iida-san, one of my part-time co-
workers, used to say that her working meant the difference between putting fruit or dessert on the table every night or only once a week. After a
visit with her and her two daughters in their small, dark apartment, I
could well imagine that her contribution to the family coffers was welcome indeed. The income brought in by Mr. Iida could not have been
terribly substantial, judging from the paucity of customers at his small
neighborhood shop which sold inexpensive slippers.

In such a milieu, the pressure to work if you are physically capable of
doing so was sometimes overwhelming. My landlady, Mrs. Hatanaka,
whose husband was quite a well-to-do white-collar executive in a
medium-sized trading company, was a part-time teacher of flower arranging, at that time more of an avocation for her than a way to make
money. She used to complain to me about the relentless pressure on her
to take some kind of job. Every time a sales person came by, she was subjected to all sorts of thinly veiled sarcasm. "You mean you're not
working—even if all your children are in school?" an insurance agent
exclaimed. The surprise was even greater if they found out that her son
was enrolled in an expensive private high school linked to one of Japan's
top private universities. But hardest to take were the comments from her
mother-in-law's friends.[11] If Hatanaka-san happened to be sitting down,
reading a book on flower arranging, for instance, the elderly widows
might comment, "Oh, so you're reading a book." "It's as though I shouldn't be reading when I could be working!" she would say to me with great
irritation. Or sometimes they asked, "What are you doing?" or "What do
you do all day?" as though housework just didn't count. "People make the
most incredible remarks," she continued. "One of my mother-in-law's
friends always comments about the expense of sending Kazuo to high
school. But last time I really got her. When she said, 'Your husband must
bring home a large salary (*kōkyūtori deshō, ne*),' I just agreed with her—
'Yes, thanks (*Hai, okagesama de*),' I said. We Japanese always downplay
things like that, especially income, but I just couldn't stand it anymore." In
fact, though, her protests notwithstanding, Mrs. Hatanaka did end up
working, as receptionist and right-hand woman to her good friend from
grade school, Yokoyama-sensei, the hairdresser. Hatanaka-san's letters to
me are now filled with energy and enthusiasm for her job and for her
new "career woman" persona. Recently, she has realized her dream of
opening up her own flower arranging school, using a room in their newly remodeled house to conduct classes.

Certainly the part-timers I knew fully embraced this imperative to work for wages. The seemingly indefatigable Teramura-san, with her two jobs, or Sakada-san, who returned to work when her children were still young, come to mind. So does Hamada-san, who did piecework at home while she raised her children. The job she had for years was assembling and making parts for a subcontractor to one of Japan's most famous manufacturers of cameras. She, too, claimed she hated to stay at home and do nothing but watch television. Financial necessity was especially acute in the cases of Itakura-san, whose husband died soon after he entered the hospital, and Akimoto-san, another widow who had been with the company for about two years. Her daughters were working as secretaries and "office ladies" in small companies in Shitamachi. Her job enabled her to get by, and judicious saving and payments on credit helped her buy her twenty-year-old daughter a lavish kimono for her coming-of-age.[12] For all these women, it appeared that part-time work was a financial necessity; it either provided the sole support of the family or critically important supplemental income.

Part-time Work and *Uchi* as a Gendered Domain

As my neighbors and co-workers showed me, work in this ward of Tokyo meant physically visible activity, especially in the form of wage labor. For the female part-timers I knew, this prevailing definition of work intersected in complicated ways with gender identity and ideologies of women's work. State-sponsored ideologies of domesticity such as *ryōsai kenbo* and more narrowly disseminated ideological precepts as embodied in, for example, the doctrines of the ethics retreat, define women in the interwar and postwar periods through their association with *uchi*, the domestic domain. This view of feminine identity prevails in the Western literature on Japanese women, and it has living significance as the image against which my co-workers, the part-timers, defined themselves. Women as a group share their commitments to the *uchi*, but these meanings are filtered through contextually specific, localized meanings of work, so that, paradoxically, for the women I knew, wage labor *outside* the home became an index of their commitment to the inside, the *uchi*.

The purest expression of devotion to the *uchi* and a recurrent image in the literature on postwar Japanese society (cf. E. F. Vogel 1963; S. H. Vogel 1978; Lebra 1984) is the middle-class Professional Housewife, who commits herself wholeheartedly to the betterment of her *uchi*, "a lifetime career requiring training, special skills, and endless devotion" (S. H. Vogel 1978, 16). This career is comparable to the all-consuming career of the white-collar executive, or *sarariiman* (cf. E. F. Vogel 1963). "The middle class, educated housewife also has a job" (S. H. Vogel 1978), the job of maintaining and promoting her *uchi.* Descriptions of "the middle-class housewife" emphasize themes familiar to those who have spent any time in Japan, including numerous tasks considered men's work in the United States middle class: for example, household repairs and household finances. Financial duties include the keeping of household accounts as well as real estate transactions (buying and selling houses, looking for apartments, dealing with landlords) and playing the stock market. Many men refer to their wives as the "Finance Minister" (Ōkura Daijin), for in addition to these financial responsibilities, the wives dole out their husbands' allowances, and many are the times one can see a man trying to cajole his wife to give him a little extra money. As in the United States, "emotion work"—providing a nurturant, warm emotional environment—and "the work of kinship"[13]—keeping track of the *uchi*'s links to other *uchi*—are the province of women. And middle-class women should ideally possess certain culturally constituted attributes of femininity: gentility, politesse, skill at cooking, and skill at arts such as playing the *koto,* flower arranging, tea ceremony, or in more recent years, English conversation. These are not merely idle pastimes. For the good of the *uchi,* women can find fulfillment in attempts to be the best housewife possible, and this can involve active participation in lessons and study. In short, the Professional Housewife[14] should embody certain values emblematic of a middle-class lifestyle: clear separation of *uchi* and *soto* spheres, and a devotion to *uchi* in the form of graciousness, competence in practical affairs, a sense of the aesthetic, and cosmopolitanism.

Above all, women in general are said to be devoted to their children. In Lebra's interviews, women invoked their children as their reason for living (*ikigai*), a theme emerging as equally central in Suzanne Vogel's account of the Professional Housewife. Indeed, Lebra cites cases of mothers who spoke of their children as "part of my flesh" (Lebra 1984, 163). For middle-class housewives, this devotion to children stereotypically assumes the well-known form of the *kyōiku mama,* education mother, who dedicates herself to her children's educational success, especially their success at the college entrance exams (cf. E. F. Vogel 1963). Certainly this is a weighty obligation in a society where success is often measured by one's educational credentials, for entering the right university virtually assures men a prestigious career and a secure future, though the situation is somewhat more problematic for women. The "education mama" stereotype is of a mother who does everything in her power to ensure her children's educational success, including sending her children to tutors and cram schools (*juku*), creating a quiet environment conducive to study, providing snacks for the hard-working student, consulting with teachers, and in general, acting as enthusiastic coach to her offspring in training for the Big Event.

Not surprisingly, these hegemonic images have relatively little salience among my part-time co-workers. The women I knew at the Satō factory were obviously devoted to their *uchi*, but their economic status and the local definitions of work inflected through this precarious economic status created quite a different scenario of femininity and work. Like middle-class housewives who stayed at home, the women I knew took responsibility for the household finances, household repairs, and real estate transactions. I remember in particular the keen interest that surrounded Iida-san's negotiations with her landlord, about the new apartment she had finally found for her family. Given these responsibilities, and adding to them an essentially 9-to-5 commitment to their jobs, few had time, money, or leisure to do much besides work in the factory, perform their domestic chores, and perhaps occasionally engage in leisure pursuits (Nomura-san was a particularly avid wrestling fan, while Sakada-san made dolls in her spare time). Housework had to be taken care of before or after their hours on the shop floor; usually the women did their laundry and aired the bedding before they arrived. "Sometimes," said Sakada-san, "something has to go. On Sundays, when the kids are home and I have to work, I just don't cook. My kids think that's what Sundays are." In fact, we all constantly complained about the hard work and the fact that the one day off—Tuesday—barely gave us a chance to renew our energy. "In one day," said Itakura-san, "we can't recover." (*Ichinichi ja tsukare ga torenai.*) "We don't even have time to rest," Nomura-san chimed in. "We always have errands to do." I remember, in particular, one Wednesday when Nomura-san came in looking tired and dispirited. "I had relatives from the country who came to visit—and on Tuesday, of all days!"

Many of the part-time workers defined themselves as occupying quite a different social location from that of the middle-class housewife. Time and again, when I asked them about their lives and their experiences at work, they would complain, but they would check themselves with the comment that *Jīto shiteru yori ii deshō* or *terebi o jīto miru yori, ii deshō;*

that is, it's better than just sitting around the house, doing nothing or watching TV. Itakura-san's warm smile and her comment, "It's good to work, too," reverberates in memory. Teramura-san's frenetic activity working two jobs and her energetic denial of her fatigue were also paired with comments about getting out of the house. And Hamada-san made a disparaging remark to me about one of my neighbors, a housewife who did not work for wages outside the home. "You see, women like that don't know what the world is like; they're just in the house all the time. They're narrow."

In this context, wifely accomplishments such as tea ceremony or flower arranging had little place. They were a luxury. "Oh, that's so *yūga,* elegant," said Sakada-san. "We here in Shitamachi don't do things like that. We'd rather have a good time (*asobu no ga suki*)." Hamada-san recounted an anecdote of her bewilderment at attending a tea ceremony. "When they served me the sweet, I just gobbled it up, and I drank the whole bowl of tea in one gulp," she laughed. In tea ceremony, the emphasis on etiquette is paramount, and guests are supposed to delicately nibble at the sweet and then drain the bowl in small sips, pausing after the first taste to appreciate the rich, astringent flavors. Hamada-san, in her refreshing way, pointed out the class bias of these pastimes when she called the tea ceremony *kidotteru,* snobbish.[15] My landlady, Hatanaka-san, corroborated their stories from the opposite point of view. "If I ever mention that I'm taking tea ceremony or teaching flower arranging, people around here always tell me how *yūga* I am. When I think of *yūga,* I think of someone who owns a villa in Karuizawa!"[16]

Nor was devotion to children in the form of encouraging educational excellence accorded much value. Conversations over the work tables revealed attitudes about human potential startlingly different from the *yareba dekiru* (you can do it if you try) ethos of the ethics center, an ethos often said to be indicative of Japanese attitudes toward achievement. Academic excellence was, according to Okamoto-san, a matter of *umare-tsuki,* innate abilities. "Yeah, pushing the kid to study doesn't do any good," Itakura-san concurred. "My kids were just born stupid!" "It's better," continued Teramura-san, "to help the family out so they have a little something special to eat every day." The differences between the statements of my co-workers and representations of Japanese mothers prevalent in the Western literature are stunning.

My interviews with schoolteachers and talks with middle-class housewives in the ward confirmed these impressions of difference. For one thing, mothers who had to work outside the home for financial reasons had little time or energy left to give to their children's education, even if they wanted to. And living conditions in many families did nothing to facilitate academic pursuits. Kaneko-san, a young schoolteacher in the ward, used to tell me about her "home visits." "So often, the shop or the machines are in the front of the house, and it's so noisy. No wonder the kids can't study," she lamented. People in my neighborhood were often unable to supply their children with the proper study atmosphere available in a more affluent home. In view of these straitened circumstances, most people chose to leave (*makaseru*) the task of education to the schools. This irritated housewives like Hatanaka-san no end. "At PTA meetings, they ask the teacher, 'What can we do? Our child just sits in front of the TV at night,'" she said shaking her head, "as if it were only the teacher's responsibility." Her own attitude could not be more sharply opposed to theirs. "My parents used to always say that even a pebble from the side of the road would shine if you polished it hard enough. They said it so often, I even had a complex—thinking I was nothing but a piece of gravel from the road!"

The class inflections are unmistakable. For middle-class executives' wives like Hatanaka-san, for whom social mobility is a goal and for whom mainstream success is in any case more probable, the notion of merit, limitless human potential, and hard work legitimates their class position. Supplied with the proper environment, the proper coaching, and passionate dedication from both mother and student, children may indeed succeed in gaining admission to the right university and thus achieve mainstream success.[17] The part-timers, and my co-workers generally, had quite a different view. They seemed resigned in many ways to their place in life as people who work with their hands, not with "paper and pencil," in the words of one young artisan. Their children were simply "stupid," and as parents, there was nothing they could do to compensate for this basic lack of ability. Their emphasis on innate ability and their correspondingly less optimistic stance on human capacities for self-improvement, both reflect and help to reproduce their lower position in Japanese society.

The discourse on gender identity is thus crosscut by class structure. Japanese women could be said to share an identity as women—those who are defined by and dedicate themselves to the *uchi* world. But economic and social differences mean that this defining devotion to *uchi* will be expressed in very different ways. Indeed, when one is delineating the various cleavages among women, class differences are replayed in a powerful, distilled form. For the part-time workers, middle-class housewives embodied middle-class wealth and leisure—the ability to completely dedicate themselves to the *uchi* as inside, to engage in elegant pursuits, and to throw themselves into the task of coaching their children for academic success. If these mothers do participate in activities outside the home, they justify those activities by arguing that the increased experience and knowledge will allow them the opportunity to develop themselves as persons and as better housewives.[18]

The women I knew were also defined in terms of their commitment and loyalty to their *uchi,* but for them, this devotion had to assume the paradoxical form of stepping into the *soto* world of wage labor. Contributions to the *uchi* through money earned outside, in the *soto* sphere, was expected as an expression of their commitment to their families. This was permissible, even desirable, so long as the women's expressed motivations were guided by culturally shaped definitions of domesticity. In one sense, part-timers thereby expand the definition of women's proper place, and they are acutely aware of postwar changes for women who want to work. In a discussion of politics with the young artisans, the part-timers in the Western sweets division argued that the development of part-time work, though exploitative, was momentous and basically a good thing. "It used to be," said Iida-san, "that women had to stay at home—*josei wa uchi ni iru mon da.* It's a lot better now." Yet it is still true that all my co-workers justified their decision to go to work in terms of commitment to the *uchi,* filtered through a high local value placed on physical activity and wage labor.[19]

Commitment to *Uchi:* Company or Family?

The part-timers' commitment to *uchi* as family is, in the workplace, justification for their tenuous status in the company. Because their primary loyalties belong to *uchi* as family, they cannot be counted on, the story goes, and hence are not full-fledged, committed members of the company. Managers, then, are provided with legitimate justification for the paltry wages, lack of benefits, and other exploitative conditions accompanying part-time work. Glenda Roberts cites the case of managers at the lingerie factory where she conducted fieldwork, who both rail against the putative impaired productivity of married women with children, on the one hand, and extol the virtues of female domesticity and motherhood, on the other. In managers' eyes, women should quit work before retirement. Although these practices are economically rational, costing the company less in wages for workers with seniority, their rationality resonates with cultural convention. Roberts relates managerial practices directly to culturally shaped gender ideologies associating women with child care and the home; managers at the lingerie factory appeared to sincerely believe in women's role in socializing the younger generation, expressing their fears that Japanese society would disintegrate should too many women enter the work force (1986, 19–21).

These sentiments are startlingly similar to the situation Beechey and Perkins describe on the basis of their extensive study of part-time work in Coventry, England.

> Part-time women workers were always seen in terms of their domestic and family responsibilities. Although the assumption was commonly made that part-time workers were married, it was not primarily marriage per se (i.e. responsibility for a house and a husband) but responsibilities for children (or occasionally some other dependent) which were proposed as an explanation as to why it was women who worked part-time . . ." (1987, 112).

Interestingly, Beechey and Perkins found that only *part-time* women workers are thus defined by their domesticity. Gender ideology and organizational structure intersect, so that managers never seem to worry about the plight of full-time women workers. A part-timer, especially, is defined in terms of her image as a woman with young children who demand most of her time. Her job is to get her out of the house and to give her some pin money, and part-time work suits her needs for flexible hours: "When part-timers were employed during the day they were seen as needing hours which fitted in with school times. When they were employed in the evenings or at weekends they were thought to need hours which enabled their husbands to look after the children. And the employers often implied that they were doing women a favour by giving them part-time work" (1987, 117–18).

Part-timers in both Britain and in Japan are defined by their presumed overriding loyalties to their domestic roles. Their tenuous commitment to work is often taken as axiomatic—at least by managers and by the writers of the literature on industrial work. But what about the part-timers themselves? How did the women I knew construe their loyalties to the company and what was their commitment to performance on the job? I will argue for my part-time co-workers' key position as the performers of the unrecognized, time-consuming labor so essential to the everyday task of supplying the shop with attractively packaged, high quality products. They assumed responsibility for critically important functions such as quality control; they felt a strong commitment to the company and took great pride in their work.

To examine the issue of part-time work more closely, we should return to the shop floor and to a day on the job, to explore the ways labor is organized at the factory.

A Day at Work

In both the Western pâtisserie and the Japanese sweets divisions, daily and seasonal work rhythms were primarily dictated by the need to produce fresh goods.

Consequently, the mornings in both divisions were spent largely making up and getting out the day's supply of fresh confections. For instance, by the time the part-timers arrived at the factory around nine, the baking of the day's cakes—"shortcake," decoration cakes of various sorts— would be at least partially finished, and we could spend our time doing *shiage*—finishing—of these products. Often this meant wrapping and packaging, a not inconsequential task in a society which prizes aesthetics and is well-known for its artistic creativity in wrapping everyday goods, especially popular gift items like confections. The primary morning task was to wrap individual slices of cake with cellophane. Though seemingly simple, this task was hard to do without disturbing the frosting decorations, difficult to accomplish in one smooth, deft movement. My first day on the job, I remember the division chief, Akita-san, coming out from his room after I'd been wrapping for a half hour or so. "Relax your shoulders!" he said, with a concerned look on his face. "Don't worry—you'll get the hang of it before long." But it took a month before he could tell me, "Looks like you've gotten used to it. You're quicker, and you don't seem to get as tired as you did before."

Other aspects of packaging required substantial attention. They might include placing pastries like éclairs or petits fours in their cups of silvered paper, or glazing a cake with apricot jam, or cutting the stems from strawberries and placing each one on its mound of white frosting atop the shortcake. Of an afternoon, we would fold up tiny boxes, decorated with scalloped edges and printed flowers, and then fill each with its rounded pastry, wrapped in gold paper—the wrapping, again, done by hand. Afternoons were also the time for cutting "Baum Kuchen," a log-shaped cake, into sections and placing them in their individual round cellophane wrappers. Sakada-san was usually the one who operated the small stamping machine, a device that sealed a wrapper shut when you pressed the pedal with your foot. Every so often, much to my dismay, we had to wrap a long, cylindrical sweet called a "ferry boat." Its distinctive paper, thick and recalcitrant to attempts at wrapping, had to be carefully folded in accordion pleats and then twisted so the ends resembled the prow and rudder of a ship. This (supposedly) accomplished, the folded and twisted ends were tied with slender yellow ribbons. Again, Sakada-san was the expert at this task, which befuddled even some of the full-time male artisans. I remember trying to disguise my smile of amusement and empathy/sympathy when Kitano-san, a young man in his twenties who was in his second year with Satōs, came over to help us when his "hands were free." Try as he might, he was no better—indeed, even worse—than I was at making crisp pleats in the stiff paper and twisting them at just the right angle. Matsumoto-san, the chief of the baking division, stepped over to look over our handiwork. "*Omae, zenzen kiyō ja nai, ne,*" he observed. "You (highly informal form) just aren't any good with your hands, are you." Red-faced, the abashed Kitano-san could only gaze at his sadly rumpled approximations of a ferry boat and mumble: "*Sō desu, ne.*"

In *wagashi,* Japanese sweets, the routine was similar. The male artisans would arrive around 7:30 to begin pounding the rice for *mochi* (glutinous rice cakes) and making the *anko* (sweetened bean paste), the two staples of Japanese confections. By the time we part-timers arrived around 9:00 or 9:30, work was already well underway. Our first task was usually to make *anmitsu,* a common Japanese dessert composed of cubes of *kanten* (agar-agar), balls of *anko,* various fruits, and honey. But most of the morning and often a good deal of the afternoon we spent in filling and packaging the *monaka,* baked pastry shells filled with various types of *anko.* We would dip our flat, wooden spatulas into large tubs of *anko,* fill the shells, place each *monaka* in its proper paper wrapper, and then take a sticker, labeled with the Satō factory's logo, to seal the small packet. In short, we did all of this by hand.

Afternoons in *wagashi* were sometimes more of the same, depending on the day's orders, but more often than not we would have to package the bulk gift items. When I began working in *wagashi,* the company had recently added a new sweet to its repertoire: a small type of *manjū* (a baked bean-paste sweet) molded in the shape of a chestnut, glazed a deep, shiny brown, and filled with a single chestnut and white bean paste. We were to gather five of these into a cellophane package, seal the package with the stamping machine, and fold the top of the package into pleats, gathering them into neat folds with pink and blue bows. The slippery stiffness of the cellophane made the bows slip off easily, and the pleats often refused to stay in properly. These "clusters of chestnuts," as they were poetically called, were the bane of the afternoons, at least for us part-timers. The task demanding the most relentless pace and concentration, though, was the "assembly line": placing batches of *manjū* on the conveyor belt to be encased in plastic. Summers were the busy period for this kind of work, for they were slack seasons when we could stock up the freezers with hearty frozen confections ready for the fall and winter. An hour or two feeding *manjū* two by two to the conveyor belt, attending carefully to see that I placed them exactly two spaces apart, was quite enough to make me dizzy and disconnected. My discomfort must have seemed obvious, for each time I finished the task, the chief artisan, Ohara-san, would say, with considerable amusement, "*Gokurōsan deshita*" (Thanks for your trouble).

But perhaps the part-timers' most important duty was quality control. If the *anko* were too old, crusted over with sugar, or, in extreme cases, if they sported a coating of mold, it was the part-timers who noticed. If the decorations were lopsided, they would tell the artisans. Because we were the last to handle the sweets before they were carried off in trays to the shop, we had charge of the final, perfect presentation of the product, and it was a duty my co-workers took deadly seriously. My own slightly more casual attitude earned me a severe reprimand from Itakura-san, the oldest part-timer who was known for her critical eye. I placed a small packet of *monaka* into the tray, a packet with the tiniest, barely discernible smudge of bean paste on the back corner. "Look at that!" she told me sharply. "What will the customers think? It will reflect badly on the company." Carelessness on the part of any worker, including the part-timers, thus affected the reputation of the company as a whole. We were thus fully part of the firm in terms of our responsibilities to our co-workers and to the company's reputation, despite our structural marginality. In this way, part-timers did identify with the company, did assume substantial responsibility, and did feel committed to the company and to their jobs.

Moreover, as in other parts of Japan and elsewhere, part-time meant close to eight hours of work a day. The women came at 9:00 or 9:30 and left at 5:00 at the earliest, more often at 6:00 or later. Still, it is true that they could not work on the astounding overtime shifts required of the full-time male artisans during the busy periods of the New Year and during March, when several holidays converged, or when there were un-

289

usual numbers of special orders. Many times, we part-timers would arrive to find that the artisans had been up since 4:00 or 5:00, on *hayade*, coming out early. And sometimes, as I have noted, the artisans worked until midnight or after, though those occasions were rare. Regular hours for the male artisans were from about 7:00 in the morning until about 7:00 at night.

The part-timers were also aware that their more tenuous status in the firm and their lower rates of pay were linked to greater freedom and flexibility, at least when their duties were compared to the stringent demands made on the male artisans. For example, Itakura-san moved away from our neighborhood a few months before I left Japan. She had finally been selected in a housing lottery for an inexpensive apartment complex on the far outskirts of Tokyo, a good thirty-minute subway ride from where the Satō factory stood. Having at one point lived on the same subway line, and remembering the crushing crowds during rush hours, I asked her whether she had asked the *shachō* for some sort of compensation for her troubles, like a commuting allowance or at least a small subsidy. She replied, "I could, but I won't. If I get more money, that means I'll be obligated to come in without fail. This way, I can take off a few days if I want, quit if I want."

Flexibility was limited by social pressure and expectation, but what flexibility existed seemed to take on considerable significance for the part-timers. When I asked about wages, I named a figure of ¥90,000 as a possible monthly salary for them. Of course, no one responded directly with a figure, but Nomura-san just laughed. "To make that much, you'd have to come everyday from nine until five, without a lunch break and without ever being late!" "Yeah, it's just not worth it," concurred Teramura-san. "Today, for instance, I was ready to leave, even had my purse in my hand, but I wanted to finish watching my favorite TV show. So I just plopped myself down in front of the TV until it was over. Our pay is lousy, and we don't get our three o'clock tea like the artisans do. If you can't take time to sit and finish watching your program once in awhile, it's just not worth working."

Commitment to the company and to our co-workers did make it necessary for us to consider the impact of our absence on others, but vacations and time off were quite easily taken; this was unlike, for example, Roberts' experience (1986) in a much larger firm, where people had to publicly apologize to the others for being absent. Usually for us, a word to the division chief was sufficient. The visits of relatives, children's illness, graduations, and my erratic schedule of interviews at other companies, did not seem to daunt the supervisors, who almost always were ready to let us go. Only rarely—during the busiest times—would there be a plea to stay. "*Tasukarimasu*" (it would help us out), Akita-san or Ohara-san would say. Still, it was hard to request leaves for Saturdays and Sundays, because these were the busiest days, when everyone could use the help. And busy seasons were equally difficult. Near the New Year, when I took a trip to Kanazawa with the Sakamotos to visit a Zen priest, I took my vacation early. Mrs. Satō insisted that I come by to receive my New Year's supply of *omochi,* glutinous rice cakes, which are auspicious New Year's symbols and the base for *ozōni,* the traditional New Year's breakfast. I popped my head into the factory, where everyone—including a couple of the Satō daughters and two high school girls hired for the holidays—was hard at work. Fatigue pervaded the room. The scene haunts me still: the weary faces of my co-workers as they glanced up at me, their cheerful greetings, the trays and boxes of confections stacked high around them, occupying every inch of counter space.

Sakada-san must have experienced similar feelings of guilt when she took an extended leave of absence. She had had a fight the night before with Akimoto-san and Iida-san, when they walked home together from work. They stopped at a counter selling *yakitori,* skewered chicken, and Sakada-san bought two large bags worth to bring home with her. "Are you going to eat all that?" Akimoto-san reportedly asked. Apparently Sakada-san found this to be an offensive question, for she snapped back, "If we weren't going to eat it, I wouldn't buy it!" And after that, she didn't come to work for a month or more. As each day passed, one or another of us would comment on her absence. "Every day she's gone, it must get harder to come back," observed Akimoto-san. But one morning, Sakada-san appeared, smiling, apologized to all of us for her long absence (a standard greeting in Japanese) and resumed work. She told us that she had been having problems with high blood pressure. "I'll bet," said Iida-san slyly to me. "With a temper like that, no wonder." In short, there is no doubt that the part-timers indeed had a more flexible work schedule than did the full-time male artisans, and that they therefore did not—nor did they wish to—assume the same degree of responsibility or the same number of hours as did their full-time counterparts. But it is equally true that social pressures—most important, obligations to one's co-workers—limited the flexibility we could actually enjoy.

Our shared exploitation sometimes provided the basis for commonality and sympathy. The paltry pay was often a subject of discussion, as I have described in chapter 6. My co-workers and I were especially aware, however, of the toll our jobs took on our bodies. We constantly complained of our sore feet, especially sore heels from standing on the concrete floors. And a company-sponsored trip to the seashore revealed even more occupational hazards. At one point, as we all sat down with our rice balls and our box lunches, the part-timers pulled up the legs of their trousers to compare their varicose veins. In our informal contest, Hamada-san and Iida-san tied for first prize. The demanding pace and the lack of assured work breaks formed another subject of discussion. At most of the factories in the neighborhood where I conducted extensive interviews, work stopped at ten in the morning and at three in the afternoon, so workers could have a cup of tea and perhaps some crackers. Nothing of the sort occurred at the Satō factory, although the artisans were, if the pace of work slackened, able to escape the workroom, sit on their haunches, and have a smoke, or grab a snack if they were out doing deliveries or running up and down the stairs to the other divisions. Informal restrictions on the part-timers' movement and time seemed much greater. Rarely, if ever, was there an appropriate slack period where all of us could take a break. Yet our energy, predictably, slumped in the afternoon. After my first few months in *wagashi,* Hamada-san began to bring in small containers of fruit juice, so we could take turns having a five-minute break to drink the juice and eat some seconds from the factory. Informal, mutual support enabled us to keep up our energies, as we each began to bring in juice or snacks for our tea breaks.

The company itself did nothing formally in this regard, but informal gestures of thoughtfulness and friendliness among co-workers surely redounded to the company's benefit, for they fostered our sense of intimacy and obligation to our fellow workers. The tea breaks are one example, but so are the many times we part-timers would stop off at Iris, our favorite coffee house, to sip banana juice or melon juice and trade gossip. We talked about other people in the company, about family, about things to do in the neighborhood. On one memorable occasion, I was sitting with the Western division part-timers in a booth near the window. A car honked as it went by, and Sakada-san grimaced and shouted loudly, "*Shitsurei yarō*—rude bastard!" The offender turned out to be her husband. In subsequent weeks, Sakada-san would delight in recounting this tale again and again, pronouncing *shitsurei yarō* with ever greater relish, and somehow, we never failed to dissolve in helpless laughter. Though most Japanese people do not often do much entertaining in their homes, especially of co-workers they do not know well, Iida-san would occasionally invite us over for tea. Her unpretentious rooms in a row house made for a relaxed atmosphere, and we had a wonderful time as we laughed and joked with her and her two daughters.

In this light, we must reassess the significance of part-timers' presumed tenuous commitments to work. In one sense, considering that they worked from virtually nine until six, with an hour's break for lunch, they could hardly be considered part-time. On the other hand, the efforts expected of them by the company and their own expectations of themselves did not obligate them to spend the astonishing number of hours on the shop floor required of the men. And a certain degree of flexibility was indeed important to the women I knew. Yet in no way does this necessarily mean that the part-timers' commitments to their work or to the company were tenuous. They took pride in a job well done, and they assumed full responsibility for quality control. Furthermore, they felt a keen sense of obligation and commitment to fellow workers, for the absence of a single person meant just that much more work for the others. Thus, for the part-timers, as for the full-time artisans, the theme of work as participatory belonging emerges strongly. But wage labor in the factory links them to two groups: they are linked to the company, as structurally marginal but functionally essential members and as co-workers engaged in relations of friendship and obligation, and to their families, as women demonstrating their loyalties to *uchi* by adding to the family treasury. Indeed, for the women I knew, work outside the *uchi* was far from a tenuous commitment. Rather, work meant dual loyalties, a double burden, and dual commitment to both *uchi* as family and *uchi no kaisha.*

Gendered Identities and the Workings of Power

We have seen some of the ways women are defined by their commitments to *uchi* and how they are also connected to the company through their important position in the labor process. At this point, let me widen my discussion to the ways people enact gender in the company, both on the shop floor and in more informal settings. Here, wider cultural meanings of gender and identity reinforce the distinction between full-time and part-time workers in the Satō company. When women strongly assert their gendered identities on the shop floor, they constitute themselves and are constituted in ways that simultaneously reinforce their marginality as workers and paradoxically make them critically important creators of a certain work atmosphere.

293

First, women were instrumental in defining the tone of what DiLeonardo (1984) calls the "work culture" at the factory: the informal social relations on the job. They did so primarily vis-à-vis the younger artisans, in their roles as surrogate mothers. Most of the younger male artisans were in their late teens or early twenties, while the part-timers tended to be women in their forties and fifties. In the Western sweets division, in particular, there was much cheerful banter among the part-timers and the young artisans, with one or two part-timers developing special relationships with some of the young men. An artisan might visit the part-timer's family at home and get a hot meal, ask her for a loan, or ask her to go to the bank on days when the men had to work through the lunch hour. On occasion, one of the women would feel sorry for the fellows, who always complained vociferously about the institutional food, and I remember a few times when Sakada-san would bring in a huge pot of *oden,* fish cake and vegetables in a salty, soy-based sauce—a very satisfying taste when all you have available to munch on are pastries. Iida-san, especially, was known for her care of the younger artisans, and some of them used to make it a practice to stop by her family's apartment of an evening to have a snack and chat. When a new artisan entered, they brought him around to her house to introduce him, asking her to treat him well in the future, the standard Japanese phrase of introduction. Ogawa, a young craftsman in the Japanese sweets division, beamed as he summed up these attitudes when, on the company trip, he invited me to sit with him and his "Tokyo mother," my co-worker Hamada-san.

Moreover, the young men seemed to depend on the women as informal sources of support and companionship. Who the *pāto* were seemed to matter as much as who the other artisans might be. When Yamada-san, the subchief of Western pâtisserie, learned of this imminent transfer to *wagashi* to finish his apprenticeship, his anxiety was palpable. "*Mazu, pāto ga okkanai*" (First of all, the part-timers are scary), he said with enormous trepidation. But in even more subtle ways the young men seemed to depend on the women as sources of companionship and support. A brief incident serves by way of illustration. One morning, Iida-san came in late, whereupon Suzuki-san, one of the youngest craftsmen, began to vilify her: "How come you're so late? Where have you been? Look at what time it is!" She patiently allowed him to finish his tirade, whereupon she simply smiled sweetly and replied, "*Omachidōsama*" (Sorry to keep you waiting). We all hooted at this, roaring even more loudly when we saw the blood rush to Suzuki-san's cheeks. Eyes downcast, he sheepishly admitted, "Well, if you see someone every day, you kind of miss them when they're gone." By creating themselves as mothers on the shop floor, women like Iida-san made themselves socially central personages at the workplace.

Women could act as companions and maternal figures for the young men, but sometimes they were cast in the culturally specific form of erot- icized mother. In Japan, relationships with mothers are considered to be especially close, and they are highly celebrated and enshrined in popular songs, cartoons, films, television shows, novels, and so on.[20] Mother-son incest, though I have never run across what I would consider accurate statistics on the matter, certainly far outweighs father-daughter incest as a subject of cultural preoccupation. Breasts, too, are eroticized maternal symbols, with more maternal connotations than would be the case in the United States.

The relationship between young men and older women was not al- ways eroticized, but one case was especially clear. Iida-san, in her early forties, had a very close relationship with Yamada-san, the twenty-one- year old handsome subchief of the Western sweets division. Often one could find them whispering softly to one another, sometimes in poses that seemed almost lover-like: his arm around her shoulders, taking her hand, for instance. Or she might, with great care and solicitude, help him fix the collar on his uniform or fluff up his permanented hair, inevitably flattened under the white hairnets we all had to wear in the workroom. Most interestingly, however, in their physical "play," I occasionally saw young Yamada try to crawl or jump on Iida-san's back: the place where mothers carry their babies in a specific posture called *onbu* in Japanese.

Women act as surrogate mothers, either eroticized or non-eroticized, as the case may be. They provide the young men with a humanized work atmosphere, a source of support and care. They do much, then, to foster a feeling of togetherness, of "company as family," where the work group, like the household, becomes a locus of emotional attachment. This posi- tion is a contradictory one, for it replays on the shop floor the notion that women are emotional workers, care-givers, and creators of an *uchi* feel- ing. Consequently, women strengthen their symbolic link to the house- hold by recreating this role in the company and continually set them- selves apart from the central story of maturity through apprenticeship and masculine toughness and skill.

At the same time, however, their position as mothers gives them some position of power over the male artisans and serves to make them important, though formally marginal, members of the company. In Ja- pan, the position of care-giver or the one who indulges the selfish whims of another (the *amayakasu* position) is actually a superordinate one, often associated with parents or bosses. By asking favors of the part-timers or by acting childish, the young artisans are placing themselves in the *amaeru* position of a child or a subordinate seeking indulgence. Because the part-timers were clearly so important to the informal tone of the work environment, one could hardly call them marginal. By casting themselves as mothers, women claim power over the younger men and stake out a central space for themselves within the informal structures of the workplace.

Women's gender was constituted in yet another way. The older men, in particular, would create women as erotic objects and receptive audiences. Our company's end-of-the-year bash—where we got together at a local drinking establishment for food and staggering quantities of *sake,* beer, and whiskey—offered one such opportunity. Ohara-san, the head of the factory, came to sit down right next to me—almost right on top of me, had I not moved out of the way—and proceeded to regale us part-timers (all women) with stories about his taste for erotica and pornography, making jokes about his sexual prowess. "My wife is no good any more," he said. "I'm just so vigorous, you know. Besides, it's no good with your wife. She thinks she has to come to you when you tell her to." Hamada-san then asked him coyly, "Which do you like better, women or *sake?*" And, pausing not an instant, Ohara-san replied, "I like *sake,* but I love women!" And he repeated, "I love women," as he made his way down the row, clapping each of us on the shoulders. Needless to say, tastes for women and *sake* are defining features of masculinity. And just as I was an appreciative audience for Ohara-san's artisanal/masculine prowess on the shop floor, all of us women at the party could serve as an appreciative or at least a captive audience for his tales of supposed sexual/masculine prowess.

Sometimes, the tales of masculine sexuality served only to make the teller look ridiculous, laughable, and pathetic, especially when the teller was the *ojisan* (old man), the only male part-timer. His job was to trundle the finished trays of sweets on his cart from the factory to the shop. One morning, as he stood waiting for the trays to be filled, he launched into his tale. "I went to a Turkish bath the other day," he said, grinning from ear to ear. "It was really something."

"Did you have the 'special service'?" asked Ohara-san, suggestively.

"Mmm," was the answer. "One day of it was great, but after two, you get awfully dizzy!" The Japanese expression for dizziness, your eyes roll around, is wonderfully evocative.

At this, the women snorted, and we all started to laugh and tease him. "What a story," said Nomura-san, sarcastically.

"How pathetic," sniffed Itakura-san.

"Yuck, can you imagine—with the *ojisan?*" Teramura-san queried, her voice dripping with distaste and revulsion.

We continued in our barbed comments for some time, breaking down every so often to chuckle over the comical vision of the *ojisan,* eyes rolling around in his head from dizziness and pleasure.[21]

Men certainly constituted women as erotic objects, but sometimes, the part-timers seemed to enjoy and facilitate this construction. One day, Iida-san was walking down the outside stairs, skirts billowing in the wind. Aoki-san, a young artisan in charge of the *anko* maker, glanced up at her, smiled, and hid his face. "I'm embarrassed," he said, coyly. "You can see."

"*Iya, ne.* Isn't it terrible, boys are always thinking about things like that," said Iida-san, obviously thinking it wasn't terrible at all.

On another occasion, Iida-san brought in photographs from a trip she and her husband had taken to the seashore about fifteen years ago. One photo of her in a swimsuit, apparently braless, attracted much attention. Suzuki-san, dramatizing his reaction, widened his eyes and exclaimed loudly, "*Dekkē, na!*" (Humongous!). Again, Iida-san smiled and reddened, in what seemed to be a combination of embarrassment and pride.

This sexual banter enacted our appropriate gendered identities. For men, it reinforced a sense of masculinity as embodied in the sexual appropriation *of* women and performing *for* women. Women were expected to be appreciative audiences and erotic objects. We women all knew how to play our appropriate identities, and thus we participated in the construction of our gender. In so doing, we inevitably facilitated our own subordination. Hamada-san, for instance, egged on Ohara-san in his transparently exaggerated tales of sexual athleticism, and Iida-san quite actively facilitated her own construction as erotic object. No one seemed to think it inappropriate that all of us were defined in these ways. We acted as the supportive backdrop for the central masculine story of artisanal/sexual/masculine prowess, all of which contributed symbolically to the centrality of male artisans in the Satō company. Yet, again ironically, without our presence, without the background, the significance and power of the masculine story would be much attenuated. Masculinity was defined in opposition to us women, and it was performed *for* us women. Without us as the "other" against whom a masculine self could be created, male artisanal identity in the Satō factory would undoubtedly have taken on rather different contours. Conversely, women need men as the audience for their performances of gender identity. Women, in enacting their genders and in being crafted by men as the receptive audience, the eroticized mother, and the undifferentiated erotic object, are marginalized and poignantly, paradoxically marginalize themselves from the central narrative of masculine work identity. Yet in so doing they also make themselves virtually indispensable to the felicitous recital of that narrative. And through marshalling these ideologies and enacting them positively, they can also create a sense of self-fulfillment and power.

Women's assertions of their gendered identities at the workplace also possess a critical edge. Acting as mothers who have links to the home provides an implicit challenge to male heroics and the masculine work ethic that would extol the virtues of 22-hour endurance marathons at the workplace. Part-time work mobilizes the women's sense of pride in a job well done, but this pride in work does not lead them to conclude that they must spend their lives centered on their jobs at the factory. Women's lives with their families command equal time and energy. Though admittedly the women have two jobs and a double burden, they shoulder these obligations and steer clear of small favors—a travel allowance, in Itakura-san's case—that would draw them into more hours at the workplace. These small refusals are also acts of critique, for women like Itakura-san had no desire to work full-time, if full-time meant *hayade* at four or five in the morning or nights that lasted sometimes until midnight. Certainly none of us part-timers (including the anthropologist) would be willing to forego the flexibility part-time work offered. For example, though Sakada-san may have been embarrassed by her month-long absence, she still saw fit to take a long break, and did so with relative impunity. Such refusals of the model of full-time work could be legitimated precisely because the part-timers called on familiar notions of gender and women's obligations to the *uchi*. A discourse on *uchi* as gendered domain could prevent the women from being further exploited in their work by allowing them to go home at a reasonable hour, just as it ensured their marginal status by defining women in terms of their allegiances to their families.

How, in the end, do we make sense of the fragmented stories I heard in snatches on the shop floor? They must be understood within complex, multilayered, mobile discourses on gendered work identities, that throw into relief the complicated ironies of constructing selves within fields of power. The central masculine story of craftsmanship is but a performative assertion, which paradoxically relies on women as an audience for the narrative and as the marginal Other against whom artisanal identities can be defined. This assertion of identity is under siege from part-timers even as it excludes them. For women, the ironies are even more apparent. A woman at any given moment may feel most comfortable, most accepted, and most integrated into the workplace as she enacts certain familiar, culturally appropriate meanings of gender.[22] At the same time, she at some level surely knows that she is thereby ensuring her exclusion. In such a situation, words like "resistance" and "accommodation" truly seem inadequate, for apparent resistance is constantly mitigated by collusion and compromise at different levels of consciousness, just as accommodation may have unexpectedly subversive effects. For it is precisely by enacting their conventional gendered identities that women also refuse to accept their structural marginality and make themselves central figures at the workplace. They use conventional definitions of *uchi* to redefine the term itself, legitimating their work outside the home by defining wage work as a contribution to the home. In so doing, my co-workers expanded the compass of *uchi.* And it is by invoking familiar conventions of women as defined by their obligations to *uchi* that my part-time co-workers could contest a masculine ethos of punishing endurance on the job. The unintended consequences of their strategies point us toward the limits and strengths of deploying conventional gender categories as oppositional forms in the particular context of the Satō factory and the political/economic/historical discursive field constituting my co-workers' understandings. The complex and often paradoxical effects of these deployments of gender lead us to reject easy definitions of accommodation which imply the complete self-subjugation of the subject, alerting us to the possibility for subversion within accommodation and drawing our attention to the multiplicity of possible points at which dominant cultural forms might be contested. Finally, they underline the always unpredictable and incomplete nature of resistance and the impossibility of constructing a transcendent space of resistance beyond discourse, beyond power, and beyond the law.

9   *The Stakes*

I have argued throughout this book that selves are crafted in processes of work and within matrices of power, and that categories such as personal and political, experiential and theoretical, personal and social are persistent North American narrative conventions unable to fully account for the complexities and ambiguities of everyday life. In the introductory chapter, I made and attempted to enact an argument that "experience" and "theory" cannot be neatly separated from one another.[1] To recapitulate my "theoretical" emphasis on the importance of understanding selves as "subject-positions" crafted within relations of power, let me end by briefly making explicit my stakes in presenting and thematizing the material as I have.

Meaningful axes of identity, such as race and gender, loom large in American society as they do in Japan, and my shifting positionings as a Japanese American woman crafting a self within a particular historical and cultural matrix have informed this work subtly but unmistakably. Certain modes of explanation and exposition seem especially comfortable or strategically important in light of these shifting positions. More specifically, "experience" leads me to a "theoretical" concern with the place of meaning and power in social life.

Culture and meaning, though for many years I had no name for these abstractions, lay in an awareness of assumptions, deeply felt, that shaped everyday life in the Japanese American community where I grew up. Mostly these assumptions had to do with the proper conduct of human relationships: the eloquence of silence, the significance of reciprocity, the need to attend closely to nuance, subtlety, ellipsis. Such deeply held orientations, imbued with moral, emotional, and intellectual significance, were sometimes at sharp variance with dominant cultural modes of action, and thus radically cast into relief the socially constituted nature of both "their" assumptions and "ours." Culture, from this standpoint, is no reified thing or system, but a meaningful way of being in the world, inseparable from the "deepest" aspects of one's "self"—the trope of depth and interior space itself a product of our own cultural conventions. These cultural meanings are themselves multiple and contradictory, and though they cannot be understood without reference to historical, political, and economic discourses, the experience of culture cannot be reduced to these nor related to them in any simple, isomorphic way.

Moreover, these meanings could never be disentangled from relations of power. For some ways of being in the world were and are more legitimate, more rewarded, more recognized than others—as anyone in a marginal or minority position will attest. My attempts to emphasize the nexus of power and meaning, then, are conditioned by my subject-positionings as a Japanese American woman.[2] As a member of a population often studied by outsiders in ways not always beneficial to the community, I am strongly convinced that no account of Japanese Americans could even begin to understand "us"—this essentialist collective identity itself a strategic assertion and a site of multiple, contested meanings—without lengthy acquaintance and a sensitive appreciation of the ways "we" define "ourselves." This account attempts to accord my Japanese friends, co-workers, relatives, and neighbors the same respect and appreciation for their lives that I would want extended to my own.

The need for this respect and appreciation seems especially acute in this historical moment, when the success of the Japanese economy has spawned a plethora of works replaying a tired ostinato of harmony, homogeneity, lifetime employment, and flattened, unidimensional portrayals of automaton-like workers happily singing the company song, burning with enthusiasm for their quality control circles, and driven by the Confucian ethic. Clearly, there is some superficial truth to these images, at least for the full-time, regular male employees in large firms. But people I knew did not belong to that much-celebrated sector of Japanese industry, and their work lives controvert many of these familiar stereotypes. My intention in choosing to work with people like the Satōs was precisely to complement/criticize images derived from the Japanese mainstream.

Furthermore, my writing strategies are deployed as an oppositional discourse to other insidiously persistent tropes that constitute the phantasm "Japan" in the contemporary United States: not only Organization Man and automaton, but submissive, subjugated Japanese Woman, domineering, sexist Japanese Man, Japanese despot, or perhaps most basically, "the (undifferentiated) Japanese." And I am in the paradoxical position of deploying what is conventionally known as an antihumanist discourse for humanist ends. That is, my emphasis on complexity, power, contradiction, discursive production, and ambiguity is invoked in part to demonstrate complexity and irony in the lives of the people I knew, in order to complicate and dismantle the ready stereotypes that erase complexity in favor of simple, unitary images. My friends and co-workers at the Satō factory, like us, forge their lives in the midst of ambivalences and contradictions, using the idioms at their disposal. This humanist argument for complexity—itself a problematic legacy of Enlightenment versions of "man"—takes on strategic importance in the light of prevailing representations of Japan and the ways those representations, like it or not, are always already embedded in larger relations of power (cf. Miyoshi 1988; Dower 1984; Said 1978). The current disturbing tendency to use martial metaphors—invasion, trade wars, beachheads—in descriptions of U.S.–Japan relations underlines the embeddedness of such representations in specific historical, political, and economic situations. As a Japanese American and as an Asian American, whom some will inevitably see as foreign[3] and whose fate is intimately tied to the state of American relations with Asia, I see the political weight of those representations take on a vivid and searing immediacy—as the extreme example of the Vincent Chin case demonstrates.[4] What and how I write is no mere academic exercise; for me it matters, and matters deeply.

My general stance, in short, is opposed to a body of literature that would reinscribe familiar narrative conventions of fixed identity and a realm of meaning beyond the reach of power, and to the stereotyped portrayals of "the Japanese" which emerge when those conventions remain unproblematized. And like all oppositional discourse, the opposition can never be pristine or transcendent, but it is always already situated within other discourses, reproducing conventions even as it problematizes them.

These points emerge clearly in my use of the first-person voice in the introduction and here, at the end. My intent is antiromantic and antinostalgic, but by invoking my "experience" as a Japanese American, or more specifically, as a Sansei, third-generation Japanese American, moments of a nostalgic rediscovery of aspects of my identity may inevitably intrude. Moreover, arguing for the complex humanity of my Japanese friends and co-workers is—within the context of a not-always-welcoming American society and an historical economic climate in which martial metaphors of Japanese invasion and trade wars abound—an argument for my own humanity. In this text, the deployment of the first-person is strategic, intended to show the ways my experiences as a Sansei woman were different from those of a white ethnographer and to argue

302

that those differences were not inert—either for the Japanese people I
encountered or in the crafting of this text. Of course these differences are
not the only ones that matter. But invoking that important difference, that
positioning, is a way of arguing for the inevitable locatedness and partiality of any understanding and for a voice acknowledging that partiality.
For most third-generation returnees to the "mother land," the temptations of romanticism or apologism are great, but our different
positionings could at the very least create the *possibility* for accounts
written from perspectives different from dominant perspectives in mainstream social science.

Some might still argue that the invocation of the first-person is itself a
nostalgic move, which acts to "create an inviolable moral space" (Butler
1988b). The authority associated with "my experience" may be a method
of "preempting" further discussion (ibid). However, the invocation of
the first-person can assume a strategic political weight within a certain
context of argument. One such move ends Carolyn Steedman's *Landscape for a Good Woman*. In a magnificent gesture of refusal, she
undermines readers' temptations to appropriate and romanticize her experience as examples of "working-class life"—paradoxically, as they will
inevitably do just that. Making a space in academic discourse for the personal and experiential (an invocation in turn never merely private, but
created by culturally and historically specific discursive conventions, including the routinization of reflexivity in contemporary ethnography)
still seems to me worthwhile in a world that valorizes conventional theoretical discussion of canonical texts and pays little attention to
experimental writing strategies, particularly if they draw upon what is
conventionally labeled "personal experience." For example, in a graduate seminar at Harvard, male students could label accounts using an
experiential, first-person voice an "immature" form of reflexivity, while
only works that displayed traditional "theoretical" prowess through a distant, third-person voice and lengthy discussions of canonical texts in
social theory earned the accolade "mature reflexivity."[5] Reproducing the
split between "personal" and "theoretical" in this conventional way in
turn reinscribes and legitimizes the generic conventions of academic discourse and the monastic conceit of disinterested objectivity in the ivory
tower, where the dispassionate, panoptical gaze of a Master Subject sur-
veys all.[6] My deployment of personal, experiential voices is opposed to
this view, and I would instead argue that the theory/experience binary is
permeable. What counts as experience is itself a discursive production
underlain by certain theoretical assumptions, and what is conventionally

considered "theory" is always already a position in which a positioned subject has "personal" stakes.

Crafting Selves makes use of writing strategies that attempt to enact its theoretical message, in service of an argument that would see "theory" as more than the discussion of texts in an introduction and a conclusion. The structure of conventional ethnography sandwiches the "data" into the body of the book, leaving "theory" for beginning and the end. I confess that I, no doubt like many readers of ethnography, sometimes take advantage of these genre conventions, turning first to the introduction and the conclusion of an ethnography, assuming that concerns of general theoretical interest will be addressed there, while the ethnographic particulars compelling only to area specialists will be confined to the middle chapters, which one can skim or read closely, according to one's degree of investment in the particular area. It is my hope that the reader has not been able to do this—at least not as easily—with this text. "The theory" is not just at the beginning and end; rather, conventional "theoretical" discussion has been scattered in different parts of the text, and the "ethnographic" vignettes and anecdotes are marshaled analytically. Tacking back and forth between "vignette" and "analysis" is meant in part to capture the shifting, multiple levels of discourse at work in my co-workers' lives. From this perspective, "theory" lies in *enactment* and in writing strategies, not simply in the citation and analysis of canonical texts.

In its writing strategies and its explicit theoretical message, *Crafting Selves* is an attempt to reconsider definitions of the self, at levels we would call collective and individual. There can be no radical rupture with the fixity and essentialism of our narrative conventions, but emphases on potential conflict, ambiguity, irony, and the workings of power in the very process of contructing identities could yield other insights and other rhetorical strategies to explore. Rather than bounded, essential entities, replete with a unitary substance and consciousness, identities become nodal points repositioned in different contexts. Selves, in this view, can be seen as rhetorical figures and performative assertions enacted in specific situations within fields of power, history, and culture.

The intertwinings of power and identity in the disciplinary production of selves in the particular Japanese contexts I described led me to confront dilemmas of representation. Is it possible to avoid the otherness of exoticism and ineffable strangeness, on the one hand, and the cultural imperialism of appropriation—"They are just like us" or "What is so Japanese about that?"—on the other? The ethics retreat is a prime example. In its vivid and exaggerated form, it is a highly culturally and historically specific phenomenon, considered extreme even in Japan. But it is a pastiche of both profoundly "Japanese" and profoundly "Western" elements, and as such it plays out in an extreme way the contradictions, ironies, and creative, coercive deployments of power at work in any crafting of identity. While plunging into icy baths, running marathons, and shouting greetings at Mount Fuji seem initially ridiculous and exotic, these extreme practices both recombine elements from a particular historical/cultural repertoire (including allusions to Gestalt therapy and the use of English to lend an exotic, contemporary flavor to the proceedings) and point us toward our everyday lives. And they do so in ways that should take us beyond stereotypes of authoritarian/submissive Japanese (or worse, "Orientals"), surpassing comparisons to EST, Outward Bound, boot camp, or even other company training programs, though these might provide instructive parallels. Rather, this experience would, I hope, occasion reflection on the ways our institutions, languages, and social formations—schools, corporations, families, and meaningful cleavages such as class, race, gender, and age—are vehicles for the disciplinary production of selves. Selves everywhere are crafted through coercions and disciplines, which offer culturally, historically specific pathways to self-realization as well as to domination.

For my friends, neighbors, and co-workers showed me that there is no place beyond power or beyond "the law." Love in the *uchi* is not separable from authority, from guilt and the weight of obligation, and from self-realization. The wrenching dilemma Masao faced threw into relief these contradictions and ironies. We saw how different people forged their lives within *ie* and *uchi,* and how these idioms offered specific—if changing and contestable—possibilities for happiness and for coercion. Obāchan, tied down to her "shitty old man," eventually became a "merry widow." Minako-san, suffering the hardships of recreating herself as a bride of the Sakamoto household, both adjusted with difficulty and set up boundaries of resistance, refusing to perfectly enact her expected role. Her life points the way toward change. The Satōs, finally, embody the cultural ideal of disciplined subjects finding fulfillment in that discipline. Life in households and family firms draw on this discourse of participatory belonging and self-fulfillment. But seeing in "the Japanese" a utopian model of human connectedness and belonging fails to see that for my neighbors—or, I would argue, for anyone else in any other setting—this belonging and connectedness is never beyond power. In this light, any idealization of family or communitarian sentiments in family firms seems highly suspect.[7]

Shifting, contradictory, multiple discourses constructed the identities of *uchi,* and once again, this collective identity is both compelling and coercive, fluid and constraining. People mobilize and deploy the idiom, but their acts are shaded by ironies and unintended consequences. Indeed, a major argument in this book is that no action has a single effect. For example, the Satōs on many levels enact in their own lives the notion that *uchi* and *kaisha* are one, but collisions with other discourses, the hierarchies of belonging to the company, and the obvious apparatuses of surveillance, create contradictions and possibilities for ironic distance and for change. Even the most successful attempts to "add the family flavor" cannot be said to work in an unproblematic way for all the employees. Oft-cited benefits such as the company trip sometimes backfire, provoking more resentment and complaint than loyal gratitude. Still, *uchi no kaisha* is far from completely undermined. Workers could use *uchi no kaisha* as an idiom through which resistance could be structured, as when they took the *shachō* to task for being inadequately familial. Pride in *uchi no kaisha,* especially a prosperous firm like the Satōs, could alternate with criticism, complaints, satire, and parody. The meanings of *uchi no kaisha* are in turn constructed by a changing political/economic context. "Company as family" meant quite different things to apprentices in a *noren uchi* during the late Tokugawa period, to the mill girls in the factories during Meiji, and to the employees of the Satō company in the 1970s and 1980s. The Meiji revolution and the deployment of household-state metaphors, the growth of capitalism, changing kinship relations, dramatic legal changes, global configurations of power—including the perceived threat from "the West"—and the outcomes of war, among other factors, indelibly mark *uchi no kaisha* and the possibilities for constructing its meaning. Moreover, the specificity of the Satō company's location—a prosperous company of problematic size, where face-to-face paternalism was desired, yet only sporadically realized, where union organization was absent, as it is in virtually all small firms—further constrained and created possibilities for the deployments of *uchi no kaisha.* The fluidity and complexities of these deployments far exceed the strictures of some Confucian ethic or unchanging cultural legacy from the Tokugawa past, and they subvert and undermine any notion of romanticized solidarity or unmitigated coercion.

At the level of what we would conventionally call "collective" identity, we see that identities are multiple, fraught with tension and contradiction, and asserted in specific performative contexts. The same is true of identities we would call "individual," as we saw in the cases of Ohara-san, Itakura-san, Satō-san, Iida-san, and Teramura-san, and in my own case. Taking cues from the linguistic ideologies underlying spoken Japanese, I have argued for a view of identities as constructed oppositionally and relationally. Selves are not referential symbols, the Transcendental Signified, but strategically deployed signifiers. Rather than universal essences, selves are rhetorical assertions, produced by our linguistic conventions, which we narrate and perform for each other. Identities on the individual level resist closure and reveal complicated, shifting, multiple facets. And selves were never separable from context: that is, from the situations in which they were performed, the audience to whom the narrative production of self was addressed, the exclusions implicit in any construction of "self", the historical and political/economic discourses, and the culturally shaped narrative conventions that constructed "the self."

If analyzing the lives of my informants leads us to a reconceptualization of the self, it also leads us to reconsider the nature of power. Again, my argument is not that there is some essential substance, power, which some people have and some people do not. Rather, power must be seen as creative, coercive, and coextensive with meaning, so that we might begin by examining the specificity of the workings of power in a given context, in the process searching out potential points of resistance. In such a view, even those who "have power"—the *shachō* and Ohara-san, for instance—are themselves dominated in the context of a changing political economy. Acts of caprice and exclusion both consolidate and undermine the power of these men in the context of the factory. Further, those conventionally defined as "without power," including the ultimate structural marginals, the part-time women workers at the Satō factory, are both marginal and central to factory life. Conventional enactments of identity provide a way for these women to assert positive strengths, just as the constitutive histories constructing idioms of gender limit possibilities for subversion.

Finally, to underline the location and partiality of this and every account, this text should be seen as the product of particular encounters among particular people with particular agendas in particular historical moments. In our efforts to understand each other, my friends, neighbors, co-workers and I asserted our own identities and attempted to force each other into comprehensible categories: to craft each other. Contradiction, multiplicity, and ambiguity emerged through my unforgettable experiences with the complicated and wonderful people who allowed me to intrude on their lives. For my relatives, neighbors, friends, and above all, my co-workers in the Satō factory showed me that my implicit, unconscious assumptions about a "concept of self," based on a notion of referential meaning, of "authentic resistance," and of the neat separability of "personal" from "political" or "theoretical," were discursively produced, the sediments of my own culture and history. Hatanaka-san, Satō-san, Itakura-san, Ohara-san, Obāchan, Minako-san, and Masao-kun, among others, helped me to realize that quests for utopian spaces of communitarianism or resistance, a bounded, essential whole subject, or neatly separable categories like "personal" and "political" are likely to prove fruitless and self-deceiving. Their lives point us toward investigations of identity which follow out the multiple ways people launch and deploy meanings within culturally and historically specific narrative fields. Above all, my Japanese friends, co-workers, and neighbors helped me to see and to appreciate the complicated tangle of ironies and ambiguities we create for ourselves, and that are created for us, as we craft our selves and our lives within shifting fields of power.

Notes

Chapter 1: The Eye/I

1. *Pachinko* is like pinball, but it is played on upright machines.

2. *Futon* are quilts which make up the Japanese bed. Generally, one or two are used underneath, as a mattress (*shikibuton*) and a larger, softer one is placed on top as a blanket (*kakebuton*). These must be aired periodically in the sun to retain their freshness and fluffiness.

3. The issue of what to call ourselves is an issue of considerable import to various ethnic and racial groups in the United States, as the recent emphasis on the term "African American" shows. For Asian Americans, the term "Oriental" was called into question in the sixties, for the reasons Said (1978) enumerates: the association of the term with stereotypes such as Oriental despotism, inscrutability, splendor, exoticism, mystery, and so on. It also defines "the East" in terms of "the West," in a relationship of unequal power—how rarely one hears of "the Occident," for example. Asian Americans, Japanese Americans included, sometimes hyphenate the term, but some of us would argue that leaving out the hyphen makes the term "Asian" or "Japanese" an adjective, rather than implying a half-and-half status: i.e., that one's loyalties/identities might be half Japanese and half American. Rather, in the terms "Asian American" and "Japanese American," the accent is on the "American," an important political claim in light of the mainstream tendency to see Asian Americans as somehow more foreign than other kinds of Americans.

4. See Merry White 1988 for an account of the families of Japanese corporate executives who are transferred abroad and who often suffer painful difficulties upon reentering Japan.

5. Most Japanese bathe in the evening, sometimes just after coming home from work. Among the people I knew, taking baths in the morning was considered a bit decadent, typical of someone who keeps very late hours.

6. This area, located at a lower level than the rest of the house or apartment, is where one leaves one's shoes before entering (literally, going up to) the house proper.

7. A *kotatsu* is a table with a quilt spread out underneath the tabletop. Electric *kotatsu* have a heating unit attached underneath, and people usually sit with their hands, feet, and legs underneath the quilt in order to warm them. In some older houses, *kotatsu* are placed above a hole in the floor, where one can dangle one's legs; the heater or brazier is located in the middle of the recessed area. At least in the majority of Japanese households, which lack central heating, it would be safe

to say that most family activity during the winter months centers around the *kotatsu.*

8. Mine, Harvard, has a very particular relationship to Japanese politics and society, especially through the presence of such well-known scholars as Edwin O. Reischauer, former ambassador to Japan, and Ezra Vogel, whose *Japan as Number One* was a best-seller in Japan.

9. See Miyoshi 1988 for an incisive analysis of this larger context of scholarship.

10. For a fascinating account of how a Japanese American man fashioned his persona as *boku* among his upper-class informants, see Hamabata (1983 and forthcoming).

11. Cf. Charles Quinn 1988 for a linguistic analysis which makes use of these terms.

12. In discussing the "epistemological paradigm"—theoretical frames that take as their point of departure a distinction between "subject" and "world," including hermeneutic perspectives and object relations theory—Judith Butler argues: "The defense of personal identity, of the stable and interior self, and of the coherent subject, thus takes up the point of view of an agent who masters its environment and the social relations it is in without ever being of that environment or of those relations. If the structure of agency, reflection, or internalization, is identical to itself throughout its travels, then it is ontologically immune from the social field that it negotiates and, in keeping with the enlightenment versions of anthropocentrism from which this subject is derived, makes itself the ontological center of a world from which it is nevertheless ontologically distinct" (Butler 1988, 23–24).

13. Judith Butler (1988a) shows how the subject/world trope circulates in theoretical frames we would label hermeneutics, psychoanalysis and object relations theory, and structuralism.

14. Gayatri Chakravorty Spivak, in her Preface to Derrida's *Of Grammatology* (1976), explains Derrida's notions of textual difference and its implications for a theory of multiple selves: "So do the two readings of the 'same' book show an identity that can only be defined as a difference. The book is not repeatable in its 'identity': each reading of the book produces a simulacrum of an 'original' that is itself the mark of the shifting and unstable subject that Proust describes, using and being used by a language that is also shifting and unstable."

15. Many analysts would further argue that the bounded, unified "whole subject" is itself far from politically neutral. Butler (1988a) and Irigaray (1985) note its "always already masculine" forms, and Takaki (1979), in an historical tour de force, examines the construction of subjectivity among nineteenth century American leaders, finding that the increasing valorization of asceticism, rationality, control, etc., was contemporaneous with the growth of capitalism and the imperialist project. The construction of a bounded, unified self was the construction of an "iron cage," and those undesirable qualities not admissible in the cage were projected outward, differentially, onto various groups: Blacks, Native Americans, Asians, women, the working class. Hollway, et al. (1984) examine the political implications of discourses in psychology that take "the subject" as presuppositional. In a Foucauldian vein, they stress the ways such discourses are

both regulative strategies and producers of disciplines, institutions, and knowledge.

16. See Weedon (1987, 21) for a similar view.

17. Feminists and people of color have been arguing this point for quite some time. (See, e.g., Fanon 1967; Moraga and Anzaldúa 1981; De Lauretis 1986.) An especially innovative example that defies genre conventions is Gloria Anzaldúa's *Borderlands/La Frontera* (1987). Anzaldúa enacts multiple levels of identity through deploying various languages—Standard Mexican Spanish, Chicano Spanish, Tex-Mex, Pachuco, English—and genres that include, among others, what could be conventionally labeled poetry, autobiography, myth, social analysis, and theoretical tract. These multiplicities are further elaborated in her notion of "the new Mestiza," an identity of fluid boundaries, ambiguity, and a tolerance for contradictions, in which conventional forms of fixity, unity, and coherence are challenged.

18. Readers may note that my inquiry has been informed in an ambivalent way by so-called poststructuralist theory, especially in its Foucauldian forms. Yet even as I "deploy" the appropriate "poststructuralist idioms," I want to ironize and problematize those idioms: in particular, Foucauldian languages of violence, war, and high-tech combat. The rhetoric of violence is part of a very specific cultural legacy, including a discourse linking eroticism to death and violence (e.g., Bataille 1986; Foucault 1979, Theweleit 1987, Stoekl 1985). Furthermore, I would suggest that the violence of "poststructuralist" language, with its emphasis on dismemberment, fragmentation, and mutilation, is predicated precisely on the existence of a "whole subject" which can then be dismembered and rent asunder. Nor is it surprising that the "whole subject" must be attacked in this way, for that subject—self-identical, coherent, bounded—still remains a compelling, powerful, culturally salient reality. When we compare it, for example, to the situationally and socially determined Japanese selves I have described, even those of us who are obviously defined in multiple ways—women, people of color, for instance—can find "the coherent self" existentially and experientially compelling as an ideal we unconsciously try to live out and in terms of which we interpret the world. In my case and in the cases of other ethnographers, the ambiguities and negotiations of identity in different cultural milieus fragment this "coherent self," whose wounds must be sutured through the writing of ethnography. Dislocation and multiplicity, in this cultural frame, can be *experienced* as fragmentation and violence. Criticisms of the "whole subject," "the coherent self," then, almost inevitably engage in a rhetoric of violence in order to tear away at what seem to be its smooth, seamless boundaries.

Yet what of cultural traditions where individuals are not necessarily defined or valorized as whole, coherent selves? Where there is no Master Subject—at least not anything like its incarnation as we would know it? Or where binarism is not opposition, but complementarity or a "sliding scale" between two poles? Where violence certainly exists, but with different meanings and sedimented histories? Or where there is a different cultural tradition with a completely different relation to the Word? Does "poststructuralism" have the same force in those instances? I would say, provisionally, no, although we can appropriate that which is of use to us. But certainly that choice must be ironized and rendered problematic (cf., e.g., Chow 1986, Haraway 1988, and the 1988 issue of *South Atlantic Quarterly,* on Postmodernism and Japan).

Chapter 2: Industries, Communities, Identities

1. For an impassioned structural analysis of Japanese society according to Marxist categories à la Poulantzas, see Steven 1983.
2. A number of analysts have tried to trace the history of industrial gradation in Japan. Shinohara argues that the category of small *and* medium industry, defined in opposition to large firms, arose during the Taisho period (1912–25), when not only indigenous small firms, but larger medium-sized ones came to be exploited by large industry. (Shinohara 1969, 327).

Other theories attempt to explain the persistence of industrial gradation. Most agree that labor market factors, such as the practices of so-called lifelong employment and wages by seniority, features in most large firms, helped to create and exacerbate wage differentials. This, in turn, is explained in various ways. Dualism in the postwar years is often labeled a response to a labor surplus, when a large population reentered the labor force. Workers could be hired for lower wages and were expected to withstand unfavorable working conditions. Differences are also attributed to the lobbying of company unions in the large firms. Because workers were worried about job security in a flooded labor market, enterprise unions in large firms lobbied for guarantees of long-term employment, thus strengthening this already existing trend in the large companies (Clark 1979, 44). Another explanation traces the growth of "lifetime employment" to cultural and historical factors, i.e., family structure and the existence of a paternalistic mode of company organization, characteristic of firms at least during the Tokugawa period (1600–1868). This paternalism assumed different forms depending on firm size. The small firms could offer personalized care for their workers. Low wages were ideally offset by these personalized relations. Such work was (and to some extent still is) conceived of in terms of an apprenticeship, where the worker was considered privileged to be taught a trade. Larger firms cannot provide such continuous personal contact with the employer, however, and consequently, more institutionalized forms of paternalism—such as lifetime employment—took on increasing importance. Certainly dualism or industrial gradation seems attributable to a complex concatenation of these and other factors, such as capital and product markets (Shinohara 1969, 329).

3. Cf. Broadbridge 1966, for a brief case study of several firms at all levels in this chain.
4. Cf. Steven 1983, for a particularly impassioned and articulate account of this perspective from a Marxist point of view, though his argument lapses into a kind of functionalism.
5. A group offering various sorts of assistance to subcontractors, including financing, advice, and introductions to parent companies.
6. Instead of the softer *sa* or *ne,* for example.
7. The phrase, *sayō de gozaimasu* (it is so) occurs in ordinary, medium polite language as *sō desu.*

8. Ura and Omote Senke are the two main branches of the study of tea, both descended from the family of the famous tea master, Sen no Rikyu. There are other "sects" or schools, as well, such as Sekishū and Enshū. They differ in minor details, such as the proper way to fold a tea cloth, which foot enters the tea room first, etc. Ura and Omote devotees each say that the other is more *hade* (showy), the most damning accusation possible in an art that, ideally at any rate, celebrates poverty and understatement.

9. An important entertainment district in the Shitamachi area. A famous temple, Sensōji, is located there, along with a well-known commercial street lined with small shops selling souvenirs and "traditional" Japanese goods. Asakusa is also known for its less wholesome pursuits—prostitution, love hotels, pornographic films, and so on. One Yamanote *ojōsan* (well-bred young lady) told me that her parents had forbidden her ever to set foot in Asakusa.

10. *Takoyaki* is usually sold at outdoor stands, especially on festival or carnival days. They are small, round, slightly doughy balls covered in a sauce; a Japanese equivalent of, say, hot dogs or other fast food one might buy at a carnival or ball game in the States.

11. Hamabata (1983) relates an amusing tale of his upper-class informants, who might nibble on delicate hors d'oeuvres and sip their single glass of champagne, only to return home to open the refrigerator and grab a beer and a hearty snack.

12. For an interesting account of these painters and their times, see Young and Smith (1966), *Japanese Painters of the Floating World.*

13. Cf. McClellan 1985, for a graceful account of one such marriage.

14. A kind of snack, made of small, round balls of pounded glutinous rice, usually served on a skewer. They can be covered with a sweet sauce of bean paste, with soy sauce, or a variety of other toppings.

15. These rates have apparently remained relatively stable; in fact, they have decreased in recent years. In 1977 there were 769 crimes committed by delinquents, down significantly from the high of 849 in 1973 (*Arakawa-ku Seishōnen Mondai Kyōgikai* 1977, 61–62).

16. For an extremely informative and complete account of the history of the ward, see Wagatsuma and DeVos 1984.

17. Interestingly, this was the plot of one of the movies. A high-powered businessman, homesick for the simple life of his country youth, skips out on his wife, child, and stressful corporate job for a few weeks. Tora-san eventually finds him and returns him to his wife and family.

18. These efforts are undoubtedly influenced by ward demographics. One crucial factor in promoting identification with the ward is length of residence. As of 1977, the population of Arakawa was 200,043, and if anything, the ward seemed to be steadily losing population. As of October 1, 1979, the population declined to 197,917; by December 1 of the following year, it had declined even further, to 194,564. Of those who remain, a substantial number are long-time residents: 24.5% of the population were born and raised in Arakawa; 61.3% had been living there for over twenty years. In addition to this relatively stable population, however, a sizeable number of people have moved in from other districts of Tokyo and from the northern provinces of Japan. Certainly identification with Arakawa

ward itself tended to vary a good deal. The factory owners and shopkeepers, many of whom had been there at least since the immediate postwar period and perhaps for generations, had strong local ties, and they also were the bulk of the officers in local merchant and block associations. People who worked in volunteer associations, many of them ward-based community groups, were also strongly identified with the ward as a community and, for the anthropologist, provided invaluable sources of information about the ward itself. But generally, as a symbolic space, not simply a geopolitical division, the ward as an entity did not recur in people's discourse as a source of powerful identifications, nor did it describe an extremely significant circle of attachment. Rather, smaller groups—the neighborhood association, the block association, family, and company (all of which make an appearance in later chapters)—take precedence. For many, the ward office's concerted efforts probably meant relatively little. The Yamanote/Shitamachi distinction most likely took on far greater significance, as it did for Kitagawa-san.

19. The disjuncture between wealth and social prestige is not uncommon. Blue-collar workers sometimes earn high wages in the United States, for example. "Class" is measured less in terms of money as such than in terms of the possession of "cultural" or "symbolic capital," a sense of taste and "distinction" (cf. Bourdieu 1984; Bourdieu and Passeron 1970). In Japan itself, this recapitulates a theme visible at least since the Tokugawa, when the samurai capped the official hierarchy, while remaining financially dependent on the merchant class, who were officially at the bottom.

20. Works on contemporary Japan often quote survey results indicating that over 90% of Japanese consider themselves middle-class. This response cries out for further deconstruction, particularly in view of my Japanese friends' and acquaintances' obvious awareness of inequality. For them, this awareness was couched not in terms of class (*kaikyū* or *kaisō*) but in terms of differences in firm size or differences between Yamanote and Shitamachi.

21. For accounts of ways people in the greater Tokyo area create and recreate collective identities as residents of Shitamachi and of a *furusato* or "hometown," respectively, see Bestor 1985, and Robertson 1985.

Notes to Chapter 3: Disciplined Selves

1. In fact, at one point during our stay at the center, participants were shown a slide show depicting this dislocation: tawdry bars, American servicemen, heavily painted prostitutes, dances, beaches.

2. In fact, such instructions are not uncommon in, for example, school assemblies, although they do not usually appear in quite so assertive a guise.

3. A popular young male singer.

4. Shouting in unison is a common practice in certain contexts. For example, at festivals, the people who bear the portable shrine rhythmically chant "*Wasshoi, wasshoi!*" as they heave the shrine up and down.

5. One does not necessarily need to specifically state the subject of a sentence in Japanese, and in this case, no subject was specified, although "I" is likely.

6. The contrast between this ultimate expression of individualism and the dis-

ciplined selves the center aimed to create is startling. How the center could use this—except for the cachet of English as young and modern, and the insistent refrain of "It's beautiful"—still puzzles me.

7. Linguistically, it occurs in countless everyday expressions to indicate feeling, disposition, and mood. For example, *ki ga mijikai,* short *ki,* means impatient. *Ki o tsukeru,* to attach *ki,* is to be careful or attentive. If one's *ki* completely changes (*kichigai*), one has gone mad. For more extended discussions, see Doi 1973; Rohlen 1978; Lock 1980.

8. These include, among others, calligraphy, poetry, flower arranging, archery, and painting, though virtually any activity, no matter how mundane, can become a means of self-cultivation.

9. I thank Matthews Hamabata for these insights.

10. Cf. Hardacre 1986, for an explication of the assumptions about selfhood shared by many of the New Religions. She summarizes their "concentric circle" model of self, located in encompassing circles of family, school, work, nation, etc. Change on individuals levels can ripple through other levels, so transforming selves eventually has implications for larger institutions in Japanese society, including the nation.

Chapter 4: Circles of Attachment

1. In Japan, one applies to a specific division or faculty of a university, such as commerce, law medicine, liberal arts, and so on. Consequently, entering students must have a reasonably clear notion of their future careers.

2. White-collar employees who earn a "salary."

3. A popular television program, depicting a sympathetic teacher who gets involved in his students' lives.

4. See Hamabata, forthcoming, for an analysis of large family enterprises.

5. For example, a long-running debate between Befu (1963) and Brown (1966) concerning the "patrilineal" or "bilateral" nature of Japanese kinship.

6. This term can be either singular or plural, as is the case with most Japanese nouns.

7. The virtual nonexistence of governmental responsibility for social welfare programs in the Tokugawa period and their continued minimal nature in contemporary Japan make "family" highly important in this regard, although some of these benefits have been taken over by the workplace. Care for the aged, in particular, is still very much considered part of the household's responsibility.

8. Ishihara (1981) uses the concept of "household directorship" to examine not simply the genealogical positions of the household head and housewife, but the division of labor within the household. It may be the case that the functions and duties assumed to be part of the headship are in fact divided among two or more members. He uses measures of (1) community concern (e.g., name of taxpayer, person in whose name the enterprise is registered); (2) assets management (ownership of various assets; principal decision maker in investing and disposing of assets; executor); (3) commodity management (who plans and who buys daily commodities and major commodities); (4) agricultural management; and (5) management of nonagricultural enterprise (Ishihara 1981, 362–63).

9. Cf. R. J. Smith 1974, Ooms 1976, and Hamabata, forthcoming, for illuminating accounts of memorializing the household ancestors.

10. Analysts must also take care not to see the *dōzoku* as the only form of *ie* organization. Hayami (1983) argues in a provocative article that the process of branching and of maintaining family continuity over generations was much more likely among landholding, wealthy families. In his study of population registers for a single village from the years 1773 to 1869, he finds that over a 97-year period, there was a substantial decrease in the number of households in the village; indeed, the number for 1869 is less than half the original number of households (p. 24). Hayami attributes this decline in large part to the extinction of households—which is also a potential choice for any *ie*. Not surprisingly, the rate of extinction is much higher for those peasants without land (35%); it is lowest (0% for this time period) for large, landowning households (ibid., 27). Hayami explains the differences as follows: "*Mizunomi* (lit., 'water-drinking,' landless) peasants, lacking landed property, traded off the social value of continuing their family lines for the economic value of the income returned by sending children off as servants and disregarded the risk of extinction" (ibid., 26).

Thus, although not all landless peasants allowed household lines to become extinct, and conversely, not all landholding families at all periods averted extinction, the tendencies are clear. Class and the holding of property are likely to produce larger *ie*-confederations, with the structure of main/branch households. Matters of household continuity will likely be more important among these households, who have more property, more responsibility, perhaps more tradition, at stake. However, extinction is always one of an array of possible choices for any *ie*, given certain social and economic conditions that might make succession to the household headship difficult or impossible.

11. For example, similar concerns were apparent among wealthy families of *dōzoku gaisha*, large family-owned firms, studied by Hamabata (1983).

12. Considerable evidence shows that such a picture of marital relations is class-related and has changed considerably over history. The Meiji period (usually what my informants mean when they say "traditional") actually saw a higher divorce rate than the postwar period in Japan. Kawashima and Steiner attribute this gradual decline over the years to the increased strength of the conjugal bond. In light of research such as that published in R. J. Smith (1983a) and Smith and Wiswell (1982) one wonders, with the complexity of marriages, divorces, etc., among the "old ladies" of Suye, whether the decline could also be attributed to the spread of middle-class propriety and the increasing cultural hegemony of the *ie* model as set forth in the Meiji Civil Code. Hamabata (forthcoming) provides an especially insightful analysis of changes in *ie* structure.

13. These conflicts take the culturally specific form of a tension between *giri*, social obligation, and *ninjō*, human feeling.

14. This is no longer the practice in Japan. *Omiai*, arranged marriage, is really arranged dating, with marriage as its aim. Either party has the right to call a halt to the proceedings, although in practice the longer the dating continues, the more difficult it is to do so. *Ren'ai*, so-called love marriage, is dating and marriage as we would know it, initiated by the couple themselves, without an intermediary.

Omiai embodies propriety; a number of young women I interviewed preferred *omiai*, so that they could have the input of others in choosing a lifelong partner. *Ren'ai* has a romantic, but risky, allure. "I'd like to try it once," said one young woman who lived in my neighborhood.

15. Please go and come back, a standard greeting given to those leaving the house. In this case, it was uttered in the most polite language, a marked contrast to the vituperative comment that followed.

16. Such conflicts are likely to occur in cases of patrilocal residence and in systems where women must gain most of their power through influencing those with authority, i.e., men. In this sense, Japan does resemble China. (See, e.g., Margery Wolf, *Women and the Family in Rural Taiwan,* 1972.)

17. It is nonetheless true that for many Japanese women, the *jikka*, natal household, is a place where one can truly relax. For childbirth—especially for the first child—it is customary for the woman to return to her natal home, a practice called *satogaeri*. (For a detailed exposition of this practice, see Ohnuki-Tierney 1984, 185–87.) This provides her with physical and psychological support at a crucial period, and gives her a vacation from the constant duties of housewifeship and, if she lives with her in-laws, from having to worry about how she is fulfilling her role as bride.

18. In this particular case, one can also see glimmers of what may be class antagonisms, for the bride, in choosing the lighter, more Western bread and coffee was choosing a more "cosmopolitan" meal suited for an office worker who need not perform heavy labor. Her behavior could be interpreted as a statement about her greater cosmopolitanism and an assertion of superiority especially offensive in a newly incorporated household member.

19. David Plath in *Long Engagements* (1980) also gives us the case of Goryōhan, a housewife who over the years has come to what seems to be an ideal accommodation with her role in the household.

20. See the next chapter for a more extended discussion on the topic.

21. More formal or informal terms can be used, depending on the speaker's status in the household, gender, and, to some degree, personal preference. *Itte kimasu,* is the so-called medium-polite form, and is probably the most commonly used. But the head of the household may say *"Itte kuru,"* using the informal form; a young daughter from a "good" family might say, *"Itte mairimasu,"* using the humble form.

22. This is a phrase much like our own "How are you?" Both the English and the Japanese utterances are notable for their roles in sustaining social interaction (their phatic function) rather than their literal or referential meanings. Few people are really asking for detailed accounts of one's health, in the American case, or one's destination, in the Japanese.

23. *Kun* is an informal suffix used only for men.

24. Obviously, the degree to which this is true depends to a certain degree on a person's gender, age, and status in the household. A young bride living with her in-laws must be careful in her social relations in the household, which often means using relatively polite language to her parents-in-law.

25. The discussion in this paragraph applies only to those families who are

wealthy enough to live in a house. Many of my informants live in small apartments, etc., where there are fewer ways to demarcate *uchi* from *soto* in the use of space. For them, linguistic and behavioral evidence is more telling.

26. Jane Bachnik (1978) in a fascinating analysis, shows the clear correlation of language levels with the use of space in the *uchi*.

27. See Bachnik 1978 and 1982, for a more detailed explication of the in-group/out-group distinction and its manifestations in language.

28. Though I have argued that the *ie* is not patrilineal, in the sense of a true lineal descent system, the priority accorded a male successor does produce a male bias, which provides the conditions necessary for the situation I describe.

29. For a detailed account of these dynamics, see Hamabata (forthcoming).

30. One should never have to pour one's own *sake*, especially if one is a guest. A host who allowed this to happen would most likely be considered neglectful and rude.

31. Had I chosen to be served, thereby acting like an important guest, I would no doubt have earned the reputation of a spoiled princess (*ohinasama*).

32. As I mentioned in the chapter on the ethics center, there is nothing particularly demeaning or unusual about this posture. Cleaning the floor is almost always done on hands and knees.

33. The continuing salience of the *ie* and *uchi* for Masao—whatever his eventual choice—warns us against the easy equation of a so-called nuclear family with the absence of *ie*-structure or consciousness. Structurally, the Kobayashis were a man, a wife, and a son—quintessentially nuclear. But Masao's concerns and his parents' hopes and desires were clearly part of a system in which *ie* and *uchi* were significant entities. Indeed, at certain points in the life cycle, a structurally nuclear family is a stage in the cycle of the *ie*.

34. For a vividly insightful account of these human dramas in the context of large-scale family enterprises in Japan, so-called *dōzoku gaisha,* see Hamabata (forthcoming).

Chapter 5: Adding the Family Flavor

1. I rely primarily on Takashi Nakano's classic accounts of merchant households (1964, 1966), based on his material from Kyoto, and more specifically, the pharmaceutical industry. (He himself is from such a family.) In Edo (later Tokyo), these *ie*-confederations were called *tana uchi*.

2. Socioeconomic status is also likely to make a difference in the degree to which specific *ie* manifest features of hierarchical *ie* organization. For instance, the sharp hierarchical distinction between successor and nonsuccessor households (in the so-called *dōzoku,* between *honke* and *bunke*) tends to be more pronounced in agricultural families among wealthy, propertied *ie*. For those *ie* with less property, and perhaps especially for an unprofitable agricultural enterprise, "succeeding to the household headship" may be seen as far less desirable than making one's way to the city or even to a foreign country (Nakane 1967, 7).

Similarly, one may surmise that among merchant households, the main/branch system was a powerful force primarily for the larger merchants, a point Takashi

Nakano emphasizes. Class differences and differences in wealth are thus other factors to keep in mind in the telling of this story.

3. Accounts differ slightly on the details. Takeuchi's version sees the *genpuku* ceremony as symbolizing the apprentice's promotion to the status of *sunma* or *hanninmae* (literally, half a portion for one person) (1962, 97). At age twenty, a *hanninmae* became a full-fledged *tedai,* who could assume the central tasks of running the shop. Nakano, on the other hand, sees the *genpuku* celebration as transforming the *detchi* into a *tedai,* and he defines *hanninmae* as an early stage in the apprentice's *tedai* status. According to Nakano, becoming a *tedai* also meant acquiring a different identity, for the master gave the *tedai* a new name, the name the *tedai* would keep for the rest of his life.

4. Please recall that a couple, a man and a woman, must succeed to the headship of any household.

5. At the bottom of the hierarchy, their low status embodied in their titles, were the *genan* (also called *otokoshi*), low man, and *gejo,* low woman or maid. They performed odd jobs, gardening, housecleaning and the like. For them, succession to the headship of a *bekke* was usually out of the question (Hazama 1969, 9). Some upward mobility seems to have been possible for a few of the maids, however, who found places as the wives of *bekke* heads, thus finding places as full-fledged *bekke* members (Nakano 1966, 24–25).

6. For example, usual lengths of service were fixed at three years in 1616; ten years later the period was extended to ten years, and in 1698, during the Genroku period, the length of service was potentially extended yet again—or at least left open-ended—by a dictum which stated that apprentices could serve as long as they consented to the arrangement. In artisanal guilds, the period of service was generally stated to be ten years, until the middle of the nineteenth century. With the advent of industrialization, these apprenticeships were shortened to five to seven years (Endō 1978, 83).

7. In trades which required unusual skills, such as the lacquerers of Wajima, who are known throughout Japan for their artistry, this period could last as long as thirteen years. (Endō 1978, 83).

8. By the 1930s in some parts of Japan, this service became shorter still. Among, for example, carpenters (*daiku*) apprentices entered at age 11 and fulfilled their term of service at 25; the corresponding figures after the Meiji Restoration (1868) were 16 and 21, respectively. In other words, the period of apprenticeship had been cut in half.

9. As in merchant households, the apprentices began by doing odd jobs. Among carpenters, for example, these tasks might include, during the first year, repairing tools, drilling holes, and using the saw. The second year, the apprentices could graduate to sharpening tools and going out to the construction site. The real learning of the techniques of the trade, however, did not occur until the fourth year (Yoshida 1976, 273).

10. Through a case study, Fruin (1983) adds complicating detail in his description of a rural *dōzoku* which eventually became the Kikkoman Corporation. Throughout the entire Tokugawa period, *ie* and enterprise were already sharply demarcated. The company employed several hundred workers, well beyond the

capacities of a single person to manage. Indeed this entire phase was characterized by the complete separation of owners and managers, as the owners left
the managerial work to their trusted *bantō*. The owners' function seemed to be
largely ceremonial: they made twice yearly visits to the factory, provided financing, and sometimes looked over the books (Fruin 1983, 2). With the formation of
a cartel, the period from 1887 to 1917 was marked by the gradually increasing
involvement of the owners in day-to-day management concerns: "purchasing
raw materials, setting wages, sorting out distribution and shipping channels, and
determining marketing territories in the countryside" (ibid., 5). The close association between family and firm really reached its peak during the period
between 1917 and 1946. At this point, owners were largely managers, and most of
them were descended from the families who had established the original company (ibid., 6). It was only at this point that the relationships of workers to the
company began to take the form of identification with the firm and the promulgation of a familial ideology.

11. In Japan, acting as go-between entails a whole series of obligations, sometimes but not necessarily involving introducing the two principal parties. Above
all, it is a ritual obligation, and people often ask an employer, teacher, or some
other senior and respected couple to take on this role. The go-betweens must be
present at the engagement (*yuinō*) ceremony and of course at the wedding. The
newly married couple should ritually acknowledge their indebtedness to the go-
betweens at the middle- and end-of-the-year gift-giving periods (Ochūgen and
Oseibo).

The importance of go-betweens is symbolized in many ways. First, it is incon-
ceivable to have a wedding without proper go-betweens, even if they did not
actually introduce the couple to each other. Second, the go-betweens take the
seat of honor at all ceremonies, in a culture where such niceties as seating arrangements are laden with the symbolism of rank and status. (See Hamabata,
forthcoming, for an explanation of this symbolism.) In a wedding portrait, for
example, the go-betweens are seated next to the bride and groom, occupying a
more central position than do the parents of the young couple (Katei Gahō 1975,
Kankon Sōsai, 50).

12. Feudal lords.

13. Midsummer festival of the dead.

14. Among subcontractors, the parallel is explicit, talked about in terms of parent and child companies.

15. A popular song genre, analogous to country and western, sung in minor
keys and treating "adult" themes: sadness and loneliness in the big city, drowning
one's sorrows in *sake,* tempestuous love affairs, and especially, lost love.

16. The *chōnaikai,* block association, performs some of the same functions for
those who are not merchants. In the commercial district where Satō-san had his
shop and factory, the two organizations overlapped considerably, since most of
the merchants were part of the same block association.

17. *Kasō,* divination based on the spatial arrangement of a building, and
kigaku, a form of divination based on directions and the positions of the stars, are
Chinese in origin. Many merchants on the local commercial street seemed to give
these notions at least some credence. Many divination practices have to do with

ensuring prosperity, so that, for example, a doorway that faces *tatsumi,* the drag-on-snake direction (east-southeast) will supposedly bring in money. The Sakamotos, the family with whom I lived for the summer, were strong believers in *kigaku,* and they would often use it to plan their movements for the day. Indeed, it seemed as though they were always moving households, back and forth from their house in the Shitamachi area of Tokyo to another house in a neighboring prefecture, depending on the positions of the stars at a certain point in time.

Chapter 6: Company as Family?

1. Translation note: The Japanese word *shachō,* head of the company or company president, is a term both of reference and address; it implies a hierarchy within the context of an organization. The "company president" is head of a collectivity of which the workers presumably are a part. *Shachō,* then, emphasizes hierarchy and the company organization or the company community, if you will, while a term like "owner" highlights the divisions between capitalist and worker.

2. This is a common practice in all Japanese and American companies; i.e., company executives are not paid by the hour, but by a fixed salary with no extra compensation for overtime.

3. Liberal Democratic Party (Jiyū Minshū Tō), the reigning conservative party.

4. According to the Labor Standards Law (*Rōdō Kijun Hō*), women were entitled to menstrual leaves. Under the new Parity in Employment Opportunity Law (passed in 1985, in effect since 1986), this provision is no longer in force.

5. A small confectionery specializing in *wagashi,* Japanese sweets, located on the same commercial street as the Satōs' shop.

6. *Ohagi* are sweets made of glutinous rice covered with sweet bean paste, and they are associated with the festivals on the vernal and autumnal equinoxes: *Ohigan.*

7. Carolyn Steedman (1986), for example, shows how a "politics of envy"—the desire for material things, and envy of the wealthy who possess them—reverberates through working-class lives. Though the desire for "things" is generally dismissed as bourgeois or apolitical, in the hands of Steedman's mother and other working-class people, this politics of envy provides tools for critique of those in power, and must be taken seriously by those who would seek to understand the working class. In another study of novel forms of resistance, Aihwa Ong (1987) documents the case of Malaysian women workers in Japanese corporations in Malaysia's export processing zones, whose response to the contradictions of their lives during late capitalism sometimes takes on the culturally meaningful form of spirit possession as a way of resisting dehumanization. Transposing the interrelations of the spiritual world and worker resistance into a slightly different key, Jean Comaroff (1985) analyzes the historical transformations of Tshidi resistance to incorporation into the South African state and into a dominant South African culture through Zionist Christian rituals which violate and reappropriate the symbols of the workplace and the dominant culture. Cultural forms (in the narrow sense) can also constitute a political aesthetic. Dick Hebdige (1979) shows how "style"—specifically, cultural forms of reggae and punk music and dress—becomes a "signifying practice" of resistance and forms the basis for

(sub)cultural, racial, and class identities. In another culture and through another expressive medium, Michael M. J. Fischer examines American ethnic autobiographies, finding in them "subversiveness of alternative perspectives (feminist, minority) for the taken-for-granted assumptions of dominant ideologies," and, in American literature, "the use of ironic humor as a survival skill, a tool for acknowledging complexity, a means of exposing or subverting oppressive hegemonic ideologies, and an art for affirming life in the face of objective troubles" (1986, 224). Arlene Teraoka (1987) analyzes a contested literary/political terrain in another cultural context: the *Gastarbeiter literatur* written by "guest workers" and their descendants in Germany. Here, even the term *Gastarbeiter* has become an arena for political struggle.

8. Scott's privileging of class relations and his desire for a more cleanly analyzable class structure (an objective class-in-itself) briefly surface in his rhetoric. Implicitly, he accepts as desirable, though not empirically realizable, a fundamental, universal notion of class, which is then mixed with other, indigenous forms: "Thus the concept of class as it is lived is nearly always an alloy containing base metals; its concrete properties, its uses, are those of the alloy and not of the pure metals it may contain" (1985: 44). Scott's methods of analysis work against his stated theoretical principles, for despite his arguments for a culturally specific, phenomenologically rich definition of class and his explicitly articulated imperative to see people in terms of multiple identities and complicated social relationships, a kind of romantic, wistful longing for a simpler notion of class and class consciousness suffuses his rhetoric. In discussing the hindrances preventing Malaysian peasants from collective action, he invokes "other cleavages and alliances that cut across class. These are the familiar links of kinship, friendship, faction, patronage, and ritual ties that muddy the 'class waters' in virtually any small community." (p. 244) The metaphor of "muddying class waters," no matter how ironically intended, still conjures up some pristine notion of class that is somehow "muddied" by other, local forms. Indeed, throughout, it is not clear precisely what Malaysians might label "class," to what extent the divisions between "rich" and "poor" are indigenous ones; whether there are intermediate gradations; and whether the notion of class as conceived in Western class analysis (itself no monolith) has any meaning at all.

9. Indeed, he argues eloquently against those who would confuse poor people's pragmatic resignation with their endowing the dominant ideology with legitimacy. The inevitable does not always become just. Though his point is well taken, one cannot help but recall, for example, the poignancy of the working-class Americans who populate the pages of Lillian Rubin's *Worlds of Pain* (1976) or Sennett and Cobb's *The Hidden Injuries of Class* (1972) where the refrain is one of at least partial acceptance of their lower position in society, precisely because they could not, somehow, measure up. And it is precisely American meritocratic, egalitarian values which legitimate their relatively low position in the class structure.

10. Like Scott, Willis premises his analysis on a particular kind of agent or subject. In his stress on the felt authenticity of the lads' oppositional culture, Willis focuses on the lads' opposition to the virtual exclusion of ways they might come to adopt—at some level, and in complex interaction with oppositional prac-

tices—a view of their position in society as lesser and themselves as less worthy. Take, for example, the ways he discusses the lads' opposition to the dominant school culture: "'The lads' of this study have adopted and developed to a fine degree in their school counter-culture specific working class themes: resistance; subversion of authority; informal penetration of the weaknesses and fallibilities of the formal; and an independent ability to create diversion and enjoyment" (Willis 1977: 84). This stress on opposition and creativity may in fact belie the ways the lads might subtly and unconsciously come to believe the "belittling and sarcastic" (p. 77) insults of the teachers, for the passion with which the lads seek revenge may be related, at least partially, to the kernel of truth they perceive in those remarks. Willis, recognizing this potential aspect of meaning not at all, instead (over)emphasizes the lads' recognition of the "coercive mode" of authority exercised by the teachers. Again, the lads are seen as true resisters in their counter-school culture, opposing and at least partially penetrating the dominant middle-class ideology of social mobility through disciplined academic work. The savage irony of the lads' situation is simply that these moments of authenticity entrap them, for they are enmeshed in a larger political/economic system which ensures the reproduction of their position in a matrix of class relations.

11. The anxiety that this approach arouses seems linked to the need for some foundational point to anchor knowledge and therefore to anchor resistance. Without this Archimedean point, some analysts fear a miasma of meaninglessness and nihilism, in which no political project can be undertaken. This Manichean dichotomy—foundation or the abyss—is a false one. On a similar point—the need to anchor values in some foundational point of departure—Chantal Mouffe argues: "Affirming that one cannot provide an ultimate rational foundation for any given system of values does not imply that one considers all views to be equal. . . . It is always possible to distinguish between the just and the unjust, the legitimate and the illegitimate, but this can only be done from within a given tradition, with the help of standards that this tradition provides; in fact, there is no point of view external to all traditions from which one can offer a universal judgment. . . . To accept with Foucault that there cannot be an absolute separation between validity and power (since validity is always relative to a specific regime of truth, connected to power) does not mean that we cannot distinguish within a given regime of truth between those who respect the strategy of argumentation and its rules, and those who simply want to impose their power" (1988, 37–8).

12. Chris Weedon underlines the importance of this point: "For feminists, the attempt to understand power in all its forms is of central importance. The failure to understand the multiplicity of power relations focused in sexuality will render an analysis blind to the range of points of resistance inherent in the network of power relations" (1987, 124). Weedon's argument for seeing the multiplicity of power relations in the domain of sexuality could be easily extended to other domains of life.

Chapter 7: The Aesthetics and Politics
of Artisanal Identities

1. See, e.g., Godelier 1980; Lévi-Strauss 1979; Vernant 1965; Cartier 1984; Kaplan and Koepp 1986; Joyce 1987; Sewell 1980; Wallman 1979.

2. See especially labor process theorists such as Harry Braverman (1974), who links the growth of capitalism to the introduction of scientific management, mass production technology, and the development of professional classes of "mental" workers. Such changes rob craftsmen of their skills, relegating them to ever more monotonous, meaningless, and atomized tasks. This teleological view of history attributes a kind of omniscience to capitalist managers, seeing the inevitable linkage of capitalism and alienation. It looks backward to a golden age of craft tradition and to a "mythic" craft worker (Stark 1982) who establishes an authentic tie with the material world. For critiques of this position, see Phillips and Taylor 1980; Wood 1982; Stark 1982; Gray 1987; Berg 1987; Rule 1987; Beechey and Perkins 1987.

3. Drinking (usually beer, *sake,* or Scotch and water) is considered a relatively masculine practice. On company parties or outings like this one, some of the men would drink from morning. Ohara-san's flask of whiskey was his constant companion during the trip. Fish is a common accompaniment to alcoholic beverages (indeed, there is an expression *sake no sakanà*—fish eaten as an accompaniment to *sake*). Men are supposed to like "salty" things, like *sake* and fish, and to disdain sweet things, which are associated with women and children. Hamabata (forthcoming) used this cultural stereotyping to create for himself a boyish persona, cultivating a liking for cakes and pastries. This came in handy whenever his Japanese informants tried to arrange dates for him with prospective marriage partners. My landlady's husband, an executive in a medium-sized trading company, would hide his taste for sweets until he made business trips to the U.S.—where he earned a reputation as Mr. Ice Cream for his constant visits to Baskin-Robbins.

4. In speaking of a collective story, I threaten to reintroduce language almost as general, abstract and totalizing as the accounts I criticize in the introduction. This is not satisfactory to me, but until I find a voice that does justice to variation and multiplicity, simply let the reader be assured that my generalizations are based on countless conversations and interviews with informants.

5. One of Singleton's informants elaborated this notion by saying: "The master would never publicly praise the work of an apprentice. It is like the husband who talks of his 'beautiful' bride—one must suspect there is something wrong with such a relationship" (forthcoming).

6. *Sake* shops also sell staples like soy sauce.

7. I never interviewed anyone who had actually experienced such deprivation, though many people claimed to know someone who did.

8. An analogous form of pedagogy, emphasizing self-realization through the learning of an art, can be found in the Zen master arts: tea ceremony, flower arranging, and the like. Even if one pays for lessons in these arts, one may have to begin—at least on occasion—with cleaning the classroom. Again, explicit instruction may be eschewed. My landlady, Hatanaka-san, now herself a teacher of flower arranging, once suffered a *shokku*—shock—which brought home to her the pervasiveness of this practice. She had studied flower arranging for a year and was already the proud possessor of a certificate of merit (admitting her to the lowest rank of learners within her sect of flower arranging), when she happened to read a book stating the relative proportions the three main branches of flowers

should have to one another. The teacher had never told her this elementary information, and Hatanaka-san had been arranging flowers for a good year in blithe ignorance of this fundamental principle. When she confronted her teacher, the teacher replied that such instruction would not benefit the student (*seito no tame ni naranai*).

9. John G. Russell (1988), in a fascinating analysis, interviewed nurses in a psychiatric hospital, who contrasted their practical knowledge, gained from experience—from the body—with the more theoretical knowledge their psychiatrist bosses possessed.

10. During the Tokugawa period (1600–1868), the apprentices' progress in honing their skills and, presumably, furthering their maturity as human beings, could be formally calibrated through a system of hierarchical ranks. Japanese artisanal careers followed the apprentice-journeyman-master progression familiar to us from the European system. A similar trajectory existed among merchant households, where young boys entered as *detchi* (apprentice), rose to the status of *hanninmae* (also *sunma*)—half a portion for one person, half a person—before the young man could become a full-fledged clerk, a *bantō,* often around the age of 30. Again, increasing competence on the job was explicitly linked with increasing maturity as a member of human society.

11. *Omiai,* or arranged marriage, is really arranged dating with marriage as a goal. Either partner can (diplomatically, if possible) veto the proceedings if the match seems unlikely to work.

12. Lebra (1976, 115) says: "Words are paltry against the significance of reading subtle signs and signals and the intuitive grasp of each others' feelings." In another work, I have also touched upon the place of silence and emptiness in Zen aesthetics (Kondo 1985). And more generally in Japan, "the ideal form of communication would be *ishin denshin,* a highly developed empathy in which mutual sensitivity obviates the need for words" (p. 304).

13. These include food and its presentation (not simply seasonally available fish and produce, but aesthetics—floating a small, green leaf in a bowl of fine, white noodles, for instance); bedding and household accessories (colors change from warmer, reddish tones in winter to cooler blues and greens in summer); plates (clear glass, for instance, is used only in summer, to impart an impression of coolness). In every case, the degree of elaboration involved is far greater and far more pervasive in every socioeconomic class than would be the case in the United States.

14. Bachnik (1978) describes the pervasiveness of this interconnection in everyday Japanese life. She reported a broken heater to her host family, using what would be in English the most impersonal of tenses—the passive, stating that "the heater became broken" (*sutōbu ga koshō ni narimashita*). Her family was insulted, indeed infuriated, interpreting her statement as an accusation that they had failed in their responsibility to care for her. Later, she learned that she should have assumed blame, saying "I broke the stove." Then the family would immediately have reassured her that no, it was really their fault, and cheerfully replaced the defective appliance. Bachnik suggests that objects were not seen as atomistic entities, separate from the people to whom they belonged. They were embedded in human relationships. Moeran (1984) also refers to the tendency for the potters

he studied to discuss their creations in terms of larger social relations, though he never elaborates on this tantalizing insight. For consideration of this relationship in cultures other than Japan, see, e.g., Appadurai 1986; Munn 1977; Tambiah 1984; Taussig 1980.

15. The only male part-timer was a retired worker in his sixties, whose duty it was to bring the finished sweets across the alleyway to the shop.

16. Cf. James Scott 1985, who calls attention to the critical potential in any culturally meaningful idiom.

17. For one such exemplary investigation, see Lynn Hunt and George Sheridan, 1986.

18. See Judith Butler, 1987a and 1989, for a performative, nonessentialist view of gender identities.

19. Cf. Barthes, *S/Z* (1974) and Barbara Johnson's illuminating analysis of the illusory, empty, arbitrary nature of "unified identity" (the transcendental signified) in Barthes's analysis of Balzac's tale, in *The Critical Difference* (1980).

Chapter 8: *Uchi*, Gender, and Part-Time Work

1. Cf. Carolyn Steedman, *Landscape for a Good Woman* (1986), and Julie Taylor's unpublished manuscript, 1988.

2. See Audre Lorde, "The Master's Tools Will Never Dismantle the Master's House," in Cherríe Moraga and Gloria Anzaldúa, editors, *This Bridge Called My Back: Writings by Radical Women of Color,* 1981.

3. An area in central Tokyo.

4. An establishment that serves drinks and edible accompaniments such as *yakitori,* grilled chicken on skewers.

5. A group of leading Meiji intellectuals, including such luminaries as Fukuzawa Yukichi, founder of Keio University, and Mori Arinori. Their Meiji Six society was named after the year in which the group was founded. They are known as leading thinkers of "civilization and enlightenment", and key interpreters of Western ideas and their possible implications for Japanese society. Most interesting for our purposes, the Meiroku group engaged in heated debates about the place of women in the new Japan, often in the pages of *Meiroku Zasshi,* the well-known and influential journal they published (cf. Sievers 1981 and 1983; Braisted 1975).

6. Indeed, while I was in the midst of fieldwork, this was the subject of a feature film, starring Ōtake Shinobu and other popular young actresses.

7. Uno (1988) takes another view of the relationship of *ryōsai kenbo* to industrialization, suggesting that the separation of workplace and home left the domain of the household increasingly under the stewardship of women.

8. It is important to note that so-called part-time is a status rather than a reflection of the number of hours spent at the job. The Labor Ministry often uses the criterion of "less than 35 hours a week" as its definition of part-time work, but more accurately, part-time work means work accorded fewer benefits, lower wages, and a more tenuous status in the company than the work performed by permanent employees. "Temporary" work also seems slightly inaccurate as a translation, for part-timers often remain with a single employer for many years.

9. Four-year college graduates are considered more costly and more of a risk, since they have fewer years to work before marriage.

10. The construction used is the so-called suffering passive, indicating that the speaker will be adversely affected by the actions of others. The sentence, roughly translated, would then become: "It will be thought I'm not doing anything, which will cause me inconvenience."

11. These women had themselves worked, either in family businesses or doing piecework at home, until their children were grown.

12. Coming-of-age is at twenty in Japan. On January 15, ward offices in Tokyo hold ceremonies for the twenty-year-olds in the ward, and the young adults turn out in their finest clothes: suits for men, a *furisode* (*kimono* for unmarried women, distinguishable by its long sleeves that almost reach the ground) for the women.

13. See DiLeonardo 1984 and Lamphere 1987, for analyses of the "work of kinship" performed by American women. Hamabata (forthcoming) offers a rich, insightful analysis of women's lives in large-scale family enterprises in Japan; among their important duties are taking care of the household's ties to other households/companies.

14. Plath (1980) in his introduction to the volume on *Work and Lifecourse in Japan,* gently tweaks these prevalent images in the Western literature, calling them "the Organization Man and his mate, the Professional Housewife."

15. Cf. Bourdieu 1984, for the role of taste—including leisure activities—in the semiotics and the reproduction of class distinctions.

16. A mountain resort in the Japan Alps, Nagano prefecture, popular with the upper middle class and Japan's Beautiful People.

17. See, e.g., Rohlen (1983) for a cogent account of high schools in Japan, including their role in reproducing class inequalities. See also Bourdieu and Passeron (1970) on the role of education in the reproduction of social class in France, and Bowles and Gintis (1976) for the United States.

18. Lewis (1978) notes that study groups of housewives have in some cases led to political action through investigating consumer issues. These study groups and the subsequent entry into politics were justified in terms of a mother's role: specifically, that of household budgeting and food preparation. Imamura (1978) studied the participation of housewives in outside activities. Again, mothers invoked the housewife's role as justification for their actions.

19. Glenda Roberts (1986) in her study of part-timers at a Japanese lingerie manufacturers, found similar attitudes expressed by her co-workers. "Their primary reason for working is to contribute to household income—they see work as necessary to their livelihoods, and their roles as workers in a way are extensions of their roles as household managers. They take their roles as housewives and mothers seriously, and view their working as contributing to the household rather than diminishing it. From their standpoint, one can infer that women's increasing participation in the workforce is a broadening of the concept of the homemaker's role rather than either a rejection of or emancipation from it. The women with whom I worked had not sought employment out of a desire for autonomy. Rather, they worked to maintain or increase their family's living standard" (p. 21).

20. See, e.g., Buruma 1984, and my review of Buruma (1984).

21. The reproduction of hierarchy intrudes here. Note that we directed our scorn toward the *ojisan,* who was as structurally marginal as we; consequently, we could tease him with impunity. Never would such remarks be directed at the *shachō,* for instance, or toward Ohara-san or Akita-san, our bosses.

22. My thanks to Julie Taylor for helping me to clarify this point.

Chapter 9: The Stakes

1. A handful of anthropologists have explicitly discussed these issues. Notable among them are moving works by R. Rosaldo (1984) and Taylor (1988).

2. I am not arguing here that all Japanese American women would embrace the same point of view. Even given similar histories, mine is only one of a variety of possible stances. But given certain subject-positionings, it is a predictable stance.

3. Every Asian American, no matter how many generations resident in the United States or how adept verbally, has undoubtedly encountered some variation on the remark, "Oh, you speak English so well."

4. Vincent Chin, a Chinese American, was beaten to death on the eve of his wedding by two unemployed Detroit auto workers, who blamed Japan for the loss of their jobs. Filmmakers Renee Tajima and Christine Choy have created a moving documentary based on the case, entitled "Who Killed Vincent Chin?" The so-called relocation—forced imprisonment—of American citizens of Japanese ancestry during World War II is another example of the ways the fate of Asian Americans seems inextricably tied to U.S.–Asian relations. These different histories and subject-positionings of Japanese Americans create potentially very different relationships to American history, so that for us, December 7 is less a "day of infamy" than a day that led to relocation, and a day when we are still reminded—sometimes forcibly, as in the case of a Sansei colleague whose car was regularly defaced on December 7—of our difference from the dominant culture and our positionings within relations of power.

5. Perhaps not incidentally, the "immature" account was written by a woman, the "mature" account by a man.

6. Donna Haraway (1988) appropriately calls this convention "the god trick."

7. One such idealization occurs in Piore and Sabel (1984). Arguing against teleological explanations of industrialization which privilege large firms and mass production, they make a case for "flexible specialization" in smaller firms as a solution to contemporary capitalism's dilemmas. The choice now facing late capitalism they label the "second industrial divide." But in putting forth their case for flexible specialization, they romanticize communitarianism, solidarity, and familialism, citing Japanese family enterprise and other familial styles of management in approving terms. As I have argued, this solidarity, harmony, and communitarianism is a far more ambiguous and complicated matter for the people who actually work in these small firms.

References

Abegglen, James C. 1958. *The Japanese Factory: Aspects of Its Social Organization.* Glencoe, Ill.: Free Press.

Anzaldúa, Gloria. 1987. *Borderlands/La Frontera: The New Mestiza.* San Francisco: Spinsters/Aunt Lute.

Appadurai, Arjun. 1986. *The Social Life of Things: Commodities in Cultural Perspective.* Cambridge: Cambridge University Press.

Arakawa-ku Seishōnen Mondai Kyōgikai. 1977. *Seishōnen no Seikatsu no Jittai to Shakai Taiō Chōsa* (Survey on the actual conditions of the lives of youth and society's response). Tokyo: Arakawa Council on Youth Problems.

Arichi, Tōru. 1974. "Meiji Minpo to ie no saihensei" (The Meiji Civil Code and the reformation of the Japanese household). In *Kazoku,* edited by Aoyama, Takeda, Arichi, Emori, and Matsuhara. Tokyo: Kobundō.

Bachnik, Jane M. 1978, "Inside and Outside the Japanese Household (*Ie*): A Contextual Approach to Japanese Social Organization" Ph.D. diss., Department of Anthropology, Harvard University.

————. 1982. *Deixis and Self/Other Reference in Japanese Discourse.* Working Papers in Sociolinguistics 99. Austin: Southwest Educational Development Laboratory.

————. 1983. "Recruitment Strategies for Household Succession: Rethinking Japanese Household Organization." *Man* (n.s.) 18: 160–82.

Barthes, Roland. 1974. *S/Z.* New York: Hill and Wang.

Bataille, Georges. 1986. *Erotism, Death and Sensuality.* San Francisco: City Lights.

Beechey, Veronica, and Tessa Perkins. 1987. *A Matter of Hours.* Minneapolis: University of Minnesota Press.

Befu, Harumi. 1963. "Patrilineal Descent and Personal Kindred in Japan." *American Anthropologist* 65(6): 1328–41.

Bennett, John W., and Iwao Ishino. 1963. *Paternalism in the Japanese Economy.* Minneapolis: University of Minnesota Press.

Berg, Maxine. 1987. "Woman's Work, Mechanisation and the Early Phases of Industrialisation in England." In *The Historical Meanings of Work,* edited by Patrick Joyce. Cambridge: Cambridge University Press.

Bernstein, Gail Lee. 1983. *Haruko's World: A Japanese Farm Woman and Her Community.* Stanford: Stanford University Press.

Bestor, Theodore C. 1985. "Tradition and Japanese Social Organization: Institutional Development in a Tokyo Neighborhood." *Ethnology* 24 (2): 121–35.

Blacker, Carmen. 1975. *The Catalpa Bow: A Study of Shamanistic Practices in Japan.* London: George Allen and Unwin.

Bourdieu, Pierre. 1984. *Distinction: A Social Critique of the Judgment of Taste.* Translated by Richard Nice. Cambridge: Harvard University Press.

Bourdieu, Pierre, and Jean-Claude Passeron. 1970. *La réproduction: éléments pour une théorie du système d'enseignement.* Paris: Éditions de Minuit.

Bowles, Samuel, and Herbert Gintis. 1976. *Schooling in Capitalist America.* New York: Basic Books.

Braisted, William R. 1975. *Meiroku Zasshi: Journal of the Japanese Enlightenment.* Cambridge: Harvard University Press.

Braverman, Harry. 1974. *Labor and Monopoly Capitalism: The Degradation of Work in the Twentieth Century.* New York: Monthly Review Press.

Broadbridge, Seymour. 1966. *Industrial Dualism in Japan.* Chicago: Aldine.

Brown, Keith. 1966. *Dōzoku* and the Ideology of Descent in Rural Japan." *American Anthropologist* 68(5): 1129–51.

Buruma, Ian. 1984. *Behind the Mask.* New York: Pantheon.

Butler, Judith. 1987a. "Variations on Sex and Gender: Beauvoir, Wittig and Foucault." In *Feminism as Critique,* edited by Seyla Benhabib and Drucilla Cornell. Minneapolis: University of Minnesota Press.

———. 1987b. *Subjects of Desire: Hegelian Reflections in Twentieth-Century France.* New York: Columbia University Press.

———. 1988a. "Gender Identity and the Discourse of Inner Truth." Paper presented at the Institute for Advanced Study, Princeton, N.J.

———. 1988b. "The Future of Women's Studies: Theoretical Directions." Remarks, Rockefeller Foundation conference, The Institute for Advanced Study.

———. 1989. *Gender Trouble: Feminism and the Subversion of Identity.* New York: Routledge.

Cartier, Michel. 1984. *Le travail et ses représentations.* Paris: Éditions des Archives Contemporaines.

Caudill, William, and David Plath. 1966. "Who Sleeps by Whom? Parent-Child Involvement in Urban Japanese Families." *Psychiatry* 29:344–66.

Chodorow, Nancy. 1978. *The Reproduction of Mothering.* Berkeley: University of California Press.

Chū-shō kigyō chō, eds. 1978. *Chū-shō kigyō hakusho* (White paper on small and medium enterprises). Tokyo: Ōkurashō.

Chow, Rey. 1986. "Rereading Mandarin Ducks and Butterflies: A Response to the 'Postmodern Condition.'" *Cultural Critique* 5:69–71.

Clark, Rodney. 1979. *The Japanese Economy.* New Haven: Yale University Press.

Comaroff, Jean. 1985. *Body of Power, Spirit of Resistance: The Culture and History of a South African People.* Chicago: University of Chicago Press.

Crapanzano, Vincent. 1977. "On The Writing of Ethnography." *Dialectical Anthropology* 2:69–73.

———. 1980. "Rite of Return: Circumcision in Morocco." In *The Psychoanalytic Study of Society,* Vol. 9, edited by Warner Muensterberger and L. Bryce Boyer. New York: Library of Psychological Anthropology.

———. 1982. "The Self, The Third, and Desire." In *Psychosocial Theories of the Self,* edited by Benjamin Lee. New York: Plenum.

References

Daniel, E. Valentine. 1984. *Fluid Signs: Being a Person the Tamil Way.* Berkeley: University of California Press.

DeLauretis, Teresa. 1986. *Feminist Studies/Critical Studies.* Bloomington: Indiana University Press.

Derrida, Jacques. 1976. *Of Grammatology.* Translated by Gayatri Chakravorty Spivak. Baltimore: The Johns Hopkins University Press.

———. 1978. *Writing and Difference.* Chicago: University of Chicago Press.

DeVos, George. 1985. "Dimensions of Self in Japanese Culture." In *Culture and Self,* edited by Anthony J. Marsella, George DeVos, and Francis Hsu. New York: Tavistock.

DiLeonardo, Micaela. 1984. *The Varieties of Ethnic Experience: Kinship, Class and Gender Among California Italian-Americans.* Ithaca: Cornell University Press.

Doi, Takeo, 1973. *The Anatomy of Dependence.* Tokyo: Kodansha.

———. 1986. *The Anatomy of Self.* Tokyo: Kodansha.

Dore, Ronald. 1958. *City Life in Japan.* Berkeley: University of California Press.

Dower, John. 1984. *War Without Mercy.* New York: Pantheon.

Dumont, Louis. 1980. *Homo Hierarchicus: The Caste System and Its Implications.* Chicago: University of Chicago Press.

Endō, Motō. 1978. *Shokunin no teshigoto no rekishi* (The history of artisanal manual work). Tokyo: Tōyō Keizai Shinbunsha.

Fanon, Frantz. 1967. *Black Skin, White Masks.* New York: Grove Press.

Fischer, Michael M. J. 1986. "Ethnicity and the Post-modern Arts of Memory." In *Writing Culture,* edited by James Clifford and George Marcus. Berkeley: University of California Press.

Foucault, Michel. 1979. *Discipline and Punish.* New York: Pantheon.

———. 1980. *Power/Knowledge.* New York: Pantheon.

Fruin, W. Mark. 1983. *Kikkoman: Company, Clan, and Community.* Cambridge: Harvard University Press.

Geertz, Clifford. 1973. *The Interpretation of Cultures.* New York: Basic Books.

Genovese, Eugene. 1974. *Roll, Jordan, Roll: The World the Slaves Made.* New York: Pantheon.

Gilligan, Carol. 1982. *In a Different Voice: Psychological Theory and Women's Development.* Cambridge: Harvard University Press.

Gluck, Carol. 1985. *Japan's Modern Myths: Ideology in the Late Meiji Period.* Princeton: Princeton University Press.

Godelier, Maurice. 1980. "Work and its Representations: A Research Proposal." *History Workshop* 10: 164–74.

Gordon, Andrew. 1985. *The Evolution of Labor Relations in Japan: Heavy Industry 1853–1955.* Cambridge: Harvard University Press.

Gray, Robert. 1987. "The Languages of Factory Reform in Great Britain, 1830–1860." In *The Historical Meanings of Work,* edited by Patrick Joyce. Cambridge: Cambridge University Press.

Hamabata, Matthews. 1983. "From Household to Economy: the Japanese Family Enterprise." Ph.D. diss., Department of Sociology, Harvard University.

———. Forthcoming. *For Love: Choice, Commitment and Fulfillment in the Japanese Household.* Ithaca: Cornell University Press.

———. n.d. Unpublished field notes.

References

Harada, S. I. 1975. "Honorifics." In *Syntax and Semantics 5: Japanese Generative Grammar,* edited by M. Shibutani. New York: Academic Press.

Haraway, Donna. 1988. "Situated Knowledges: The Science Question in Feminism and the Privilege of the Partial Perspective." *Feminist Studies* 14 (3): 575–600.

———. 1989. *Primate Visions: Gender, Race and Nature in the World of Modern Science.* New York: Routledge.

Hardacre, Helen. 1986. *Kurozumikyō and the New Religions of Japan.* Princeton: Princeton University Press.

Hayami, Akira. 1983. "The Myth of Primogeniture and Impartible Inheritance in Tokugawa Japan." *Journal of Family History* 8 (1):3–25.

Hazama, Hiroshi. 1969. *Nihon rōmu kanrishi kenkyū* (Studies in the history of Japanese labor management). Tokyo: Dayamondo-sha.

Hebdige, Dick. 1979. *Subculture: The Meaning of Style.* London: Methuen.

Hirota, Masaki. 1982. "Bunmei kaika to josei kaihōron" ("Civilization and enlightenment" and debates over the liberation of women". In *Nihon Joseishi* (A history of Japanese women), edited by Joseishi Sōgō Kenkyū. Vol. 4, *Kindai.* Tokyo: Tokyo Daigaku Shuppankai.

Hirschman, Albert. 1989. "Two Hundred Years of Reactionary Rhetoric: The Case of the 'Perverse Effect,'" *Tanner Lectures on Human Values,* Vol. 10. Salt Lake City: University of Utah Press.

Holden, Karen C. 1983. "Changing Employment Patterns of Women." In *Work and Lifecourse in Japan,* edited by David Plath. Albany: State University of New York Press.

Hollway, Wendy, Julian Henriques, Cathy Unwin, Couze Venn, and Valerie Walkerdine. 1984. *Changing the Subject: Psychology, Social Regulation, and Subjectivity.* London: Methuen.

Hunt, Lynn, and George Sheridan. 1986. "Corporatism, Association, and the Language of Labor in France, 1750–1850." *The Journal of Modern History* 58 (4):813–44.

Ikeda, Yoshihiro, 1982. "Meiji Minpo to Josei no Kenri" (The Meiji Civil Code and women's rights). In *Nihon Joseishi* (A history of Japanese women), edited by Joseishi Sōgō Kenkyū. Vol. 4, *Kindai.* Tokyo: Tokyo Daigaku Shuppankai.

Imamura, Anne. 1978. "The Active Urban Housewife: Structurally Induced Motivation for Increased Community Participation." In *Proceedings of the Tokyo Symposium on Women,* edited by Merry White and Barbara Molony. Tokyo: International Group for the Study of Women.

Irigaray, Luce. 1985. *Speculum of the Other Woman.* Translated by Gillian Gill. Ithaca: Cornell University Press.

Ishida, Takeshi. 1984. "Conflict and Its Accommodation: *Omote-Ura* and *Uchi-Soto* Relations." In *Conflict in Japan,* edited by Ellis Krauss, Thomas Rohlen and Patricia Steinhoff. Honolulu: University Press of Hawaii.

Ishihara, Kunio. 1981. "Trends in the Generational Continuity and Succession to Household Directorship." *Journal of Comparative Family Studies* 12 (3): 351–63.

Isono, Seiichi and Fujiko Isono. 1958. *Kazoku Seido* (The family system). Tokyo: Iwanami Shoten.

References

Itō, Tsuneko. 1982. "Sengo kaimei to fujin kaihō" (Postwar reforms and women's liberation). In *Nihon no Joseishi* (A history of Japanese women), edited by Joseishi Sōgō Kenkyū. Vol. 5, *Gendai*. Tokyo: Tokyo Daigaku Shuppankai.

Johnson, Barbara. 1980. *The Critical Difference: Essays in the Contemporary Rhetoric of Reading*. Baltimore: The Johns Hopkins University Press.

Joyce, Patrick, ed. 1987. *The Historical Meanings of Work*. Cambridge: Cambridge University Press.

Kanter, Rosabeth Moss. 1977. *Men and Women of the Corporation*. New York: Basic Books.

Kaplan, Steven, and Cynthia J. Koepp, eds. 1986. *Work in France: Representation, Meaning, Organization and Practice*. Ithaca: Cornell University Press.

Katei Gahō, eds. 1975. *Kankon Sōsai* (Ceremonial occasions). Tokyo: Sekai Bunkasha.

Kawashima, Takeyoshi. 1950. *Nihon no Kazokuteki Kōsei* (The familial structure of Japan). Tokyo: Nihon Hyōron Shinsha.

Kawashima, Takeyoshi, and Kurt Steiner. 1960. "Modernization and Divorce Rate Trends in Japan." *Economic Development and Culture Change* 9 (1):213–40.

Keller, Evelyn Fox. 1985. *Reflections on Gender and Science*. New Haven: Yale University Press.

Kitaoji, Hironobu. 1971. "The Structure of the Japanese Family." *American Anthropologist* 73:1036–57.

Kondo, Dorinne, K. 1982. "Work, Family and the Self: A Cultural Analysis of Japanese Family Enterprise." Ph.D. diss., Department of Anthropology, Harvard University.

———. 1984. Review of *Against the State*, by David Apter and Nagayo Sawa; *Behind the Mask*, by Ian Buruma; and *The Japanese*, by Jean-Claude Courdy. *The New York Times Book Review*, September 16.

———. 1985. "The Way of Tea: A Symbolic Analysis." *Man (N.S.)* 20:287–306.

———. 1986. "Dissolution and Reconstitution of Self: Implications for Anthropological Epistemology." *Cultural Anthropology* 1(1):74–88.

Kumagai, Fumie. 1983. "Changing Divorce in Japan." *Journal of Family History* 8(1):85–108.

Kumagai, Hisa. 1981. "A Dissection of Intimacy: A Study of 'Bipolar' Positions in Japanese Social Interaction, Amaeru and Amayakasu, Indulgence and Deference." *Culture, Medicine, and Psychiatry* 5(3):249–72.

Lacan, Jacques. 1977. *Écrits*. New York: Norton.

Lamphere, Louise. 1987. *From Working Daughters to Working Mothers: Immigrant Women in a New England Industrial Community*. Ithaca: Cornell University Press.

Lanham, Betty. 1979. "Ethics and Moral Precepts Taught in Schools of Japan and the United States." *Ethos* 7:1–18.

Lebra, Takie. 1976. *Japanese Patterns of Behavior*. Honolulu: University of Hawaii Press.

———. 1984. *Japanese Women: Constraint and Fulfillment*. Honolulu: University Press of Hawaii.

Lévi-Strauss, Claude. 1979. *Kōzō, Shinwa, Rōdō* (Structure, myth, labor). Tokyo: Misuzu.

References

Lewis, Catherine. 1978. "Women in the Consumer Movement." In *Proceedings of the Tokyo Symposium on Women,* edited by Merry White and Barbara Molony. Tokyo: International Group for the Study of Women.

Lock, Margaret. 1980. *East Asian Medicine in Urban Japan.* Berkeley: University of California Press.

Lorde, Audre. 1981. "The Master's Tools Will Never Dismantle the Master's House." In *This Bridge Called My Back: Writings by Radical Women of Color,* edited by Cherrie Moraga and Gloria Anzaldúa. Watertown: Persephone.

Lutz, Catherine. 1988. *Unnatural Emotions.* Chicago: The University of Chicago Press.

McClelland, Keith. 1987. "Time to Work, Time to Live: Some Aspects of Work and the Reformation of Class in Britain, 1850–1880." In *The Historical Meanings of Work,* edited by Patrick Joyce. Cambridge: Cambridge University Press.

McClellan, Edwin. 1985. *Woman in the Crested Kimono:The Life of Shibue Io and Her Family.* New Haven: Yale University Press.

MacLendon, James. 1983. "The Office: Way Station or Blind Alley." In *Work and Lifecourse in Japan* edited by David Plath. Albany: State University of New York Press.

Marcus, George E. 1986. "Contemporary Problems of Ethnography in the Modern World System." In *Writing Culture,* edited by James Clifford and George Marcus. Berkeley: University of California Press.

Marcus, George E., and Michael M. J. Fischer. 1986. *Anthropology as Cultural Critique: An Experimental Moment in the Human Sciences.* Chicago: University of Chicago Press.

Mauss, Marcel. 1938. "Une categorie de l'esprit humain: la notion de personne, celle de 'moi,'" *Journal of the Royal Anthropological Institute* 68:263–82. "A Category of the Human Mind: The Notion of Person; the Notion of Self," translated by W. D. Halls. In *The Category of the Person: Anthropology, Philosophy, History,* edited by Michael Carrithers, Steven Collins, and Steven Lukes. Cambridge: Cambridge University Press, 1985.

Meiji Civil Code. *See* Sebald.

Miller, Jean Baker. 1976. *Toward a New Psychology of Women.* Boston: Beacon.

Miller, Roy Andrew. 1967. *The Japanese Language.* Chicago: University of Chicago Press.

Ministry of International Trade and Industry. 1984. *MITI Handbook.* Tokyo: Japan Trade and Industry Publicity.

Miyoshi, Masao. 1988. "Against the Native Grain: The Japanese Novel and the 'Postmodern' West." *South Atlantic Quarterly* 87(3):525–50.

Moeran, Brian. 1984. *Lost Innocence: Folk Craft Potters of Onta, Japan.* Berkeley: University of California Press.

Moraga, Cherríe, and Gloria Anzaldúa, eds. 1981. *This Bridge Called My Back: Writings by Radical Women of Color.* Watertown: Persephone.

Mouffe, Chantal. 1988. "Radical Democracy: Modern or Postmodern?" In *Universal Abandon? The Politics of Postmodernism,* edited by Andrew Ross. Minneapolis: University of Minnesota Press.

Munn, Nancy. 1977. "The Spatiotemporal Transformation of Gawa Canoes." *Journal de la société des océanistes* 33:39–53.

References

Nagahara, Kazuko, 1982. "Ryōsai kenboshugi kyōiku ni okeru ie to shokugyō" (Occupation and household in "good wife, wise mother" education). In *Nihon no Joseishi* (A history of Japanese women), edited by Joseishi Sōgō Kenkyū. Vol. 4, *Kindai*. Tokyo: Tokyo Daigaku Shuppankai.

Nakamura, Takafusa. 1981. *The Postwar Japanese Economy: Its Development and Structure*. Tokyo: Tokyo University Press.

Nakane, Chie. 1970. *Japanese Society*. Berkeley: University of California Press.

———. 1983. "*Ie*." *Kodansha Encyclopaedia of Japan* 3:259–61. Tokyo: Kodansha.

———. 1967. *Kinship and Economic Organization in Rural Japan*. London: Athlone.

Nakano, Takashi. 1964. *Shōka dōzokudan no kenkyū* (Research on merchant household groups). Tokyo: Miraisha.

———. 1966. "Merchant *Dōzoku* of Japan: Process of their Change from the Tokugawa Period to Pre-War Times." Unpublished manuscript.

Ohnuki-Tierney, Emiko. 1984. *Illness and Culture in Contemporary Japan*. New York: Cambridge University Press.

Okimoto, Daniel. 1971. *An American in Disguise*. New York: Weatherhill.

Ong, Aihwa. 1987. *Spirits of Resistance and Capitalist Discipline: Factory Women in Malaysia*. Albany: State University of New York Press.

Ooms, Herman. 1976. "A Structural Analysis of Japanese Ancestral Rites and Beliefs." In *Ancestors,* edited by William Newell. The Hague: Mouton.

Ouchi, William, 1982. *Theory Z*. New York: Avon.

Outlaw, Lucius. 1987. "African 'Philosophy': Deconstructive and reconstructive challenges." In *Contemporary Philosophy: A New Survey,* edited by G. Floistad and G. H. Von Wright. Dordrecht: Martinus Nijhoff Publishers.

Pascale, Richard, and Anthony Athos. 1981. *The Art of Japanese Management*. New York: Warner Books.

Patrick, Hugh, and Thomas P. Rohlen. 1987. "Small-scale Family Enterprises." In *The Political Economy of Japan, Vol. 1: The Domestic Transformation,* edited by Kozo Yamamura and Yasukichi Yasuba. Stanford: Stanford University Press.

Pelzel, John C. 1970. "Japanese Kinship." In *Family and Kinship in Chinese Society,* edited by Maurice Freedman. Stanford: Stanford University Press.

Pharr, Susan. 1980. "Soldiers as Feminists: Debate Within U.S. Occupation Ranks over Women's Rights Policy in Japan." In *Proceedings of the Tokyo Symposium on Women,* edited by Merry White and Barbara Molony. Tokyo: International Group for the Study of Women.

Phillips, Anne, and Barbara Taylor. 1980. "Sex and Skill: Notes Toward a Feminist Economics." *Feminist Review* 6:79–88.

Piore, Michael J. and Charles F. Sabel. 1984. *The Second Industrial Divide*. New York: Basic Books.

Plath, David W. 1980. *Long Engagements*. Stanford: Stanford University Press.

———, ed. 1983. *Work and Lifecourse in Japan*. Albany: State University of New York.

Quinn, Charles. 1988. "*Uchi/Soto:* Tip of a Semiotic Iceberg." Paper presented at panel, *Uchi/Soto:* Shifting Linguistic and Social Boundaries." Annual meeting of the Association for Asian Studies, San Francisco, California.

References

Rancière, Jacques. 1986. "The Myth of the Artisan: Critical Reflections on a Category of Social History." In *Work in France: Representation, Meaning, Organization, Practice,* edited by Steven Kaplan and Cynthia Koepp. Ithaca: Cornell University Press.

Reynolds, David. 1980. *The Quiet Therapies.* Honolulu: University Press of Hawaii.

Roberts, Glenda. 1986. "Non-trivial Pursuits: Japanese Blue-collar Women and the Lifetime Employment System." Ph.D. diss., Department of Anthropology, Cornell University.

Robertson, Jennifer. 1985. "The Making of Kodaira: Being an Ethnography of a Japanese City's Progress." Ph.D. diss., Department of Anthropology, Cornell University.

Rōdōshō (Ministry of Labor). 1980, 1984. *Fujin Rōdō no Jitsujō.* Tokyo: Ōkurashō.

Rohlen, Thomas P. 1974. *For Harmony and Strength: Japanese White-collar Organization in Anthropological Perspective.* Berkeley: University of California Press.

———. 1978. "The Promise of Adulthood in Japanese Spiritualism." In *Adulthood,* edited by Erik Erikson. New York: Norton.

———. 1983. *Japan's High Schools.* Berkeley: University of California Press.

Rosaldo, Michelle Z. 1980. *Knowledge and Passion: Ilongot Notions of Self and Social Life.* Cambridge: Cambridge University Press.

———. 1984. "Toward an Anthropology of Self and Feeling." In *Culture Theory: Mind, Self, and Emotion,* edited by Richard Shweder and Robert LeVine. Cambridge: Cambridge University Press.

Rosaldo, Renato. 1984. "Grief and a Headhunter's Rage: On the Cultural Force of Emotions." In *Text, Play and Story: The Construction and Reconstruction of Self and Society,* edited by Edward Bruner. Washington, D.C.: The American Ethnological Society.

———. 1987. "Politics, Patriarchs, and Laughter." *Cultural Critique* 7:65–86.

Rubin, Lillian. 1976. *Worlds of Pain.* New York: Basic Books.

Rule, John 1987. "The Property of Skill in the Period of Manufacture. In *The Historical Meanings of Work,* edited by Patrick Joyce. Cambridge: Cambridge University Press.

Russell, John G. 1988. "The Descendants of Susano: Marginalization and Psychiatric Institutionalization in Japan." Ph.D. diss., Department of Anthropology, Harvard University.

Said, Edward. 1978. *Orientalism.* New York: Vintage.

Satō, Seizaburō, Yasusuke Murakami, and Shumpei Kumon. 1979. *Bunmei to shite no ie shakai.* (Familial society as civilization). Tokyo: Chūō kōronsha.

Saussure, Ferdinand de. 1966. *Course in General Linguistics.* New York: McGraw-Hill.

Schneider, David. 1968. *American Kinship: A Cultural Account.* Englewood Cliffs: Prentice-Hall.

Scott, James. 1985. *Weapons of the Weak: Everyday Forms of Peasant Resistance.* New Haven: Yale University Press.

Scott, Joan. 1988. *Gender and the Politics of History.* New York: Columbia University Press.

Sebald, William J., trans. 1934. *The Civil Code of Japan.* Kobe: Thompson.

References

Seidensticker, Edward. 1983. *Low City, High City: Tokyo from Edo to the Earthquake, 1867–1923*. New York: Knopf.

Sennett, Richard and Jonathan Cobb. 1972. *The Hidden Injuries of Class*. New York: Vintage.

Sewell, William. 1980. *Work and Revolution in France: The Language of Labor from the Old Regime to 1848*. Cambridge: Cambridge University Press.

Shinohara, Miyohei. 1969. *The Role of Small Industry in the Process of Economic Growth*. The Hague: Mouton.

Shore, Bradd. 1982. *Sala'ilua: A Samoan Mystery*. New York: Columbia University Press.

Shweder, Richard. 1984. "Anthropology's Romantic Rebellion against the Enlightenment, or There's More to Thinking Than Reason and Evidence." *Culture Theory: Essays on Mind, Self, and Emotion,* edited by Richard Shweder and Robert LeVine. Cambridge: Cambridge University Press.

Sider, Gerald M. 1986. *Culture and Class in Anthropology and History: A Newfoundland Illustration*. Cambridge: Cambridge University Press.

Sievers, Sharon. 1981. "Feminist Criticism in Japanese Politics in the 1880s." *Signs* 6(4):602–16.

———. 1983. *Flowers in Salt: The Beginnings of Feminist Consciousness in Modern Japan*. Stanford: Stanford University Press.

Silverstein, Michael. 1979. "Language Structure and Linguistic Ideology." In *The Elements: A Parasession on Linguistic Unity and Levels*. Chicago: Meetings of the Chicago Linguistic Society.

Singleton, John. Forthcoming. "Japanese Folkcraft Pottery Apprenticeship: Cultural Patterns of an Educational Institution." In *Anthropological Perspectives on Apprenticeship,* edited by Michael Coy. Albany: SUNY Press.

Smith, Robert J. 1960. "Pre-industrial Urbanism in Japan: A Consideration of Multiple Traditions in a Feudal Society." *Economic Development and Cultural Change* 9(1):241–57.

———. 1974. *Ancestor Worship in Contemporary Japan*. Stanford: Stanford University Press.

———. 1983a. "Making Village Women into 'Good Wives and Wise Mothers' in Pre-war Japan." *Journal of Family History* 8(1):70–84.

———. 1983b. *Japanese Society: Tradition, Self, and the Social Order*. Cambridge: Cambridge University Press.

Smith, Robert J. and Ella Lury Wiswell. 1982. *The Women of Suyemura*. Chicago: University of Chicago Press.

Smith, Thomas C. 1988. "The Right to Benevolence: Dignity and Japanese Workers, 1890–1920." In *Native Sources of Japanese Industrialization*. Berkeley: University of California Press.

Spivak, Gayatri Chakravorty. 1988. *In Other Worlds: Essays in Cultural Politics*. New York: Routledge.

Stark, David. 1982. "Class Struggle and the Transformation of the Labour Process: A Relational Approach." In *Class, Power, and Conflict,* edited by Anthony Giddens and David Held. Berkeley: University of California Press.

———. 1986. "Rethinking Internal Labor Markets: New Insights from a Comparative Perspective." *American Sociological Review* 51:492–504.

References

Steedman, Carolyn. 1986. *Landscape for a Good Woman: A Story of Two Lives.* London: Virago.

Steven, Rob. 1983. *Classes in Contemporary Japan.* Cambridge: Cambridge University Press.

Stoekl, Allan. 1985. *Politics, Writing, Mutilation: The Cases of Bataille, Blanchot, Roussel, Leiris, and Ponge.* Minneapolis: University of Minnesota Press.

Sumiya, Mikio. 1955. *Nihon chin rōdō shi ron* (A discussion of Japanese wage labor). Tokyo: Tokyo Daigaku Shuppankai.

Suzuki, Haruo. 1969. *Chū-shō kigyō ni hataraku hitobito* (People who work in small and medium enterprises). Tokyo: Nihon Rōdō Kyōkai.

Suzuki, Takao. 1978. *Japanese and the Japanese: Words in Context.* Translated by Akira Miura. Tokyo: Kodansha.

Swidler, Ann. 1977. "The Concept of Rationality in the Work of Max Weber." *Sociological Inquiry* 43(1):35–42.

Takaki, Ronald. 1979. *Iron Cages: Race and Culture in 19th-Century America.* New York: Knopf.

Takeuchi, Hideo. 1962. "Hōkōnin, Yatoinin, Totei," (Apprentice, employee, apprentice). *Nihon Minzokugaku Taikei* (An outline of Japanese ethnology). Tokyo: Heibonsha.

Tambiah, Stanley J. 1979. "A Performative Approach to Ritual." *Proceedings of the British Academy* 65:113–69.

———. 1984. *The Buddhist Saints of the Forest and the Cult of Amulets.* Cambridge: Cambridge University Press.

Taussig, Michael. 1980. *The Devil and Commodity Fetishism in South America.* Chapel Hill: University of North Carolina Press.

Taylor, Julie. 1987. "Tango." *Cultural Anthropology* 2(4):481–93.

———. 1988. "Elite Socialization as Sequence and Collage: The Gaucho and Europe in Argentina." Paper presented at the panel, Elite Socialization. American Anthropological Association Meetings, Phoenix, Arizona.

Teraoka, Arlene. 1987. "*Gastarbeiterliteratur*: The Other Speaks Back." *Cultural Critique* 7:77–101.

Theweleit, Klaus. 1987. *Male Fantasies, Vol. 1: Women, Floods, Bodies, History.* Minneapolis: University of Minnesota Press.

Tsurumi, E. Patricia. 1984. "Female Textile Workers and the Failure of Early Trade Unionism in Japan." *History Workshop* 18:3–27.

Tyler, Stephen. 1986. "Post-modern Ethnography: From Document of the Occult to Occult Document." In *Writing Culture,* edited by James Clifford and George Marcus. Berkeley: University of California Press.

Uebayashi, Takujirō. 1976. *Chūshō reisai kigyōron* (Theories of very small, small and medium-sized enterprise). Tokyo: Moriyama.

Uno, Kathleen. 1988. "Good Wives and Wise Mothers in Early Twentieth-Century Japan." Paper presented at the panel, Women in Prewar Japan. Pacific Coast Branch of the American Historical Association and the Western Association of Women Historians joint meeting, San Francisco, California.

Vernant, Jean-Pierre. 1965. *Mythe et pensée chez les grecs: Études de psychologie historique.* Paris: Maspero.

References

Vogel, Ezra F. 1963. *Japan's New Middle Class*. Berkeley: University of California Press.
————. 1979. *Japan as Number One*. Cambridge: Harvard University Press.
Vogel, Suzanne H. 1978, "Professional Housewife: The Career of Urban Middle-Class Japanese Women." *Japan Interpreter* 12(1):16–43.
Wagatsuma, Hiroshi, and George DeVos. 1984. *Heritage of Endurance: Family Patterns and Delinquency Formation in Urban Japan*. Berkeley: University of California Press.
Wallman, Sandra. 1979. *Social Anthropology of Work*. London: Academic Press.
Weedon, Chris. 1987. *Feminist Practice and Poststructuralist Theory*. London: Basil Blackwell.
Wetzel, Patricia. 1984. "'Uti' and 'Soto' (In-Group and Out-Group): Social Deixis in Japanese." Ph.D. diss., Department of Linguistics, Cornell University.
White, Geoffrey, and John Kirkpatrick, eds. 1985. *Person, Self and Experience: Exploring Pacific Ethnopsychologies*. Berkeley: University of California Press.
White, Merry. 1987. *The Japanese Educational Challenge: A Commitment to Children*. New York: Free Press.
————. 1988. *The Japanese Overseas: Can They Go Home Again?* New York: Free Press.
Willis, Paul. 1977. *Learning to Labour: How Working-class Kids Get Working-class Jobs*. Westmead: Saxonhouse.
Wolf, Margery. 1972. *Women and the Family in Rural Taiwan*. Stanford: Stanford University Press.
Wood, Stephen, ed. 1982. *The Degradation of Work?: Skill, Deskilling and the Labour Process*. London: Hutchinson.
Yanagida, Kunio. 1957. *Japanese Manners and Customs in the Meiji Era*. Translated by Charles Terry. Tokyo: Obunsha.
Yoshida, Mitsukuni. 1976. *Nihon no shokunin* (Japan's artisans). Tokyo: Kadokawa.
Young, Martie W. and Robert J. Smith. 1966. *Japanese Painters of the Floating World*. Ithaca: The White Art Museum, Cornell University.

Index

Adachi (artisan, division subchief), 76, 81, 87–88

Adoption: of bridegroom, 125–26; of married couple, 127; as succession strategy, 125–26. *See also* Marriage; Succession

Akimoto (part-timer), 59, 111, 280, 291

Akita (division chief), 114, 184, 188, 287, 291

Amae (seeking indulgence), 149–52, 296

Anzaldúa, Gloria, 311n.17

Aoki (artisan), 297

Apprenticeship: artisanal, 235–41 (*see also* Artisanal work; Gender; Self); contracts and, 165; and masters, 165, 236–37; in Tokugawa period (1600–1868), 165–66; and capitalism, 168; changes in meanings of, 254; journeymen-apprentice relations, 166; *kurō* (hardship) and, 235–38, 240; length of, in Tokugawa period, 319n.6; in merchant households, Tokugawa period, 163–65

Arakawa ward: as bedroom community, 69; changes in, 69; demographics, 313, 314n.18; and Shitamachi identity, 68, 70, 71; and small enterprise, 53–54, 68; as socially marginal, 69; and symbolic pollution, 68

Ariga, Kizaemon, 29–30

Artisanal work: aesthetics of, 231–34, 244–47; and artisanal spirit, 239–40; definitions of, in Shitamachi, 234–35; historical sketch of, 234; and identity, 45, 214–18, 246 (*see also* Apprenticeship; Self; Company as family); and language, 58; and masculinity, 232, 240–41 (*see also* Gender); and material objects, 244–46; and mobility, 165–66, 232–33, 239; narratives and performances of, 232–41, 249–50; and nature, 233; politics of exclusion and, 230, 247–53; and political-economic context, 231, 254–55; and seasons, 241–44; as self-realization, 234–41; and Shinto, 246–47; stereotypes of, 232, 240; as symbols of national identity, 235; as symbols of "tradition," 232, 235; vs. white-collar work, 63 (*see also* Dual structure; Small and medium-sized enterprises; Shitamachi/Yamanote); young artisans' attitudes toward, 233–34, 254–55. *See also* Apprenticeship, artisanal; Ohara

Athos, Anthony, 50

Bachnik, Jane, 26, 27, 122, 125, 147, 175, 325n.14

Beechey, Veronica, 286

Boissonade (and Meiji Civil Code), 169

Bourdieu, Pierre, 61

Braverman, Harry, 324n.2

Butler, Judith, 33–34, 225, 310nn.12, 13, 15

Chikamatsu Monzaemon, 65

Chū-shō kigyō. See Small and medium-sized enterprises

Clark, Rodney, 53

"Class", 44; and education, attitudes toward, 284 (*see also* Gender); and gender, 280–85; and language, 58–59; Japanese inflections of, 314nn.19, 20; merchants vs. white-collar workers, 120; and small enterprises, 49. *See also* Arakawa ward; Dual structure; Self, and power; Power; Shitamachi/Yamanote; Small and medium-sized enterprises; Power

Comaroff, Jean, 321n.7

Company as family, 44–45; and artisanal pride, 216–17; and capitalism, impact of, 166–69; and company benefits, 179–91; contradictions in idiom, 176; history of, in Satō factory, 176–77; idealization, dangers of, 328n.7; and large industry, turn-of-the-century, 172–73; Meiji period, changes during, 166–74; meanings summarized, 198, 202–6, 306; as "parental" care, 179–80; and part-time workers, 175; and recruitment practices, 178; in small

341

Index

Company (*continued*)
enterprise, 113–14, 166–69; and suppliers, 191–94; spatial symbolism of, 177; in Tokugawa period, 162–66; workers' vs. owner's appropriations of, 203–6, 212–14, 218–19. *See also* Household; Household confederations; Resistance; Satō; *Uchi*; Work

Confections, Japanese: and seasons, 243–44; as symbols of "tradition," 232; as "too traditional," 254; wrapping of, 287–89

Crapanzano, Vincent, 32

Daniel, E. Valentine, 39–40
Derrida, Jacques, 36, 310n.14
DeVos, George, 149
Divorce, 170–71
Doi, Takeo, 149–51
Dual structure: as culturally meaningful, 53–54; defined, 51; as economic buffer zone, 52; history and persistence of, 312n.2; and identity, 56; problematized, 52; workers' comments on, 201. *See also* Class; Shitamachi/Yamanote; Small and medium-sized enterprise

Enryo (restraint), 150
Equal rights amendment, 273
Essentialism, 10, 25, 42, 304, 307; and the unified subject, 33–37; problematized, 257; in textual strategies, 36–41. *See also* Referentiality; Self, and essentialism; Subject, unified; Textual strategies

Ethics movement: cultural institutions, relationship to, 92–93, 110; daily schedule, 83; discipline, 80–81, 84, 94, 112; discipline, physical, 92–93, 95–96; disciplinary production of subjects, 98, 106–8, 114; encounter sessions, 82, 99–100; fees, 79; filial piety, 86–87, 93–94, 99–100; and hierarchy, 79–81, 86–87; history of, 78; and nature, 87, 89; parody of, 87, 94, 103, 112; participants, 79; pedagogy, summarized, 91, 106; reactions to, 77, 82, 86, 90, 95, 98–100, 114–15, 216; resistance to, 87–88, 90–91, 94–95, 98, 111; as ritual experience, 110–11; self, theories of, 104–6; seminars described, 78–79; and small business, 113; and work, 14, 77, 85–87, 90, 95–97, 106, 113

Ethnography: narrative conventions of, 7–10, 46, 304; innovation in, possibilities for, 41–43, 46; as process, 8–26. *See also* Evocation; Experience; Reflexivity; Self/society trope; Setting trope; Textual strategies

Evocation, 8. *See also* Experience; Textual strategies

Experience: as oppositional practice, 203–4; and understanding, 18–24; as theory, 8, 24, 48, 300–301, 303–4. *See also* Participation; Reflexivity

Feminism, 10; analytic dilemmas, 258; and critique of the subject, 32–33, 43; in Meiji period, 267–68; and relational selves, analysis of, 32–33. *See also* Gender; Power, poststructuralist approaches to; Self, and power

Fischer, Michael M. J., 34, 322n.7
Foucault, Michel, 161, 212, 225, 310n.15, 311n.18, 323n.11
Fruin, Mark, 172–73, 319–20n.10
Fujimoto (dry cleaners), 5
Fukuzawa (*puresuyasan*), 57, 245, 129–30

Geertz, Clifford, 9
Gender, 45–46; and class, 280–85; changes from Tokugawa to Meiji, 266–67; context, historical, legal, and political-economic, 264–77; expectations of ethnographer, 14–17; "good wives, wise mothers," 266–68; and industrialization, 268–74; job discrimination, 277; and labor force, postwar, 274–77; and language, 27, 58; in law, 264–68; middle-class housewives, 280–85; masculinity, performances of, 229, 232, 240–41, 245–47, 249–50, 296–97; and neo-Confucianism, 266; and resistance, 259, 298–99; and skill, 230, 250–53, 256; and state, 267–68; as subject-positions, 44; women and family business, 137–40; women's performances of, 259, 293–99; and Western models, 266. *See also* Artisanal work, and masculinity; Feminism; Household; Part-timers; Power; Resistance

Geomancy, 196
Gluck, Carol, 173
Gordon, Andrew, 172–73, 239
Guilds, 164–65, 168–69. *See also* Apprenticeship; Artisanal work

Hamabata, Matthews, 126, 159, 173, 245–46
Hamada (part-timer), 60–61, 87, 183, 186, 199, 201, 208, 211, 280, 282, 292, 294, 296–97

Index

Haraway, Donna, 42, 46, 225
Hashimoto (violinist), 83, 86, 95, 98, 102
Hatanaka (landlords), 17–22, 28, 63, 145, 217, 283–84, 279
Hayashi (shoe-store owner), 63
Hazama, Hiroshi, 164
Hebdige, Dick, 321–22n.7
Hegemony, 202–3. *See also* Resistance
Henriques, Julian. *See* Hollway et al.
Hirota, Masaki, 265–66
Holden, Karen, 274
Hollway, Wendy. *See* Hollway et al.
Hollway et al. 310n.15
Household: childrearing practices in, 148–49; debates over, in Meiji period, 173; as corporate group, 122; defined, 121; and elite practices, 173–74; linguistic markers, 142–43; as locus of identity, 141–59 (*see also* Uchi); nuclear family, differences from, 122, 318n.33; patrilineal descent groups, difference from, 122–23, 127; and postwar legal changes, 174; significance summarized, 153, 159, 174; spatial symbolism of, 143–45; state-household metaphors, 173–74; and work, 121–22; as zero-point of discourse, 145–47. *See also* Adoption; Company as family; Gender; Household confederations; Succession
Household confederations: and changes under capitalism, 166–68; and class, 318–19n.2; defined, 123; and kinship, 162; main-branch relationships, 123, 162–64, 166–68; *noren wake* (dividing the shop curtain), 162–64; as work organization, 163
Household Registry Law of 1871, 265
Humanism, 301–2

Identity. *See* Self; Subject. *See also* Artisanal work; Company as family; Gender; Shitamachi/Yamanote; Small and medium-sized enterprises
Ie. See Household
Iida (part-timer), 97–98, 186, 279, 282, 285, 291–92, 294–95
Ikeda, Yoshihiro, 265
Imperial Rescript on Education, 173, 263
Inazawa (high-school student), 83
Irigaray, Luce, 310n.15
Itakura (part-timer), 54–55, 181, 186, 200–201, 204–7, 233–34, 260, 280, 282–83, 289–90, 297–98
Itō (artisan), 54, 199, 208

Japan, stereotypes of, 50–51, 301–2
Japanese American: as ethnographer's subject-position, 11–17, 23–24, 300–301; as historical political identity, 309; and politics of representation, 328n.4

Kaneko (schoolteacher), 284
Kikkoman, 173, 319–20n.10
Kimura (artisan), 94
Kinship. *See* Company as family; Household; Household confederation; *Uchi*
Kirkpatrick, John, 9
Kitagawa (artisan), 72–73
Kitahara (former employee), 180–81
Kitano (artisan), 111, 208, 210, 215, 251, 288
Kōno (artisan), 111
Kumagai, Hisa, 150
Kurō (hardship). *See* Apprenticeship, *kurō* and; Ethics movement, disciplinary production of subjects
Kurokawa (artisan), 97–98

Labor Standards Law, 215, 273
Lamphere, Louise, 223–24
Lebra, Takie, 32–33, 281
Lutz, Catherine, 40–41

Machines: as extensions of self, 244–47; mechanization, 208–9; for surveillance, 176, 210
Maebara (part-timer), 189–90
Marcus, George, 34
Marriage: meanings of, 140; as succession, 125, 132–40; women's experiences of, 132, 134, 137–38. *See also* Adoption; Gender; Household; Succession
Maruyama Toshio, 28
Masanori (part-timer's son), 189–90
Masao (high school student), 119–21, 128, 131, 153, 158
Material world. *See* Self, and material world
Matsuda (supplier), 185, 188–89, 190–92, 197
Matsumoto (baking chief), 215, 239, 288
Mauss, Marcel, 34–35
Meiji Civil Code: and changes in household structure, 169–72; and women's status, 169–71, 265–66, 268
Merchants' Association, 194–96
Misono (real-estate agent), 99
Miwata, Masako, 267
Miyake (dormitory caretaker), 181
Mori (former employee), 191–92

Index

Motherhood. *See* Ethics movement, filial piety; Gender; Household; Part-timers
Mouffe, Chantal, 323n.11

Nagahara, Kazuko, 268
Nakagawa (*sushi* maker), 197
Nakamura, Masanao, 266–67
Nakamura, Takafusa, 274–75
Nakane, Chie, 122, 126, 151, 171, 278
Nakano, Takashi, 163, 166–69, 172
Narrative. *See* Ethnography, narrative conventions of; Setting trope; Self, as narrative convention; Self, as narrative, assertion, and performance; Self/society trope; Textual strategies
Nomura (part-timer), 181, 191, 199, 200–201, 205, 207, 210, 252, 262–63, 282, 297

Obāchan (merry widow), 132–34, 305
Occupation of Japan, 273–74
Ogawa (artisan), 76, 79, 81–83, 85, 87–88, 102, 180–81, 183, 187
Ohara (chief artisan), 54, 183, 187, 199–200, 217, 244, 246, 289, 296; and creation of hierarchy, 247–52; and narrative production of self, 229–34, 255–57; performances of masculinity/artisanal identity, 249–50, 247–50, 252–53
Ojisan (male part-timer), 283
Okamoto (part-timer), 283
Omachi (cosmetics salesperson), 102
Ong, Aihwa, 321n.7
Ouchi, William, 50

Participation: and collapse of identity, 23; demands of, 21; and emergence of theoretical problem, 23–24. *See also* Experience
Part-timers, 45–46; artisans' attitudes toward, 252; cultural significance, 175; defined, 326n.8; education, attitudes toward, 284; employers' reasons for hiring, 275–76; as erotic objects, 296–98; and flexibility, 276; growth in numbers, 274–77; home and work, 276, 282–83; hours, 289–90; managers' attitudes toward, 285–86; and marital status, 276; relationships among, 291–93; and resistance, 199–218; as surrogate mothers, 294–96; and women's roles, extensions of, 285; and work, commitment to, 289–93; and work culture, 294; work day, described, 287–93; work

histories of, 260–64. *See also* Gender; Work; Resistance
Pascale, Richard, 50
Peirce, Charles Sanders, 40
Pelzel, John, 122
Performance. *See* Self, as narrative, assertion, and performance; Textual strategies
Perkins, Tessa, 286
Person. *See* Self, and person; Subject
Pharr, Susan, 273–74
Phillips, Anne, 256
Piore, Michael, 328n.7
Plath, David, 33
Poststructuralism: problematized, 311n.13. *See also* Foucault; Butler; Haraway; Feminism; Subject; Power, poststructuralist approaches to
Power: as creative and coercive, 10–11, 221, 224–25, 304–8 and *passim* (*see also* Class; Company as family; Ethics movement; Household; Self; Subject); and ethnography, 7, 17, 24, 42–43; as coextensive with meaning, 24, 221, 300–301; poststructuralist approaches to, 45–48, 258, 323nn.11, 12, and *passim;* as repressive, problematized, 221, 224–25; as social reproduction, 222; and Shitamachi/Yamanote discourse, 73–74 (*see also* Class; Shitamachi/Yamanote); and role in understanding, 10–17, 24–25, 307–8. *See also* Hegemony; Resistance

Referentiality: and essentialism, 35–37; in ethnography, 34–43. *See also* Essentialism; Ethnography; Self, and essentialism; Subject, unified
Reflexivity, 307–8; and emergence of theoretical problem, 8–10; routinization of, 303; and subversion of narrative conventions, 48, 302–4; as textual strategy, 7–11; as theory, 8, 25. *See also* Experience; Evocation; Participation; Textual strategy
Representation, politics of, 42–43, 50–51, 258, 301–5, 328n.4
Resistance: contradictory nature of, 213–14, 298–99; in household, 153–59; and narrative conventions, 46; possibilities and limits of, 46, 48, 221–22, 259 (*see also* Power); poststructuralist approaches to, 47, 322nn.11–12 and *passim* (*see also* Hegemony; Poststructuralism; Power); problematized, 42, 222–25, 298–99, 308; on shop floor, 199–202, 212, 298–99; social

344

Index

science narratives of, 218–25, 321–22n.7; of women workers, Meiji period, 270–72. *See also* Company as family; Gender, and resistance; Household; Part-timers

Rhetoric. *See* Ethnography; Textual strategies

Roberts, Glenda, 285–86, 290

Rohlen, Thomas, 104, 108

Rotary Club, 196

Ruriko (relative), 28, 149

Sabel, Charles, 328n.7

Sakada-san (part-timer), 260–61, 280, 282, 287–88, 291–92, 294, 298

Sakamoto, 12–13, 15–17, 61; Minako (bride), 134–35, 136–37, 139–40, 143, 144–46, 151–55, 194, 242, 291, 305

Satō, 4, 7, 18, 308; and assertions of authority, 207–12, 213–14, 224–25 (*see also* Power; Resistance); company history, 138–40; and ethics movement, 14, 77, 94, 114 (*see also* Ethics movement); and "familial" management, 176–93, 195–98 (*see also* Company as family); language use, 28–29, 147; and patron/client ties, 196–97 (*see also* Merchants' Association; Rotary Club); recruitment practices and, 178; succession, 138–39, 155–59, 193, 211, 291 (*see also* Household; Succession); Workers' complaints about, 199–202, 206, 210–12 (*see also* Resistance)

Saussure, Ferdinand de, 35–36; Derridean critique of, 36; Peircean critique of, 39

Scott, James, 219–21; notions of agency and subjectivity in, 322n.9; assumptions about "class," 322n.8; power as repression in, 221

Seasons: in Satō factory, 243–44; markers of, 241–44

Sekiguchi (soapmakers), 6

Self: and agency, 48, 224–25; concept of, in anthropology, 10, 34–43; emergence of topic, 9, 18, 22; and essentialism, 33, 35, 37, 304 (*see also* Essentialism; Referentiality; Subject, unified); fragmentation of ethnographer's, 16–17; and material world, relation to, 234; multiple 24, 36, 42–49, 51, 224–25, 257, 304, 306–8, 310n.14, 311n.17; as narrative convention, 25–26, 29, 32, 47, 304; as narrative rhetorical assertion, and performance, 10, 41, 46–48, 229–35, 257–64, 293–99, 304, 306–8; and power, 10, 24–25, 42–48, 112–14, 255–57, 304–5 (*see also* Subject, disciplinary production of); and

person, 34–35; as process, 48; semantic load of, 42; as subject-positions, 44, 46, 300, 304; Japanese, 26–33, 107–8. *See also* Gender; Subject; Self/society trope

Self/society trope, 9, 22, 24; in anthropological literature, persistence of, 37–43; problematized, 22, 25, 32–33, 39, 42–43, 106, 257, 310nn.12, 13. *See also* Self; Butler

Setting trope, 3–6; discussed and problematized, 7–9. *See also* Ethnography, narrative conventions of

Shintō, 246

Shitamachi, 65; culture, in Tokugawa period, 64–66; setting described, 3–6, 18–22; nostalgia and, 6–8, 72; pastimes, 283; and small companies, 72–73; "spirit," 195; Tora-san as embodiment of, 67–68, 72; townsmen, Tokugawa period, 64–66

Shitamachi/Yamanote: as class discourse, 58, 71–74; and cultural capital, 58–62; defined, 57; history of, 58; and language, 58–60; stereotypes of, 19, 63–64

Shweder, Richard, 37

Sievers, Sharon, 264–65, 269–72

Sincerity. *See* Self; *Tatemae/honne*

Singleton, John, 232

Skill: artisanal, in Tokugawa period, 166 (*see also* Apprenticeship; Artisanal work; Gender); challenges to, 249, 252–55; as creativity, 248, 250; gender and, 230, 250–53; and hierarchy, 230, 247–53; as physical knowledge, 238–39; and maturity, 239; and degradation of work, 324n.2; pride in, 56. *See also* Part-timers

Small and medium-sized enterprise: in Arakawa ward, 53–54; artisan vs. white-collar workers, 56–57; definition of, 50; and identity, 53; moral values associated with, 53–54; owners of, interviews with, 55–57; as proportion of Japanese businesses, 50. *See also* Dual structure

Smith, Robert J., 29, 62, 65, 170, 266

Smith, Thomas C., 173

Spivak, Gayatri Chakravorty, 310n.14

Steedman, Carolyn, 303, 321n.7

Subcontractors' Association, 55–56

Subject: disciplinary production of, 10, 12–14, 26, 43, 108–9, 159–60 (in household), 235–41 (artisanal), 304–7 (*see also* Self, as narrative convention; Self, and power); and poststructuralist languages of violence, 311n.18; unified, 29, 32–33, 35–37, 44–45,